OPERATIONAL
FLYING

AN AIRLIFE PILOT'S HANDBOOK

OPERATIONAL FLYING

A Professional Pilot's Manual based on the Joint Airworthiness Requirements

PHIL CROUCHER

Airlife
England

First published in the UK in 2001
by Airlife Publishing Ltd

British Library Cataloguing-in-Publication Data
A catalogue record for this book
is available from the British Library

ISBN 1 84037 295 8

Typeset by Phoenix Typesetting, Ilkley, West Yorkshire
Printed in England by Biddles Ltd., Guildford and King's Lynn

Airlife Publishing Ltd

101 Longden Road, Shrewsbury, SY3 9EB England.
E-mail:airlife@airlifebooks.com
Website:www.airlifebooks.com

Table of Contents

Table of Contents

Table of Contents

Introduction

This book has very little to do with flying, but everything to do with being a pilot – and the sort of training and information you need after you get your licence, but don't always get. Certainly, no-one tells you that aviation runs on paperwork, and that you need to be a bit of a lawyer just to read the regulations. Flying schools don't teach interview techniques, either! If you work, or are going to work, for a small charter company, or in the corporate field, it's mainly written with you in mind, but those working in larger outfits (like airlines) should still benefit. The idea is to catch you, if you've just qualified, at the same point as when you left school, where your education really begins. For more experienced pilots, it is hoped that some of the tips and tricks will make your job that much easier. It will be especially useful to operations staff, who often have to put themselves in a pilot's shoes, such as when inspecting Pleasure Flying sites.

Smaller companies can't afford to spend too much time or money on training, although naturally they meet minimum requirements (with the emphasis on minimum, because it costs money which is usually never recovered). Not only that, they tend to be rather short on staff as well, needing people who can be quite versatile. You could frequently find yourself (especially in a helicopter company) out in the field dealing directly with customers and making decisions on your company's behalf. Would you feel up to this? It's hard enough to maintain your basic flying skills, let alone become part of the management. It's well known that what customers think of your company depends not only on how you fly the aircraft, but also on your interaction with them. As an aviation advert once said, there's nothing like a curly sandwich to make your passengers query your ability as a pilot! They will expect you to know the answers to all their questions, which will range from how long you can fly on full tanks to the type of form Customs need for the goods they wish to import.

You might not think it's fair, but you will rapidly find you're not really a pilot at all – you'll also be a combination of handling agent, freight agent, manager and salesman, amongst other things. Mastering the aircraft is only half the job.

If you're going to be in a remote place with no supervision, or be a corporate pilot with no commercial experience to fall back on, but are nevertheless faced with operating an aircraft on your own, this should be the ops manual you don't have the incentive to write for yourself – all the information needed to run a flight department professionally is inside, in plain English as far as possible, which leads me to another reason for writing it.

The content of operations manuals is being standardised, at least within Europe, in line with *Joint Airworthiness Requirements* (JAR), and is therefore being written by committee, with very little thought given to the people who have to use them. Any attempt at making the task easier for the target readership is actually frowned upon, so some sort of translation is needed, especially as, in many sections, no deviation from the text supplied is allowed (particularly with *Flight Time and Duty Hours),* which seems to have been written by people whose native language is not English. Of course, no self-respecting pilot likes reading manuals anyway, but it's part of the job and should be made as easy as possible.

To help things along, this book loosely follows the JAR format for ops manuals, containing all the stuff the authorities wouldn't let me put in the manuals I wrote for several companies, including humour – the bits that are written in legalese can be slotted straight into your own manual when you get lumbered to write one (where you *can* read it, just change the wording to make it incomprehensible). So, as well as passing on a few tricks of the trade, it's a commentary on operations manuals, or at least the sort of common-sense one I would like to have seen when I started.

Although the contents are largely based on UK operating procedures, the basics of professional flying are the same everywhere, and the differences will largely be in terminology; for example, what the CAA calls an *Air Operator's Certificate* (AOC) is sometimes called an *Operating Certificate* in Canada. My point is that, wherever you are, you won't be wasting your time reading it, because there's something for everyone inside, especially as JARs are 'harmonised' with CARs (*Canadian Aviation Regulations*) and based in part on American procedures anyway.

One day, some of you will be chief pilots, or at least have a hand in running a company, however large. That's why there are some parts of the book, such as *Obtaining an Air Operator's Certificate* or *Setting Up a Company* (which take you over to the management side of the fence) that may not seem all that relevant at the moment, but you should read them anyway, as they will give you a greater insight into what your employer had to do to get into a position to pay your salary, as well as helping you understand how your company works – maybe they will help you with your own when the time comes. You are definitely of more value if you are commercially minded and can save money (which doesn't mean cutting corners).

Also not necessarily relevant at this stage is the chapter called *Going for a Job*. Like other pilots, you will find after a few years that your CV (*résumé*) will read like a patchwork quilt. Usually, this is no fault of yours, but management often doesn't see things the same way as Real People, so you may find that useful too. Luckily, modern companies seem to expect a little change and a few gaps here and there – at least it proves you're flexible.

Whatever parts you read (all of them, I hope), this book should help you find your way round when it all seems Very Strange, and hopefully help you realise *why* certain things happen the way they do.

Finally, being about as politically correct as Attila the Hun, I make no apologies for not distinguishing between genders, because long-winded phrases would ruin the flow of the text, so the pronoun 'he' also includes 'she', as it does in most legislation. Otherwise, the ladies fly just as well as anyone else.

Good luck and best wishes!

Phil Croucher

PS – If you feel that any of your experiences would be a useful contribution, or you feel I've got something wrong, please get in touch at **www.electrocution.com**.

After reading one of the early proofs, John Bulmer sent me this:

> *'Never allow your ego, self-confidence, love of flying, pressure from a customer, boss or co-pilot, or economic need to interfere with your good judgement during any stage of a flight. There is no amount of pride, no thrill, pleasure, schedule or job that is worth your licence or your life and the lives of your passengers. Complacency kills, and so does being a cowboy.*
>
> *That all may seem obvious and unnecessary, but I learned it the hard way during the foolishness of my youth. I may not have listened to that advice then, but if I had your book, who knows?'*

What Sort of Company Do You Keep?

Wherever you end up, you will have to get used to having no real influence except when actually flying. In other words, you may be the boss in your own office (the cockpit), but it will seem as if everyone else is in charge of you otherwise, especially in smaller companies, where you end up amending publications, etc. as a secondary duty; you're being paid anyway, so when you're not flying you end up in the pool of cheap labour. No sitting at home when you're not needed!

Companies differ in what they allow you to get away with. In some, being away from base with a problem may mean ringing Operations before you make any kind of a move. On the other hand, you may be able to make decisions on their behalf there and then, which the ops manual (next chapter) is supposed to help you with. Some airlines won't even allow personal items or conversation in the cockpit.

There are three types of flying – Commercial Air Transport, Aerial Work and Private.

Being a professional (well, potentially, anyway), you will only be concerned with the first two. Commercial Air Transport exists where payment (usually by a passenger) is given for the use of an aircraft, which in this context means the same sense as a taxi, as opposed to self-drive car hire. You need to be aware that there is considerable legal argument as to when a flight is Public Transport, or Commercial Air Transport, to use the new phrase, and you will find it summarised later in Chapter 14, *Legal Stuff*. As it is such a complex subject, any further discussion will be continued there.

Aerial Work covers other situations where payment is still given, but in specialised roles not involving the usual passenger or freight carriage, such as photography or flying instruction, or any other situation where you're getting paid to fly.

Private flying speaks for itself, its most distinguishing feature being that no payment exists, other than by the pilot, for the right to use the aircraft in the first place, although this in itself could cause problems (you can take money for some 'private flights', but see *Legal Stuff*).

Within the above limits, the companies you could get involved with will also fall (broadly) into three categories, with some blurring in between, in the shape of Scheduled, Charter or Corporate Flying.

Scheduled

'Scheduled Flying' is a legal definition describing services that run at predefined times with certain conditions imposed on them, such as being open to all classes of passenger and the flights always running, even though they may be empty (many companies use this as a form of sabotage, by sending someone on a rival's flight just to ensure the flight goes, otherwise they might develop a 'technical problem' if there are no passengers, cancel it, and save some money).

This would mean that, although holiday flights and oilfield helicopters do indeed move at predefined times, they are not subject to the other restrictions and are not therefore 'Scheduled', but as the difference is mostly transparent, I'll treat them as the same. Let's just say they are regular services.

Similarly, whilst airlines can provide charter flights, the word commonly covers the Air Taxi companies within General Aviation, which itself is a vague term – it usually means anything below 5,700 kg (12,500 lb) Max All-Up Weight, encompassing Air Taxi, Flying Club and personally owned aircraft, although the ICAO definition excludes aerial work.

Scheduled Flying is said to be boring (actually it is), but it does have the advantage of being organised anything up to four weeks in advance, so you can at least have some sort of planning in other areas of your life; this is strictly enforced by the authorities, and is covered more in Chapter 7, *Flight Time And Duty Hours*. Well, at least you know when you're going, even if you're not sure when you'll be coming back! The only qualification to this depends on the size of the company.

As the size of the operation decreases, and sometimes with it the aptitude of the operations department, you will end up wondering why they bother issuing duty rosters at all. Very often, in this sort of company, they are thrown straight into the bin, as the crews know they bear no resemblance to what will actually happen.

Congratulations! You are probably in a charter company (or a flying club) disguised as an airline, of which there are several. That is, they might have a lot of aircraft, but they will only be capable of managing a few. You will need a well-developed sense of humour here, as the worst aspects of both types of company will come to the fore, namely little time to yourself and very little information filtering down to the coal face, i.e. you. You can tell you're in one of these when your workload increases to keep them out of trouble.

Charter

If scheduled flying is like bus driving, then charter flying is a taxi service, which means you are on call twenty-five hours a day with everything geared to an instant response to the customer, leaving you unable to plan very much. Don't get me wrong; this can be fun with plenty of variety and challenge in the flying, but the downside is an ops department that lets you do all the work yourself, and being left hanging around airports or muddy fields while your passengers are away (with missed meals, getting home late, etc.). Charter flying is also where your other skills as salesman and/or diplomat come into play, as you will be very much involved with your passengers, who are more than just self-loading freight!

Thus, while you can move relatively easily from Charter to Scheduled, it's not so straightforward the other way round. As an airline pilot, you rarely see your passengers, and the flying is very different. Charter (or Air Taxi) is intensive, single-handed and stressful work in the worst weather (you can't fly over it) in aircraft with the least accurate instruments. It can be quite a culture shock for an airline pilot, looking forward to pottering around in a small aircraft until retirement, to find there's twice as much work as before and it's all happening at the same time.

As a pilot, therefore, you can have two types of working day, depending on the flying you do. In Scheduled, there is relatively little to do before departure as a lot of it is done by others – for instance, ground staff check-in and weigh the passengers whilst engineers look at the aircraft, although you still need a working knowledge of what they do, because in aviation the buck stops at the bottom.

A day flying charter, however, is a different story. You could be working at almost any time, provided the duty hour limits are not exceeded (again, see Chapter 7). Departures are inevitably very early, as businessmen need to be where they're going at approximately the start of the working day and return at the end of it, so some days can be very long.

As you're only allowed a certain number of hours on duty, there's a continual race to minimise them, sometimes working like a one-armed paper-hanger to keep up with everything. The flight plan has to be filed, the weather checked (as well as the performance and the aircraft itself), the passengers' coffee and snacks must be prepared and they must be properly briefed and looked after (that's just the start).

Usually, the only thing that can usefully be done the day before is to place the fuel on board, and even that can be difficult if the aircraft is away somewhere else. The flight itself is busy, too. As it's single-pilot, you do the flying, navigation and liaison with ATC. By contrast, the time at your destination is very quiet – after you've escorted your passengers through security and seen them safely on their way (the terminal's naturally miles away from the General Aviation park) you have to walk back to tidy up, supervise the refuelling, do the paperwork and have your own coffee (if there's any left) while preparing for the return journey.

If you're in a place you haven't been to before, you could always see the sights, but airfields are usually well away from anything interesting, with very few buses to get you there anyway. After a while, all you remember will be the same shops, so the general thing is to join the rest of the 'airport ghosts', or other pilots in the same boat as you, and find a quiet corner to read a book. You may as well go to the terminal, because you have to meet your passengers there, but constant announcements could drive you out to the aircraft again.

However, while you may be on time to meet them, your passengers will very rarely be on time to meet you. One trick that many pilots adopt is to hand them a slip of paper (keeping a copy!) stating when they must be back, and giving a reason, which may be weather or duty hours. Then, if they're not back in time, they have very little recourse if you either decide to go home without them or stay the night. In Charter, it's also a luxury to have more than one day off in a row, and those you do get are needed by law, or turn up by surprise where you don't fly if business is bad, even though you've still gone into the office. Some companies don't allow any leave at all during summer, which is the height of the busy season, and only a week at a stretch if you do get it.

Corporate

Corporate flying, where you run the flight department for a private company, is similar to Charter, but out of the Commercial Air Transport sphere, so the requirements (and paperwork!) are not so strict. Having said that, most flight departments are run to Commercial Air Transport standards, or better, and there is, naturally, no excuse for letting your own standards slip. One distinguishing feature is the way the Corporate world regulates itself – high-performance intercontinental aircraft follow essentially the same rules as single-engined General Aviation ones, and it's a credit to the people in it that things run so well.

In the Corporate world there are two types of company. The first is the large conglomerate, where the aircraft is just as much a business tool as a typewriter is. You are genuinely a company employee, people are used to the aircraft, you collect customers and move company personnel around, from the chairman to the workers, and your decisions as a professional are respected. There is a high degree of job satisfaction in this type of work, especially as you will build up relationships with regular passengers.

On the other hand, you might end up where the aircraft is the personal chariot of the chairman, with you as its chauffeur (or, if you look at the books carefully, a gardener!), in which case nobody else is able to use it and what you think doesn't matter, because the sort of person who is dynamic enough to run a large company single-handed also thinks the weather will change just for him, and you're constantly under pressure to try and find the house in bad weather, which, naturally, hasn't got a navaid within miles of the place.

Unless you can establish a good personal relationship with your passenger, or have an extremely strong character, you are unlikely to get much job satisfaction here, especially if the company is family-run and you have to take the kids to horse shows, etc. at weekends.

Having said all that, there are some decisions that are not yours to take, whoever you work for. Unfortunately, you are only in command where technical flying matters are concerned. If it's legal to fly, then, strictly speaking, it's nothing to do with you whether it's sensible or not – it's an operational decision. If the chairman (or Ops) wants you to fly and risk themselves being left to walk if conditions get too bad, then it's entirely up to them – it's their money.

For example, say you check the weather the night before and advise your passengers to go by car, because, while the destination and departure will be OK, the bit in the middle is iffy and there's no real way of knowing what it's like unless you go there and have a look (this is assuming a VFR flight in a helicopter, although the same principles apply to anything larger). However, they must get there and the timings mean they can't delay things till the weather gets better, so it's the car or flying – a straight choice. If your man wants to try and fly, and risks missing the meeting at the other end because you refuse to either start or carry on when it becomes impossible, then that, I suggest, is up to him. Similarly, an airline could be viewed as employing you right down to decision height; you might very well be aware that your destination is socked in, but it's not your place to say 'I'm not going', unless you have no alternates, or you think it unsafe for any reason. If your company says 'Try anyway', then go down to 200 feet (or whatever) and come all the way back again – they're paying the bills and you get the hours in your logbook. This situation may arise if the weather reports at the destination must legally reflect the worst conditions, but local effects will always ensure there's actually a good chance of getting in, which is a common situation in the Channel Islands. Of course, you can't plan to go without an alternate, or to land if the weather is below limits, but this is a typical workaround.

Another one airline pilots use when pressured to go in bad weather in the USA, where thunderstorms are common, is to taxi from the terminal, so the departure is technically on time, and wait by the take-off point until the weather clears. Mind you, I wouldn't want to be on the receiving end of passenger complaints.

Please note that I'm *not* advocating flying in bad weather as a normal procedure! The problem is not just your ability to fly in those conditions, but what might happen later, such as fifteen minutes afterwards, when you can't find your way back.

Minor digression: Another thought springs to mind, having mentioned a VFR flight in a helicopter, with regard to met forecasts. You have to check the weather before you go, that's the law, but the information for such a flight in an area forecast is actually pretty useless. You might get told, for instance, the 'visibility will be 500 m in hill fog'. Well, of course it will, but where is the hill fog, and when might you see it? Will it actually be there at all? You will find weather forecasts are often full of such woolly phrases, that in reality mean nothing at all when you get right down to it (rather like a speech from a politician), so there is often no other way but to go and have a look. This will apply especially in the Arctic or in mountainous regions.

A major plus point about Corporate Aviation is the way companies spend money on their flagship. It's a curious fact that, despite the higher standards that Commercial Air Transport demands, I have never yet seen a badly maintained Corporate aircraft and very few badly run Corporate flight departments, but decidedly the opposite has often been the case in the commercial world.

Corporate work sometimes pays the most, at least where smaller aircraft are concerned, but the jobs are less stable, as the aircraft is usually the first thing to go when the company gets into financial difficulties (which is more often a wrong decision than you think). This often depends on how it is perceived by other parts of the organisation, so perhaps you could add marketing to your list of occupations.

1

The Operations Manual

Almost the first thing you might see in your new company will be the operations manual. This is usually fairly badly written, often being a copy of somebody else's, which will no doubt include their bad English ('acquiring' ops manuals is a favourite form of industrial espionage). You'll probably also find items in the most illogical places, after being added willy-nilly over the years with no thought to content. It might also have been typed by someone wearing boxing gloves.

It wouldn't be so bad if you were given time to read it, but you're usually expected to do so overnight, at the same time as learning the rest of the company procedures and studying for the exams you will no doubt be expected to sit the following morning (as you've probably discovered already, everything happens yesterday).

The operations (or ops) manual is like the standing orders or SOPs (Standard Operating Procedures) issued by any military unit, hospital or other type of large organisation. It's a book of instructions that are constant, so that company policy can be determined by reference to it, containing information and instructions that enable all operating staff (i.e. you) to perform their duties. As part of the operating staff of a company, you are subject to the rules and requirements in it, and it's your responsibility to be fully conversant with the contents at all times. You will be expected to read it at regular intervals, if only because it gets amended from time to time.

The chief pilot is usually responsible for the contents and amendment policy (he may well have written it as well, so be careful when you criticise the English). Amendments, when they're issued, consist of dated and *printed* replacement pages on which the text affected is marked, ideally by a vertical line in the margin. On receipt of an amendment list, those responsible for copies of the manual incorporate the amendment in theirs and record it on the form in the front. You should find a proposal form for changes somewhere as well.

The manual will have been compiled from several sources: first of all, as I said, there are other people's, but after that comes experience, and documentation issued by the authorities. In the UK, a sample manual is available as a book, with the text on a floppy disk inside the cover, in Microsoft Word 2.0 format, which sometimes crashes Windows. This, in turn, has been based on the requirements in *JAR Ops Part 1* (*Part 3* for helicopters), which tells you what should be in a manual, and which replaces CAP 360, although I do detect an American influence.

Unfortunately, you can't use the sample manual straight away, as it needs to be personalised for your company; regard it as a shell into which you put your own information. When doing this, don't just cut out sections you don't need – it's very important to keep the numbering system, as one reason for the Joint Requirements is to make it easier for pilots to move between companies and find information in different manuals, so replace the text in the paragraphs you don't need with the words 'Not required', or a similar pair with the same meaning.

You can also expect to look at CAP 371 (and its amendments), which talks about Flight Time and Duty Hours (Chapter 7), and any operating handbooks for your aircraft. Another good source of information is *Notices to AOC Holders* (NTAOCH), but, when writing the manual initially, you don't officially have access to them, as you don't yet have an AOC. On top of all that, you might find various extracts from other manuals discreetly left on your desk after one of your inspector's regular visits. In Canada, most of the information you need is in CARs (Canadian Aviation Regulations), which has separate sections for Airline, Commuter, Air Taxi and Aerial Work operations.

JAR, by the way, stands for Joint Airworthiness Requirements, which works on the premise that aviation is the same in most civilised countries, and can be standardised to a certain extent. Essentially, certain European countries have agreed upon common procedures to help with importing and exporting aircraft, type certification and maintenance between them, based on existing European regulations and FARs (from the FAA in the USA), where acceptable. In fact, the maintenance side of JAR, 145, is directly drawn from FAR Parts 43 and 145. Naturally, there's a committee somewhere that jollies things along, which is somewhere in Holland, and the bottom line is that your company will find it easier to use foreign aircraft. The Canadian equivalent of JAR (and FAR) is CAR.

The prime objective for the ops manual being written in the first place is to promote safety in company flying operations. As the authorities are involved, it's therefore compiled in accordance with the law (in fact, as far as you are concerned it is the law) and all flights should be conducted to the Public, uh, *Commercial* Air Transport, standards set out in it. There should be a definition of Commercial Air Transport, which, officially, is an aircraft operation involving the transport of passengers or cargo for remuneration or hire, which definition does not include Aerial Work or Corporate Aviation. Also, there will be a declaration of who you're actually working for, which may sound daft, but many companies trade under several aliases, and they will be pinned down as to their real identity somewhere in the first few pages.

Some parts of an ops manual apply even when you think you're flying privately, because the aircraft will still be operated by an *air transport undertaking*. There should be an indication of what bits relate to what types of flight, but most companies apply the same rules to everything – it makes life easier. Usually consisting of several parts, the manual can be the size of a single volume with a small operator, or several in the average airline.

The separate parts will consist of:

Part	Contents
A	The main volume, with company administration and operating policy.
B	Flight Manuals and performance schedules for each type of aircraft operated.
C	Flight Guides (Jeppesen, Aerad, etc., or even your own).
D	Training Manual.

Manuals are notoriously difficult to navigate around, so a good index is important, as is a table of contents. This helps two people: you, trying to find the answer to a question in a hurry, and the ops inspector when reading the thing in the first place.

Although the manual will be supplemented by statutory instructions and orders, not all of them will be mentioned. It doesn't mean that you should ignore those that aren't, but being acquainted with all regulations, orders and instructions, issued by whoever, is all part of your job. Naturally, references made to any publication (such as Air Navigation Orders of whatever year) should be taken as meaning the current editions, as amended. When they are mentioned in the ops manual, they acquire the same legal force.

There will be several copies of the operations manual around, the numbers issued differing with the size of the company, but the typical distribution list below should be regarded as a minimum; each aircraft will have its own copy. All must be clearly marked for amendment purposes, and there's no reason why you can't have small versions for small aircraft, but remember they must all have the same text.

Copy No	Who has it
1	Master copy – operations manager
2	Relevant authority (Flight Operations Inspectorate)
3	Chief pilot
4	Training captain
5	Maintenance organisation
6+	One per aircraft or pilot

A large airline is likely to have its own print shop just to produce ops manuals and amendments.

Flying Staff Instructions and Crew Notices

Minor or temporary changes to company procedures are brought to your attention by Flying Staff Instructions (FSIs), to save too many amendments to the ops manual. They are among the list of items to be checked before each flight and will be found on the ops room notice board and in the back of the manual (with a copy sent to the authorities). FSIs are displayed either until they are not relevant, or for six months, whichever is the sooner, after which time they will either be destroyed or incorporated in the ops manual.

Anything of a non-flying nature, that is, pay and admin, is likely to be dealt with by Administrative Notices.

Operating Regions

These will be specified for the types of aircraft flown and may be shown by a map if it's not obvious. For example, you may be licensed to operate in a particular state or province, and just stating its name will be sufficient, as the details can be extracted from any atlas; if you operate in a specific area inside, you may have to describe it. There are several internationally defined areas covering other parts of the world, and different rules apply if you wish to operate in them. Examples will be in the back of JAR Ops 1.

Company Personalities

An effective management structure is regarded as essential, especially in the operations department (it's a mistake, by the way, to skimp on operations – if you ever start your own company, by all means

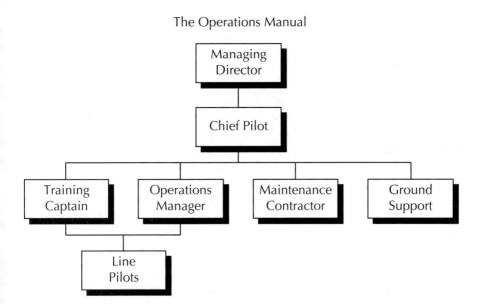

spend money on decent pilots, but not at the expense of a good ops manager).

The company will have appointed certain people to undertake particular tasks, and you will find some described below. Naturally, some will change, depending on your setup, and one person's functions may be combined with another's, but most companies will be laid out as above, bearing in mind that names of appointment holders will be included. Larger companies may swap the ops manager and chief pilot positions in terms of seniority. In Canada, the people described here must have qualifications listed in the Commercial Air Service Standards (CASS).

You must also supply a list of contact telephone and fax numbers for all company personalities, who can only act under one AOC.

For a police operation, expect to see a Chief Constable in charge, who will appoint an executive officer for day-to-day running.

The Managing Director

This person will have the ultimate responsibility for the efficiency, organisation, discipline and welfare of the company, ensuring that all activities are safe and legal and that the company is commercially viable. This will therefore include marketing and projection of the company image.

The Chief Pilot

Next in line is the chief pilot, who is the main point of reference to whom inspectors and other officials will relate, and they will expect to see him with some measure of control of the day-to-day happenings of the company, although technically the job is just to keep things legal. However, to do that, there will have to be some involvement in the more commercial aspects. (In Canada, this position, that is, next one down from the MD, may actually be occupied by the ops manager, for which see below.) The chief pilot is responsible to the managing director for the overall safety, legality, efficiency and economy of flying operations by the establishment of proper drills and procedures, and for ensuring that people (well, pilots, anyway) are properly qualified, so he will be responsible for hiring and firing.

Whilst the managing director is responsible for the administrative acceptability of work, the chief pilot has the technical side of things to worry about, like keeping control of the Flight Time and Duty Hours Scheme (sometimes by random inspection of returned flight documentation) in addition to supervising aircrew currency, maintaining aircrew records, compiling and updating the ops manual, raising occurrence reports and flying staff instructions.

Randomly inspecting returned flight documentation is a real chore, and is done for three reasons. The first is that it's part of the company's Quality Assurance Scheme (see Chapter 3), and the second is to ensure that you're doing your job properly. The third, and most important, is to eliminate nasty surprises when the inspector drops in for coffee. You will greatly endear yourself to your chief pilot if you make sure that *all* boxes on *all* forms are filled in (whether or not you think they're relevant), especially on the technical log, loadsheet and navigation log (Plog), and *not at the end of the day*, because you might get ramp-checked before then.

Digression: When ramp-checking, inspectors are looking for (amongst other things) altimeter settings, holes in the dashboard, approach plates out (or not), general condition of the aircraft, cleanliness, etc. and *scruffy paperwork*, with parts not filled in. They will especially be interested in weight and balance calculations.

With regard to the above items, where a signature is required, produce one, and always ensure that your departure fuel in the tech log agrees with the fuel load in the loadsheet (all tanks) and the nav log, and that fuel usage throughout the flight is consistent with time: that is, that you're not using mysterious amounts of fuel that would indicate somebody's fiddling the books (some companies give bonuses if you use less fuel, or bollockings if you use more). Especially make sure that the fuel loads on the tech log and loadsheet are *above* that required for the trip as specified on the nav log. The same rules apply to passenger and freight loads, and you should *always* check your figures, especially when adding up in hours, minutes and seconds – many engineers don't let pilots add up because it messes up the paperwork – they do all the entries themselves.

Lastly, don't write defects down on the nav log and forget to put them in the tech log at the end – that's a dead giveaway to your inspector, as almost every aircraft goes unserviceable when it gets back to base as if programmed, so use simple psychology – occasionally use the deferred defect procedure away from base, not forgetting to use a new tech log sheet, so that the inspector thinks your procedures are working (then again, he may not, because he's probably done it himself).

The chief pilot also liaises with the maintenance contractor on airworthiness matters, and may designate a suitable person within the company (guess who!) to carry out, or be responsible for, any of the above duties. That person would be directly responsible to the chief pilot (as is everybody else).

The chief pilot may also have the secondary function of:

The Flight Safety Officer

Or FSO, who operates any Mandatory Occurrence Reporting Scheme (MORS) and maintains a vigorous Flight Safety policy. That entails collecting information from the various sources that publish it, and spreading it around the company, probably by giving lectures and convening regular meetings with management, in accordance with (you guessed it!) the Quality System; this may also involve conducting internal investigations when somebody has an accident, and cooking up Root Cause Analysis reports. The reason for spreading things around is part of the reason for accident investigation, i.e. *that it doesn't happen again!* Safety management involves plenty of communication: as a flight safety officer, you have to encourage people to speak to you, so your personality is quite important. It's more than just a desk job.

The Chief Training Captain

This person co-ordinates flying training (the FSO may do Emergency and Survival), arranges periodical checks and examinations, selects training staff, and ensures that all aspects of flying training meet statutory requirements, if necessary by liaising with the authorities, in addition to compiling and maintaining flying training records.

Where training captains are thinly spread between companies, meaning that you don't see them from day to day, the chief training captain may simply be the chief pilot wearing another hat, to provide some consistency.

The Fleet Manager

A pilot with management responsibilities, reporting to the chief pilot, in charge of a fleet of the same type of aircraft.

The Base Manager

A sort of mini chief pilot/ops manager, in charge of a remote base, responsible to the ops manager or chief pilot for its day-to-day running and local marketing, keeping customers happy, altering your documentation, etc.

The Maintenance Contractor

The maintenance contractor (who must be specified) maintains and valets company aircraft in accordance with directions and laid down procedures or, more simply, mends what you bend. As to what laid down procedures is a good question, since they are supposed to develop the maintenance schedule. More about this in *Techie Stuff* (Chapter 13). If your company does its own maintenance, you will find instead a maintenance manager and chief engineer, who will have to order spares and schedule maintenance in a timely fashion, together with everything else needed to run an efficient organisation. Engineers and storemen will also be mentioned.

The Operations Manager

Although the operations manager may be technically under the chief pilot, in practice they have more or less equal status, and some companies may have one person occupying both positions. Having said that, Ops have to acknowledge your ultimate authority as aircraft commander. In addition, where ops managers must have certain qualifications, such as in Canada, and may therefore have more than the chief pilot anyway, you may find that the ops manager is well and truly in charge and the chief pilot a few steps down in the pecking order. Look for this situation in larger companies, where you will also find ops assistants doing most of the work described below.

Operations will provisionally accept work and, in liaison with the chief pilot, confirm it. As a result, they organise the flying program, including pilot duty and rest days, so you want to keep on their good side. Ops will ensure that duty times are in limits by keeping a record of flight crew flying and duty hours, and are supposed to ensure that you receive a written briefing (including NOTAMs, etc.) before going anywhere, and that all passenger and cargo manifests and tickets are completed as required.

The ops manager must keep in touch with the maintenance contractor to ensure scheduling for maintenance, forwarding completed tech log sheets and other relevant documents to them at the end of each flight. This is not the same as mentioned for the chief pilot, who does it on a more lofty level – all the ops manager is expected to do is monitor the aircraft hours so that nothing gets behind, and everything gets serviced on time. This is usually done by circulating coloured copies of the tech log after a flight.

Operations will also maintain carnets and aircraft documents (collectively referred to as aircraft libraries), an up-to-date stock of maps, route guides and aeronautical charts covering all areas of company operations, Flight Information Publications (such as NOTAMs, *UK Air Pilot*, AICs, Royal Flights, the Landing Site Register, etc.), and arrange exemptions and clearances for particular tasks.

Note: Although Ops are supposed to ensure the validity of all licences, medicals, periodical checks and training, you still have to keep your own up to date.

The ops manager also ensures that company accident and incident procedures are followed, processes amendments of the operations manual, assesses landing sites, categorises airfields, calculates specific weather minima, obtains met forecasts for planned routes and destinations and arranges overnight accommodation for night stops, amongst other things. Most important is the arrangement of an accurate and up-to-date flight watch of all company aircraft movements and a standby telephone coverage outside normal working hours. This is not legally required under some circumstances, such as Day VFR in Canada, but is still good practice.

A company that actually gets the ops manager to do all that is setting quite a high standard (naturally, the above duties may be delegated). Unfortunately, what happens is that whoever owns the company has a nephew, niece, girlfriend or whatever, who ends up doing the job instead. In that case, the best thing you can do is either leave the company, or leave this book around! In Canada, ops managers must hold, or have held, a pilot's licence for one of the types flown, or have appropriate experience, and rightly so. While on the subject, the biggest thing you need out of Ops is information, so try and make sure they get it from the customer, or you will continually find yourself having to fix other people's problems illegally, as when you turn up for a sling job expecting a 200 lb load and find it's actually nearer 600, which means pressure on you to go over-weight to get the job done.

The Quality Assurance Manager

The quality assurance manager (who may well be the chief pilot in disguise) ensures that the company's quality system is established and implemented, in this respect assuming the role of 'management representative', or a focal point for staff to refer to.

Duties include the issue and withdrawal of all quality system documents and forms, and maintaining a list of them, together with the aforementioned regular checks of documentation, etc. Routine flights should also be accompanied occasionally to confirm that normal procedures are being followed, but this will probably take the shape of a training captain doing a line check. A typical job is to ensure that new pilots joining the company have their paperwork done correctly. More about Quality in Chapter 3.

The Company Pilot

In small companies, it will be policy to operate on a single-crew basis as far as possible (less wages to pay), with the designated commander occupying the captain's seat as detailed in the relevant flight manual. It's therefore important to maintain your own standards, because you'll be on your own a lot.

You may think it a little over the top to see somebody with large amounts of gold braid emerging from a small aircraft and be wondering on what occasions you can call yourself 'Captain'. As far as I can make out, it used to be a convention that if you had either 5,000 hours, an ATPL of some description or a training (IRE) qualification, you were entitled to do so. The trouble was that as smaller airlines became popular, they didn't have people so qualified, and passengers were wary of flying with pilots who didn't have the requisite amount of the shiny stuff on their sleeves. Thus, the various rank gradings have become blurred and you're a commander if you're in charge of any aircraft, in the same way that people in charge of smaller seagoing vessels are ship's masters, as opposed to captains.

You may also be wondering why the commander has to be designated – this is so that the subsequent Board of Inquiry can pin the blame on the right person. In the USA, for example, under certain circumstances, four people can claim PIC time, including those in the passenger seats! This would naturally include whoever is doing the poling, but if someone in another seat has better qualifications, or is the owner or operator, that would qualify, too, especially in court (so watch it). Certainly, in the RAF, the captain has never been necessarily the first pilot (it could easily be a wing-commander in a passenger seat), since the captain is responsible for the final disposition of the aircraft (which, when you think about it, could also include a purser). So, there is a difference between acting as PIC and logging PIC time, and it should be spelt out clearly to save legal trouble later.

As an aircraft commander, you are first and foremost subject to any Air Navigation Orders or Aviation Regulations that may be in force. Inside the company, you are responsible to just about everybody else (but especially the fleet/base manager or chief pilot) for ensuring that aircraft are flown with prime consideration for the safety of passengers and persons on the ground; not negligently or wilfully causing an aircraft to endanger persons or property while ensuring it is operated in accordance with performance requirements, flight manuals, checklists, State authority regulations, the operations manual, Air Traffic Regulations, *UK Air Pilot*, Aeronautical Information Circulars and NOTAMs.

Seems a bit much, doesn't it? Hang on . . .

It's also up to you to keep your licences and personal flying logbooks up to date, and to ensure you are medically fit for your duties (a Board of Inquiry or insurance company may interpret the words 'medically fit' a little differently than you think if you fly with a cold or under the influence of alcohol).

You must keep customers and the company informed of any accidents, incidents and alterations caused by bad weather or other reasons. In remote areas, this will include a position report every hour or so.

Yours is the final responsibility for supervising the loading, checking and refuelling of your aircraft and making sure that all passengers are briefed on emergency exits and the use of safety equipment (see later), although you also have the right to exclude certain persons, such as drunks, etc.

You must check that the aircraft is serviceable with a current Certificate of Release to Service and with previously reported defects notified in the technical log as being rectified or transferred to the Deferred Defects lists by a person so qualified. Any defects must be allowed for in the Minimum Equipment List (MEL) or CDL.

You must ensure that no weight limitation is exceeded, that the C of G will remain inside the envelope at all times, and that performance is sufficient to complete the flight, as well as leaving a duplicate copy of the loadsheet and technical log (or operational flight plan, in Canada) with a responsible person before each flight, and ensuring that all documents are correctly completed and returned to Ops at the end (all documentation must remain valid throughout the flight). Of course, nobody ever does this, but you are supposed to.

You should not permit any crew member to perform activities during take-off, initial climb, final approach and landing that are not required for safe operation, and take all reasonable steps to ensure that before take-off and landing, the flight and cabin crew are properly secured in their allocated seats (cabin crew should be secured in their seats during taxi, except for essential safety-related duties).

Whenever the aircraft is taxiing, taking off or landing, or whenever you consider it advisable (such as in turbulent conditions), you should ensure that all passengers are properly secured in their seats, and all cabin baggage is in the approved stowages.

In an emergency situation (that is, requiring immediate decision and action), you should take any action considered necessary under the circumstances, which means you can break all the rules in the interest of safety. You can apply greater margins to minima at any time.

You should ensure that a continuous listening watch is maintained on appropriate radio frequencies at appropriate times, which, officially, is whenever the flight crew is manning the aircraft for the purpose of commencing and/or conducting a flight, and when taxiing.

You should not permit a flight data recorder or cockpit voice recorder to be disabled, switched off or erased, especially after an incident or accident, unless you need to preserve what's on the CVR (because it erases automatically when power is reapplied).

Although it's part of Ops' job to get a met forecast, it's actually your responsibility, so you may as well do it yourself.

Your behaviour and representation of the company in front of actual and potential clients must be exemplary.

Finally, here's a little gem, from about 1919, which comes from *Recollections of an Airman*, by Lt.-Col. L. A. Strange. Nothing changes!

> '. . . As a pilot of a machine, you are responsible for that machine all the time, and it is always your fault if you crash it in a forced landing occasioned by any failure, structural or otherwise, of the machine or its engine. It is your fault if, in thick weather, you hit the top of any hill that has its correct height shown on your map.
>
> It is entirely your fault if you run out [of petrol] when coming home against a headwind after four or five hours [of flying], or if you fail to come down on the right spot after a couple [of] hours cloud flying.

It is your fault if you have nowhere to make a landing when the engine fails just after you have taken off; in the event of a forced landing, your machine is a glider that should take you down safely on any possible landing place.

It is your fault – well, it is a golden rule to assume that whatever goes wrong is your fault. You may save yourself a lot of trouble if you act accordingly.'

The First Officer

For legal, safety, weather or duty reasons, a second pilot may occupy the other seat, performing the duties described here. Although two-crew operations are meant to be based on teamwork, sometimes the flight will actually be operated on a single-crew basis, despite the first officer's presence (we're talking small aircraft here). Whether this happens or not depends on company policy, and you may actually find the equivalent of a pilot's assistant in the other seat (see below).

Much of any pilot's job consists of cross-checking and monitoring, which is even more important when there are two crew in a complex aircraft. To minimise errors, set procedures are used for multiple crews, for which see Chapter 8. In fact, every commander has a management role, which includes training, and allowing P2s to gain experience whilst retaining the ability to recover from any situation.

First officers must know of the duties and responsibilities of the commander in case of incapacitation, so they will more than likely find themselves preparing and maintaining the navigation and fuel logs in flight, because they should be fully aware of the intended route, weather, etc. that may affect it. Constant briefings from the commander are essential, as the FO naturally must know the game plan if there is going to be a takeover at any stage. This even extends to the routes to be flown, minimum safety altitudes, overshoot action, etc. All this 'interaction' is part of Crew Resource Management, of which more later. In addition, first officers carry out checks (the commander reads them, or vice versa), make radio calls, cross-check altimeters and other instruments and monitor each flight continuously.

They're supposed to advise you (as commander) of any apparently serious deviations from the correct flight path, such as specific warning if, on an instrument approach, the rate of descent exceeds 1,000 feet per minute or the ILS indicator exceeds half-scale deflection, or of any instrument indicating abnormal functioning. In addition, they carry out secondary checks on engine power after the throttles have been set.

If, for any reason, you become incapacitated, they should be prepared to assume command, further described in Chapter 8.

They also supervise the loading and refuelling of the aircraft and prepare the loadsheets for the commander's signature before each flight, if it's not already done by a handling agent. When it's raining, they do the pre-flight check.

First officers are also supposed to 'support the commander' during interactions with the remainder of the crew, including helping him out of the bar. See also Chapters 4 and 8.

The Pilot's Assistant

In aeroplanes, particularly when pilots are in short supply, some companies may use an extra crew member to ease your workload, mainly completing paperwork as you go along, who won't be a pilot, but be called a 'safety pilot', to confuse things. Naturally, what they're allowed to get up to depends on their experience, but, unless in dire emergency, if they do not hold an appropriate professional licence (with all relevant checks), they are not allowed *any* part in the physical controlling of any aircraft flying for Commercial Air Transport.

In the light of this, their duties should be clearly spelt out in the ops manual, possibly more than anybody else's. For example, those with an RT licence may carry out radio calls at certain less critical points, under your supervision. Other duties may include preparing flight plans, looking after refuelling, keeping logs, reading check lists, tuning and identifying radio aids, briefing passengers, checking doors and seat belts, etc. They will only be used if you have a serviceable autopilot, and certain minimum qualifications, such as 1,000 hours' total flying, which must include 400 hours' P1. If not, you will need a fully qualified first officer.

Minimum qualifications will be something like a PPL with valid IMC rating and a flight radiotelephony operator's licence.

Cabin Attendants

These are needed when you have more than a certain number of passengers (see Chapter 6).

Cabin attendants are responsible to the purser, or No. 1, who is responsible in turn to the commander for ensuring that catering is ordered for flights to which they are allocated, and that such stores are correctly used in proper cabin service to the passengers.

It's their job to make sure that all passengers are briefed before take-off on the items detailed in the passenger briefing card (or video), which includes being properly seated with safety belts fastened for take-off and landing or any other times in flight as and when instructed. They must also ensure that doors and emergency exits are kept clear of obstructions during take-off and landing, and that loose articles are in overhead lockers or underneath a seat, if applicable.

Of course, they serve meals and refreshments as well, but don't underestimate their qualifications – a proper training course is quite rigorous. The old RAF joke about a coffee machine being a flight simulator for a loadmaster is *not* appreciated!

In the UK, there isn't a cabin crew licence as such; any certificates are granted internally by the company.

Others

There may well be other staff around, such as flight dispatcher, flight follower, ramp officer, senior steward(ess), etc. who are not catered for here, but it shouldn't be hard to deduce what they get up to, given the above examples. There isn't a specific qualification for flight dispatchers in the UK, either, but sometimes they get a whole week's training.

2

Admin

Otherwise known as Operational Control and Supervision in the ops manual, this section would deal generally with company matters of a non-flying nature.

Supervision of Company Operations

Somebody has to decide how many people are needed to operate your aircraft. For a small outfit, one manager may supervise more than one department, and whoever it is will be lumbered here.

Additional Instructions and Information

As mentioned before, instructions and information not already in the ops manual are made the subject of flying staff instructions, with copies distributed to all departments on a 'need to know' basis. For non-operational matters, watch out for Administrative Notices.

Accident Prevention and Flight Safety Programme

Flight safety awareness will be fostered by circulating accident reports, incident bulletins, General Aviation Safety Information Leaflets (GASILs) and flight safety magazines. Incidents and accidents involving aircraft types or equipment operated by the company should be highlighted, and the flight safety officer (FSO) should bring to the attention of the appropriate manager(s) anything that may involve revising procedures.

The FSO's responsibilities have been described in Chapter 1.

Operational Control

The procedures for this are normally overseen by the ops manager.

Public Relations and Press Enquiries

As mentioned in the Introduction, how a company is perceived by its customers depends on its image, which in turn depends on its employees. How you conduct yourself with respect to potential clients (including on the telephone) helps too. Very often, whether a company gets work or not isn't based on price or service, but on whether it has a good image. Advertising, for instance, is not geared to making you buy a particular product directly, but by enhancing your view of it. So it is with your company, and you are one of its least expensive and most important ways of advertising – it's not a good idea to be seen too often in the local bar in uniform, at least, not an identifiable one.

Formal statements should not be made to the press or other sections of the media without management instructions.

Expenses

Aviation is an expensive business, even for those who ordinarily wouldn't be expected to invest in it; the effects filter down quite markedly. It's common practice for pilots to pay landing fees and suchlike as the trip progresses (some airfields won't let you go until fees are paid, and sometimes the Mafia will have their hand out), and the subsequent shock to your bank account may be quite severe unless you've been given a float which is topped up weekly. Expect a sizeable one, and try and get it repaid as often as possible – there's no reason why you should subsidise the company (you may be lucky and get a company cheque book or credit card).

The taxman also allows companies to pay a tax-free subsistence allowance per duty hour, but some may pay meal allowances instead. These are for missed meals and the fact that you wouldn't necessarily choose to eat at such expensive places as airport cafeterias, which unfortunately are usually the only places available when things are busy. Also, you will find your life insurance gets loaded, and this will help to offset the cost.

Sometimes there may be an allowance negotiated by your union, but you may find it's for airline pilots only.

3

Quality System

Life these days is very complex, and operating aircraft is no exception. Indeed, the rate of change is such that legislators can hardly keep up with avionics, and inspectors are even further behind, so the onus is on companies to self-regulate, which is where the quality system comes in. Anything affecting goods or services delivered to customers is subject to it, based on ISO 9000, which is supposed to ensure that the company product is of the 'required quality' or, in officialese, is 'assured as conforming to specified requirements and is supplied in accordance with the company's quality policy and procedures'.

ISO 9000 is an internationally recognised standard for quality systems, previously known as BS 5750 in the UK, where 'quality' is defined as satisfying the customer's needs – as far as ISO is concerned, a product or service is of the required quality if it performs the function it was designed for. Well, a cheap watch performs a function, but I think Rolex would have something to say about it being 'quality'! The truth of the matter is that the system was designed for manufacturing, to produce low return rates, which doesn't always translate well to service industries.

The International Standards Organisation is Geneva-based, and 9000 has been around since 1987. It is a generic management system standard which doesn't have much to do with the end product, except for ensuring its production under sound management procedures, leading to efficiency and consistency, and, ultimately, cost reductions. Side benefits are improved employee motivation and customer relations and better perception of the company image.

You need some sort of internal auditing system, in which all company functions are continuously monitored. Certification, by the way, is not actually done by ISO, but by consultants appointed by it. Documented working procedures are officially a Good Thing for controlling the business (like checking that your suppliers are up to scratch) and ensuring that everyone knows their job, which, in the case of aviation, is mostly in the ops manual anyway, so all this is arguably a duplication of effort, aside from Accounts and Admin.

For now, you can safely skip this chapter, because it's mostly boring, but is here in case you want to use it in your own manual one day and are wondering where to get the text from. To save time for now, this whole chapter is encapsulated in the next paragraph . . .

Translation: All staff must help to streamline company procedures, which will be investigated and corrected at an appropriate level, as well as being audited regularly. The quality assurance manager will monitor and record the details and present them in management reviews at least twice a year.

Quality Policy Statement

This is a statement from senior management demonstrating commitment to the process, unfortunately, in the case of some companies, being extremely pompous (check out a very senior UK airline). It's supposed to let customers know that the company knows what their needs are. Look for something on the company noticeboard called a mission statement.

It should be company policy that all staff shall strive to maintain the highest standard of service to customers and adhere to, maintain and improve the quality system. Effective corrective and preventative action to eliminate non-conformances shall be an essential part of the company's quality system, and all personnel shall be made aware of the need to identify and rectify deficiencies. Any deficiency noted or brought to the attention of the company shall be investigated at a level commensurate to the seriousness of the problem, and effective corrective action shall be taken.

Procedures shall be established to provide for the control, monitoring and analysis of corrective and preventative actions employed by the company.

Corrective and preventative actions in response to company deficiencies shall be analysed by the quality assurance manager, who shall be responsible for ensuring the recording and analysis of non-conformances, including customer complaints, and identifying specific areas that may require action to prevent and eliminate the causes.

A review of corrective and preventative actions for effectiveness shall be included in management review procedures.

Management Reviews

A programme of reviews shall be implemented by the quality assurance manager to ensure compliance with all aspects of the quality system, and to ensure its continuing suitability and effectiveness in satisfying the requirements of 'the standard', together with the company's stated quality policy and objectives. Recorded follow-up action is taken as necessary to verify that deficiencies are corrected and to ensure that repetitions are avoided.

At least twice a year management shall hold a review of the quality system and shall complete a report with actions required, timescales and responsibilities for implementation.

Information regarding the effectiveness of the quality system shall be obtained from the records of internal quality audits, non-conformance reports and customer/supplier complaints, together with reports from members of the company's staff, which shall be regularly sought by management.

Documentation

All documents must be issued, amended, revised and controlled in accordance with procedures monitored by the quality assurance manager. Prior to issue, documents shall be reviewed and approved for adequacy and fitness for purpose by the quality assurance manager and the personnel concerned with the function of the document in question. Up-to-date issues of appropriate documents shall be available at all locations where operations require their use, and obsolete documents shall be removed from all points of issue or use.

All changes to, or introduction of, computer generated documents that comprise part of the quality system shall be subject to the procedures above. The nature of the computer system means that obsolete documents will no longer be generated once changes are made. Each document shall be identified with an issue number, date and unique description. A master record of controlled documents shall be maintained so the current issue number and date can be identified.

A document shall be re-issued if any amendment affects the intent of it. Changes shall be highlighted in the text with the amendment history records being updated to reflect the latest issue. Grammatical or spelling changes need not necessitate another issue change. Changes in computer-generated document or forms format or content are not highlighted, but by their very nature comprise a re-issue.

Supervisors

Supervisors shall carry out regular checks of pre-flight planning, returned flight documentation, flight and duty time records and technical documentation. Appropriate flying personnel (e.g. chief pilot, nominated training captains) should accompany a selection of routine flights to confirm that normal operating and flight deck procedures are being followed.

Auditing

All activities are subject to internal quality audits, the results of which form an integral part of the input to management reviews. Audits confirm the relevancy of procedures and identify unsatisfactory ones before they cause trouble, comparing how the operation is run against how it should be.

Internal audits shall be planned and documented so that all aspects of the quality management system are reviewed to ensure continued effectiveness (obvious, really). The frequency of such audits shall be determined according to the results of previous audits and the significance of individual aspects of the system. Whatever happens, all aspects of the quality management system should be audited at least twice a year.

Audits shall be performed with check lists identifying key elements, such as:

- ❏ Activities, processes, work areas, materials storage
- ❏ Computer data integrity and accuracy
- ❏ Documentation and technical data
- ❏ Compliance with industry standard practices
- ❏ Compliance with regulatory authority requirements

Audits of specific areas shall be carried out by a suitably qualified and experienced person who is not directly responsible for the day-to-day operation of the audited function. That person may be contracted-in from outside the company; in this case he shall submit proof of training, experience and qualifications to the quality assurance manager who shall assess his suitability to carrying out internal audits. The person, or the company that employs him, shall be included on the list of company-approved suppliers if assessed as suitable for the task.

Audit findings shall be documented on the audit report form. Audit reports will be reviewed by the quality assurance manager who will instigate corrective actions and changes to procedures as necessary. Subsequent instigation and evaluation of required actions taken shall be his sole responsibility, but will be monitored by the internal auditor.

Reviews

A review of the quality management system to assess its suitability and continued effectiveness shall be undertaken twice yearly at a meeting of the managing director and all staff concerned with the operation of the system.

The review shall view objective evidence of internal audits, non-conformance documents, customer complaints records and supplier performance.

Specific recommendations and actions shall be logged and these shall be completed within agreed timescales.

Details of methods, responsibilities and documentation shall be defined in written procedures.

See – told you it was boring!

4

Crew Composition

The minimum flight crew should never be less than that in the certificate of airworthiness, or flight manual, in that order. You might regard that as stating the obvious, but such words are legally required in an ops manual. Anything registered in the UK over 5,700 kg needs two pilots for public transport, but otherwise:

IFR

Aeroplane

Two pilots
In IFR or at night, you need two pilots on turbo-jets, pressurised turbo-props and multi-engined turbo props capable of carrying more than nine passengers (or fewer than ten without pressurisation).

Single pilot
You can fly single-crew in IFR or at night in unpressurised multi-engined aircraft if you have been trained and checked in the single-crew role (with particular reference to cockpit management), the autopilot is serviceable with at least altitude hold and heading mode, you have a headset and boom microphone with a control column transmit button, and there is a conveniently placed, illuminated chart holder.

Helicopter

Two pilots
You must have two crew if more than nine passengers are carried, and both must have an IR. The commander must also have an ATPL(H).

Single pilot

Only if fewer than nine passengers are carried, and you must have an IR, and a serviceable autopilot with at least altitude hold and heading mode, a headset and boom microphone with a control column transmit button, and a conveniently placed, illuminated chart holder, as well as being trained in the single-crew role, with particular reference to cockpit management.

VFR

Aeroplane

You must have a minimum of 500 hours or an IR to operate on your own as a CPL holder when more than 50 nm from the departure aerodrome.

Helicopter

You must have two crew if over nine passengers are carried, and an ATPL (H) if you're the boss. Otherwise a CPL(H) will do.

Cabin Crew

Cabin staff are required in aeroplanes carrying more than twenty passengers, or capable of carrying more than thirty-five, when at least one is present. The minimum number should be about one for every fifty, or fraction of fifty, passenger seats installed.

Designation of Aircraft Commander

No matter how many pilots are carried, one will be nominated as commander. See Page 10 for reasons why.

Incapacitation

See Chapter 8.

5

Qualifications

These are sometimes dictated by the insurance company, customer requirements (such as large oil companies with their own safety departments), or, in a large company, the personnel department, who mostly don't have a clue. The minima will vary according to supply and demand, but here is what the CAA will expect. Naturally, any licence you need must be valid – for example, medical certificates are not mentioned here because the licence requires one anyway.

Commanders

Aeroplane

The minimum requirements are:

- ❏ successful completion of the single-crew or command course
- ❏ an ATPL, or a CPL and 500 hours total time (or valid IR) when carrying passengers under **VFR** more than 50 nm from a departure aerodrome. For a multi-engined aeroplane in **IFR**, this changes to 700 hours total time, including 400 PIC, which includes 100 IFR, of which 40 must have been on a multi (the 400 hours PIC can be 800 P2 if gained in an established multi-crew system)
- ❏ 50 hours IFR on type, of which 10 as PIC, for single crew
- ❏ Valid IR (when IFR) and recurrent checks.

Recency
A minimum of three take-offs and landings in the past ninety days, which may be done in an approved flight simulator; ninety days may be extended to 120 if accompanied by a TRI or TRE when line flying. As single pilot under IFR or at night, a minimum of five IFR flights, including three instrument approaches in the past ninety days, or an IFR instrument approach check.

Helicopter

700 hours on helicopters, of which 300 must be PIC, and 100 hours instrument time (10 as PIC). The 300 PIC can be 600 P2 if obtained in an established two-crew system. You must also have twenty-five hours in the environment concerned.

Helicopters under 5,700 kg MAUW, in IMC or at night with visual ground reference, must have either two pilots or one pilot with an autopilot.

Recency

Three take-offs, three circuits and three landings in the preceding ninety days (can be done in an approved simulator), or 120 days by supervised line flying. If relevant, at least five IFR flights including three instrument approaches on the type in the last three months.

Co-Pilots

ATPL or CPL, valid IR (when IFR) and recurrent checks.

Recency

Must have flown aeroplanes on the relevant type during take-off and landing in the past ninety days. For helicopters, three take-offs, three circuits and three landings in the preceding ninety days (can be done in an approved simulator), or 120 days by supervised line flying.

Cabin Crew

Minimum age is eighteen years, and must be medically fit. Additional qualifications may be required for senior cabin crew member, or operation on more than one type.

6

Crew Health Precautions

People holding (flying) medical certificates should not exercise licence privileges if they suffer from any illness, injury or disability, are taking a drug or receiving medical treatment that could impair their ability to safely exercise those privileges.

Whilst nobody should object to you taking a drink or two the evening before a flight, you should remember that it can take over three days for alcohol to clear the system (it remains in the inner ear for longest). Within twenty-four hours before a planned departure, you should not drink alcohol at all; certainly not on standby. The maximum blood level is officially 0.2 mg per ml, a quarter of the driving limit in the UK, but it's not only the alcohol that causes problems – the after-effects do as well, like the hangover, fatigue, dehydration, loss of blood sugar and toxins caused by metabolisation.

As far as passengers are concerned, although they get cabin service, persons under the affluence of incohol or drugs, of unsound mind or having the potential to cause trouble should not be allowed on board – certainly, no person should be drunk on any aircraft (people aren't generally aware that one drink at 6,000 feet is the same as two at sea level). This is not being a spoilsport – drunks don't react properly in emergencies and could actually be dangerous to other people (which is why I always get an aisle seat – I don't have to get round people in the way). Therefore, it's not just for their own good, but that of others as well. If you need to get rid of obstreperous passengers, you can always quote the regulations at them (or even use sarcasm), but don't forget to fill in a mandatory occurrence report.

Although the symptoms of colds and sore throats, etc. are bad enough on the ground, they may actually become dangerous in flight by either distracting or harming you by getting more serious with height (such as bursting your eardrums, or worse). If you're under treatment for anything, including surgery, not only should you not fly, but you should also check there will be no adverse effects on your physical or mental ability, as many preparations combine chemicals, and the mixture could make quite a cocktail. No drugs or alcohol should be taken within a few hours of each other, as even fairly widely accepted stuff such as aspirin can have unpredictable effects, especially in relation to hypoxia (it's as well to keep away from the office, too – nobody else will want what you've got). Particular ones to avoid are antibiotics (penicillin, tetracyclines), tranquillisers, antidepressants, sedatives, stimulants (caffeine, amphetamines), anti-histamines and anything for relieving high blood pressure, and, of course, anything not actually prescribed. Naturally, you've got to be certifiable if you fly having used marijuana, or worse, but it seems that people do in the USA, which is why your medical results are faxed to a central office.

Pilots generally are discouraged from giving blood when actively flying, and some dental anaesthetics can cause problems for up to twenty-four hours or more, as can anything to do with immunisation. If you do give blood, try to leave a gap of forty-eight hours, including bone marrow donations. Although your blood volume is restored in a very short time, and for most donors there are no noticeable after-effects, there is still a slight risk of faintness or loss of consciousness (syncope). After a general anaesthetic, check with the doctor first.

You shouldn't fly within forty-eight hours of deep-sea diving to more than ten metres. Food poisoning can also be a problem, and not just for passengers – the standard precaution (as in *Airplane!*) is to select different items from the rest of the crew, even in the hotel.

Don't forget to inform the authorities (in writing) of illnesses, personal injuries or presumed pregnancies that incapacitate you for more than twenty days (you can fly up to the thirtieth week of pregnancy in Canada, if your doctor agrees, but wait for 4–6 weeks afterwards before flying again). There's also an upper age limit of sixty that affects commanders on commercial air transport (can you sue for age discrimination?). Pilots involved in accidents should be medically examined before flying again.

7

Flight Time and Duty Hours

Your personal performance diminishes as you get tired – but you don't need me to tell you that. Nor do you need to be told that, on average, at least seven hours' sleep is needed per night where peak performance requires about nine. However, scientists are also beginning to think it's not so much the amount of sleep you get, but when you get it that counts, so fatigue is just as likely to result from badly planned sequences of work and rest, rather than the actual duration of duty.

The problem with fatigue is that it's difficult to legislate for. Not only that, your performance can start to fall off well before you actually feel tired. Variations while crossing time zones, for instance, can vary anywhere between 8 and 70 per cent. Some people can cope with vastly disrupted work patterns – most of us can't.

A surprising number (over 300) of bodily functions depend on the cycle of day and night – we have an internal rhythm, which is modified by such things. You naturally feel best when they're all in concert, but the slippery slope starts when they get out of line. The best known form of desynchronisation is jet lag, but it also happens when you try to work nights and sleep during the day – bright light can fool your body into thinking it's day when it's not, and is actually used for circadian rhythm disorders.

One day for each time zone crossed is required before sleep and waking cycles get in tune with the new location, and total internal synchronisation takes longer (kidneys may need up to twenty-five days).

Even the type of time zone change can matter – six hours westward requires (for most people) about four days to adjust – try seven for going the other way! This eastward flying compresses the body's rhythm and does more damage than the expanded days going west; north–south travel appears to do no harm.

Symptoms of jet lag are, naturally, tiredness, faulty judgement, decreased motivation and recent memory loss. They're aggravated by alcohol, smoking, high-altitude flight, overeating and depression, as found in a normal pilot's lifestyle.

In view of all this, you have a maximum working day laid down by law, intended to ensure you are rested enough to fly properly. It's similar to truck drivers' hours, except that there's no tachograph; companies and pilots are trusted to stick to the ops manual, and the authorities reserve the right to spot check the paperwork at regular intervals, mainly looking to see that flights are *planned* within the company's scheme (if you don't see a flight ops inspector for long periods, then you can assume that your company is well regarded in this respect).

In the UK corporate pilots (or unpaid instructors) have no legal protection, apart from any basics under the ANO in Canada, private operators are covered in CARs, and have approximately the same limitations as their commercial brethren. Consequently, you could find yourself in continuing battles with company executives, to whom working twenty-eight 12-hour days non-stop is *not* uncommon – if you are moonlighting from the military, you must count that time as well. It's fair to point out, though, that it's difficult to introduce duty hours into a corporate environment – the schedule changes so often that you would need a lot of extra staff to cope with it. I suppose you could point out that if the aircraft is not flown in accordance with the ANO, the insurance becomes invalid.

Depending on the size of the company, the FTL Scheme, as it's known, will be written in consultation with various interested parties such as staff unions, but most just insert the relevant documentation (CAP 371 in the UK) into their ops manual as it stands, as (while recognising differences between companies) there's actually very little latitude allowed in what goes into this section, despite the fact that the requirements were origi-nally written 'in basic form with reasonable freedom to apply them with common sense' (with apologies to Douglas Bader, who had a hand in writing them originally).

Since the second edition of CAP 371 was published, several things have changed (due to the opening up of Third World countries, night freight and increased pilot mobility, amongst others) and flight up to maximum limits and beyond are now the norm. There are, therefore, amendments to CAP 371 which reflect new working practices and have many anom-alies removed, while trying to keep the same structure of the document; you'll mostly find them in Notices to AOC Holders, as well as Sub-part Q of JAR Ops 1 & 3.

It's unlikely that general aviation pilots (or any in a non-scheduled en-vironment) will notice much difference, though, as GA rarely changes. Most of this chapter is geared towards outfits in the sole-use charter busi-ness, where the passenger seats available are nineteen or fewer, so it has to cater for a wide variety of aircraft and circumstances. Mainly, though, it assumes that company operations are confined to an area within which local time doesn't vary by more than two hours, and there's no in-flight relief to extend duty hours.

In some countries, such as Canada, knowledge of flight time limitations is actually part of the commercial pilot exams, whereas in the UK you don't really start finding them out until you join a company. Also, before we start, this section is not necessarily in the same order you would find in a manual, as I have tried to put it into a more logical sequence, so that you can understand it better. Definitions, for example, have been placed where the terms they relate to actually arise, rather than in one lump at the beginning.

Put simply, there is a basic working day, which generally is ten hours long (fourteen in Canada). This may be longer or shorter, depending on the time you start and the number of crew you have; the earlier you start, the less time you're allowed, but this could be offset by carrying extra crew, when appropriate. Within the resulting duty period there may be a maximum number of flying hours which cannot be varied, such as seven hours' helicopter flying within twelve on duty. If you need an exceptionally long working day, you can always apply for an exemption to cover it.

In Canada, the initial description of this subject is in CARs, Part VII, Subpart 0, so start looking at Paragraph 700.14. It's further amplified in CASS (*Commercial Air Service Standards*), in Paragraph 720, etc. These are the only two places you will find it mentioned. Further differences will be found in your ops manual, as the company can get exemptions for special situations. The reason why it's as high as fourteen hours a day in Canada is because the flying season is so short, especially in the North, and full use must be made of the time available. That doesn't mean you can abuse the rules, though – there are stiff fines for breaking the limits, for companies and pilots, so beware. You can do as many hours as you want in the basic 14-hour day, limited only by refuelling, eating, etc., but if you extend to 15 hours, you can only do 8 hours' flying.

Cabin staff also have duty hours, which are essentially the same, but up to an hour longer at the start of the day, as they have to prepare the aircraft for passengers.

Your Responsibilities

These stem from various provisions of the ANO and CAP 371 and/or JAR Ops 1 or 3, or CARs in Canada. Firstly, you must inform the company of all your flying (including Aerial Work, which in turn includes paid, or remunerated, flying instruction), except private and military flying in aircraft under 1,600 kg MAUW. Exempt military time must be for the Royal Air Force Cadet Organisation, that is, air experience flights.

It's also up to you to make the best use of any opportunities and facilities for rest provided, and to plan and use your rest periods properly – you should inform Operations if you can't sleep properly, for example. They might arrange for you to see a specialist.

Then there's the Aircraft Crew and Licensing part of the ANO (CARs in Canada) which says that you're not entitled to act as a member of a flight crew if you know or suspect that your physical or mental condition renders you temporarily unfit to do so (what about if you're permanently unfit?).

All this means you should not act as a crew member (and should not be expected to) if you believe you are (or likely to be) suffering from fatigue which may endanger the safety of the aircraft or its occupants.

Company Responsibilities

Duties must be scheduled within the company's approved scheme, and rostering staff must be given adequate guidance. Work patterns must be realistic with the intention of avoiding, as far as possible, over-running limits. As a result, they must avoid such nasties as alternating day and night duties and positioning that disrupts your rest.

Unless you're in an airline or on the North Sea, it's obviously difficult to schedule much in advance, but companies must advise you of work details as far ahead as they can (though not less than seven days), so that you can make arrangements for adequate and, within reason, un-interrupted pre-flight rest. Away from base, it's normally the company's job to provide rest facilities (the legal definition is 'satisfactory in respect of noise, temperature, light and ventilation'), but they may lumber you with finding them, as you're on the spot – they are allowed to claim that short notice precludes them doing it. Note that bush and fire-fighting camps must also meet the definition of 'suitable accommodation', which, in Canada, at least, should start as a single-occupancy bedroom subject to minimum noise, but can change to something suitable for the site and season, so you can't win. On seismic support, for example, the only place you could manage to hide is inside the back of your helicopter.

All this being said, it must be pointed out before we go on that very, very few companies below a certain level are actually honest about their duty hours. The reason is fairly simple in most cases – if you kept to the letter of the law you would duty-hour yourself out of business, especially when there's not a lot of staff around. Otherwise, the companies simply have no respect for the law or their employees; many are cheapskates and beat down the room price, so you will get the noisiest and hottest for 'suitable accommodation'. Also, believe it or not, some companies don't regard Vancouver or Seattle as being on the West coast of N. America (haven't they got an atlas?), so their minimum rest periods can be reduced to twenty-five hours rather than the two local nights needed for San Francisco.

Discretion here is the better part of valour, but falsifying duty hours is but a short step removed from doing it to other documents, such as technical logs, and that would never do. It's hard to give you any advice, except to point out that being pedantic can often be counter-productive – that is, sometimes you just have to swallow things.

Maximum Permissible Duty Period (FDP)

A *Duty Period* is any continuous period through which you work for the company, including any FDP (see below), positioning, ground training, ground duties and standby duty.

A *Flying Duty Period* (FDP), on the other hand, is any duty period during which you fly in an aircraft as crew. It includes positioning immediately before or after a flight (say in a taxi or light aircraft) and pre/after-flight duties, so the start will generally be at least thirty minutes before the first scheduled departure time and the end at least fifteen minutes after last chocks on or rotors last stopped time, though these may vary between companies (see also Pre- and Post-Flight Activity and Positioning). In Canada, flight duty time starts when you report for a flight or standby and finishes when the engines stop after the final flight of the day, including time used for duties prior to the reporting time. Presumably, after-flight duties aren't included, as there are no specific times laid down.

If a flying duty period immediately follows ground or other duty, the FDP commences from the start of the other. With split duties (see below), the intervening time on the ground is also included.

The maximum rostered FDPs are in tables in the ops manual which actually come from CAP 371 (The Guide to Requirements on the Avoidance of Excessive Fatigue in Aircrews). These tables (only two reproduced below) give limits dependent on acclimatisation (or not) to the local time zone. You're considered to be acclimatised if you've had three consecutive local nights free of duty within a local time zone band of two hours (for a definition of 'local night' see under Duty Cycles).

Maximum FDP – Fixed-wing; single pilot

Sectors Up to	4	5	6	7	8+
0600–0759	10	9½	8½	8	8
0800–1259	11	10¼	9½	8¾	8
1300–1759	10	9¼	8½	8	8
1800–2159	9	8¼	8	8	8
2200–0559	8	8	8	8	8

Maximum FDP – Helicopters; single pilot

Local start	Max FDP	Max Flying
0600–0659	9	6
0700–0759	10	7
0800–1359	10	7
1400–2159	9	6
2200–0559	8	5

FDPs for aeroplanes are more flexible than for helicopters because the latter involve relatively short flights during which several sectors are flown without stopping rotors, giving you a high workload. In fact (as you can see), in a helicopter, there's a maximum number of hours you can fly within any FDP, in view of the lack of sector limits, and the fact that four hours' helicopter flying is the equivalent of eight hours' hard labour, and double that when long-lining. In Canada, that sort of restriction seems to come with heli-logging or spraying.

Helicopter pilots doing repetitive short sectors at an average rate of ten or more landings per hour (e.g. pleasure flying or load slinging) should have a break of at least thirty minutes away from the aircraft within any continuous period of three hours (you need it, too). After three hours' offshore shuttle operations in conditions other than day VMC, you should get a thirty-minute rest free of all duty.

As the objective of these restrictions is to ensure that you're adequately rested *at the beginning* of each flying duty period, it follows that flexibility should be applied at the end. All FDP limits can be stretched by Split Duties, In-flight Relief or Extensions, which are described below. Extensions can be used on the day at your discretion, to cater for unforeseen delays, etc., but the others must be planned.

Discretion to Extend a Flying Duty Period

There are always delays in aviation, for anything from technical to weather reasons, and a flying duty period may be extended if you think you can make the flight safely and have consulted the other members of the crew about their fitness. However, the normal maximum is based on the *original* reporting time, and calculated on what *actually* happens, not what was planned to happen (everything must be planned properly). Sometimes, for example, you may have to exercise it if a lower-performance aircraft is used instead of a larger one, and consequently takes longer to get round the route. This discretion is yours (as commander), but some companies will make the decision for you before the first flight of the day, which is not when it should be used. In these circumstances, you may only extend the FDP by 1.5 hours, saving the remainder of the three normally permitted for later.

In the UK, extensions up to three hours are regarded as the absolute limit, except in emergencies, which are situations that, in your judgment, present serious risks to health and safety, such as air ambulance flights, where the patient may be put at risk by the delay caused by a rest period. In such cases, the figures may be extended by up to four hours, provided that no in-flight relief has been allowed for and the previous rest period has been taken in full.

There must be at least forty-eight hours between air-ambulance flights, and a spare (qualified) commander must be carried if you plan to extend by more than two hours of the permitted four. The need for the trip itself must also be certified by a competent medical authority, and no passengers (other than next-of-kin of the patient) must be carried. Once the patient has been de-planed, you can't use any further discretion over the permitted four hours to get you home. You can only do three of these flights in any consecutive twenty-eight days.

Whenever discretion is exercised, the circumstances should be reported to Operations on the discretion report form (in the ops manual). If the duty period is extended for more than two hours, the report should also be forwarded to the CAA within thirty days.

In Canada, most people extend to 15 hours, if the following rest period is extended by the same amount (1 hour) *or* you do less than 8 hours' flying a day. Transport Canada can issue a special permission for 15 hours, so check your ops manual – in this case, it appears that your next rest period must also be an hour longer, or you can't do more than 8 hours flying the *next* day. Spray pilots are restricted to 14 hours anyway (and must have 5 days off in every 30).

Minimum Rest Periods

As well as having a maximum number of hours on duty, there's also a minimum rest time between duty periods.

A *Rest Period* is time before a flying duty period which is intended to ensure that you're adequately rested *before* a flight. It doesn't include excessive Travelling Time (over ninety minutes or so) or Positioning. During it, you should be free from all duties, not interrupted by the company, and have the opportunity for a minimum number of consecutive hours' sleep (eight, in Canada) in suitable accommodation, plus time to travel there and back, and for personal hygiene and meals.

In Canada, the minimum rest period is defined in only one place in CARs, right at the front, under *Interpretation*, where it says that you should be free from all duties, not be interrupted and be able to get at least eight hours' sleep in suitable accommodation, travel there (and back) and take care of personal hygiene. Realistically, therefore, the rest period should be about nine hours long. It's an hour extra anyway for spraying, with 5 hours of sleep taking place between 2000 and 0600 hours. Time spent on essential duties required by the company after duty are not part of any rest period.

You should have your rest periods (see also Duty Cycles) rostered enough in advance to get your proper rest. Minimum rest periods should be at least as long as the preceding duty period, and not less than twelve hours (in the UK), except when accommodation is provided by the company, in which case the minimum may be eleven, subject to any exemptions you have. Rest starts from the end of the duty period and not the flying duty period (see earlier for the differences). A rest period must include a Local Night if it follows a duty period longer than eighteen hours.

Discretion to Reduce a Rest Period

You can reduce rest periods below the minimum, but like extending duty time, it's at your discretion, and can only be done after consulting the crew. In any event, you must be able to get at least ten hours at the accommodation where you take your rest, subject to the requirements of travelling time. Use of discretion for reducing rest is considered exceptional and shouldn't be done to successive rest periods (it's very much frowned upon). In general, you're better off extending an FDP than reducing a rest period if at all possible. Also, at no time should a rest period be reduced if it immediately follows an extended duty period, *or vice versa* (this is even more frowned upon).

Your discretion to reduce a rest period (following a non-extended FDP) should not be for longer than one hour. If a rest period is reduced, a written report should be submitted to Operations on the discretion report form (again, in the ops manual). If the reduction is by more than one hour, both you and the company must forward the report to your inspector within thirty days.

Split Duties

You can extend a duty day by other means than discretion, though, and you can do it on duties with a long time gap between flights. Technically, a split duty is a flying duty period with two or more sectors separated by less than a minimum rest period, typically being a situation where you deliver people to a place and wait for them to come back. In other words, you can claim some of the period spent hanging around in the middle as 'rest' and tack it on to the end of the basic working day. What's more, you can plan to do this from the start, extending the FDP by half of the 'rest' taken if it's between 3 and 10 hours (inclusive, providing the hours are consecutive). In Canada, the extension is up to three hours, so you need 6 hours off.

The company should make arrangements for a quiet and comfortable place (not open to the public, which doesn't mean the aircraft) for the rest to be taken. If your rest is longer than six consecutive hours, they should also provide a bed in the previously mentioned 'satisfactory accommodation'.

The rest period doesn't include any time required for immediate post- and pre-flight duties, typically fifteen minutes for each (see also Pre- and Post-Flight Activity).

If the rest period gets to be longer than ten hours, just start a new FDP (but see also Minimum Rest Periods). Also, there's nothing to stop you having two split duties within one FDP – the only proviso is that the different sectors (and their duty periods) should be separated by more than three hours to claim the extra.

In Canada, you can go beyond 14 hours by half the rest period up to 3 hours, *if* you have been given advance notice *and* you get 4 hours in suitable accommodation, and are uninterrupted. This means that the maximum time you can possibly be on duty is 17 hours, if you have 6 hours off during the day. Your next rest period must be increased by at least the extended time.

In-Flight Relief

Although small operators don't require it (because their aircraft don't generally have the endurance), just in case you were wondering, this works in a similar way to split duties, in that you can extend the working day by using a proportion of 'rest' taken within it, but you must be away from both flight deck and passengers, and it's subject to certain limitations outside the scope of this book.

If you've been relieved and have no further duties on the flight, then the remainder of the FDP is treated as positioning.

Positioning

Positioning means being transferred from place to place as a passenger in surface or air transport, usually before or after a FDP, but also at any time as required by the company (this shouldn't be confused with normal travel from home to work – see Travelling Time below). Many airlines use taxis for this, but you may be lucky and get a comfortable bus or a light aeroplane.

All time spent on positioning is classed as duty, and when it comes immediately before a flying duty period is included in it, so the subsequent rest period must account for (and be at least as long as) the total FDP and positioning. Positioning is not, however, counted as a sector, and in case I haven't mentioned it before, a sector is the time between an aircraft first moving under its own power until it next comes to rest after landing (there are no sector limits for helicopters).

Travelling Time

Travelling time (that is, not positioning but normal travel from home to work) is not classed as duty and therefore not included in the totals, but should your journey exceed 'a lengthy period' (about ninety minutes), you should make arrangements to get nearer. When away from base and travelling times between the aerodrome and sleeping accommodation exceed thirty minutes each way, the resulting rest period should be increased by the excess (or a lesser time) enough for a minimum of ten hours (nine for cabin crews) there.

If you have to travel from your home to an aerodrome other than your normal one, the actual time between the two aerodromes (if any) is also positioning (for example, your normal trip to A is twenty minutes, but it takes ten to get to B from A, so there's ten minutes' extra to add to the

FDP). You must also include excess travel to the new aerodrome over and above your normal travelling time.

Standby Duty

Aside from crews actually flying, resting or taking time off, some must be available for emergencies, like sickness or extra flights. Standby is when the company requires you to be on call and able to report within, say, ninety minutes, but not where you need merely to be contactable for notification of a duty that starts ten or more hours ahead.

Should you get called out, your maximum duty period is what your maximum allowable FDP should be, according to the tables, plus six hours for the standby itself, which presumably means that if you haven't been called out after that, you're safe. The ensuing rest period must be based on the combined length of standby, FDP and positioning. Standby alone should not exceed twelve hours, and all standby time counts towards cumulative totals, except when a predetermined amount of notice has been given before reporting, when it can be halved.

In Canada, you can be On Standby, On Call, On Reserve or Free of Duty. For the first, you must be in a specified location to be available at less than an hour's notice; for the second, the location requirement is removed (these really apply to commuter/airline work); and the third allows a notice period of more than one hour, with each day having an uninterrupted rest period scheduled in advance, giving you the chance of at least 8 hours' sleep. There are three ways of dealing with this:

- You get 24 hours' notice of when your rest period will start, and how long it will be. It cannot start more than 3 hours earlier or later than the preceding rest period, or more than 8 hours in a week (that's 1.1 hours a day). So, if your first rest period starts at 2000 hours, the next one must start between 1700 and 2300 hours, and those for the rest of the week around 1900–2100 hours.

- You get at least 10 hours' notice, free of all duty.

- You do not get any duties and are not interrupted between 2200 and 0600 hours.

Most companies use the third. If the above cannot be complied with, that is, you get no notice at all, your maximum duty time is 10 hours, and the next rest period must be increased by 5 hours (actually half the duty time).

Cumulative Limits

UK

Your weekly total of duty hours should not exceed fifty-five (sixty for helicopters), with an occasional increase to sixty, counting everything (flying duty, ground duty, split duty, standby and positioning). In any twenty-eight consecutive days, it's 190 (200).

The number of early starts and late finishes must not exceed three consecutively, or four in a week. Officially, early starts and late finishes arise from duty periods that impinge on the period 0100–0700 local acclimatised time, to cover ringing your customers at between 2300 and 0700 hours before you propose to fly, and letting them know if you can go or not because of weather. If this go/no go time is earlier than one hour before the proposed start of the FDP, it must also be added to the FDP.

Your total hours during the previous twenty-eight consecutive days should not exceed 100 (90 for helicopters) *at the beginning of any flight*, but the expiry of the twenty-eight days is at the end of the day the flight begins, so a bit of bad drafting makes things confusing, because you don't know what you're going to do that day. Also, a helicopter pilot shouldn't do more than eighteen hours in three days, thirty in seven and 240 in 84 (3 × 28).

You shouldn't do over 900 hours (800 helicopter) in any twelve consecutive calendar months.

Canada

Here the limits are 1,200 flying hours a year, 300 every 90 days, 120 hours every 30 days or, if you're on call, 100 hours every 30 days. For aircraft other than a helicopter forty hours a week, or sixty hours otherwise. For single-pilot IFR, eight hours a day. There are no cumulative limits for duty hours.

Duty Cycles

Days off are periods available for leisure and relaxation that are not part of a duty period (that is, not rest periods, although their function is the same; the essential phrase is free from all duty). A single day off includes two local nights (defined below) and should be at least thirty-four hours long. Subsequent days off will include a further local night for each additional one, the first being at least twenty hours long and the rest twenty-four. A day off may include a rest period. A *Local*

Night is a period of eight hours falling between 2200 and 0800 local time.

If the company can't manage to schedule much in advance (although they must make the effort), days off must be rostered at least seven days ahead and may only be given up with your permission, assuming that rostering limits are not exceeded. If you lose a day off you must have one to make up for it inside the next twenty-eight days (days off are intended to be sacrosanct).

You should not work more than seven consecutive days between days off and must have two consecutive days off in any consecutive fourteen. You should also have at least seven days off in any consecutive four weeks and an average of at least eight days off in each consecutive four-week period, averaged over three such periods.

Helicopter pilots (as always, a special case) should also have two consecutive days off after seven consecutive days on duty and at least three days off in any consecutive fourteen (a single day off for helicopter crews may only follow up to a maximum of six days duty).

In Canada, for commuter and airline operations using aeroplanes, or when on call, the figures are at least 36 hours a week or 3 days every 17 days (all in one go). For aerial work, air taxi and helicopters, 13 days every 90 or 3 every 30, although you can be assigned duty for up to 42 days after 5 days off instead of the latter requirement. You must, in any case, have 5 days off after every assignment over 27 days. In other words, before and after any assignment of duty over 27 days, you must have 5 days off, and the maximum assignment is 42 days.

Records to be Maintained

Operations are responsible for completing your Record of Flying and Duty Hours from the information you give them at the end of each flight. Try and resist maintaining them on their behalf, as this will ensure that, if somebody is fiddling the hours, it won't be you that gets it in the neck first (I once worked for a company whose totals were consistently 100 hours per month fewer than my own figures).

Records must contain information concerning the beginning, end and duration of each FDP (and the function performed during that period); the duration of each duty period (whether or not it includes a FDP); the duration of each rest period prior to a FDP or standby duty period; the dates of days off and weekly totals of duty. These must be preserved for twelve calendar months from the date of the last entry, while discretion reports are kept for at least six months. There's a seven-day example of an FTL record below. The left-hand side deals with flying hours and the right with duty hours.

Record of Flight Time and Duty Hours

Date	T/O	Ldg	Total	On	Off	Split Duty Hrs	On	Off	Total	Remarks

Total Flying Hours

Total Duty Hours

Pre- and Post-Flight Activity

Pre-flight activity (for flight planning, etc.) is about thirty minutes before the first departure; post-flight activity is about fifteen minutes after last chocks on/rotors last stopped time. For a split duty, they are about fifteen minutes each. All these may be shorter if the flight is *dispatched* (that is, the work is done by other people).

Delayed Reporting Time

If you're informed of a delay to your reporting time before leaving your place of rest, the new FDP commences four hours after the original reporting time, or at the new time, whichever is earlier. The maximum permitted re-scheduled FDP, however, is based on the original reporting time from the tables.

In Canada, if the delay is over three hours, your flight duty time starts three hours after the original reporting time.

Pleasure Flying

Briefly (because it's dealt with more fully in Chapter 12), pleasure flying involves short flights which take off and land at the same aerodrome (not including photography). This presumably includes load slinging from helicopters. Under these circumstances (if you only do pleasure flying), a single FDP shouldn't exceed ten hours, but you can stretch this to twelve if you're positioning to and from base. Within that FDP, you should not spend more than a total of seven hours at the controls, except for up to an additional two when *positioning only* (in any case, you should not be at the controls continuously for more than three hours). Also, you should have breaks at least thirty minutes long according to this:

FDP Duration	Rest
up to 6 hours	at least 1 hour
6–8 hours	at least 1.5 hours
over 8 hours	at least 2 hours

Split duties do not apply, but normal rest periods do.

Definitions

A couple of stray definitions that I couldn't fit in earlier:

Week

A *week* is seven consecutive days starting at 0001 local time on any set day of the week, as determined by the company (the set day must be specified in the manual, so why not say Monday?).

Rostering Period

A rostering period normally comprises four consecutive weeks.

Rostered, Scheduled or Planned Duties

Single or a series of duty days notified to you in advance.

8

Operations Procedures

How a company operates, from weather minima to de-icing . . .

Flight Planning

Proper Planning Prevents Poor Performance. Quite true. As we're not strictly talking about drawing lines on maps (which you should know about already), I've combined the operational planning that technically is up to you with the procedure for setting up a charter, since they are both part and parcel of the same thing. With any luck, Ops will have done their part for you, but there will always be some overlap which will have to be sorted out amongst yourselves.

Procedure for Charter Queries

You may be the only one in the office one day, and a customer wants to go somewhere. How do you quote for a job? There's no substitute for experience in what is really the function of Ops or Sales, but the following is based on sound practice. All quotes given (including sub-charters) should be recorded – there will be a quotes book or file somewhere, and your figures must be entered under the appropriate headings. Initially, you need to know:

- ❏ Customer's name
- ❏ Contact telephone no.
- ❏ Date of trip
- ❏ Route details
- ❏ Load details
- ❏ Timings
- ❏ Alternative action if diverted

The last one is quite important, as you will quite often have to make that decision on their behalf, and the more knowledge you can get before you go, the better you will look if things go wrong.

This information (and more) is put on the flight brief, a document you get before you take off, telling you what you're going to be doing. The charterer shouldn't be expecting a service that's illegal or unsafe – the most common is landing without permission ('It's all right, he's a friend of mine') and flying overweight ('We got it all in last week'), not to mention bad weather at the destination ('I can see the end of the garden'). It's too easy to get a reputation as a cowboy company when attempting to give customers what they want, and they'll drop you in it if something happens, so why bother? Actually, whilst on this subject, if a customer insists that the last pilot managed to do the job, check that he wasn't using something a lot bigger ('Oh yes, now you mention it, it was an Astar' Duh).

When quoting, try to give the information they want, so that they will be less likely to go elsewhere. If you have to call back, do so within, say, fifteen minutes. *Always* ring back when you say you will, even if it's just to say you haven't got the information yet – it's all salesmanship! Quotes should be valid for about seven days, because things have a tendency to change, as if you didn't know already.

Invoicing is based on flight times, so keep them and costs down, which is as much for the customer's benefit as yours. It's hard enough to sell flying, but once you start the add-ons, they often start to back off. Normally, just take the hourly rate and multiply it by the flying time, rounded up to the nearest five or six minutes (the latter for decimal accounting). The aircraft speed for flight planning purposes should be in the Flight Planning or Technical section of the ops manual, and hourly rates should be on a chart in the office. Some companies have precalculated figures for frequent destinations in a spreadsheet or on the wall somewhere.

You will then need to add up everything else that costs money, namely landing fees, handling charges, Customs/Special Branch, etc., not to mention purchase taxes, except for foreign trips and those in aircraft with more than twelve seats, which are exempt (more details on going overseas later, but don't forget to claim the fuel drawback).

Payment should be made in advance, as it would be if they went by train, though some approved customers may be invoiced afterwards, but even then a written or faxed confirmation of the booking, or the equivalent of a purchase order, is required. **This next bit is VERY important**: *The more rush on the part of the customer, the greater must be your insistence on payment first!* If they can't pay in advance (no credit cards, cheque book eaten by the dog, whatever) politely refer them somewhere else; you won't look very good if you incur a bad debt, as, once the panic's over, they'll probably complain about the weather, service, etc., and make every excuse not to pay. The company should accept all major credit cards anyway.

Tip: Some customers say they're going to put a lot of work your way and want a discount as a result. There's nothing wrong with that, it's normal business practice, but don't give the discount straight away, otherwise you'll find they have only one or two trips and disappear, effectively getting cheap flying. The best way to deal with anyone who may be half-serious is to give a retrospective discount, such as every thirteenth hour free, or a cheque for 10 per cent of the money spent every fortnight. If he's any sort of businessman, your customer will understand. If he doesn't, then he may cause other trouble as well, like arguing about the bill. For photographers, take the money first and refund it when their stuff is published.

It's also a good idea to have some sort of system where the customer signs for the flying received so that there's no argument later.

There may or may not be a minimum charge for your company's services, but, if it's busy, make it one hour per half day, as the machine can't be used elsewhere. If business is slack, compromise a little, but remember that passengers are rarely on time, so don't do too much tight scheduling; refuelling at some airports, like Birmingham, can take up to an hour and a half, not because the refuellers don't know what they're doing, but because you've got to walk all over the place, through security, paying landing fees, booking out, etc.

Having gone through the stuff below, don't start a flight unless you're satisfied that the aircraft is airworthy, its configuration is as per the Minimum Equipment List (MEL) or Configuration Deviation List (CDL), documents and forms, ops manual, maps, charts, etc. are on board, and fuel, load and balance are OK.

You must also complete an ICAO/ATS flight plan, discussed elsewhere. Now let's look at the rest of it:

❏ Is the load acceptable? Is it dangerous cargo? (If so, see Chapter 9).

❏ Aircraft and crew availability. How many hours to the next maintenance and are there enough for the flight? Have you enough crew and are they cleared into that airfield (check the Airfield Categorisation File – later)?

❏ Crew duty hours are not too near weekly or monthly limits. When did they come off duty and when does the rest period end?

❏ Departure and destination points are open. Early or late movements will incur extension fees, which can be hefty (at Heathrow, all sorts of variables ranging from the time of day you fly to the direction you approach from can affect the price), and they will probably charge a minimum. Think about getting an indemnity for out-of-hours use if the aircraft is small enough not to need a licensed airfield (below 2,730 kg).

❑ Prior permission is obtained for landing at the departure and destination – you must get the *owner's* consent to use any landing site, which is assumed with a licensed airfield – it's part of the terms under which a licence is granted. See also Helicopter Landing Sites in this chapter.

❑ Handling for departure and destination is available *and booked.* Handling charges are really only applicable at Gatwick and Heathrow in the UK when meeting, interlining or departing passengers onto domestic or foreign flights. Self-handling is permitted at Heathrow, but not at Gatwick (even for refuelling), where you have to nominate a handling agent. Handling agents available include airlines as well as private companies, so try those if you get stuck. Handling is actually a sore point amongst many operators (as are Eurocharges) so be careful before you incur the charges. On the other hand, self-handling is a pain to the pilot, but some customers won't pay for what is essentially an expensive taxi ride, despite the inconvenience the use of a handling agent avoids.

❑ Always expect handling charges when abroad (see International Operations in this chapter).

❑ Eurocharges. Use of the airways costs money, and the larger the aircraft, the more it will cost, but below a certain weight (2,000 kg) it's free, so a Partenavia gets away with it, and an Aztec doesn't. Naturally, if you go VFR you don't get charged, but even if you only cross an airway en route the civil servants will have their hands out, so there may be pressure to fly VFR everywhere to escape the charges, even to the extent of flying at 1,000 feet through Amsterdam in cloud claiming to be visual or over the Channel at 500 feet claiming to be VFR at 1,000. (Both true. Sigh.)

❑ Fuel available (and booked on a tight schedule or opening-hours extension). With a full load, you will have limited endurance, so you may need a top-up somewhere. You should offer a choice of refuelling en route, which is usually cheaper, or flying away while the customer's on business, which is more convenient, and gives you something to do, but don't forget the extra flying and landing fees go on the bill.

❑ Site/performance characteristics. Check the runway length! (Airfield Categorisation File again.) When quoting for a helicopter trip, unless there's clear access, don't include landings in built-up areas, which technically can include open areas, such as golf courses, though this hasn't been proved in court yet, as far as I know. Hotels are always a good bet, and farms are also worth trying, as are the local police, as they may know somebody.

❑ Grid references (for helicopters) correct. Pick a site with good transport access, as you don't want to wade through muddy fields. A description of the site is useful, as is getting it marked.

❑ Exemptions or dispensations are valid and the conditions therein can be complied with.

❑ Police and other services notified as a courtesy – this is a legal requirement where the public has access to sites. In Canada, you have to inform the local municipality as well.

❑ Security arrangements at the destination, such as Prevention of Terrorism Acts, where you have to notify your departures and arrivals.

❑ Correct seating and bar, with drinks, fitted – see Engineers.

❑ Paperwork correct (for a full list see later this chapter):
  ❑ Captain's briefing sheet
  ❑ Navigation log
  ❑ Trimsheets/Loadsheets
  ❑ Terrorism cards
  ❑ WX ordered on telex or fax
  ❑ OS maps
  ❑ Customs documentation

❑ All the above (as required) should be placed in a large envelope for whoever's going to do the job. See Chapter 15, *Setting up a Company*, for more about paperwork.

Sub-Charters

This is where another operator gets you to do a job, or where you pass one on and take a commission, typically when a customer wants a plane you haven't got and you can't quite bear to turn away the trade.

Unfortunately, having commissions everywhere can get complicated, and too many fingers in the pie leads to confusion and a dissatisfied customer (actually, if you do have to turn down work, pleading full commitment rather than unavailability gives a better impression). It can be lucrative, though – five-figure commissions are not unusual, for the sake of a phone call, and a company can often make more money by not flying at all. However, if you want to become a broker, be aware that you need considerable credibility before flying companies will deal with you.

If you do get involved, just invoice the commission to whoever you pass it on to. Sometimes you will get a net quote, which is the minimum that they want, so add your figures on top.

Minimum Flight Altitudes

These may be governed by national regulations, ATC, or hard objects (obstacles), in that order. The highest of them will determine the minimum altitude for that route or sector (that is, each intended track between reporting points), which will ultimately depend on the accuracy of your position, your maps and the characteristics of the area, in terms of weather or terrain. There are different definitions of this, depending on the airspace you are in, but they all provide you with a lowest safe altitude you can use in an emergency.

You should already be familiar with the low flying rules, but an ops manual will still have to state them, just to tighten things up legally – Rules Of The Air would be in Section 12.

Minimum Obstacle Clearance Altitude (MOCA)

The lowest altitude for an airway or route segment in which an IFR flight may be conducted. In Canada, it gives you 1,000 ft of clearance above all obstacles inside the lateral limits defined by navaids (see below), in non-mountainous regions, but does not account for reception range, as does the MEA, which will be higher. Otherwise (for JARs), start with the highest ground or obstacle within 5 nm, add 1,000 ft when under 6,000 ft, or 2,000 when over, and round up to the next 100. Two thousand feet is the minimum over land anyway, but try for 1,500 over water, assuming the highest obstacle is under 500 ft.

Navigation aids

You naturally use navaids to fix your position, but their information becomes less reliable the further away you get from them, so corridors are defined, within which the signals can be counted on.

For **VORs**, the corridor width starts 5 nm either side, diverging at 4 degrees for 70 nm, until 20 nm wide. The width remains constant between 70 and 140 nm, where it diverges again at 4 degrees until a width of 40 nm is reached at 280 nm out, at which point it remains constant.

For **NDBs**, the corridor starts 5 nm either side, diverging at 7 degrees until a width of 20 nm is reached at 40 nm out, remaining constant between 40 and 80 nm out, thereafter diverging at 7 degrees until 60 nm wide at 245 nm, then remaining constant.

In Canada, VHF airways (i.e. defined by VORs) are 4 nm wide either side of the centreline, increasing where 4.5 degree lines cross the width. For LF/MF airways, using NDBs, substitute 4.34 and 5 degrees.

Minimum Off-Route Altitude (MORA)

This is a minimum altitude calculated from the highest ground or obstacle in every Lat/Long square on the map, plus 1,000 ft up to and including 6,000 ft, or 2,000 ft above that. You must enter MORA figures in the nav log, both as a reminder, and so that they can get you at the Board of Inquiry. When in IMC en route you should not fly below MORA until your position is established on an approved procedure, after which you must stick to the minimum altitude specified.

Minimum Sector Altitude

Found on approach plates, based on a 25 nm circle round a navaid, for the procedure turn, giving you 1,000 feet above the highest obstacle.

Allowance for Wind Speed

Within 20 nm of ground over 2,000 ft amsl, increase the standard MOCA/MORA by:

Elevation	0–30 kt	31–50 kt	51–70 kt	+ 70 kt
2,000–8,000 feet	+ 500 ft	+1,000 ft	+1,500 ft	+2,000 ft
+ 8,000 feet	+1,000 ft	+1,500 ft	+2,000 ft	+2,500 ft

This is to safeguard against the Venturi effect over a ridge making the altimeter misread, as well as causing turbulence and standing waves. A combination of all this, plus temperature errors (see below), can result in an altimeter overreading *by as much as 3,000 feet*.

Temperature Correction

When the surface temperature is well below ISA, correct MSAs by:

Surface Temperature (ISA)	Correction to MOCA/MORA
−16 C to −30 C	+ 10%
−31 C to −50 C	+ 20%
−51 C or below	+ 25%

In the discussions that follow, I will assume you're not going to land at any aerodrome or heliport unable to take your aircraft in terms of weather or performance (always allowing for ice systems), that you're not going to run engines outside their rated limits, and you can come to a complete stop using normal procedures, so the term *suitable aerodrome* will do as shorthand, instead of the long-winded repetitions you might otherwise find. I will also assume that the weather remains as expected, and that weight limits will not be exceeded (common sense, really).

Aeroplanes

Single-engined
If the engine fails, you should be able to continue the flight above MOCA/MORA to 1,000 feet above a suitable landing point.

Multi-engined
If an engine fails, you must be able to continue to a suitable landing point, maintaining at least the MSA with a positive gradient of climb at a particular height above it, which depends on your aircraft's performance (see below). Some aircraft, of course, can't maintain much height with one engine out, let alone two or more, and there will be charts in the flight manual to indicate your expected rate of descent with respect to weight and temperature, etc. Drift Down, as it's called, is discussed further later in this chapter under Performance, where you will also find definitions explained. For (JAR) performance purposes, aeroplanes come in three classes:

❑ *Class A*. All multi-engined turbojets and turboprops capable of carrying more than nine passengers, or which are heavier than 5,700 kg. A turboprop lighter than this may use Class B.

❑ *Class B*. Propeller-driven aeroplanes capable of carrying fewer than nine passengers, and lighter than 5,700 kg.

❑ *Class C*. Piston-engined aeroplanes capable of carrying more than nine passengers, or heavier than 5,700 kg.

Class A
One Engine Inoperative En Route Net Flight Path
If one engine fails, you must be able to maintain a positive net flight path (that is, be able to climb, however slowly) at least 1,000 feet above all ground and obstructions (and clear them vertically by at least 2,000 feet) within 5 nm (9.3 km) of the intended track, to a suitable aerodrome. In

other words, at any given point, you must be able to maintain a climb at OCH + 1,000 ft, all the while clearing obstacles by OCH + 2,000 ft.

Two Engines Out , Three or More Engines
You should never be more than ninety minutes (at the all-engines long-range cruising speed at standard temperature in still air) from a suitable aerodrome, and be able to continue, clearing vertically, by at least 2,000 ft, all terrain and obstacles 9.3 km (5 nm) either side of the track. If navigation is less than 95 per cent, increase the margin to 18.5 km (10 nm). The net flight path must have a positive gradient at 1,500 ft above the suitable aerodrome.

Safe fuel jettisoning is allowed if you can land with the proper reserves – the expected weight where the two engines are assumed to fail must include enough fuel to arrive at least 1,500 ft over the landing area and fly level for fifteen minutes afterwards. You should dump fuel at least 2,000 feet above the highest obstacle within 5 nm, to allow for adequate vaporisation. Ideally, it should be undertaken over a relatively less populated area, clear of heavy traffic, on a constant heading. You should tell ATC as well, so that they can warn other people.

Class B
Multi-Engined
If an engine fails, you must be able to continue at or above MSA to 1,000 feet above a suitable aerodrome. You cannot assume more than a 300 feet-per-minute climb rate, and you must subtract 0.5 per cent from the gross gradient.

Single-Engined
If the engine fails, you must be able to reach a point 1,000 feet above a place where you can make a safe landing, so don't fly above cloud that extends below the MSA. You cannot assume more than a 300 feet-per-minute climb rate, and you must subtract 0.5 per cent from the gross gradient.

Class C
All Engines Operating
You must have a climb rate of at least 300 feet per minute, with all engines below maximum continuous power, at the minimum altitudes used for Classes A and B.

One Engine Out
You must clear all obstacles within 5 nm (9.3 km) either side of track vertically by 1,000 feet, when the ROC is zero or greater, and 2,000 feet when

below. Increase the width margin to 10 nm (18.5 km) if navigational accuracy is below 95 per cent.

Your performance figures must provide a positive slope at 1,500 feet (450 m) above the landing point. As far as this paragraph is concerned, the available rate of climb is assumed to be 150 feet per minute less than the gross. You can jettison fuel safely if you can land with proper reserves.

Two Engines Out , Three or More Engines

You should never be more than ninety minutes (at the all-engines long-range cruising speed at standard temperature in still air) away from a suitable aerodrome, and you must clear all obstacles within 5 nm (9.3 km) of the intended track vertically by at least 2,000 feet. If accuracy of navigational is less than 95 per cent, increase the margin to 10 nm (18.5 km).

Your performance figures must provide a positive gradient at 1,500 ft above the suitable aerodrome. The available rate of climb is assumed to be 150 feet per minute less than the gross.

Safe fuel jettisoning is allowed if you can land with the proper reserves – the expected weight where the two engines are assumed to fail must include enough to arrive at least 1,500 ft over the landing area and fly level for fifteen minutes thereafter.

Helicopters

For (JAR) performance purposes, helicopters also come in threes:

❑ Class 1. Can land on the rejected take-off area, or safely continue, depending on when the failure occurs.
❑ Class 2. Can safely continue, except before a defined point after take-off or after a defined point before landing (in other words, some sort of committal point), in which case a forced landing may be required.
❑ Class 3. If a power-unit fails, a forced landing must be performed (i.e. single-engined).

Classes 1 and 2

On top of the minimum altitudes already listed, if you plan to fly out of sight of the surface, you must be able to maintain at least 50 feet per minute ROC at 1,000 feet (2,000 in mountains) above all obstacles within 10 nm either side of the track (0.5 nm if day VMC in sight of the surface), or continue to 1,000 feet above a suitable heliport, clearing all obstacles as above (drift-down techniques can be used). You must allow for winds, safe fuel jettisoning (not below 1,000 feet agl) consistent with reaching the heliport with required reserves, and you may reduce the width margins to 5 nm if navigational accuracy is good enough.

Class 3

You must be able to continue without flying below MOCA, but, if an engine fails, you must land without danger to persons or property on the surface. The minimum cloudbase must be 600 feet, visibility 800 m, you must be in sight of the surface not beyond ten minutes from land, and must not be at night or operating from a helideck or heliport in a hostile environment, which is where more stringent rules apply: that is, a safe forced landing is impossible, you cannot be protected from the elements, SAR is lacking or there is unacceptable endangering of persons or property on the ground (the sea areas north of 45N or south of 45S are considered hostile).

When VFR, most pilots (ex-military, anyway) fly above 1,200 feet or so agl (a bit more at night) unless under instructions from ATC or on a specialist task such as filming (with suitable exemptions). This is a hang-over from avoiding small-arms fire, but is also good for keeping the neighbours happy and not disturbing wildlife, particularly caribou, if you're in Canada, because running reduces their winter reserves. It's also worth noting that you find fewer birds at 1,500 feet.

Aerodromes and Heliports

All destinations or alternates, naturally, must be adequate and suitable for the aircraft using them; in this context, 'adequate' means that runway/FATO (Final Approach and Take-Off Area) dimensions and significant obstacles do not interfere with performance, but it also means that services, such as ATS, lighting, communications, navaids, weather and emergency services should be there as well.

For IFR, an approved approach procedure must be available for each destination and alternate, with up-to-date copies of the plates for each pilot. Under VFR, minimum operating visibilities and cloud ceilings must be clearly stated on your flight brief; the letters 'VFR' by themselves imply compliance with VFR minima in the ops manual.

Airfield Categorisation

Airfields are graded as to suitability for the average pilot, depending, amongst other things, on surroundings and local weather. Actually, proper grounds for classification into one area or another include lack of details in the normal flight guides, performance restrictions (runway conditions or obstructions), complex departure procedures and political problems.

They should be colour coded and graded in ascending order of difficulty, and the pilots' self-briefing file on them kept in the Operations office, being reviewed quarterly by Ops based on advice from the chief pilot and feedback from crews. On return from a flight, it is your responsibility to check that the information concerning the airfield is correct. Where changes have occurred, you should inform Operations; temporary ones will be recorded in the file, while those of a more permanent nature will go in the ops manual. Anything not mentioned should be checked out with the chief pilot.

Of course, if you ask for all that you may well get a puzzled silence. In practice, any briefing will be something like:

Chief Pilot: 'Been there before?'
You: 'No.'
Chief Pilot: 'Well, I'm sure you'll enjoy it.'

Category A – GREEN
Airfields with no undue difficulties and an approved let-down procedure, a non-performance-limited runway with night capability, and circling minima below 1,000 feet agl. You may operate into these airfields at any time provided you're signed up as current on your Route Competency certificate. No prior briefing is required and this category is unrestricted.

Category B – YELLOW
Airfields with some degree of difficulty, like non-standard approach patterns, high ground, unusual weather, performance limitations or other peculiarities. You may operate into them if you're specifically briefed (by a little something in your flight brief) and certified as competent into each named airfield. Where the problem is only runway length, that is, the field would otherwise be in the A list, you can just record satisfactory performance data before you go.

Category C – RED
Especially difficult airfields without recent familiarity, either in terrain, met or non-standard procedures (e.g. Hong Kong before it changed). You may fly into them only if you (or an accompanying pilot) have done so in the last thirteen months as an observer, and/or take instruction in an approved simulator.

Other categories

Airports are also allocated a three-letter code by IATA for commercial purposes, such as reservations, ticketing and baggage labelling. It's used on signals sent over the Aeronautical Fixed Telecommunications Network (AFTN). For example, YWG stands for Winnipeg.

In the same way, ICAO issues a four-letter code, and you will already be familiar with the EG codes on flight plans – see Chapter 14, *Legal Stuff*, for the differences between IATA and ICAO. As you will have gathered, the first two letters stand for the country and the last two the particular airport. There may be two others added for a specific address within the airport.

Alternates

Twins

At one-engine-out speed in still-air ISA conditions, take-off alternates should be within one hour's flight time, based on the actual take-off weight, or two hours or the ETOPS diversion time (see later), whichever is the less.

3- and 4-engined aircraft

The time is two hours still-air flight time at one-engine-inoperative cruising speed in ISA, based on the actual weight at take-off. The remaining engine max continuous power speed can be used as an alternative.

IFR

There must be at least one destination alternate for each IFR flight, unless you will be flying for less than six hours, or the destination is isolated with two separate runways, where you can do a VMC approach and landing from MSA for one hour either side of the ETA – runways are separate when a blockage of one will not affect the other and each has an approach procedure based on a separate aid. If the weather will be below minima for an hour either side of the ETA, or no met information is available, you must have two alternates.

Alternates must be specified in the nav log.

Helicopter Landing Sites

Ideally, flights should be undertaken from licensed sites, but most will be unlicensed, as helicopters are more able to make use of them.

In the UK, aircraft below 2,730 kg MAUW don't need a licensed aerodrome, provided the flights do not begin and end at the same place, take place at night, are not for training or are not regular services. Otherwise, licensed aerodromes must be used for scheduled services and training.

The owner of a piece of land does not need special permission to use it as a Helicopter Landing Site provided certain conditions are met. Naturally, it must not be in a congested area, otherwise you will come up against the ANO. It must also be only for private or business use, that of any employees, or people specifically visiting for social or business purposes. Finally, no structure must be erected in connection with its use for helicopters, aside from temporary ones (such as windsocks), otherwise the Planning Permission (Zoning) people will become interested – there's no need to notify them of anything unless the land is to be used as a helipad on more than twenty-eight days in any year. In fact, current planning regulations allow a helicopter to be used for personal, business and leisure uses 'as many people use a private car' from the owner's dwelling house without limitation, making it exempt from planning control, provided the use is incidental, or ancillary to, the principal use of the land. Also, the local police should be informed, as well as the other emergency services, especially where the public would normally have a right-of-way (such as a park).

In the USA, and probably Canada, you can land a helicopter anywhere that has not been declared as illegal, with the usual provisos about low flying and reckless operation, but be aware that local restrictions may well override any laid down by the FAA or Transport Canada.

If you use an unlicensed site, a landing site card should be raised and kept in the landing site library, possibly as part of the airfield categorisation file, which is the equivalent. This may then be used with the OS map for others to self-brief before using it.

However, making more than four movements at a place in a relatively short time (a movement is a take-off *or* a landing) makes it a 'feeder site', and subject to stricter standards than pleasure flying – relevant if you're performing shuttle flights at a special event, such as the Grand Prix.

Sites should allow you to make emergency landings without danger to persons or property on the surface, or significant risk to the helicopter and its occupants. An alternate site for a twin should meet single-engined requirements.

Performance **Group A** (JAR Class 1) helicopters need sufficient take-off space for the weight to be carried, and take-off, landing and reject areas must be prepared surfaces on which you must be able to land safely before the CDP, or continue to an alternative afterwards. You must be able to land safely on the planned area after LDP.

Group A (Restricted) (JAR Class 2) machines may have to make a forced landing before CDP or after LDP. For A (Restricted) and **B**, a prepared surface is not required, but there must be somewhere to land in the event of a reject that will cause no risk to third parties. If the site is too small, and/or with obstructions, you can downgrade to the next Group. It works the other way round, as well – given room to manoeuvre, you could upgrade and carry more payload.

The type of take-off will depend on the size of the area. Class 1 take-off techniques should be used when the area is restricted, and clear climbout paths should be available. They should also be used from elevated sites without obstructions so that you can land back on the site if an engine fails before the critical decision point.

Although an air or ground inspection is needed for all this, it's not always possible, so the charterer should be asked to supply a large-scale map of the landing site and approaches. If, on arrival, you decide that the area is not suitable, you shouldn't use it (which is easier said than done), so it's most important that the customer is fully aware of your company's requirements and that he will be charged for an abortive flight should the landing site not meet the required standards.

How do you tell how suitable a site is from the air? Difficult, that. The easy answer is to suck it and see, but confined or congested areas don't meet Performance requirements for Commercial Air Transport, and you may be contravening the famous Rule 5 as well (low flying). Your customer wants to land. You, on the other hand, have a licence to protect. If you're at all unsure, do a couple of flypasts and feel your way down – confined areas are further discussed under Mountain Flying.

The following criteria should apply to all unlicensed sites, which are technical requirements that do not necessarily allow for anything like Rule 5. The ANO regards a congested area as one 'substantially used for recreational and residential purposes', etc., which officially makes a golf course one, though you would be forgiven for thinking otherwise. A rule of thumb is 60 per cent buildings and trees, but specifics haven't been tested in court yet.

There should be at least one approach and departure lane containing either no or only isolated obstacles – a downwind component is not acceptable. The lanes and landing areas should be big enough to ensure you can land, take off and reach a safe height so that you can touch down into wind following an engine failure, while avoiding obstacles by a safe margin.

Try not to have marshland underneath the lanes because, while it may be soft, skids or wheels may sink in during an emergency landing, which is the last place you want dynamic rollover. In other words, the ground beneath the lanes must be suitable for emergency landings with respect to slope, softness, frangible obstructions, etc. Water is OK, provided the performance group is suitable or you've got the usual lifejackets, floats, etc.

The landing pad itself should be level, drained, with a grass or solid surface that does not blow up dust at the slightest provocation (you should be able to drive the average car over it). Its diameter should be at least twice the length of the largest helicopter to use it, including rotors, as you will need to turn round your tail. Watch out for anything that may snag the skids, particularly on take-off. Some people like the touchdown area marked with an H, but provided the grid reference is accurate enough, it shouldn't be too hard to find it.

If you're wanting to land where there's a gathering of 1,000 or more people at an organised event, remember that no landings at unlicensed sites should be undertaken within 3,000 feet of that assembly without written permission from the CAA and the event organisers (as per Rule 5 (1) d (i)).

Pleasure flying and feeder sites are considered elsewhere (Chapter 12). Finally, a couple of points to watch if you're ever tempted to land across or near railway lines, as you might if they're the only firm place around. The first is that your skids more often than not will complete an electrical connection used for signalling, and you may cause some confusion in the local signal box. The other is that trains do use the track outside published schedules, so don't be surprised to see a humungous diesel bearing down on you unexpectedly.

Airways Manuals

You need a route guide so that you can get around the airway system without messing things up for anybody else.

The ultimate airways manual is the *UK Air Pilot*, being the source from which all others get their information. If you ever end up in court, this will be the one introduced in evidence, but that's not to say that others are no good. They're all potted versions of it to varying degrees, but with better presentation. You can even produce your own, which is more economical if you have only one or two routes to cater for.

The commercially available ones are really as good as each other, whichever one you get started on probably becoming your favourite. In addition to the best known ones, *Jeppesen* and *Aerad*, the RAF do their own as a little sideline, which are worth a look at.

All of them, however, may contain non-approved letdowns, so inclusion of a procedure in a Flight Guide (other than the UKAP) doesn't necessarily mean it can be used for commercial air transport flights.

The above guides are intended for IFR work – for VFR you'll need to carry your trusty *Pooley's* or *Flyer's Guide* or, if you're wealthy, *Bottlang's*, but *Bottlang's* doesn't carry helipad information.

Operating Minima

There are weather conditions under which you're not allowed to land, attempt to land, or take off. A minimum cloud base and visibility will be laid down by the company for each airfield or heliport it intends to use, taking into account the navigation aids available, terrain, obstacles, type of aircraft, crew experience and State legislation. You don't have to do all the hard work: the above airway manuals will have all the calculations done for you, but how they are derived is described below in case you have to roll your own.

These regulations aren't only for safety, they also save your customers money and inconvenience. Speaking from experience, if you find the departure time creeping back because of weather, after about two hours, advise them to go twenty-four hours later. They're still going to take the same time at the destination – after all, there is a job to do which is the whole point of them going. If you don't, you will find the day getting unacceptably long and the company will still clock you on thirty minutes before take-off, regardless of the time you came in.

Some companies will pressure you into going just to get the money, knowing you won't get anywhere. In this case, leave the choice up to the clients. Offer no guarantees, but point out that there will still be a charge if the whole exercise is a waste of time. You therefore pass the ball into their court, and there's a chance you will be appreciated for not wasting their time, which must be expensive otherwise they wouldn't be flying.

In any case, you are responsible for ensuring that before take-off you've got weather minima for the relevant times at every destination and at least one suitable alternative, which must be noted on the nav log if you intend to use them (this can mean up to eight airfields if you include take-off alternates – see below). For Commercial Air Transport, foreign airfields are also subject to UK rules, and minima which apply to you will be the highest of:

❏ Those established by the State in which you are flying
❏ UK minima, as shown in the airway manual
❏ Basic minima established by your company

Remember that foreign airfields tend to close down automatically when the weather gets too bad, whereas an airport authority in the UK may only close down on their own initiative in the case of snow or a blocked runway – however, attempts to land in marginal weather are reported back to the authorities.

While you're not allowed to reduce the limits given, you are actively encouraged to increase them if you think it's necessary. As they're calculated for fog conditions with little or no wind, you should make due allowance for rain and/or crosswinds.

Naturally, minima are not valid if anything affecting their calculation has been changed through NOTAMs, or as instructed by ATC.

Minima not in the airways manual can be worked out with figures in the ops manual. In this case, one copy of your calculations must be retained in Ops, and another carried on board. However, airfields used regularly in this way should be permanently in the manual, and it's the company's responsibility to self-check them.

Calculations from the ops manual will be higher than anything pre-calculated, because they come from blanket figures which allow for aircraft in lower performance groups avoiding obstacles visually if an engine fails on take-off, so cloud ceiling figures will vary according to where you can start to construct your net flight path data (see Performance later in this chapter). If that happens at 300 feet (that is, your engines are assumed to be working till then), expect a 300 ft cloud ceiling.

The same principle goes for RVR figures, which are related to the time required to see and avoid obstacles – if you're going at ninety knots, 1,500 m RVR will give you thirty seconds between seeing and missing anything. RVR is the distance you can see in the direction of take-off or landing, determined by a certain procedure, usually with the aid of a transmissometer, and based on runway lights at setting 3. The distance given is taken as the RVR for the time being, that is, only valid for a short time. If the reported RVR is below your expected minima, you're not allowed to start an approach past the outer marker (or at least descend below 1,000 feet above the aerodrome elevation), even if you've established visual reference above that height. As they say, there is an *approach ban* (see the Glossary). Remember the minimum visual approach visibility is 800 m, to guard against shallow fog, and you need to increase the limits if the autopilot is unserviceable.

It's a good idea, in a commercial environment, to have something up your sleeve as well, by which I mean what do you do if the ILS goes off halfway down an approach? In training, you would probably go around, but that's expensive and the commercial department will love you if you keep adding ten-minute sectors to each flight. Many ILSs use an NDB as an outer marker, so why not be prepared to convert to an ADF approach? or a VOR (or whatever)? Most professional pilots don't expect to land from an approach, which means they don't get fixated and try to get in when they shouldn't.

Any non-standard minima must be retained with flight documentation for three months.

Planning Requirements

Take-Off/Alternates

If your multi-engined aeroplane can either stop or continue to 1,500 feet above the aerodrome while clearing all obstacles by the required margins, the take-off minima may not be less than:

Facilities	RVR (m)	Vis (m) Cat D
Nil (Day Only)	500	–
Runway Edge Ltg and/or Centreline Marking	250	300
Runway Edge and Centreline Lighting	200	250
Runway Edge, Centreline Ltg and Multi RVR	150	200

At night, at least runway edge and end lights are required. RVR/Vis for the initial part may be replaced by your own assessment. If you need to re-land immediately, and therefore see and avoid obstacles in the take-off area, refer to the table below. The height at which your engine fails may not be lower than that from which the *one-engine-inoperative net take-off flight path* can be constructed. When RVR/met vis is not available you cannot take off unless the actual conditions satisfy the applicable take-off minima.

Eng Fail Ht (ft)	<50	51–100	101–150	151–200	201–300	>300
RVR/Vis (m)	200	300	400	500	1,000	1,500

Use the higher of the tables according to circumstances.

For Class 1 helicopters (Group A) minima may not be less than:

Onshore heliports with IFR departure procedures	RVR/Visibility
Nil Facilities (Day)	250 m*
Nil Facilities (Night)	800 m
Unlit/unmarked defined runway/FATO	200 m
Rwy edge/FAT lighting and centreline marking	200 m
Rwy edge/FATO and centreline lighting, RVR info	150 m
Onshore heliports without IFR dep procs	800 m

*or rejected take-off distance, whichever is greater

With no reported met vis or RVR, you can only commence a take-off if they are equal to or better than required minimum (obvious, really). For

Class 2 (A) (Restricted) minima must be at least 800 m RVR/Vis, remaining clear of cloud during take-off or until reaching Class 1 capabilities. For Class 3 (Group B), try at least 600 ft cloud ceiling and 800 m RVR/Vis.

You must nominate a suitable alternate (on the nav log) to return to when weather conditions at the aerodrome you're departing from are below those required for landing, in case you have to return in a hurry. Favourable landing conditions at this alternate must be reported and forecast to be *at or above landing minima* one hour either side of ETA, and it must be within a certain time at one-engine-out speed, typically thirty minutes for a twin-piston and sixty for a turbine (the terrain and weather conditions en route must permit this, that is, your single-engined climb performance may not get you over obstacles in the way). For helicopters, it's an hour at normal, twin, IMC cruising speed.

If there is no suitable diversion, delay the flight until one is, or the departure weather improves. In fact, without an alternate, departure minima should be not less than those for landing at the same aerodrome. If you have to see and avoid obstacles on departure, a cloud ceiling should also be specified.

Take-off minima depend on many factors, including the performance group or class of the aircraft, availability of markings, lighting, runway surface and width, distances available and your experience (inexperienced crews should add 100 feet and 200 m to these figures).

Destinations

Landing distance requirements must be satisfied on both the most suitable runway for landing in still air and any you may need because of forecast wind conditions. You must not descend below the en route minimum altitude (MOCA) until your position has been positively identified, and you must reconfirm it afterwards (well, you would, wouldn't you?). You should also have a copy of the let-down plate available, with all required ground and airborne aids being serviceable. When in IMC, you should not descend below MSA (as on the chart) until established in the approach or hold procedure. As the safe altitude is based on correct entry procedures, it will cover a certain area of ground, so if you're given something non-standard, such as a very long downwind leg that takes you off the chart, beware!

The *Decision Height* (or *Minimum Descent Height*, depending on the sort of approach) is the height at which you must go around if you can't see anything vaguely resembling a runway. If the cloud ceiling is lower than this, you may (unless prohibited by national regulations) carry out one approach to check if you can see anything (known in the trade as 'assessing the visual reference available'), but missed approach action *must* be taken at decision height on a precision approach if you can't.

A *precision approach* is an ILS or PAR. A *non-precision approach* is basically anything else, such as VOR or ADF, which only has azimuth guidance (that is, only left or right, without up or down). It is characterised by large steps, that is, major descents at certain stages requiring large power changes that can be a pain with an engine out. It's often a good idea to keep a consistent glide path as much as possible throughout a non-precision approach – the minimum heights at each step are just that – minimum heights. There's nothing to stop you being above them if you are actually descending under control (300 feet per mile gives you three degrees).

On non-precision approaches, if visual reference has not been established by minimum descent height, you may fly level at that height if your heading is within 15 degrees of the runway QDM, and you may go down further if you can see where you're going, if you can land at normal touchdown speed. This, unfortunately, raises the temptation of a dirty dart for the runway if you see it, without really being in a position to cope with the situation – you are in a high drag landing configuration, and have been for some time. There are no performance figures for go-arounds under those conditions.

If you can't see anything by your estimated time of reaching the threshold, you must go around. After two successive overshoots you're allowed no more attempts until a significant improvement in the weather is reported – the meaning of 'significant' is left to common sense, but you can have a third go if you've previously used an autopilot, or you have an emergency.

You may abandon an instrument approach in favour of a visual one if you have the aerodrome continuously in sight, you are below all cloud, and conditions are equal to or better than those for circling (bear in mind, though, the minimum RVR of 800 m, even when visual, which is to guard against shallow fog reducing the visibility in the final stages).

For destinations, forecasts must indicate that the weather will be at or above the minima for one hour either side of ETA. For a non-precision or circling approach, the ceiling must also be at or above MDH.

Destination and En Route Alternates

Should the weather deteriorate below acceptable limits you must consider diversion, but if things are improving, you can request holding at the optimum level for up to half of your holding allowance before going elsewhere. If you eat into this, you should have two alternates available, with enough fuel to reach one of them (a minimum of 60 nm away) with forty-five minutes' holding fuel on arrival.

You can use an Isolated Aerodrome procedure instead of alternate fuel for destinations with no suitable alternate, which means you must carry significantly more fuel than normal, that is, about two hours' worth as opposed to forty-five minutes'. The amount of the reserve is related to statistical information about local weather conditions, and is covered more fully later.

Met reports and/or forecasts must indicate that the weather at the aerodrome will be at or above the planning minima below for an hour either side of ETA:

Type of Approach	Planning Minima
Cat II and III	Cat I (RVR)
Cat I	Non-Precision (RVR with ceiling at or above MDH)
Non-Precision	Non-Precision (RVR with ceiling at or above MDH) plus 200 ft/1,000 m
Circling	Circling

Decision Height/Minimum Descent Height

The starting point for decision height is the obstacle clearance height for the landing aid, or circling minima as an alternative (circling height should be regarded as MDH/DH for any instrument approach followed by circling). Add ten feet (sink allowance) to that, plus the Pressure Error Correction for the type, which will be in the Flight Manual, so DH = OCH + PEC + 10 feet. If the ILS is offset, the DH must be at least the height at the middle marker.

The OCH for non-precision approaches should include a fudge factor for sink and PEC, so you can read OCH directly as the Minimum Descent Height (MDH for non-precision approaches being the same as DH for precision approaches), or MDH = OCH. If you're a newbie, that is you have less than fifty hours' P1 on the relevant type, expect to increase your DH or MDH by 100 feet.

Non-Precision Approaches (Onshore)

The MDH for a non-precision approach must be higher than the OCH/OCL for the category of aircraft, the system minimum (see table below), or any State minima.

Approach Aid	System Minimum (ft)
ILS No Glide Path	250
SRA (0.5 nm)	250
SRA (1 nm)	300
SRA (2 nm)	350
VOR	300
VOR/DME	250
NDB	300
NDB/DME	300
VDF (QDM & QGH)	300

Visual reference

You cannot continue below MDH unless you can see (and identify) at least one of:

❏   elements of the approach or runway lights
❏   the threshold or touchdown zone, their markings or lights
❏   visual glideslope indicator(s)

It's worth noting that MDH is a height *below which you must not descend*, and not a height at which you must fly to comply with the procedure: that is, you don't have to descend immediately to it. For a 3-degree glide slope, you should be 1,642 feet above the threshold elevation at 5 nm (including a 50-foot screen height). At 10 nm, the height should be 3,234 feet. Put more simply, for every nautical mile, you can descend about 300 feet (actually 318), which will help with power changes.

Required runway visual range (RVR)

You may get an RVR report with three values, covering the touch-down, middle and stop end of the runway, respectively. The touch-down one must be at least equal to landing minima, but the others need merely be enough to stop safely, provided they are more than that required for take-off. The RVR for landing from a visual circuit is 800 m, or the lowest Cat 1 RVR for the intended runway, whichever is the less, regardless of approach lighting, time of day or type of aircraft. As mentioned, this is for shallow fog, where you may see the airport from height, but lose sight of it as you descend on the approach (a visual approach must be authorised by ATC).

The minimum RVR for a non-precision approach depends on the

MDH, approach and runway lighting as shown below. At night, at least runway edge, threshold and runway end lights must be on.

Non-Precision Approach Minima – Full Facilities
With runway markings, 720 m + of high- or medium-intensity approach lights, runway edge lights, threshold and end lights, which must be on.

MDH(ft)	Aeroplane Category and RVR(m)			
	A	B	C	D
250–299	800	800	800	1,200
300–449	900	1,000	1,000	1,400
450–649	1,000	1,200	1,200	1,600
650 +	1,200	1,400	1,400	1,800

Non-Precision Approach – Intermediate Facilities
With runway markings, 420–719 m HI/MI approach and other lights.

MDH(ft)	Aeroplane Category and RVR(m)			
	A	B	C	D
250–299	1,000	1,100	1,200	1,400
300–449	1,200	1,300	1,400	1,600
450–649	1,400	1,500	1,600	1,800
650 +	1,500	1,500	1,800	2,000

Non-Precision Approach Minima – Basic Facilities
With runway markings, <420 m of HI/MI approach lights, runway edge, threshold and end lights, which must be on.

MDH(ft)	Aeroplane Category and RVR(m)			
	A	B	C	D
250–299	1,200	1,300	1,400	1,600
300–449	1,300	1,400	1,600	1,800
450–649	1,500	1,500	1,800	2,000
650 +	1,500	1,500	2,000	2,000

Non-Precision Approach Minima – Nil Facilities
Runway markings, edge, threshold and end lights, or none.

MDH(ft)	Aeroplane Category and RVR(m)			
	A	B	C	D
250–299	1,500	1,500	1,600	1,800
300–449	1,500	1,500	1,800	2,000
450–649	1,500	1,500	2,000	2,000
650 +	1,500	1,500	2,000	2,000

Notes: Tables only apply to approach slopes under 4°. Steeper ones will normally require VASIs or similar to be seen from MDH. RVR is either reported RVR, or met vis converted as below. The MDH above refers to its initial calculation. RVR doesn't need to be rounded up to the nearest ten feet, as when converting to MDA.

Performance Class 1 and 2 helicopters

	Onshore Non-Precision Approach Minima Facilities		
MDH(ft)	Full	Intermediate	Basic
250-299	600	800	1,000
300-449	800	1,000	1,000
450 +	1,000	1,000	1,000

Notes: Refer to aeroplane tables for description of facilities. Tables only apply to conventional approaches with gradient below 4°. Will normally require VASIs or similar to be seen from MDH. Figures are reported RVR or met visibility converted as below. Where MAP is within 0.5 nm of the threshold, minima for full facilities may be used regardless of length of approach lighting, but you still need runway edge, threshold and end lights and runway markings. At night, ground lighting must illuminate FATO and obstacles. Single pilot, min RVR is higher of 800 m or Table 3.

Converting reported met visibility to RVR

Lighting in Operation	RVR = Met Visibility X	
	Day	Night
HI Approach and Rwy Lighting	1.5	2.0
Any lighting other than above	1.0	1.5
No Lighting	1.0	N/A

Note: Don't use this table for calculating take-off of Cat II/III minima, or when a reported RVR is available.

Precision Approaches (Onshore)

For these, a Cat I operation uses ILS, MLS or PAR with a DH not lower than 200 feet, and RVR above 550 metres (500 for helicopters). The DH shall be at least the highest of:

- ❏ the OCH/OCL for the category of aircraft
- ❏ minimum DH in the flight manual (AFM), if any
- ❏ the minimum height without visual reference
- ❏ 200 feet, or any State minima

Visual reference

You cannot continue a precision approach below a DH determined as above, unless you have at least one of these visual references (for the intended runway) visible and identifiable:

- ❏ elements of the approach or runway lights
- ❏ the threshold or touchdown zone, their markings or lights
- ❏ visual glideslope indicator(s)

Runway visual range

The minimum RVR is governed by the DH and the approach lighting and runway lighting/marking available shown below. At night, at least runway edge, threshold and runway end lights must be on.

RVR for Cat 1 Approach versus Facilities and DH

DH	Facilities/RVR			
	Full	Intermediate	Basic	Nil
200	550	700	800	1,000
201–250	600	700	800	1,000
251–300	650	800	900	1,200
301 +	800	900	1,000	1,200

Notes: Refer to aeroplane tables for facilities. Nil approach light facilities comprise runway markings, runway edge, threshold and end lights or no lights at all. RVR values either as reported, or vis converted as above. Figures only apply to conventional approaches with slope below 4°.

The DH refers to initial calculation; associated RVR does not have to be rounded up to the nearest ten feet, as when converting to DA.

Performance Class 1 and 2 helicopters

DH(ft)	Full	Intermediate	Basic
Onshore Precision Approach Minima – Category 1 Facilities			
200	500	600	1,000
201–250	550	650	1,000
251–300	600	700	1,000
301 +	750	800	1,000

Notes: Refer to aeroplane tables for facilities. Figures are reported RVR or met vis converted using the above. Figures only apply to conventional approaches with glideslope up to and including 3.5 degrees. At night at least runway edge lights must be available.

The DH refers to initial calculation; associated RVR does not have to be rounded up to the nearest ten feet, e.g. when converting to DA. The DH applied must not be less than 1.25 × minimum-use height for the autopilot. Single pilot, minimum RVR shall be at least 800 m, except when using a suitable autopilot coupled to an ILS.

Single-pilot operation

Minimum RVR may not be less than 800 m, unless a suitable autopilot, coupled to an ILS or MLS is used, in which case RVR above may be used, but DH must be not less than 1.25 × the minimum-use height for the autopilot.

Commencement and Continuation of an Approach

An approach may be started irrespective of the RVR, but not continued past the outer marker (or equivalent – see note) unless the reported controlling RVR/visibility is equal to or better than the minimum required. Once past the outer marker, you can continue if your visual reference has been established at the DH/MDH, and is maintained. With no outer marker, you must make the decision to continue or abandon before descending below 1,000 feet above the aerodrome on final approach.

Note: The 'equivalent position' is a DME distance, a suitably located NDB or VOR, SRE or PAR fix, or anything else that independently establishes your position.

Visual Manoeuvring (Circling)

Circling is visually manoeuvring to a runway or FATO (for helicopters) after an instrument approach to another one, or the same one if the approach is not straight in (more than 30° off, in fact). Minima for this will give the necessary obstacle clearance, but in mountainous areas, account will also be taken of its height and effect on turbulence. Remember the minimum RVR is 800 m.

Circling height will be in the airway manual, precalculated to a standard formula; otherwise, just add 300 feet to the highest obstacle within 5 nm of the airfield (provided the result is above 500 feet agl).

You can get a reasonably accurate circling visibility in metres by multiplying the circuit speed in knots by 20, that is, if speed = 120 knots, then visibility must be 2,400 m. You should not descend below minima until aligned with the runway, except down to 500 feet agl on base leg at your discretion if you have the whole of the runway continuously in sight. The minimum MDH and visibility for visual manoeuvring are 250 ft and 800 m for helicopters, and as per this table for aeroplanes:

Aircraft Category	A	B	C	D
MDH (ft)	400	500	600	700
Min Met Vis (m)	1,500	1,600	2,400	3,600

Visual Approach

The minimum RVR for a visual approach is 800 metres.

Aerodromes Without Approach Aids

If your destination doesn't have any aids (unserviceability, perhaps), you can either fly to your destination in VMC, or under IFR to where you can carry out an instrument approach, then continue under VFR to your original destination, which must be within twenty-five miles.

In the latter case, permission must be obtained from ATC at the letdown point, and forecast weather between the two aerodromes must be better than 1,000 ft cloudbase agl and 3 nm visibility. This also means that if you don't maintain the above VFR conditions, you will be flying below 1,000 feet above decision height en route, or if you're over the sea, actually below DH where you should really be under an approach ban (see Glossary). You should not be below MSA unless you can identify your position, and since you're flying towards an aerodrome without approach aids, you could find that difficult. Your company may apply some rules in this case, but you will more than likely have to apply your own.

Airborne Radar Approach (ARA) – Helicopters Overwater

You cannot undertake this unless your radar is good enough to provide course guidance for obstacle clearance (cloud ceiling must also be good enough for a safe landing). Before starting, a clear path must exist on the radar screen for the final and missed approach segments. If lateral clearance from any obstacle will be less than 1 nm, you should either approach to a nearby target structure and proceed visually, or make the approach from another direction leading to a circling manoeuvre.

Minimum descent height (MDH)

This is determined from a radio altimeter. It must be at least 200 ft by day and 300 ft by night. The MDH for an approach leading to a circling manoeuvre shall be at least 300 ft by day and 500 ft by night.

Minimum descent altitude (MDA)

May only be used if the radio altimeter is unserviceable, and shall be at least MDH + 200 ft, based on a calibrated barometer at the destination or the lowest forecast QNH for the region.

Decision range (DR)

At least 0.75 nm unless you can convince the CAA otherwise.

Visual reference

You cannot continue an approach beyond DR or below MDH/MDA unless you are visual with the destination.

Single-pilot operations

The MDH/MDA for a single-pilot ARA shall be 100 ft higher than the above – DR shall not be less than 1 nm.

Note: An ARA to a rig or vessel under way is only permitted for multi-crew.

Heliport Minima for VFR/IFR, Onshore/Overwater

When VFR, if you are slow enough to see other traffic and obstacles in time, that is, get a one-minute visual reference ahead at 120 knots, the in-flight visibility should be at least 2 nm. Out of sight of land, flight visibility must be at least 1,500 m during daylight and 5 km by night. Special VFR flights shall not normally be commenced when the visibility is less than 3 km and not otherwise conducted when less than 1.5 km.

Flights to helidecks or elevated heliports have a max windspeed limit of 60 kts.

VFR En Route Minima

Helicopters

On land, helicopters should have a minimum cloud-base of 600 feet agl (1,500 feet at night) and 1,000 m visibility (3 km). In reduced visibility, adjust your airspeed to maintain a one-minute visual reference ahead, e.g. at 120 knots, the in-flight visibility should be at least 2 nm. A US Army study indicates that it takes about five seconds to perceive a problem, make a decision and start a correction. At 80 kts TAS, therefore, you will move 676 feet and get still closer as you turn away from an obstacle, the distance being equal to the radius of the turn, which, in this case, would be 984 feet, assuming 30 degrees of bank, giving you a total distance of 1,660 feet to cope with, which is not good if your visibility is only 1,000 feet!

Flying VMC on top of cloud is not allowed because performance rules require that, if an engine fails, you must remain in sight of the surface, and be able to carry out a safe forced landing, but in twins it may be undertaken by non-Instrument Rated pilots if the cloud within 10 nm of the destination is forecast to be less than 5/8 at 1,000 feet, with a minimum visibility of 1,000 m (VFR OTT is only allowed with a permit in Canada). The forecast should be valid from take-off until 2 hours after ETA. DO NOT LOSE SIGHT OF THE GROUND AT ALL IN THE ARCTIC.

Special VFR should not be *started* below 3 km and *conducted* below 1.5 km.

Over water
When crossing estuaries, it's a good idea to see the other side before leaving the side you're on, so that you get as little of the goldfish-bowl effect as possible. Try also keeping sight of the shoreline. Out of sight of land, the visibility must be greater than 1,500 m by day and 5 km by night.

Single-engined aeroplanes
If an engine fails, you must be able to continue at or above MSA to 1,000 feet above a place *on land* where you can make a safe forced landing. Since you will be gliding, flight above cloud extending below MSA is not a good idea.

Aeroplanes will require 1,000 ft cloud-base agl (1,500 over water or at night) and 3 km visibility at all times.

Multi-engined aeroplanes

For minima, aeroplanes come in five speed categories based on nominal threshold speeds, defined as 1.3 times the stalling speed in the landing configuration, or 1.23 times VS $_{1G}$ for JAR 25 certificated aeroplanes, at maximum certificated landing mass. The five categories are:

Category	Threshold Speed (Kts)
A	Less than 91
B	91 to 120
C	121 to 140
D	141 to 165
E	166 to 210

A and B can operate under VFR between 3 and 5 km visibility in Class G airspace if the IAS is below 140 kts. Special VFR flights shall not be commenced when the visibility is less than 3 km, and not otherwise conducted when less than 1.5 km. All flights must be conducted in accordance with Rules 24–27 of the Rules of the Air.

Presentation and Application of Operating Minima

If your flight guide does not contain the information you need for a particular aerodrome, the details must be included in your flight brief. For precision approaches, this will be in terms of decision height (or Decision Altitude when landing on QNH) and RVR. For non-precision approaches, it will be MDH (or Altitude for QNH settings) and RVR. For circling, the minimum descent height/altitude will be shown together with a minimum in-flight visibility (IFV).

You can always operate to higher minima at any time in the interests of safety, and you must always be prepared to amend the intended minima if the status of any aid changes, which brings me back to the previous idea about having something up your sleeve.

Altitude correction

Pressure altimeters indicate true altitude under ISA conditions, so where the temperature is higher, true altitude will be higher than shown and vice versa (errors may be significant in extremely low temperatures).

Interpreting Meteorological Information

Some codes (e.g. for wind velocity) use the same figures as the values being reported, so a wind from 280° at 15 knots is 28015KT. Otherwise, lettered abbreviations are used, as described below.

METARs

Routine actual weather reports (METARs) are compiled half-hourly or hourly while the met station is open. Missing information may be indicated by oblique strokes.

Horizontal Visibility

The minimum is in metres, followed by one of the eight points of the compass if there is a difference in visibility by direction, as with 4000NE. If the minimum visibility is between 1,500 and 5,000 m in another direction, minimum and maximum values, and their directions will be given, e.g. 1400SW 6000N. 9999 means 10 km or more, while 0000 means less than 50 metres.

Runway Visual Range (RVR)

An RVR group has the prefix R followed by the runway designator, then an oblique stroke followed by the touch-down RVR in metres. If RVR is assessed simultaneously on two or more runways, it will be repeated; parallel runways are distinguished by L, C or R, for Left, Central or Right parallel respectively, e.g. R24L/1100 R24R/1150. When the RVR is more than 1,500 m or the maximum that can be assessed, the group will be preceded by P, followed by the lesser value, e.g. R24/P1500. When less than the minimum, the RVR will be reported as M followed by the minimum value, e.g. R24/M0050.

Cloud

Up to four cloud groups may be included, in ascending order of bases. A group has three letters for the amount ('FEW' = 1 to 2 oktas, 'SCT', or scattered = 3 to 4 oktas; 'BKN', or broken, = 5 to 7 oktas, and 'OVC', or overcast = 8 oktas) and three for the height of the cloud base in hundreds of feet above aerodrome level. Apart from significant convective clouds (CB), cloud types are ignored. Cloud layers or masses are reported so the first group represents the lowest individual layer; the second is the next individual layer of more than 2 oktas; the third is the next higher layer of more than 4 oktas, and the additional group, if any, represents significant convective cloud, if not already reported, e.g. 'SCT010 SCT015 SCT018CB BKN025'.

CAVOK and SKC

CAVOK will replace visibility, RVR, weather and cloud groups when visibility is 10 km or more, there is no cloud below 5,000 feet or below the highest MSA, whichever is the greater, and no cumulo-nimbus; and there is no precipitation, thunderstorm, shallow fog or low, drifting snow. Otherwise, the cloud group is replaced by 'SKC' (sky clear) if there is no cloud to report.

Air Temperature and Dewpoint

Shown in degrees Celsius, separated by an oblique stroke. A negative value is indicated by an 'M' in front of the appropriate digits, e.g. '10/03' or '01/M01'.

Pressure Setting

QNH is rounded down to the next whole millibar and reported as a four-figure group preceded by 'Q'. If less than 1,000 mb, the first digit will be '0', e.g. 'Q0993'.

Recent Weather

Significant weather seen since the previous observation, but not currently relevant, will be reported with the standard present weather code preceded by the indicator 'RE', e.g. 'RETS'.

Windshear

Included if windshear is reported in the lowest 1,600 feet, beginning with 'WS': 'WS TKOF RWY20', 'WS LDG RWY20'.

Runway State

For snow or other runway contamination, an eight-figure group may be added at the end of the METAR.

Trend

For when significant changes are forecast during the next two hours. The codes 'BECMG' (becoming) or 'TEMPO' (temporarily) may be followed by a time group (in hours and minutes UTC) preceded by one of 'FM' (from), 'TL' (until) or 'AT' (at). These are followed by the expected change using the standard codes, e.g. 'BECMG FM 1100 250/35G50KT' or 'TEMPO FM 0630 TL0830 3000 SHRA'. Where no such significant changes are expected, the trend group will be replaced by the word 'NOSIG'.

DENEB
Fog dispersal is in progress.

Aerodrome weather forecasts (TAFs)

These describe forecast conditions at an aerodrome for between nine and twenty-four hours. The validity periods of many longer forecasts may not start for up to eight hours after the time of origin, and the details only cover the last eighteen hours. Nine-hour TAFs are updated and re-issued every three hours, and twelve- and twenty-four-hour TAFs, every six hours, with amendments issued as and when necessary. They are not available for offshore operations.

A TAF may be sub-divided into two or more self-contained parts by the abbreviation 'FM' (from) followed by the time UTC to the nearest hour, expressed as two figures. Many groups in METARs are also found in TAFs, but differences are noted below:

Validity Period

A METAR reports conditions at a specific time, but the TAF contains the date and time of origin, followed by the start and finish times of its validity period in whole hours UTC, e.g. 'TAF EGLL 130600Z (date and time of issue) 0716 (period of validity 0700 to 1600 hours UTC).

Horizontal Visibility

Only minimum visibility is forecast; RVR is not included.

Weather

If no significant weather is expected, this is omitted. After a change group, however, if the weather ceases to be significant, the abbreviation 'NSW' (no significant weather) will be inserted.

Cloud

For clear sky, the cloud group will be replaced by 'SKC' (sky clear). When no CB, or cloud below 5,000 feet or the highest MSA, whichever is greater, are forecast, but 'CAVOK' or 'SKC' are not appropriate, 'NSC' (no significant cloud) will be used instead.

Significant Changes

In addition to 'FM' and the time (see above) significant changes may be indicated by 'BECMG' (becoming) or 'TEMPO' (temporarily). 'BECMG' is followed by a four-figure group indicating the beginning and ending of the period when the change is expected. The change is expected to be permanent, and to occur at an unspecified time within it. 'TEMPO' will similarly be followed by a four-figure time group, indicating temporary fluctuations in forecast conditions. 'TEMPO' conditions are expected to last less than one hour in each instance, and in aggregate, less than half the period indicated.

Probability
Probability of a significant change, either 30% or 40%. The abbreviation 'PROB' will precede the percentage, followed by a time group, or a change and time group, e.g. 'PROB 30 0507 0800FG BKN004', or 'PROB40 TEMPO 1416 TSRA BKN010CB'.

Amendments
The amended forecast will have AMD inserted between TAF and the aerodrome identifier, and will cover the remainder of the validity period of the original forecast.

Fuel, Oil and Water Methanol

Fuel and oil consumption rates and weights for flight planning should be in Part B (the flight manual). It's usual to keep a check on the fuel contents during flight to see if things are going according to plan, thus keeping track of fuel consumption; it's written down on the flight progress log (Plog) every hour or so on long trips, but not required (for obvious reasons) in single-engined unstabilised helicopters. Special conditions apply under IFR and, needless to say, you shouldn't think of going IMC on VMC fuel reserves, talking of which . . .

IFR

Journeys are split into specific phases, such as start, checks, and taxi (that is, before take-off), take-off and climb (another phase), cruise and descent (yet another), approach and landing, plus 10 per cent, plus missed approach and diversion to the alternate. Then there's holding at the alternate, unusable fuel and contingency fuel, which covers errors in forecast winds, navigation, ATC restrictions and individual variations from standard fuel consumption. By arrangement, block figures can be used which ignore the take off and climb. Fuel flow will have to be adjusted if you plan to use specialised equipment in flight, such as heaters, or not use anything essential, such as an engine. More about Critical Points and Points of No Return against 'wet footprints' are in International Operations later in this chapter.

Helicopters

Helicopters don't need aerodromes, and minimum figures reflect this. However, they are calculated for level aircraft. Odd attitudes, say when slinging, may cause a fuel boost pump to become uncovered and give you a nasty surprise just when you don't want it. On a 206, the unusable fuel after a boost pump failure can be up to 10 US gal, which is uncomfortably close to the figures below.

By day, use the IFR ones as above, but without missed approach and loiter fuel. The contingency fuel can be 5 per cent if over non-hostile terrain, and 10 per cent otherwise (non-hostile in this context means where fuel is available). By night, add loiter fuel as well.

Final reserve fuel

An emergency exists when your fuel has reduced to the point where you should land without delay. This is at least the sum of:

- ❏ for VFR by day, twenty minutes at best range speed
- ❏ for IFR, or VFR and navigating by other means than visual landmarks or at night, thirty minutes at holding speed at 1,500 ft above the destination heliport in ISA, calculated with the estimated mass on arrival above
- ❏ extra fuel, at your discretion

This total is what you should have left when you arrive at your destination.

Isolated heliports

Where an alternate does not exist, the fuel required is the sum of:

- ❏ Taxi fuel
- ❏ Trip fuel
- ❏ Contingency fuel (see Standard Procedure, below)
- ❏ Additional fuel if required, but not less than two hours' worth, based on normal cruise consumption over the destination, or 45 min for piston-engines, plus 15 per cent of planned cruise time
- ❏ Extra fuel, at your discretion

Fixed Wing

The plan should be to arrive over the destination in a position to make an approach, overshoot and fly to an alternate, and still have enough to hold for forty-five minutes (thirty if a turbo jet) at the alternate. Even then, you must still be able to carry out an approach and landing, so you should carry enough for the estimated time to the destination, plus 5 per cent for contingencies, time to alternate, and holding fuel, which may be a set minimum amount, not forgetting the start-up and unusable fuel allowances for type.

Fuel Planning

Based on figures in the flight manual, or data from the company fuel consumption monitoring programme, if you've got one, from which contingency fuel is calculated, the fuel on board at the start of each flight must cover the elements listed below. Sometimes this can mean considerable forward thinking – for example, fuel for a there-and-back trip means considering max landing weight at the first destination, how much you can accept when you get back (so that you don't need to defuel for a heavy load next time) and whether or not you can claim tax drawback from Customs.

Standard procedure

The fuel required is the sum of:

❑ Taxi fuel, that is, the total amount you expect to use before take-off, including ice protection systems and the APU

❑ Trip fuel, including take-off and climb for the expected departure routeing, cruise from top of climb (TOC) to top of descent (TOD), TOD to initial approach point according to the expected arrival procedure, and approach and landing at destination

❑ Contingency fuel, which must be the higher of:
   ❑ 5 per cent of planned fuel or that for the rest of the flight, which may be reduced to 3 per cent with en route alternate, or
   ❑ fuel for twenty minutes, based on the planned trip fuel, supported by data from the FCMP, or
   ❑ fuel for at least fifteen minutes' hold at 1,500 ft above the destination in ISA supported by data from FCMP, or
   ❑ five minutes' hold at 1,500 ft above the destination in ISA

❑ Alternate fuel, to include
   ❑ a go-around to missed approach altitude, based on the proper procedure
   ❑ climb from missed approach altitude to cruising level
   ❑ cruise from TOC to TOD
   ❑ TOD to initial approach point, based on the expected arrival procedure, and

❏ approach and landing at the alternate

With two alternates, use the figures for the one that needs the most fuel. The departure point can be used as an alternate.

❏ Final reserve fuel, or enough for forty-five minutes for a piston-engined aeroplane, or thirty minutes at 1,500 ft above aerodrome elevation in ISA for turbo-props and turbo-jets, based on the estimated landing weight

❏ Additional fuel, dictated by the operation, e.g. ETOPS. Only needed if the fuel calculated above is not enough for fifteen minutes' holding at 1,500 ft above the aerodrome in ISA (when IFR) without an alternate, and following an engine or pressurisation failure at the most critical point en route, covering descent as necessary to a suitable aerodrome, fifteen minutes' hold at 1,500 ft in ISA and approach and landing

❏ Extra fuel, at your discretion

Decision point procedure

For an en route decision point the fuel required is the greater of:

For the destination

❏ Taxi fuel
❏ Trip fuel, via the decision point
❏ Contingency fuel of at least 5 per cent of estimated fuel from decision point to destination
❏ Alternate fuel, if required
❏ Final reserve fuel
❏ Additional fuel, if required, and
❏ Extra fuel, at your discretion

For the alternate

❏ Taxi fuel
❏ Trip fuel via the decision point
❏ Contingency fuel of not less than 3 per cent of the trip fuel
❏ Final reserve fuel
❏ Additional fuel, if required, and
❏ Extra fuel, at your discretion

Isolated aerodrome procedure

Where an alternate does not exist, the fuel required is the sum of:

❏ Taxi fuel
❏ Trip fuel
❏ Contingency fuel (see Standard Procedure, above)
❏ Additional fuel if required, but at least two hours' worth, based on normal cruise consumption over the destination, or 45 min for piston-engines, plus 15 per cent of planned cruise time
❏ Extra fuel, at your discretion

Predetermined point procedure

Where the distance between the destination and alternate means you can only go through a predetermined point, use the greater of:

For the destination

❏ Taxi fuel
❏ Trip fuel to the destination via the predetermined point
❏ Standard contingency fuel
❏ Additional fuel if required, but not less than two hours' worth, based on normal cruise consumption over the destination, or forty-five minutes' for piston-engined aircraft, plus 15 per cent of planned cruise time
❏ Extra fuel, at your discretion

For the alternate

❏ Taxi fuel
❏ Trip fuel from the departure aerodrome to the alternate, via the predetermined point
❏ Standard contingency fuel
❏ Additional fuel if required, but at least forty-five minutes' for piston-engined aircraft, or thirty minutes' hold at 1,500 ft in ISA including final reserve fuel for turbo-props and turbo-jets, and
❏ Extra fuel, at your discretion

Oil

Just check before flight that the engine has been topped up according to the manufacturer's recommendations, and that no excess oil consumption has taken place between flights.

Water Methanol

See the flight manual.

Mass and Centre of Gravity

Loading presents similar problems for all aircraft, but heavier types will have things like maximum zero fuel weight to contend with, aside from larger areas in which to place loads and present more chances for mistakes to happen. Some aircraft have a proper cargo fit, but problems arise where one that normally carries passengers is used without modification, which is why you may need to be certificated on your training forms as being cleared to change the aircraft layout. Naturally, in small aircraft where the emergency exits are obvious, this really only involves removing the seats, because the aim is just to substitute loads that use the same fixtures and locations, but where you get involved in removing galleys and otherwise converting the cabin in larger ones, the exercise becomes a little more difficult (just because a flight manual contains details of freight loading limitations, don't assume that any modifications you make are permitted – those figures may only have been used for basic certification).

There are two aspects to loading, the weights and their distribution, and you sometimes get some nasty surprises – fuel in wings means unusually shaped fuel tanks, so you won't get a straight line variation with weights against moment arms; every fuel load will have a different moment figure, principally because the fuel tanks have a C of G system all of their own, running separately from the aircraft. In this case, it's not enough just to subtract the closing fuel moment from the start – for example, say 1,000 lb has a moment of 1,843 and 300 has 558. The result for 700 may not be 1,843 – 558 (1,285), but an actual figure of 1,294, which is enough of a difference to cause an insurance company to have qualms about paying up if you have an accident.

Basic weight is that stated on the weight and centre of gravity schedule (in the flight manual), which must be established by actual weighing before the machine is used for commercial air transport, and reweighing every four years, unless fleet masses are used, in which case try every nine years. The figures are used to calculate a DOM (Dry Operating Mass) and C of G for each machine or fleet, as appropriate.

Note: Newer documentation uses the word *Mass* instead of *Weight*.

The maximum taxi (ramp) weight (mass) is the max permitted weight at which the aircraft may be moved, under its own power or otherwise. The maximum take-off weight (mass) is that in the flight manual, which is not necessarily the maximum permitted take-off weight, or maximum structural take-off mass, the max weight at the start of the take-off run that varies due to performance factors such as length and slope of runway, temperature, humidity, obstacles and altitude. Any maximum take-off weight less than the full maximum due to performance factors is known as the restricted (or regulated) take-off weight (RTOW) and is the starting point for calculating maximum payload available. Sometimes, of course, RTOW is the same as MTOW, but this will only tend to happen at larger airfields or landing sites with plenty of room. Maximum taxi weight can therefore be higher than maximum take-off weight, and you should be able to burn off the difference before getting airborne.

It's well known that all aircraft will fly overweight to a certain extent, if only because there's a tolerance range in any performance figures given – ferry flights frequently do so, with the extra weight being fuel, but having the physical ability doesn't mean that you should. You will at some stage be under some pressure to take an extra bit of baggage or top up with that bit of fuel that will save you making a stop en route, but consider the implications. Firstly, any insurance cover will be invalid if you don't fly the aircraft within the limits of the flight manual, and, secondly, you will be leaving yourself nothing in hand for turbulence and the like, which will increase your weight artificially. The designer will have allowed for sixty-degree turns all the way up to MAUW, but not heavier than that.

Maximum structural landing mass (max landing weight) speaks for itself, and is there to help prevent the impact with the runway being trans-mitted through the undercarriage to the rest of the aircraft, which can only happen if the weight is kept within certain limits (it also assists you to reduce the downward velocity at the point of landing, such as with autorotations in a helicopter). This weight may very well be restricted performance-wise in a similar way to take-off weight, and could equally be a factor in further reducing your payload at the start of a flight.

As fuel is carried in the wings of most aeroplanes, excessive payload (in the cabin) relative to fuel weight will increase the design bending moment, being most critical with a full load and zero fuel. A maximum zero fuel weight (mass) will limit the weight in the cabin, being a weight beyond which any increase in load must consist entirely of fuel, or, in other words, the maximum permissible mass with no usable fuel. This is to ensure that the wings are forced downwards during flight, and is why using inboard tanks first is often recommended.

As well as the above technical weights, there are operational weights, the most important being the aircraft prepared for service weight (APS), which is the basic weight plus or minus changes to seat layouts, fixed equipment, unusable fuel and crew equipment, such as flight guides. It's the basis of the loadsheet, and is sometimes the same as the dry operating mass (DOM), an APS weight that also includes the crew, their baggage, catering equipment, etc. Wet operating weight, on the other hand, includes usable take-off fuel plus engine additives.

The traffic load is the weight of cargo, passengers and baggage, and will include loading equipment (pallets, nets, etc.). The allowed traffic load (not necessarily the same thing) is just the payload, which is calculated by subtracting the operating weight from the RTOW. With under twelve seats, without dispensation, you must use actual weights for passengers, whereas otherwise a statistically derived standard weight (which will include baggage) may be used (see the following section). The maximum compartment weight is the most you can have in any specific compartment, subject to restrictions on floor loadings, and loose equipment weight is additional equipment which may or may not be included in APS.

You can use standard or actual masses for the crew and baggage in the DOM and actual figures for everything else, not forgetting the engine oil. Actual figures must also be used for freight or ballast. The fuel load must be calculated using actual or standard density values of 0.71 for gasoline, 0.79 for JP1 and 0.76 for JP4. On-board fuel must always be compared with that remaining before refuelling plus the amount uplifted, as a gross error check.

Standard Mass Values

Aeroplane
Passengers, 20 seats or more

Passenger Seats	20 +		30 and more
	Male	*Female*	*All Adult*
Flights, not charters	88 kg	70 kg	84 kg
Holiday charters	83 kg	69 kg	76 kg
Children (2–12 years)	35 kg	35 kg	35 kg

Holiday charter means part of a holiday package.
Passengers, 19 seats or fewer

Passenger Seats	1–5	6–9	10–19
Male	104 kg	96 kg	92 kg
Female	86 kg	78 kg	74 kg
Children 2–12 years	35 kg	35 kg	35 kg

With no hand baggage, or if separate, deduct 6 kg from male and female masses. (Overcoats, umbrellas, small handbags, reading material, etc. not relevant here.)

Checked baggage, 20 or more seats

Type of Flight	Baggage standard Mass
Domestic	11 kg
Within Europe	13 kg
Intercontinental	15 kg
All Other	13 kg

With nineteen passenger seats or fewer, use actual mass. Here, *domestic flight* means one with origin and destination(s) within the borders of one state, *within Europe* means flights, other than domestic ones, whose origin and destination are within the EEC, and *intercontinental flight*, other than within Europe, means with origin and destination in different continents.

Mass values for crew

Crew Position	Std Mass inc Hand Bge
Flight Crew	85 kg
Cabin Crew	75 kg

Helicopters

Use actual values, but see below (you might have an Arrangement). Engine oil will be in the APS or DOM, so ignore it for balance purposes. When possible, specific gravity of the fuel uplifted should be used for the fuel load, but standard values are 7.2 lb/imp. gal. (0.72 kg/litre) for Avgas and 7.9 lb/imp. gal. (0.79 kg/litre) for JP4. For notional weights, tables below include infants under two years carried by an adult on one passenger seat. Infants in separate seats are regarded as children.

Passengers, 20 seats or more

Passenger Seats	20 +*		30 +*
	Male	*Female*	*All Adults*
All flights	82 kg	64 kg	78 kg
Children (2–12 years)	35 kg	35 kg	35 kg
Hand Baggage (if any)		6 kg	
Survival Suit (if any)		3 kg	

Passengers, 10 to 19 seats

Passenger Seats	10 to 19		
	Male	*Female*	*Child (2–12 yrs)*
All flights	86 kg	68 kg	35 kg

Passengers, 9 seats or fewer

Passenger Seats	1 to 5			6 to 9		
	Male	*Fem*	*Child*	*Male*	*Fem*	*Child*
All flights	98 kg	80 kg	35 kg	90 kg	72 kg	35 kg

Checked baggage, 20 or more seats

Passenger Seats	20 or more*
	Checked Baggage
All flights	13 kg

* With twenty or more seats, the values apply to each piece of checked baggage. With nineteen or fewer, use actual mass.

Mass values for crew

Crew Position	Standard Mass Inc Hand Baggage
Flight Crew	85 kg
Cabin Crew	75 kg

Canada

Summer		Winter
182 lb	Males (>12)	188 lb
135 lb	Females (>12)	141 lb
75 lb	Children (2–11)	75 lb
30 lb	Infants (0–<2)	30 lb

Distribution

Right, now we come to weight distribution. Incorrect loading naturally affects aircraft performance, and will possibly prevent the thing from even getting airborne. A centre of gravity too far forward will make it more difficult to raise the nose on take-off (or landing), possibly overstress the nosewheel as a result, and make the flight less economical by excessive use of trim tabs, which causes more drag. There are certain advantages to having the C of G towards the rear (by making the tailplane contribute to total lift, which also reduces the power required), but too much will make the aircraft less stable, more fatiguing to fly and cause similar drag and nosewheel problems (but in reverse) as excessive forward C of G. Also, if you don't have enough elevator movement to get yourself out of a stall, you could end up in a flat spin you can't get out of. Don't forget that there will also be local weight restrictions concerning the strength of the fuselage at a particular point, so an otherwise ideal C of G may have to be adjusted.

Passenger seats occupy the whole floor space evenly; this load-spreading principle needs to be borne in mind with freight (cargo is best distributed like passengers would be), which makes it easier to provide decent restraint on each pack, because access areas to exits above and around the cargo are needed for when the load has moved *after* an emergency stop. You may find it helpful to line the floor with something waterproof if you're not sure what you're carrying – people who use the Royal Mail don't know about Dangerous Goods Regulations and may send flimsy items that leak something 'orrible all over the place. Loads must be restrained with nets or straps (or a combination of both) and must distribute the load over available fixtures, such as seat attachments.

A company mass and balance document should be raised in duplicate for each commercial air transport flight. One copy must be on the aircraft, with another available on the ground for at least three days. It must contain details of all loaded items, including fuel, and indicate whether standard or actual values have been used. Whoever's supervising the loading must confirm by signature that the load and its distribution are as stated on the mass and balance document, which must also have the name of the person who prepared it. The document must be acceptable to, and countersigned by, the commander, to whom late alterations must be passed, and entered in the 'last-minute changes' spaces. Of course, this won't be so necessary if you make several trips with loads that don't change very much, in which case a load plan system is more practical (see below).

There are many ways of expressing C of G position, ranging from a simple statement of fact (like 75 inches from a specified point), through using a graph in the flight manual (which will give an envelope in which it may be plotted), to using index numbers on larger aircraft which are more manageable than the telephone numbers you would get if calculations were done conventionally.

However, fine detail is outside the scope of this book, and we are dealing with smaller aircraft anyway. There are ways of making life easier with regard to these, the most common of which is a load plan.

The Load Plan

Used to save the constant working out of C of G on loads that are fairly standard. Weight ranges need to be worked out, as the aircraft will frequently be loaded by non-technical staff (like oil rig workers or slashers), who will want as little detail and as much flexibility as possible (these weight ranges should not be confused with standard weights, mentioned above). C of G limits in load plans will therefore be more stringent. Your inspector will want to see pre-worked examples for worst case situations (including full and empty tank positions). Flights outside the load plan will need the C of G and a loadsheet to be worked out in full.

Sample load plan

The following example plans may be used for the Bell 206 helicopter with the fuel and payloads as shown (just adapt the method to suit other aircraft). The load plan number should be included in the tech log before flight. The figures assume an APS weight of *up to* 2,100 lb and a maximum weight of 3,200 lb. Pilot and passenger weights may be *up to* 200 lb including baggage (remember, not a standard weight). With fewer than four passengers, baggage may be loaded on the rear seats or in the hold, but maximum weight in the baggage hold is 250 lb. Fuel loads above seventy-five gallons assume a range extender is fitted.

Load Plan	Pax	Fuel(gal)
B3	3	50
B2	2	83
B1	1	93

Passengers will be loaded front to rear as follows:

FIRST	Forward passenger seat
SECOND	Starboard rear passenger seat
THIRD	Port rear passenger seat
FOURTH	Centre rear passenger seat

As you can see, everything needs to be spelt out so that anybody can get it right with all possibilities catered for. If you need to reduce weight, manipulate the payload, not the sector fuel, although commercially you might find you can make a tech stop.

Loadsheets

These are not required for aircraft below 2,730 kg, nor for training, positioning or private flights, but you will still need to know your C of G as a matter of airmanship. Loadsheets should be drawn up outside the conditions imposed by a load plan and should account for all items of the laden weight. Generally, they could be used in the circumstances below, although you could probably think of more. The position of the laden C of G must be specified, together with the load distribution, but noting its position within a range will be enough, unless it's required for other purposes, such as airworthiness or performance. A copy should be left behind with a responsible person or organisation, or placed in a fire-proof container with the tech log on a helicopter.

You need loadsheets:

- ❏ outside load plan provisions, such as with more than anticipated baggage
- ❏ with any combination of doors removed
- ❏ with camera mount and cameraman on board
- ❏ with an underslung load
- ❏ With freight only
- ❏ When parachute dropping

When you're overweight in one section and want to redistribute the load, here's how to calculate how much to move and where:

$$X = \frac{W \times D}{d}$$

where:

X	Weight to be moved
W	Gross weight of aircraft
D	Distance the C of G is out
d	Distance between old and new locations of load moved

So, if your gross weight is 3,000 lb, your load is 1.5 inches outside the envelope (aft), to be moved from the baggage compartment to the rear seats, all of 34 inches, you need to move 133 lb to get back in limits:

$$133 = \frac{3000 \times 1.5}{34}$$

Paperwork

Alterations should be done so that the original entry can still be seen, with a note as to why the alteration was made, when and by whom.

ATS Flight Plan

There are many reasons for filing flight plans – first of all, they help get you slotted into the system, even if it isn't quite the route you asked for. Next, they help with radio failures, as, once you're in the pipe, so to speak, everyone knows where you're supposed to be going and can act accordingly. Then there are forced landings, where an educated guess may be made as to your position, followed by statistics, and, finally, because the law says you must.

A flight plan must be filed for all commercial flights, except those under VFR taking off and landing at the same aerodrome. Just to clarify, this includes positioning, private and line training. You can, of course, file one at any time at your discretion, but don't forget to close it properly if required (e.g. in Canada), otherwise you will be overrun by C130s. Booking out is enough for other flights, such as local area training flights, or air tests. The company must have someone on the ground responsible for monitoring flight progress, and for alerting the emergency services if you do not arrive within one hour of ETA. You are responsible for ensuring that a plan has been filed, and being fully aware of the details.

In Canada, because of the land surface (it's huge), you must file at least a VFR flight plan or flight itinerary wherever you go, unless you are within 25 nm of the aerodrome. The latter can be left with a Responsible Person, who undertakes to notify the relevant authorities if something happens.

International flights always require a flight plan, but flights from Canada to the USA are not considered as such for this purpose, so there is a different form to use.

Operational Flight Plan

A navigation log and fuel flight plan (sometimes known as a progress log, or Plog) is used for all IFR flights. There are many variations on this theme, but there is a suggested sample on Page 93 for you to adapt as necessary. There are occasions when a reusable one is appropriate, such

Flight Progress Log

Aircraft Reg	Pilot	Chocks off	Date
		Chocks on	

From	Freq ID	ATA	Awy	FL	MSA	To	Freq ID	ETA	FOB	Track [M]	Dist [nm]	W/V	Hdg [M]	G/S	Time	Fuel Flow	Fuel Reqd
TOC						TOC											

Alternate →

Info		Departure		Arrival		Item	Wt	Datum	Mom	Notes
Start/taxi	Time	ATIS	ATIS			APS Weight				
Climb	W/V	Ground	Ground			Front Row				
Cruise	Visibility	Tower	Tower			2nd Row				
Descent	Lo Cloud	Approach	Approach			Hold				
Landing	Med Cloud	**En Route**	**En Route**			Fuel (6 lbs/gal)				
Contingency (5%)	Hi Cloud					Total Wt/Mom				
Alternate	Temp/Dewpoint					T/O CG (mom/wt)				
Final Reserve	Altimeter					Burn Off (-)				
Discretionary	Runway					Ldg Wt/Mom				
Total Fuel										

as on certain schedules and trips under 100 nm, but it's easier just to use a new one all the time. In a helicopter you may not need one anyway. The company will normally issue a prepared plan for each flight, but you may have to produce your own, in which case you need at least the following information:

❏   aircraft registration, type and variant
❏   date and identification of flight
❏   names of flight crew members, and their duty assignments
❏   places and times of departure and arrival (actual off-block time, take-off time)
❏   type of operation (ETOPS, VFR, ferry, private, training, etc.)
❏   route and segments with checkpoints; waypoints, distances, time and tracks
❏   planned cruising speed and flying times between check-points/ waypoints. Estimated and actual times overhead
❏   safe altitudes and minimum levels
❏   planned altitudes and FLs; the actual height should be entered on each leg – check it's not below the MSA! If it is, 'V' (for VFR) should follow the level entered, which you would if you've any sense.
❏   fuel calculations (i.e. records of in-flight fuel checks). For flights more than one hour, fuel contents should be recorded roughly every hour, but use discretion where a natural sector break occurs before or after this time by five or ten minutes.
❏   fuel on board when starting and shutting down engines
❏   alternate(s) for destination, take-off and en route. These should be shown immediately after the destination airfield workings, leaving one line blank. It's normally enough to enter the straight track distance between the destination and alternate, the MSA, track and calculated flight time, a five minute let-down allowance and the leg fuel calculation. However, although straight-line diversions are often adequate, they should be realistic and include SIDs, STARs, etc. where they complicate the issue, because if you need an alternate, you will need it badly, and it doesn't pay to skimp on the planning
❏   initial ATS clearance and subsequent re-clearance(s)
❏   in-flight re-planning calculations
❏   relevant met information. There is a requirement to record pre- and in-flight weather for the destination and alternates. Minima must be calculated and entered prior to departure if less than twice the minima is forecast (weather obtained for flight-planning purposes should be carried on the flight and included in the voyage report)

If you've got room, leave a blank line between each sector to help deal with reroutings and direct clearances. When given changes in heading, altitude, squawk or radio frequency, write them down and cross the old one out. It's too easy to forget when things are busy.

Aircraft Technical Log

A system for recording defects and maintenance between scheduled servicing, as well as information relevant to flight safety and maintenance. In other words, it's the formal means of communication between flight crews and engineering. In Canada, the equivalent is the journey log – the tech log is not allowed to accompany the aircraft.

The types of tech log (as they're known) are many and varied, from those with many sectors per page, to a page per sector – it all depends on the amount of information required, which in turn depends on the complexity of the aircraft – a tech log can contain other documents, such as a propeller or airframe log.

Actually, many tech logs are hopeless, being badly designed and obviously concocted to satisfy legal requirements with no thought for people who use them. If you ever design one, please resist the temptation to include a loadsheet with it – keep it separate if you can. The main reason for tech logs being bad is that people try and cram too much information on them; if your aircraft are below a certain weight, loadsheets are not required anyway.

Examples

An official example is in the sample ops manual from the CAA, but the one included on Page 97 is a practical multi-sector one typically used by small operators.

A different page is used for each day, but successive flights by different pilots may be entered on the same one (because provision has been made to identify the pilot in each case).

It's your responsibility to ensure that the Check A (Daily Check) slot is signed, preferably by the engineer or pilot conducting it (see later this chapter for more about Check As), but you should be given an ID number by your maintenance organisation to use in the Authority box. Talking of engineers, you must also check that previous defects have been rectified (or deferred – see later) by a person so qualified. In addition, check the validity of the Certificate of Maintenance Review and the Certificate of Release to Service before flight (both issued by your maintenance contractor). To assist in keeping track of servicing requirements, the next Maintenance Due date should be entered from the Certificate of Release to Service in Box 1, being immediately comparable to the current date, which is in the box to the right, Box 2.

The hours at which that maintenance is due are also entered in Box 3. The aircraft hours brought forward (from Box 7 of the previous page) are then entered in Box 4 and the total of Box 3 minus Box 4 is then entered in Box 5. This gives you an indication of the hours required to the next check, which should be compared against the proposed flying for the day. It's your responsibility to ensure that the aircraft has enough hours (and days) to do what you want before the next maintenance check is due.

The aircraft fuel state and uplifts must be correct (and make sure they match with those on the nav log and the load sheet!). The Acceptance Signature certifies that the foregoing have been checked, the loading is satisfactory and that the aircraft is accepted for flight.

Before take-off, one copy of the technical log should be left behind at the point of departure (in Canada, they are not carried on the aircraft). If this isn't possible in a helicopter, the copy must be carried in an approved fireproof container with the rest of the aircraft documents.

There is some controversy about fireproof containers. They're only really relevant in helicopter operations where sometimes it really is impractical to leave a copy behind, as passengers tend to board with the engine running and don't want to waste time while you close down and find a suitable stone to leave the paperwork under (some helicopters need a two-minute rundown before stopping the engine). Trials have taken place with a bag made of that shiny stuff that airport firemen use as uniforms, but it only preserves documents if a sheet of cardboard is inserted either side of them. All the bag seems to do is ensure that everything burns up inside without harming anything outside (a bit like fireproof flying suits).

Place perforations at the top of the form, otherwise you're continually undoing the whole book to extract a copy.

After each flight, enter the take-off and landing times and the duration of each flight. Defects should be entered next, and the aircraft is grounded until they're either cleared or deferred under current regulations. If there are none, just write 'Nil Further Defects', or 'NFD' for short.

Whenever a defect is entered, start a new page. If this is not possible (lack of sheets, maybe), include the sector number.

A new sector line should be used when either fuel is uplifted, a landing away is carried out, the engine has been shut down or a new pilot is used. If there is no way of identifying the pilot on each sector, a new page must be started every time the pilot changes. A new page must also be started (in addition to entering a defect) if a new Check A or de-icing procedure is performed.

| A/C Type | | | | | DATCON Start | | | | Next Check (type) Due Date | | | Current Date | **1** | | | Serial No | **2** |
| Reg | | | | | | | | | | | | | | | | | |

	Oil Uplift	Fuel (lbs-ltrs-gals*)			Type of Flight	Pilot Name	Acceptance Signature		From	To	Dfct No	After Flight Sign		T/O	Ldg	Time	Eng Cycles
		Arr	Up	Dpt													
Load Plan																	
1																	
2																	
3																	
4																	

The Pilot's Acceptance Signature
confirms correct completion of preflight inspection and ground anti-de-icing, acceptance of aircraft and defect state and sufficient fuel and oil for the planned flight.

◀

Certificate of Release to Service
Certifies that the work specified except as otherwise specified was carried out in accordance with JAR-145 and in respect to that work the aircraft/aircraft component is considered ready for release to service.

➤

No	Defect	Sign	Action Taken	Signature	Authority	Date

6	Daily Total	
3	Next Check due at (hrs)	
4	A/c hrs b/f	
5	Hrs to next check	
7	Total A/c Hrs	

Check A/Daily Inspection
Certifies that the work specified except as otherwise specified was carried out in accordance with JAR-145 and in respect to that work the aircraft/aircraft component is considered ready for release to service.

Sign   Authority   Date

Ground Anti/Deicing
Aeroshell 07+up to 50% water by volume

Start   Mix Ratio

Finish   Sign

* Delete where inapplicable

97

At the end of the day's flying, the total hours are added to comprise Box 6, and the totals of Box 6 and Box 4 are added to give a/c total hours which should be entered in Box 7 and then transferred to Box 4 of the next page. After that, a copy of the completed log is transmitted to the maintenance contractor by whatever means your company uses.

Documents, Forms and Information to be Carried

The stuff listed below should be carried on all commercial air transport flights (if you're going abroad, you also need to read International Operations later in this chapter). It's quite an exhaustive list, which after a time becomes automatic, but it does save embarrassment when you get ramp-checked!

These documents must be carried on each flight (* may be copies):

- ❏ Certificate of Registration*
- ❏ Certificate of Airworthiness*
- ❏ Noise Certificate (if applicable)*
- ❏ Air Operator Certificate*
- ❏ Aircraft Radio Licence*
- ❏ Third Party Liability Insurance Certificate(s)*
- ❏ Valid flight crew licences with appropriate rating(s)
- ❏ Operations manual, which must be readily accessible (i.e. not in the baggage hold!)
- ❏ Flight manual, or part B of this operations manual
- ❏ Technical log (not in Canada – try journey log instead)
- ❏ Certificate of Release To Service. Issued after overhauls, repairs, replacements, etc. to certify that work has been carried out properly. Normally on the tech log page
- ❏ Certificate of Maintenance Review. For Commercial Air Transport or Air Work, saying that maintenance has been carried out on time, including modifications and inspections, and that defects have been rectified or deferred. Again, normally somewhere on the tech log page
- ❏ Details of any filed ATS flight plans
- ❏ Appropriate NOTAM/AIS briefing documentation
- ❏ Appropriate meteorological information
- ❏ Mass and balance documentation
- ❏ Notification of special passengers, such as security personnel, if not considered as crew, handicapped persons, inadmissible passengers, deportees, persons in custody
- ❏ Notification of special loads, including dangerous goods
- ❏ Current maps and charts and associated documents

- ❏   Cargo/passenger manifests, etc.
- ❏   Reporting forms (MORS, etc.)

Maintenance of Records

The paperwork must be preserved! Keep the following for the times stated:

Document	Time
Certificates of Maintenance, Review and Release to Service	2 years after expiry
Aircraft, propeller and engine log books	2 years from withdrawal
Certificate of Compliance	2 years after expiry
Weight schedule	6 months
Tech log sheets	2 years after last entry
Pilot training records	3 years after leaving
Duty records, discretion reports	15 months from last entry
Flying log books	2 years from last entry
Flight documentation (nav logs, etc.)	3 months
Loadsheets	6 months

Ground Handling Procedures

Fuelling Procedures

Jet and piston fuels mix differently with contaminants (particularly water), which is due to variations in their specific gravities and temperature. The s.g. of water, for example, is so close to Avtur that it can take up to 4 hours for it to settle out, whereas the same process may take as little as half an hour with Avgas. As a result, there is always water suspended in jet fuel, which must be kept within strict limits, hence two filtration stages, for solids and water. The latter doesn't burn, of course, and can freeze, but it's the fungi that gather round the interface between it and the fuel that are the real problem – they turn into a dark-coloured slime which clings to tank walls and supporting structures, which not only alters the fuel chemically but will block filters as well. Not much water is required for this – trace elements are enough.

It has been found that when visible water is present in jet fuel containing anti-icing additive, the additive will separate from the fuel and be attracted to the water. After a certain amount, thought to be about 15 per cent,the density of the new liquid changes so much that it is not identified as water, and will therefore pass through water filters, and will not be detected by water-finding paste. Where the ratio becomes 50 per cent, as much as 10 per cent of whatever is going through the filter could actually be water, which is very likely to get to the engine, since the filters on the airframe itself are not as restrictive (thanks to Northern Mountain Helicopters for the information).

Fuel is actually a combination of various (very toxic) substances – pound for pound, it's more explosive than dynamite. Jet A, standard for commercial and general aviation, is narrow-cut kerosene, usually with no additives apart from anti-icing chemicals. Jet A1 has a different freezing point and possibly something for dissipating static, used for long-haul flights where the temperature gets very low. Jet B is a wide-cut kerosene containing naphtha, so is lighter and has a very low flash point. It contains static dissipators and is widely used in Canada. JP4 is like Jet B but also has a corrosion inhibitor and anti-icing additives. It was the main military fuel, but is being superseded by JP8, at least in the USA. JP5 has a higher flashpoint than JP4, and was designed for US navy ships. JP8 is like Jet A1, but has a full set of additives (or e-numbers, if you like).

Aircraft parked overnight should ideally have tanks completely filled to stop condensation, but this is impractical if you expect a full load the next morning and don't have room for full fuel as well, in which case be prepared to do *extensive* sampling from the tanks. Half-filled drums left overnight should not be used for the same reasons, but, in remote places (like the Arctic), fuel is a precious commodity and you think more than twice before discarding any (as it happens, drums are scarce too, and they may get used for all sorts of things, so beware). Full drums are usually delivered to a remote cache by Twin Otter or something, and they should be sealed straight from the refuellers – as you tend to use any remainder in a very short time, this can be minimised somewhat. Look for a fill date, as fuel over two years old should be looked at sceptically. Also look for a large X, which is the accepted symbol for contamination, although not everyone has a black marker with them.

Drums should not be stored vertically, because the bungs are not airtight, even though they might stop fuel from leaking out. When the contents contract as the air cools overnight, water inside the rim and collecting around the bung can be sucked in as well, so either store the drums on their sides, with openings at 3 or 9 o'clock, or stick something underneath at 12 o'clock that causes the drum to slant enough to stop rainwater collecting and covering the bungs. Other openings or connections should be protected with blanks or covers, or at least have their openings left facing downwards. Drain plugs, valves, filter bowls, sumps and filter meshes should be checked daily for sediment, slime or corrosion. Always have spare filters.

Each day before flying, and when the fuel is settled, carry out a water check in aircraft and containers (but see below, for drums). Collect samples in a transparent container and check for sediment, free water or cloudiness—if there is only one liquid, ensure it is not all water. The instructions for using water detectors are displayed on the containers. In the Arctic, unless there is a thaw in summer, separated water will be frozen in the bottom of the drum, and you will only have to worry about that in suspension. Water-finding paste, however, will not detect suspended water, and is used as an additional test, not a replacement for a proper inspection.

Naturally, only competent and authorised personnel should operate fuelling equipment, who must also be fully briefed by their company. In practice, of course, refuellers know very well what they're doing, but you should still be in full communication with them. In general, the following precautions should be taken:

❏ Documentation must reflect the fuel's origins and its correct handling
❏ Vehicles used for transportation must be roadworthy and regularly inspected
❏ Fire-extinguishing equipment must be available and crews familiar with its use
❏ Barrels, when used, must be undamaged and in date (give-aways for this include faded labels). Over long periods, (like 2 years or so), a fungus can grow, which will clog fuel lines. When checking a drum, have it standing for as long as possible, but at least half an hour. Then draw a sample from as far down as you can through a water detector (but don't actually put the pump right to the bottom). *Smell* the contents just to make sure it's the right stuff – don't trust the labels or colours if the seal's been broken. An X on the drum means contamination. Secure it afterwards so that it doesn't roll all over the place
❏ Run fuel for a few seconds to clear the pipes of condensation and bugs, etc., that may be downstream of the filters
❏ Maintain a clear exit path for removal of fuelling equipment in emergency
❏ The aircraft, fuelling vehicle, hose nozzle, filters or anything else through which fuel passes should be electrically bonded *before* the fuel cap is removed. The proper procedure is drum to ground, drum to pump, pump to aircraft, nozzle to aircraft *then* open the cap. The reverse when finished. Be particularly careful when it's cold, as the air will probably be dry, and airborne snow particles will add their own friction

- ❏ Don't refuel within 100 feet of radar equipment that is operating. Only essential switches should be operated, with radio silence being observed when fuelling is taking place
- ❏ Avoid fuelling during electrical storms, and don't use bulbs or electronic flash equipment within the fuelling zone. Non-essential engines should not be run, but if any already running are stopped, they should not be restarted until fuel has ceased flowing and there is no risk of igniting vapours
- ❏ Brakes or chocks should be applied, but some places require brakes off when near fixed installations
- ❏ Take out rescue and survival equipment so that if the thing blows up you have something to hand

The most important thing is daily checks, before flying. If you spill anything, either use a neutralising agent, move the aircraft or wait for it to evaporate before starting engines again.

Fuel can burn you. High vapour concentrations will irritate the eyes, nose, throat and lungs and may cause anaesthesia, headaches, dizziness and other central nervous system problems. Ingestion (like siphoning when defuelling) may cause bronchopneumonia or similar nasties, including leukaemia and death. If you get it on your clothes, ground yourself before removing any and rinse them in clean water. Fuel spills on the ground must be covered with dirt as quickly as possible.

Otherwise, everybody not involved in the process should keep clear – at least 50 m away, but for exceptions see later.

At base
Confirm with Ops that the fuel ordered is enough for your flight, and during the pre-flight confirm that:

- ❏ The correct grade of fuel is used – 80/87 Avgas is red, 100/130 is green and 100LL is blue
- ❏ Fuel drains are checked for water, and left properly closed
- ❏ A visual check of tank contents, or a dipstick check, reveals the correct amount of fuel on board within reason
- ❏ Fuel tank caps are properly secured
- ❏ Fuel gauges indicate the required levels, and
- ❏ Details are correctly entered in the tech log and a gross error check is carried out

A turbo-prop may not be refuelled or defuelled with an engine running, but, if done in exceptional circumstances, the prop brake must be on and the precautions above observed. Hot refuelling (as it's called) a helicopter from drums is particularly not a good idea, but if you ever do, the drum can 'oilcan' suddenly and throw anything on top of it into the rotors, so don't leave spanners, etc. lying around.

En route

A flight crew member should normally be present, and as well as confirming that the requirements above are met, should ensure that:

❏ Particular care is taken to advise the refuellers of the type, grade and fuel quantity, especially units of measurement

❏ The bowser or whatever is earthed to the aircraft *before* the hose is extended, and remains so until refuelling is complete

❏ Smoking is not permitted within 15 m

❏ The correct quantity of anti-freeze is added

❏ The bowser readings at the start and finish reflect the uplift as on the aircraft gauges, and a gross error check is carried out; particularly important in some countries, where they try and swindle you

With wide-cut fuels, electrics should be switched off before refuelling starts, and remain off until it finishes and hoses have been removed.

Passengers on board

Not normally, especially when the engines are running, but in certain circumstances (i.e. casevac, bad weather, no transport, or on an oil rig) it may be permitted, provided that:

❏ Passengers are warned that they must not produce ignition of any substance by any means (including electrical switches). They must also remain seated, with belts/harnesses unfastened, until refuelling has been completed

❏ 'Fasten Seat Belt' signs are off, and NO SMOKING signs on, with sufficient interior lighting to identify emergency exits

❏ A responsible person is at each main door, which should be open and free from obstacles

❏ Fuellers are notified if fuel vapour is detected in the cabin

❏ Ground activities do not create hazards, e.g. the fuel bowser/installation should not stop people leaving in a hurry

❏ ATC and the Fire Authority are informed

❏ Fire extinguishers are close at hand

Note: Don't re/defuel with Avgas or widecut fuel (e.g. Jet B or equivalent) or a mixture, when passengers are embarking, on board or disembarking.

Handling Procedures Related to Safety

Anyone responsible for ground handling, including handling passengers and freight, must have detailed guidance about their duties. The commander is responsible for briefing non-company people.

Passengers
These come in three groups:

Likely to assist evacuation
Reasonably fit and strong people, who should be the only ones next to self-help (Type III and Type IV) exits – an exit door may weigh up to 53 lb. They should understand instructions.

Likely to impede evacuation
These should be seated where they will not obstruct emergency equipment or exits, or otherwise get in the way, such as:

- ❏ Persons of restricted mobility, due to physical incapacity, intellectual deficiency, age, illness, etc. Must not exceed those able to assist with evacuation
- ❏ Physically or mentally handicapped people who would have difficulty in moving quickly if asked to
- ❏ Those with impaired sight or hearing who might not understand instructions
- ❏ Children and infants, whether or not accompanied by an adult (suggest those under fifteen)
- ❏ Those in custody and/or being deported (i.e. in handcuffs)
- ❏ Those whose physical size prevents quick movement

Passengers unlikely to affect evacuation
Those with no seating restrictions except as above.

Note: Multiple occupancy is only allowed when one is an infant under two and the other is a responsible adult over sixteen.

Transport arrangements
Passengers should be either taken to the aircraft in approved transport, or escorted by a crew member, company employee or representative of the handling agent. Once there, they should be guided to their seats in a way that keeps the aircraft stable. Once seated, a flight or cabin crew member should close the door(s) and/or confirm it by inspection. At the

destination, passengers should remain on the aircraft until the engines have been shut down, or rotors stopped, and they can proceed to the terminal by vehicle, or with an escort. If rotors are turning, competent people must escort them by a safe route outside the rotor disc (similarly with propellers). They must remain in a unified group, refrain from smoking, and keep well clear of main and tail rotors, and jet engine intake, propeller and rotor wash and exhaust danger areas while on the movement area. If you have deportees or persons charged with criminal offences, special arrangements, including the provision of escorts, should be made and full details included in your flight brief. (See also Police Operations on Page 230.)

As well as having their attention drawn to the safety cards, passengers must be carefully briefed on their contents, particularly when there's no cabin crew. Emphasis should be placed on the operation of the normal/emergency exits, the use of safety belts/harnesses, the position of seat backs during take-off and landing, and general requirements for cabin security at all times.

Baggage and freight

Cabin baggage will normally be restricted to handbags, briefcases, cameras, outdoor coats and reasonably stowable items, and be within that passenger's standard allowance.

Stowage

Each item must have an approved stowage, whose limitations must not be exceeded, and whose doors must not be stopped from closing properly (i.e. not in toilets or against bulkheads that cannot cope with them shifting).

Neither must they be stowed under seats unless they (the seats) have a restraint bar, and the baggage is small enough to be restrained by it and not obstruct the seat row or impede access to emergency equipment.

Hold baggage should be stowed only where it's supposed to be, subject to floor loading limitations. However, you may have to restrict the type of luggage or the weight carried for balance rather than structural considerations.

Freight should not be carried unless the aircraft is cleared for it, and the appropriate spreader boards, freight lashings, nets and anchor points are available and approved. Dangerous Goods are covered in Chapter 9.

Ground Operations

Whenever an aircraft is to be positioned on the ramp, under tow or its own power, marshallers or wingtip/rotor guides should be used if there is any doubt about clearances. Once parked, ground support vehicles and equipment should be clear and, if possible, parallel to the centreline so that if the brakes fail they will not collide with the aircraft. In all cases, the main exit must be clear.

Engines should not be started until all passengers or freight have been loaded, doors and hatches have been closed, and all ground equipment, except for a GPU, has been removed. As for the arrival, marshallers should be available when manoeuvring in relatively confined or crowded areas of the apron. Ground staff must have been briefed on all aspects of ramp safety, with particular reference to fire prevention, blast and suction areas, and the need to be constantly alert for loose objects and/or debris.

Refusal of Embarkation

You can refuse entry to anyone who could be a hazard, such as those under the influence of alcohol or drugs, or suffering from mental or physical illnesses which could put everyone else at risk. Sufferers of known or declared illnesses may be carried if prior medical approval has been given, and qualified nurses accompany them. To help you exercise your authority, everyone engaged in passenger handling should alert you if they consider particular passengers to be a problem. Be prepared to call the police if you need them.

De-icing and Anti-icing on the Ground

Certification for flight in icing conditions
Having the equipment doesn't mean you can fly in icing conditions. On small twins it may just mean it produces no adverse effects on normal flight (though they might be nearly always overweight), and no-one could be bothered to take it off. Some aircraft are simply not happy in icing, even if the stuff is there (this is particularly true of older Barons and PA31s). Icing equipment is not certified if you are carrying deposits from ground operations or storage, so you must ensure that all hoar frost, ice and snow is removed before any attempt is made to get airborne, if only because the aircraft systems don't get really under way till then.

Ground de-icing
Use either soft brushes, fluids, or a combination (try parking behind a friendly jet with its engines idling). Priorities are control surface hinges, engine intakes or static ports. Some manufacturers, however, don't recommend using fluids at all because of the possible effect on the

bonding of composite materials. Some people recommend using warm water, but I'm not so sure about that - I know that if you want to freeze water quickly, you put it in the freezer hot.

De-icing Fluids
The two main types are AEA *(Association of European Airlines)* Type I (unthickened) with a high glycol content and low viscosity, and Type II (thickened) with a minimum glycol content of about 50 per cent which, with a thickening agent (one or two teaspoons of cornflour), remains on surfaces for longer, but remember it has to blow off before you actually get airborne. Type I fluids have good de-icing properties, but may refreeze. *Union Carbide Ultra* fluid appears to increase the times given by the tables overleaf by 1.5 over Type II and way more for Type I – they give general guidance on the use of I and II, and the likely protection you might get *on the ground*.

General Precautions
Deposits must be swept away from hinge areas and system intakes, and the sprays themselves should not be directed to them, since the fluid may be further diluted by the melting ice it is designed to remove, and may re-freeze. It may also cause smearing on cockpit windows and loss of vision during take-off.

Afterwards, confirm that flying and control surfaces are clear and move over their full range, and intake and drain holes are free of obstructions. Jet engine compressors should be rotated by hand to ensure they are not frozen in position. Propeller spinners should be checked for trapped snow or moisture, which could subsequently refreeze and cause an imbalance. Don't forget the undercarriage.

Further Precautions
Holdover time can be affected by high winds or jet blasts damaging the fluid film, and skin temperatures can be significantly lower than the OAT, which makes them a more representative entry point into the tables overleaf.

Technical Log
An appropriate entry must be made and signed in the tech log, including the start and completion times.

Type I holdover times
Approximate holdover times under various weather conditions
(hours:minutes)

OAT (°C)	Frost	Freezing Fog	Snow	Freezing Rain	Rain cold soaked wings
Above 0	0:18–0:45	0:12–0:30	0:06–0:15	0:02–0:05	0:06–0:15
0 to –7	0:18–0:45	0:06–0:15	0:06–0:15	0:01–0:03	N/A
below –7	0:12–0:30	0:06–0:15	0:06–0:15	N/A	N/A

Source: International Standards Organisation (ISO) 11076:1993(E) Table 3

Type II holdover times
Approx holdover times anticipated under various conditions
(hours:minutes)

OAT (°C)	undil fluid/ water	Frost Fog	Freezing	Snow	Freezing Rain	Rain cold soaked wings
above 0	100/0	12:00	1:15–3:00	0:25–1:00	0:08–0:20	0:24–1:00
	75/25	6:00	0:50–2:00	0:20–0:45	0:04–0:10	0:18–0:45
	50/50	4:00	0:35–1:30	0:15–0:30	0:02–0:05	0:12–0:30
0	100/0	8:00	0:35–1:30	0:20–0:45	0:08–0:20	N/A
0 to –7	75/25	5:00	0:25–1:00	0:15–0:30	0:04–0:10	N/A
	50/50	3:00	0:20–0:45	0:05–0:15	0:01–0:03	N/A
–7 to –14	100/0	8:00	0:35–1:30	0:20–0:45	N/A	N/A
	75/25	5:00	0:25–1:00	0:15–0:30	N/A	N/A
–14 to –25	100/0	8:00	0:35–1:30	0:20–0:45	N/A	N/A

Source: International Standards Organisation (ISO) 11076:1993(E) Table 4

Notes: Under extreme conditions, heat the neat fluid (60 °C) for sprayability. No significant increase is achieved with a stronger mix of Type I (AEA) fluids. Stations using Kilfrost will normally mix 50/50 or 60/40.

Flight Procedures

Flight Plan Annotation of VFR/IFR

You should normally use the most convenient airways under IFR, regardless of weather, although you can go VFR if there aren't any. Certain flights, such as aerial photography, need VFR by definition, but

IFR can still be used en route. The (operational) flight plan should indicate clearly what you use. Changes should be annotated on the flight plan, as well as where they take place. Revised clearances should be requested immediately from ATC. Obviously, maintain VMC until any IFR clearance is received.

Minimum Radar Service

When outside airways or advisory routes, a minimum of Radar Information Service should always be available. In the UK, you have:

❏ Radar Advisory Service (RAS), which gives information and advisory avoiding action from conflicting traffic. It can be requested at any time, but is usually used in IMC. This can be time wasting, especially if it's a clear day and you're continually given vectors downwind that take ages to catch up on; although you are not obliged to accept the advice, you must inform the controllers, as you must if you change heading or altitude for any reason. This can also be expensive, as you immediately become subject to Eurocharges, 100 per cent in UK (but only 25 per cent in France).

❏ Radar Information Service merely provides information about conflicting traffic. How you avoid it is up to you

❏ Radar Control Service in controlled airspace, where you do what you're told

Flight Information Service is just someone to talk to. There's no radar and very limited information about other traffic as not everybody calls up. They can, however give you weather and NOTAMs, as they're usually not as busy as radar controllers.

Procedural Service gives separation between participating traffic but without the luxury of radar. It's mainly used on approach and advisory routes.

The controller will state the type of service provided (so that it goes on tape and can be used at the subsequent Board of Inquiry), so even though you may have been identified, don't assume you have the service requested until told so. In VMC, it's still your responsibility for collision avoidance, so you will need to maintain a good lookout.

Flying VFR where weather or other circumstances demand that you should be IFR (i.e. in order to avoid Eurocharges) should be avoided. In the same vein, Special VFR should not be used to get around Rule 5: that is, you can't use a clearance of 'not above 1,000 feet' as an excuse to fly low over Birmingham, where you should be over 2,000. If you are so cleared, it's only from an Air Traffic point of view – they're assuming you know what you're doing.

Special Helicopter Zones

The London Specified Area is where you can't fly so low in a helicopter that you cannot land clear if an engine fails, so no single-engined heli-copter can operate in it unless along the River Thames. As you're over water, flotation equipment is required, together with approved life jackets for all occupants.

Specific routes for helicopters flying in the London Control Zone and through the Specified Area are shown in the *UK Air Pilot* and included in other guides. They're also overprinted on a special OS map, a copy of which you must have with you. Information on other zones with special helicopter procedures, such as Glasgow, will also be found in the *UK Air Pilot*.

Recording of Flight Times

Flight times in personal flying logbooks are from first movement under power until rotor rundown for helicopters, and first chocks away (with the intention of taking off) until final chocks on for fixed wing.

Flight times in technical logs, by contrast, are from take-off to landing only, sometimes entered in decimal hours. It's common practice, where several flights are made per hour without closing down (such as pleasure flying), to record the first take-off and last landing times and to note the actual airborne time in between.

There are many ways of doing this, the most accurate being with a stopwatch, but there is an unofficial and widely used practice (by arrange-ment with your local CAA surveyor) when pleasure flying, of using two thirds of the total time between first take-off and last landing. Accountants love it, but engineers don't, as they regard the wear and tear as still taking place. Too much of this sort of paperwork will really play havoc with servicing schedules (and profit and loss figures) as parts will wear out more quickly than anticipated, despite the 'fudge factor' allowed by the CAA when setting up maintenance requirements.

Timings should be local, unless consistently in another time zone.

Navigation Procedures

The definition of navigation is taking an aircraft from place to place without reference to the ground. Some points to note about doing it in the Arctic are that it's darker for longer and there are fewer navaids.

Mercator doesn't work, and you need to switch to Polar Stereographic, so rhumb lines are therefore not the shortest course, and you must use great circles instead. Naturally, compasses begin to get unreliable, and there is increased deviation due to the aircraft's own magnetic field.

Equipment not directly required for navigation should be tuned to ground stations to check accuracy or ground speed, so that errors can be detected and the equipment will be available in an emergency. It also keeps the circuits warm, but this is really a hangover from old steam-driven equipment that would go unserviceable if bumped around too much when cold.

Don't rely on a beacon until it has been identified and confirmed by both pilots. For computerised equipment, one pilot should read aloud the co-ordinates, tracks or distances, while the other operates the keyboard and reads them back as a cross-check. Otherwise, for single-pilot operations, a conscientious system of self-monitoring should be adopted.

Nav logs should be comprehensively completed en route, except in busy terminal areas at lower altitudes, and ETAs should be kept up to date as a matter of course, as well as diversions, including a brief description of the circumstances, the time the alteration was made, and any fuel re-planning calculations which were necessary. In general, enough information should be recorded to assist a post-flight investigation, so that problems can be avoided on future flights over the same route.

For Minimum Navigation Performance Specification (MNPS) and POLAR airspace, and that designated for Area Navigation (RNAV), you need approval from the CAA, a minimum level of navigational equipment, and specific briefing and/or training.

Altimeter Checks

Altimeters must be checked before flight as follows, ensuring that rotation of the knob through ± 10 mb produces a corresponding difference in height of about ± 300 ft in the appropriate direction.

- ❑ Both should be set to the aerodrome QFE and should indicate within ±50 feet of zero, within 50 feet of each other
- ❑ With No. 1 on QFE and No. 2 on aerodrome QNH, the difference should equal the aerodrome altitude amsl, to within 50 feet
- ❑ With both on aerodrome QNH, indications should be within ±50 feet of the aerodrome elevation, and 50 feet of each other

Note: No. 1 is the handling pilot's primary instrument and No. 2 the secondary.

Setting procedures

To avoid confusion if your altimeter does not have a decimal point on the millibar sub-scale, round down pressure settings to the nearest whole millibar; a QFE of 1002.9 mb will be set as 1002 mb.

Altimeters must be set, and cross-checked with a new setting, as follows:

Stage	No.1	No.2	Remarks
Before Take-off	QNH	QNH	Aerodrome setting
Climb & Cruise	QNH	QNH	Below transition altitude
Climb	1013.2	QNH	When cleared to flight level
En route	1013.2	1013.2	
Descent	1013.2	1013.2	When cleared to intermediate flight levels
Descent	QNH	QNH	When cleared to an altitude and no further flight level reports are required by ATC
Init App	Airfield	QNH	Aerodrome QNH
Finals	Airfield	QNH	Aerodrome QNH
Missed App	Airfield	QNH	Aerodrome QNH

Notes: When en route, Regional QNH should be set, unless below a TMA, when the Zone QNH, or suitable Aerodrome QNH can be used. Alternatively, aerodrome QFE may be used on finals, in which case it should be on the No. 1 altimeter when single-pilot, and on both otherwise. When single crew, No. 2 altimeter may remain on the relevant QNH. A third altimeter must be set to relevant QNH when at or below MOCA or MORA.

Temperature error

Pressure altimeters indicate true altitude under ISA, so you will get errors if it's too cold, about 4 per cent of indicated altitude for every 11 degrees of difference.

Altitude Alerting Systems

These include devices that give audio/visual warnings, and those that merely act as a reminder, using a digital indicator, of the required altitude or flight level. Either should be reset every time a change is made, and cross-checked by the other pilot. Exercise care with the automatic flight control system (AFCS), to prevent unplanned departures from the flight path.

Audio voice alerting device

Helicopters over water more than ten minutes from land at normal cruise must carry a radio altimeter with an audio voice warning below a pre-set height, and a visual warning that operates at a height selectable by the pilot.

Ground Proximity Warning System

This should be energised and used throughout the flight, unless it is unserviceable and the MEL allows it. GPWS is supposed to provide a warning just before you go into Terrain Impact Mode, based on excessive rate of descent or closure rate, negative climb rate or approach too close to the ground with the gear up. It is not infallible, but an immediate and positive response must be made to *all* its alerts and warnings, even if you've previously had spurious ones, leaving investigation till later. An *Alert* is a *caution*, whilst a *Warning* is a *command*, which may be *genuine*, a *nuisance* (where you are actually in a safe procedure), or *false*. This table shows the relationship between alerts, warnings and modes.

GPWS Mode	Alert	Warning	Alert	Warning
Excessive descent rate		'Whoop Whoop Pull Up'	'Sink Rate'	'Whoop Whoop Pull Up'
Excessive terrain closure rate		'Whoop Whoop Pull Up'	'Terrain Terrain'	'Whoop Whoop Pull Up'
Altitude loss after take-off or go-around		'Whoop Whoop Pull Up'	'Don't Sink'	'Whoop Whoop Pull Up'
Terrain – not in the landing configuration	Gear not locked down	'Whoop Whoop Pull Up'	'Too Low Gear'	'Whoop Whoop Pull Up'
	Flaps not ldg posn	'Whoop Whoop Pull Up'	Too Low Flaps'	'Too Low Terrain'
Descent below glideslope	'Glideslope'		'Glideslope
Below 'minimums'			'Minimums'

When you get a warning, pull up smoothly and apply thrust until it ceases.

Basic GPWS

This gives warnings, rather than alerts, in all modes except 5, Descent Below Glideslope, where activation will cause the audio warning 'Glideslope' to be repeated; you take immediate action to regain the glideslope as quickly as possible, until the alert ceases. Whenever a warning is received, the immediate response must normally be to level the wings and initiate a maximum gradient climb to MSA for the sector being flown, but see below.

Advanced GPWS

This not only indicates the mode of operation, but provides alerts as well as warnings. Do not recover the original flight path until the cause of the alert has been positively established and eliminated. Whenever a warning is received, the immediate response must be to level the wings and initiate a max gradient climb to MSA for the sector being flown, except as below.

Warnings – discretionary action by commander

Responses to warnings may be reduced to those for alerts only during the day, when 1 nm horizontally and 1,000 feet vertically from cloud, with visibility of at least 5 nm, and it is obvious there is no danger.

Limitations

There is no forward-looking facility, so you will get little or no warning of anything in front of you. Alerts and warnings in Modes 1 and 2 are only given when you are less than 2,500 ft above the local terrain. If no corrective action is taken, a maximum of some 20 seconds will elapse between the initial alert or warning and contact with the ground, which will be lessened if the rate of descent is excessive, or there is rising ground beneath you.

Unwanted warnings

Unwanted (that is, false or nuisance) warnings may be received when, for example, you are being vectored by ATC and descending into hills. A Mode 5 (glideslope) alert may be triggered when you are outside the validity area of the glideslope signal, as you would when circling. You will also get an alert/warning if the flaps are set wrongly.

TCAS/ACAS

Airborne Collision and Avoidance Systems (ACAS) provide you with an independent backup to the Mark 1 Eyeball and ATC by alerting you to collision hazards. TCAS II (Traffic Alert and Collision Avoidance System Type II) is the current equipment, which provides advice in the vertical plane, as a Traffic Advisory (TA), telling you where nearby (Mode A) transponding aircraft are, or Resolution Advisory (RA) detecting aircraft transponding Mode C, and what to do about it. TCAS III can issue horizontal suggestions. Not required in the UK, but may be used if you have it. It uses four antennae, a computer and Mode S transponder to continually survey the airspace around you and predict the flight paths of likely intruders. Mode S uses a 24-bit interrogation address, which reduces mistakes and allows the system more capacity and efficiency. It can also provide two-way data link communications on 1030 and 1090 MHz, used in this case for manoeuvre messages, but also as a back-up for VHF voice. The size of the *Caution Area* varies with your speed. A TA alerts you that an RA, requiring a change in flight path, may follow – it is displayed 35–48 seconds from the time the intruder aircraft is predicted to enter the collision area, displaying range, bearing and altitude, but remember that this system relies on transponder-equipped aircraft receiving information from others – RAs will only be generated if both use Mode C – if only Mode A is available, you will only get Traffic Advisory information. The equipment cannot resolve with complete accuracy the bearing, heading or vertical rates of intruding aircraft, so you should not rely solely on TAs. Look where the conflicting traffic is supposed to be, and get ATC to help. Otherwise, manoeuvre away from the collision risk. Once clear, advise ATC.

The *Warning Area* extends 20–30 seconds from when an intruder would enter the collision area, which is when RAs are issued. They are meant to advise you of vertical manoeuvres required for adequate separation from a threat. A *corrective advisory* calls for a change in vertical speed and a *preventive* advisory restricts it. A response should be initiated immediately, *not in the opposite direction*, and crew members not involved should check for other traffic. Once adequate separation has been achieved, or there is no longer a conflict, you should return to your intended flight path, and inform ATC. An RA may be disregarded only when you visually identify the conflicting traffic and decide that no deviation is necessary. If an RA and ATC conflict, follow the RA.

Nuisance or false advisories should be treated as genuine unless the intruder has been positively identified and shown visually to be no longer a threat. Departures from ATC clearances in compliance with an RA should be reported to the company and/or authorities.

In-Flight Fuel Management

You must carry out fuel checks, that is, record the remaining fuel, at regular intervals, such as hourly, or at convenient times when the flight is less than an hour and the cockpit workload is low. The idea is to compare actual consumption with that planned, and ensure you have enough to complete the flight with the expected fuel remaining.

For an isolated destination aerodrome, if the expected fuel remaining at the point of last possible diversion is less than the sum for diversion, contingency and final reserve fuel, you must either divert, or continue to the destination, provided it has two separate runways and the expected weather conditions are as planned. You must declare an emergency when the usable fuel on board is less than final reserve fuel.

Adverse and Hazardous Atmospheric Conditions

Thunderstorms
The airflow is greatly disturbed anywhere near a thunderstorm, usually noticeable by strong up and down draughts, together with heavy rain and lightning. Avoid them even at the cost of diversion or an intermediate landing, but should this be impossible, there are certain things you can do to help. It can be at least as dangerous up high as low – you can expect anything from lightning and turbulence to icing and hail, each with hazards of their own – lightning, for instance, could explode a fuel tank, and strikes can occur up to 20 nm from a storm cell. Not only that, even over baby ones near to larger storms, you will need at least 5,000 feet clearance. Similarly, try not to fly underneath, either, or make steep turns.

Approaching the Thunderstorm Area
Seat belts should be tightened, and loose articles stowed. One pilot should control the aircraft and the other monitor the flight instruments. Select an altitude for penetration that will keep you clear of obstacles, and use the weather radar to select the safest track. Set the power for the recommended turbulence speed, adjust the trim and note its position, so that any excessive changes from autopilot or mach trim can be quickly assessed. Height, mach, rate of climb or descent and airspeed locks should be disengaged, but the yaw-damper(s), if fitted, should be on.

Switch on the pitot heaters, de-icing, and continuous ignition system, where fitted. Disregard any beacons subject to interference, such as ADF and OMEGA (although tuning the former to its lowest frequency will give you a primitive lightning detector). Turn the cockpit lighting fully on and lower crew seats and visors to minimise the blinding effect of lightning flashes.

Within the Storm Area

As the speed of vertical air currents may well exceed the capabilities of the aircraft, fly by attitude at the recommended turbulence speed and maintain your original heading – do not correct for altitude, except for obstacles; avoid harsh or excessive control movements, particularly with power, except to restore margins from stall warnings or high-speed buffets. Do not be misled by conflicting indications on other instruments, and don't roll too much. If auto-trim variations are large, disengage the autopilot. Movement of the mach trim, where it occurs, though, is necessary and desirable. Check that the yaw-damper remains engaged. You might get temporary warnings (e.g. low oil pressure) from negative G, which should be ignored.

Air Traffic Control Considerations

Obtain clearance from, or notify, ATC so that they can separate you from others. If you can't do this, manoeuvres should be kept to a minimum, and inform them ASAP.

Take-off and Landing

Do not take off if a thunderstorm is overhead or approaching within 5 nm. At destination, hold clear or divert.

Use of Weather Radar

This detects rainfall to *avoid* (not penetrate) severe weather, as large raindrops in a small area are a dead giveaway for thunderstorms. Your decisions are therefore based on a deduction from certain facts. Turbulence can be inferred from the shape of the concentrated precipitation and how it moves, but if you're flying where there's no weather to detect, it's difficult to guesstimate where any might be (a clear area on the radar screen doesn't mean there isn't any cloud, as minute cloud droplets, ice, dry snow and dry hail have low reflective levels. On the other hand, large water droplets will totally absorb the energy as they approach the size of the wave).

Operation is quite simple, but full use on the ground should be avoided (not below 500 feet, in fact). Naturally, you've got to check the equipment before departure, but most sets have an internal procedure for this. When you do switch it on, it should be set to Standby for at least 3 minutes first, to allow things to warm up. You will have several scan ranges to choose from, possibly from 250 miles down to 5, but 80 is adequate, which is about what you would get with a 10 inch antenna, the usual fit in small aircraft. The smaller it is, the wider the beam and the dispersal of energy, which means that a lot of it will pass by whatever storm is around, giving you an indication very much less than the true hazard. You would be safe in assuming that whatever you see is one or two levels more severe.

Once airborne, there is a tilt capability which will point the antenna upwards or downwards, but don't expect to see the tops of a storm, because the crystals there won't reflect the energy in the first place, and your beam focusing will be too narrow to include it. In the same way, you will also get ground echoes, which are good for detecting the enemy coast ahead, but only because the water will absorb all the echoes and you will see a big black hole. Buildings and the like won't reflect properly at all – you might just see a mass of confusing colours.

If you haven't got the luxury of colour and computer-controlled echo highlighting (and have to rely on steam), there are certain distinctive storm patterns to look out for, such as the *hook, finger* and *U-shape,* which all look similar to a figure 6. The heaviest precipitation, and the heaviest turbulence, will show up as black holes, or red when using colour. These will be best detected in Contour mode. Remember that radar signals weaken, and might show the end of the weather falsely.

Iso-Echo produces a hole in a strong echo when the returned signal is above a pre-set value. Where the return around a hole is narrow, there is a strong gradient of intensity, so avoid all hooked echoes, especially those rapidly changing.

Avoid the brightest returns by at least 20 nm, so corridors should be at least 40 nm wide. Without radar, avoid storms by 10 nm. Intermittently monitor long ranges to avoid situations you would prefer not to be in.

Altitude (1,000 ft)	Shape	Intensity	Gradient of intensity	Rate of Change
0–20	Avoid by 10 miles echoes with hooks fingers, scalloped edges or other protrusions	Avoid by 5 miles echoes with sharp edges or strong intensities	Avoid by 5 miles echoes with strong gradients of intensity	Avoid by 10 miles echoes showing rapid change of shape, height or intensity
20–25		Avoid all echoes by 10 miles		
25–30		Avoid echoes by 15 miles		
Above 30		Avoid echoes by 20 miles		

Icing conditions

Ice adversely affects performance, not only by adding weight, but also altering the shape of lift-producing surfaces, which changes your stalling speed – autorotation in a helicopter could therefore be a lot more interesting than normal. The US Army found that half an inch on the leading edge reduces your lifting capacity by up to 50 per cent, and increases drag by the same amount. On top of that, fuel could freeze in wing tanks, as could control surfaces, and slush picked up on take-off could stop the landing gear from operating, amongst other things.

Zero degrees is actually the point at which water becomes supercooled and capable of freezing. Airframe icing happens when supercooled water droplets strike an airframe below that. Some of the droplet freezes on impact, releasing latent heat and warming the remainder, which then flows back, turning into clear ice, which can gather without noticeable vibration. On the ground this can mean ground resonance in a helicopter, and bits of ice flying off rotor blades or propellers. In flight, the extra weight and drag could cause descent and improper operation of flying controls. So – it's a good idea to avoid icing conditions, but in any case, you shouldn't go if you haven't got the equipment, which naturally must be serviceable (see the paragraph on Certification for Flight in Icing Conditions, above).

All ice should be removed from critical areas before take-off, including hoar frost on the fuselage, because even a bad paint job will increase drag, which is relevant if you're heavy, and hoar frost will have a similar effect. De-icing details should be entered in the relevant part of the tech log, including start/end times, etc. The critical areas include control surfaces, rotors, stabilisers and the like.

The ability of an object to accumulate ice is known as its *catch efficiency*; a sharp-edged object is better at it than a blunt-edged one, due to its lesser deflection of air. Speed is also a factor. Due to the speed and geometry of a helicopter's main rotor blades, their catch efficiency is greater than that of the fuselage, so ice on the outside of the cabin doesn't relate to what you might have on the blades. In fact, Canadian Armed Forces tests show that you can pick up a lethal load of ice on a Kiowa (206) rotor blade inside 1–6 minutes. It is the rate of accretion that's important, not the characteristics of the icing, although clear ice is definitely worse than rime ice, since the latter contains air bubbles and is much lighter and slower to build. It also builds forward from the leading edge as opposed to spreading backwards. Variations on clear ice are freezing rain and freezing drizzle, both of which have larger droplets and are caused by rain, snow or ice crystals falling through a layer of warmer air at lower altitudes. However, the latter's droplets have a much higher water content.

Although aircraft are different, expect icing to occur (in the engine intake area, anyway) whenever the OAT is below 4 °C. Otherwise, it can form in clear air when humidity is high. Clear ice is found most often in cumulus clouds and unstable conditions between 0 and –10 °C, and rime ice in stratiform clouds between –10 and –20.

Pitot head, static vent and fuel vent heaters should be on whenever you encounter icing, together with anything else you feel is appropriate. Try not to use de-icing boots until at least one-half inch of solid (not slushy) ice has formed, otherwise they will merely stretch the ice covering and operate inside the resulting cocoon. Waiting a while at least gives you the ability to crack the ice off. I know that some experts have determined that this is not the case, but, trust me, they're wrong. If you operate the boots too early, the ice coating on them will merely flake and stay stuck on.

You need warmer air to get rid of ice effectively – just flying in clear air can take hours, but I suppose you could at least say you won't get any more. Climbing out is often not possible, due to lack of performance or ATC considerations, and descending has problems, too – if you're getting clear ice, it's a fair bet that the air is warmer above you, since it may be freezing rain, which means an inversion, probably within 1,000 feet or so, as you might get before a warm front. In this position, landing on your first attempt becomes more important, as you are unlikely to survive a go-around without picking up more of the stuff.

You basically have three choices, to go up, down or back the way you came. Going up is a good first choice if you know the tops are nearby, if only because you won't have a chance to do so later, but you do present more of the airframe to icing risk, which is why there is often a minimum speed for climbing in icing conditions.

Before going, check that the freezing level is well above any minimum altitudes, which will help get rid of ice in the descent. Try to make sure the cloud tops are within reach as well, or that you have plenty of holes.

Turbulence

This also exists high up, not so much due to convection, but rather the passage of fronts or mountain waves. You can't see the evidence of its existence as there is little moisture to collect into cloud, hence Clear Air Turbulence.

If turbulence is likely, mention it to the cabin crew and advise the passengers to return to, and/or remain in their seats, ensuring their seat belts/harnesses are securely fastened. Catering and other loose equipment should be stowed and secured until the risk has passed. Fly at recommended turbulence speed.

Windshear

This concerns airspeed changes over about 10 kt resulting from sudden horizontal or vertical changes in wind velocity – more severe examples will change not only airspeed, but vertical speed and aircraft attitude as well. Officially, it becomes dangerous when the variations cause enough displacement from your flight path for substantial corrective action; severe windshear is considered to cause airspeed changes of greater than 15 kt, or vertical speed changes greater than 500 feet per minute. Expect it to occur mostly inside 1,000 feet agl.

Although mostly associated with thunderstorms (see above), where you have the unpredictability of microbursts to contend with, it's also present with wake vortices, temperature inversions, mountain waves and the passage of fronts, and can occur over any size of area. You can even get it where rain is falling from a cumulus cloud, as the air is getting dense from the cooling, and will therefore fall quicker. It's not restricted to aeroplanes, either – helicopters can suffer from it above and below tree top level in forest clearings, when a backlash effect can convert headwind to tailwind.

All fronts are zones of windshear – the greater the temperature difference across them, the greater the changes will be. Warm fronts tend to have less windshear then cold ones, but as they're slower moving, you catch it for longer. In general, the faster the front moves, the more vigorous the weather associated with it; if it goes slower, the visibility will be worse, but you can still get windshear even then and always for up to an hour after its passage.

One significant effect of windshear is, of course, loss of airspeed at a critical moment, similar to an effect in mountain flying, where a wind reversal could result in none at all! You would typically get this from a downburst out of a convective-type cloud, where initially you get an increase in airspeed from the extra headwind, but if you don't anticipate the reverse to happen as you get to the other side of the downburst, you will not be in a position to cope with the resulting loss. This has led to the classification of windshear as either *performance increasing* or *performance decreasing*. Windshear encountered near the ground (say below 1,000 feet) is the most critical, mainly because you can't quickly build up airspeed – remember the old saying: altitude is money in the bank, but speed is money in the pocket.

The effects also depend on the aircraft and its situation, in that propeller-driven types suffer less than jets, and light aircraft tend to be less vulnerable than heavy ones – those with a good power to weight ratio will come off best. The take-off leaves you most vulnerable because of the small scope for energy conversion, smaller amounts of excess engine power and the amount of drag from the gear and flaps, which is not to say that landing is that much better.

In extremely simple terms, where windshear is expected, you should have a little extra airspeed in hand; you can help with the following:

❏ On take-off, use the longest runway, less flap and more airspeed up to about 1,000 feet agl, but watch your climb gradient and don't use over 10 kt more than usual. If your shear is indicated by rapidly fluctuating airspeed and/or rate of climb or descent, apply full power and aim to achieve maximum lift and maximum distance from the ground. Be prepared to make relatively harsh control movements and power changes, using full throttle if you have to – new engines are cheaper than a new aircraft

❏ In a jet, you can use higher angles of attack and still get a sizeable amount of lift for a moderate increase in drag, because the wings are designed that way. Various methods are used to inform you of the stall, and you want to keep the thing flying just above that point – something that may require some practice in a simulator. Similarly, if the shear is encountered during the approach, positive application of power and flying controls should keep the speed and rate of descent within normal limits; if there is any doubt, abandon the approach and take action as above

❏ Set the prop r.p.m. to maximum (for flat pitch)

Windshear should be reported to ATC as soon as possible, for the benefit of others. It can be detected by radar, using Doppler shift to calculate how fast raindrops are moving and subsequently the pattern of air movement, specifically looking for headwind/tailwind combinations. In theory, this technology could also be used to detect turbulence at higher levels, assuming raindrops are present.

Your company has to provide a formal windshear training program. If it doesn't, there is an FAA video which is available from the CAA library to AOC holders only.

Jetstreams

Jetstreams occur at the tropopause, or the boundary between lower air (troposphere) and the stratosphere, where it collects and channels air into a high-speed stream due to a strong horizontal temperature gradient. They lie to the north of frontal systems where the temperature gradient is greatest, and are stronger in winter. To qualify for the name, the wind-speed must be at least 60 kt. A jetstream may only be a few hundred miles wide, but thousands of miles long. They have extreme turbulence associated with them, which can extend as much as 15,000 feet below the tropopause, usually on the polar side – also, headwind components will naturally increase your fuel consumption for the trip. Bear in mind that the tropopause lowers in winter, which will move the unstable air beneath the jetstream further downwards as well (it's unstable because the jetstream is sucking it up like a vacuum).

Shallow fog
In shallow fog, you may be able to see the whole of the approach and/or runway lights from a considerable distance, even though reports from the aerodrome indicate fog. On descending into the fog layer, your visual reference is likely to drop rapidly, in extreme cases from the full length of the runway and approach lights to a very small segment. This may give the impression that you're pitching nose up, making you more likely to hit the ground after corrective movements. You should be prepared for a missed approach whenever you have the slightest doubt about forward visibility. The minimum RVR for landing from a visual circuit is 800 m.

White-out
Defined by the American Meteorological Society as 'an atmospheric optical phenomenon of the polar regions in which the observer appears to be engulfed in a uniformly white glow'. That is, you can only see dark nearby objects, no shadows, horizon or clouds, and you lose your depth perception. It occurs over unbroken snow cover beneath a uniformly overcast sky, when the light from both is about the same. Blowing snow doesn't help. It's particularly a problem if the ground is rising. Once you suspect white-out, you should immediately climb or level off towards an area where you can see things properly.

Clear air turbulence
This can sometimes be avoided by simply changing the cruising level. Listen out for other aircraft reports.

Rain, snow and other precipitation
On the ground, you may need slower taxiing speeds and higher power settings to allow for reduction in braking performance and the increase in drag from snow, slush or standing water, so watch that your jet blast or propeller slipstream doesn't blow anything into nearby aircraft.

When Taxiing

Try not to collect snow and slush on the airframe, don't taxi directly behind other aircraft, and take account of banks of cleared snow and their proximity to wing- and propeller-tips or engine pods. Delay flap selection to minimise the danger of damage, or getting slush on their retraction mechanisms.

On the Runway

A contaminated runway has significant amounts of standing water, ice, slush, snow or even heavy frost along its surface. The most important factors are loss of friction when decelerating, and displacement of (and impingement drag when accelerating through) whatever is on it, so it may be difficult to steer, and take-off and accelerate-stop distances may be increased due to slower acceleration, as will landing distance because of poor braking action and aquaplaning, which is a condition where the built-up pressure of liquid under the tyres at a certain speed will equal the weight of the aircraft.

Higher speeds will lift the tyres completely, leaving them in contact with fluid alone, with the consequent loss of traction, so there may be a period during which, if one of your engines stops on take-off, you will be unable to either continue or stop within the remaining runway length, and go water-skiing merrily off the end (actually, you're more likely to go off the side, so choosing a longer runway won't necessarily help). The duration of this risk period is variable, but will vary according to your weight.

A rough speed at which aquaplaning can occur is about nine times the square root of your tyre pressures, 100 pounds per square inch therefore giving you about 90 kt – if this is higher than your expected take-off speed you're naturally safer than otherwise. The point to note is that if you start aquaplaning above the critical speed (for example, when landing), you can expect the process to continue below it; that is, you will slide around to well below the speed you would have expected it to start if you were taking off.

Most factors that will assist you under these circumstances are directly under your control, and it's even more important to arrive for a 'positive' landing at the required fifty feet above the threshold at the recommended speed on the recommended glideslope than for normal situations. Under-inflating tyres doesn't help – each 2 or 3 lb below proper pressure will lower the aquaplaning speed by one knot, so be careful if you've descended rapidly from a colder altitude.

Aquaplaning aside, it's obviously a good idea to avoid using a contaminated runway, but if this isn't possible, there are techniques that may assist you to reach a speed at which you can continue if an engine fails, or stop in the shortest practicable distance, which will include not taking off with a tailwind component or carrying unnecessary fuel. The recommended maximum depth of slush or water for take-off should not exceed 15 mm, and of dry snow 60 mm. Wet snow should be treated as slush.

The airfield must have either a paved runway having an Emergency Distance Available of not less than 1.5 × TODR (say a PA23) or 2 × TODR (an AA5) or 1,500 feet, whichever is the greater; or a grass runway having an Emergency Distance Available of not less than 2 × TODR (PA23) or 2.66 × TODR (AA5) or 2,000 feet, whichever is the greater. The minimum cleared width should be 70 feet (see Performance later in this chapter for definitions).

There should be provision for you to identify the point on the runway which is 40 per cent of EDA from the start of take-off as a check against acceleration. If 0.85 V_2 has been achieved by this marker, continue the take off, rotating at 0.9 V_2. V_2 should be achieved by 50 feet. If you can't get that, then the take-off should be abandoned, keeping the nosewheel in contact with the runway, the throttles closed and maximum (safe) braking applied.

The maximum depth of slush or water for landing should not exceed 3 mm, with limitations for snow being the same as for take-off.

Touchdown should be made firmly and at the beginning of the touchdown zone, the nosewheel lowered as early as possible, and any retarding devices such as spoilers, lift dump or reverse thrust used before applying the brakes, to give the wheels time to spin up. Maximum anti-skid systems should be used immediately. Crosswind components should be well below the normal dry runway figure. However, release the brakes if you have difficulty steering, as anti-skid will reduce cornering forces for directional control.

Also, allow the engines to spool down when changing from reverse thrust to forward idle, or they will transition to forward thrust at a higher setting.

Runway Braking Action

Critical fluid depths for aquaplaning can vary from approx. 0.1 to 0.4 in., depending on the surface. The effects of water or liquids on a runway that may affect braking action are:

Condition	Description
Damp	Surface colour changed due to moisture
Wet	Surface soaked, no significant standing water visible
Water Patches	Significant standing water patches visible
Flooded	Extensive standing water patches visible

Sandstorms

To be avoided. On the ground, aircraft should be under cover, or at least have engine blanks and cockpit covers fitted, as well as those for system and instrument intakes and probes. These should be *carefully* removed before flight so accumulations of dust are not deposited in the places the covers are designed to protect. The stuff gets everywhere!

Volcanic ash

Flight through this can cause abrasion to all forward-facing parts of the aircraft, enough to impair visibility through the windshields and severely damage aerofoil and control surface leading edges. Airspeed indications may also be completely unreliable through blocking of pitot heads, and engines may become choked enough to shut down.

Known areas of ash-producing volcanic activity are found in NOTAMs, as deduced with the help of a Cray computer. Flight into them should be avoided, particularly at night or in IMC when ash clouds won't be seen – don't expect weather radar to help. If you end up in one, the immediate action is to keep all or some of the engines running and find the shortest route out, which may be downwards.

Mountain waves

Where a high mountain range exists with an airflow greater than twenty knots over it in stable conditions, standing waves may exist downwind, noticeable by turbulence and strong persistent up and down draughts.

Waves form in the lee of a range of mountains when a strong wind (over 20 kt) is blowing broadside on (within about 30 degrees). They are usually standing waves, with several miles between peaks and troughs, extending 10 or 20,000 feet above the range and up to 200 or 300 miles downwind, although the effects, such as turbulence and strong up and down draughts reduce with height. At normal cruise altitudes, mountain waves are usually free from clear air turbulence, unless associated with jetstreams or thunderstorms.

Watch out for long-term variations in speed and pitch attitude in level cruise (the variations may be large). Use the autopilot height-lock to maintain altitude, but change power as well. Bear in mind that at cruise height the margin between low and high speed limits can be relatively small. Near the ground in a mountain wave area, severe turbulence and windshear may be encountered. This region is known as a *lee wave rotor*, and is caused by flow separation behind the mountain range (see also Mountain Flying in Chapter 12). Take-off or landing should not be attempted. The quickest way out of severe turbulence is up, with the next best directly away from the range. Fly parallel to the range in an up-draught, avoiding peaks.

Significant temperature inversions
Performance is affected by variations in temperature, and inversions will affect it adversely. Large ones encountered shortly after take-off can seriously degrade climb performance, particularly when heavy. Even a small inversion in the upper levels can prevent you reaching a preferred cruising altitude. At lower levels, expect deteriorating visibility, as an inversion can prevent fog clearance for prolonged periods. Another good reason for avoiding the top of an inversion is that all the industrial pollutants collect there, especially in the stubble-burning season, which may include incinerated pesticides.

Wake turbulence
A by-product of lift behind every aircraft (including helicopters) in forward flight, particularly severe from heavy ones. Wake vortices are horizontally concentrated whirlwinds streaming from the wingtips, from the separation point between high pressure below and low pressure above the wing. The heavier and slower the aircraft, the more severe they will be, and flaps, etc. will only have a small effect in breaking them up. The effects become undetectable after a time, varying from a few seconds to a few minutes after the departure or arrival, although they have been detected at twenty minutes. Vortices are most hazardous to other aircraft during take-off, initial climb, final approach and landing. Although there is a danger of shockloading, the biggest problem is loss of control near the ground. You are safest if you keep above the approach and take-off path of the other aircraft, but, for general purposes, allow at least three minutes behind any greater than the light category for the effects to disappear (but see the table below).

Wake generation begins when the nosewheel lifts off on take-off and continues until it touches down again after landing. Vortices will drift downwind, at about 400–500 f.p.m. for larger aircraft, levelling out at about 900 feet below the altitude at which they were generated. Eventually they expand to occupy an oval area about one wingspan high and two wide. Those from large aircraft tend to move away from one another, so, on a calm day, the runway itself will remain free, depending on how near the runway edge the offending wings were. They will also drift with wind, so your landings and take-offs should occur upwind of a moving heavy aircraft and before the point of its take-off and after the point of landing. Although ATC will normally suggest an interval, use these tables as a guide:

Successive Aircraft on Final Approach

Leading Aircraft	Following Aircraft	Min dist (miles)
Heavy	Heavy	4
	Medium	5
	Small	6
	Light	8
Medium	Medium (see Note)	3
	Small	4
	Light	6
Small	Medium or Small	3
	Light	4

Note: If the leading medium aircraft is a B575, increase to 4 miles, as they are difficult to slow down and lose height with, and often fly steeper approaches. BV234, Puma, Super Puma, EH 101 and S61N helicopters are small. Bell 212, Sikorsky S76 and smaller machines are light.

Departing Aircraft
Applies to both IFR and VFR flights.

From same or parallel runways less than 760 m apart (inc. grass)

Leading	Following	Departing From	Min spacing
Heavy	Med/Sm/Lt	Same take off posn	2 min.
Medium/Small	Light	Same take off posn	2 min.
Heavy	Med/Sm/ Lt	Intermediate posn	3 min.
Medium/Small	Light	Intermediate posn	3 min.

Runways with displaced landing thresholds where flight paths cross

Leading		Following		Min spacing
Heavy	Arrival	Med/Small/Light	Departure	2 min.
Heavy	Departure	Med/Small/Light	Arrival	2 min.
Medium	Arrival	Light/Small	Departure	2 min.
Medium	Departure	Light/Small	Arrival	2 min.

Crossing and diverging or parallel runways over 760 m apart.

Leading	A/c Crossing Behind	Min Dist	Time Equiv
Heavy	Hvy/Med/Sm/Lt	4/5/6/8 miles	2/3/3/4 min.
Medium	Med/Sm/Lt	3/4/6 miles	2/2/3 min.
Small	Med or Sm/Lt	3/4 miles	2/2 min.

Opposite-direction runways

There should be at least two minutes between a light, small or medium aircraft and a heavy one, and between light and a small or medium when the heavier is making a low or missed approach and the lighter is using an opposite-direction runway for take-off, landing on the same runway as in the opposite direction, or landing on a parallel opposite-direction runway separated by less than 760 m (a grass strip is a runway).

Weight Parameters (Maximum Take-off Mass in kg)
Mass categories for wake vortex separations

Category	ICAO and Flight Plan	UK
Heavy (H)	136,000 or greater	136,000 or greater
Medium (M)	<136,000 and >7,000	<136,000 and >40,000
Small (S)	–	40,000 or less and >17,000
Light (L)	7,000 or less	17,000 or less

Helicopters
Rotor downwash is wake turbulence from helicopters, which is easy to forget when hovering near a runway threshold or parked aircraft with little wind.

Downwash also creates dust storms and can lift even heavy objects into the air, instantly presenting foreign object damage (FOD) hazards to engines, main and tail rotor blades (so don't bolt your FOD, it gives you ingestion! – old RAF joke, on which I hope there's no copyright). Plastic bags or packaging sheets are FOD, too.

Generally speaking, the larger the helicopter, the greater the potential danger (obvious, really). Still-air conditions permit vortices to persist and travel considerable distances.

Crew Members at their Stations

Duty stations should be occupied from when an aircraft starts to move at the beginning of its flight until stationary on its allocated parking stand.

In level cruise and during rotors-running turnrounds in helicopters, any one member may, with the commander's permission, leave an assigned station for an agreed purpose and period, if there is more than one pilot. However, there may be a situation where a passenger is about to walk into a running tail rotor or propeller (or otherwise be out of control) and there's nobody to assist you if you're by yourself. In the same way that it's illegal for fire engines to be driven across red lights, but they do in an emergency, you can't legally leave your seat and the aircraft unattended, but it is justifiable afterwards if something dangerous is about to happen.

Cabin crew
Seating positions should be evenly distributed, be close to a floor-level exit and provide a good view of the passenger cabin, in that order.

Use of Crew/Passenger Safety Belts/Harnesses

Crew
During take-off and landing, and whenever you consider it necessary, crew members must be at their stations, properly seated and secured by their harnesses. Otherwise, flight deck occupants must keep seat belts fastened.

Passengers
Each person on board must be briefed before take-off on how to fasten and unfasten safety belts and harnesses. Before take-off and landing, and whenever you think it prudent, you must ensure that they each occupy a seat with safety belts and harnesses properly secured.

Multiple occupancy of seats is not permitted other than by one adult and one child younger than two, properly secured by a child restraint device.

Admission to Flight Deck or Cockpit

Where your office is separate from the cabin, passengers are not normally allowed to move forward into it, except in the single-pilot case noted below. At your discretion and in suitable cruise conditions, individual passengers may be allowed into the flight deck, during which times both pilots must remain seated at the controls and have their seat belts fastened. However, this very much depends on company policy.

Authorised inspectors can enter and remain on the flight deck when suitable facilities exist (e.g. unoccupied second pilot's seat, or 'jump' seat), on official business, assuming the safety of the flight will not be compromised, as can staff members, both on and off duty, at your discretion. You have the absolute authority to refuse admission to and/or carriage on the flight deck for whatever reason.

Use of Vacant Crew Seats

If the aircraft requires two pilots, this is obviously not allowed, but for single pilot, where dual controls are fitted, the second pilot's seat may be occupied by a non-crew member if flight manual limitations are observed, the person has the permission of the ops manager and/or the commander, with a valid passenger/staff ticket and can operate self-help exits. You must also ensure that the person is personally briefed on safety procedures and equipment, by you, the commander, and the importance of using the full harness, occasions when it remains fastened and the need for the lap restraint to remain fastened at all times. The person should also remain clear of the flying controls and not use pedals as a foot rest, so, if you can, remove them completely. When the co-pilot's seat is unoccupied, secure the harness away from the controls, so that it doesn't get caught, by fully fastening it.

Incapacitation

There is always a danger that whoever is in the other front seat may become incapacitated; in the obvious case, they collapse and fall across the controls. Less noticeable is the sort that comes with boredom or lack of mental stimulation on longer trips, where you may physically be in the cockpit but mentally miles away. Even disorientation during instrument flight is included. There's not much you can do against the first type, aside from levelling the aircraft and returning to a safe flight path, then ensuring that the unfit pilot cannot interfere. Call for a crew member or passenger to help if need be and tell ATC what's going on. Land as soon as you can under the circumstances, which is not as daft as it sounds – you might find it prudent to divert to a place with better aids or weather, which is further away, despite what the company says about landing where it has a base. *Do not be rushed* into an approach before you are ready, especially at an unfamiliar airfield. Your greatest responsibility is to the passengers.

The second type depends on the cause, most commonly (in the normal pilot's lifestyle) the low blood sugar caused by missed meals and the like. Although you may think it's better to have the wrong food than no food, be careful when it comes to eating choccy bars in lieu of lunch, which will cause your blood sugar levels to rise so rapidly that too much insulin is released to compensate, which drives your blood sugar levels to a lower state than they were before – known in the trade as 'rebound hypo-glycaemia'. Apart from eating 'real food', you will minimise the risks of this if you eat small snacks frequently instead of heavy meals after long periods with nothing to eat. Complex carbohydrates are best.

Incapacitation can be gradual or sudden, subtle or overt, partial or complete and may not be preceded by any warning. According to the 'Two Communications Rule', you are deemed to be incapacitated if you do not respond appropriately to a second verbal communication associ-ated with a significant deviation from a standard operating procedure or flight profile. So there.

Partial or gradual
This bit concerns any medical symptoms affecting your handling ability, to the extent that you have to hand over control. These might include severe pain (especially sudden severe headache or chest pain), dizziness, blurring or partial loss of vision, disorientation, vomiting or diarrhoea (airline food again!). Temporary symptoms often indicate more severe illness to follow, so don't be tempted to take control again.

Two pilots
You must immediately inform the other pilot and hand over control, then inform the destination, base or whoever else and divert, bearing in mind the nature and severity of the symptoms and the availability of medical facilities. Naturally, as with any emergency, the company would prefer you to carry on (minimum inconvenience to the passengers) or return to base (minimum inconvenience to them), but appendicitis waits for no man!

You should not take control again, and your harness must be locked to stop you falling over the controls if you get worse. Neither must you fly again (as a crew member, at least) until a medical examination has taken place, or, with diarrhoea or vomiting, you've had no symptoms for twenty-four hours.

Single pilot
You should react before any illness becomes severe enough to affect your handling, so an immediate radio call is essential. The first consideration must be for the safety of the passengers, so medical assistance for you must be a lesser priority, though the former may well depend on the latter.

Sudden or complete

This may be subtle or overt, and give no warning; Murphy's Law dictates that fatal collapses occur during approach and landing, close to the ground. Detection of subtle incapacitation may be indirect, that is, only as a result of some expected action not being taken, so when you die maintaining your body position, the other pilot may not even notice until the expected order of events becomes interrupted.

Two pilots

Crew members should closely monitor the flight path, especially in the critical stages of take-off, initial climb, final approach and landing, and immediately question any deviations. The fit pilot should assume control, assuming the controls are not interfered with, which is why you should always wear full harness, which should be locked in place, and the seat slid back if there is any trouble, as a matter of priority (use passengers or other crew to help if required). First aid should be delayed until the immediate operational problems have been sorted out, then the aircraft should be landed as soon as practicable.

Cabin Safety

How to handle passengers in general is very much a matter of company policy. Some like to be spoken to, some don't, but there are some small attentions you can give without being obtrusive. Just going round checking seat belts and doors helps (*never* trust a passenger to shut doors properly), as is a look over your shoulder before take-off and occasionally during the flight.

People new to flying are fairly obvious, and they may not appreciate such commonplace occurrences (to you, anyway) as noise, turbulence, pressure changes, strange noises from the front (stall warnings, gear coming up and down, etc.), or lack of toilets.

However, the ANO imposes on you the responsibility for the safety and well-being of your passengers. You will find you are supposed to brief them before every flight, or at least take all reasonable steps to do so, although what you can do with the nose of your helicopter in the side of a mountain and your hands on the controls is a bit different from what you can do on the ground with a bit more time, so try and get as much done as possible beforehand.

A lot depends on what your passengers are going to do at the destination – if you're going to shut down, then tell them to stay seated until everything stops (it helps to explain why you have to sit there for two minutes). If it involves a running disembarkation (other than pleasure flying), one passenger should be briefed to operate the baggage door and do the unloading. Everyone else must leave the rotor disc area. Similar action must be taken with a running pickup.

Nobody should enter the area of ground covered by the main rotor disc of a helicopter without your permission (indicated by 'thumbs up' during the day, or a flash of the landing light by night). Movement in and out of this area should be to the front or at 45 degrees to the longitudinal axis, ensuring that all movement is within your field of vision. Additionally, no movement should be allowed during startup or rundown (due to the dangers of blade sailing) and nobody should approach the rear of a helicopter AT ANY TIME (unless it's a Chinook). You can help by landing in such a way that passengers have no choice but to go forward, but watch that the doors aren't forced against their stops if the wind is behind you.

Tip: When pleasure flying in a helicopter, do not reduce the throttle to ground idle when passengers are getting in and out, so that when one of them decides to run round the back (they will), you can lift into the hover to move the tail rotor out of the way.

In any aircraft, transistor radios, tape recorders and the like should not be operated in flight as they may interfere with navigation equipment. If you don't believe me, tune to an AM station, as used by ADF, on a cheap radio and switch on an even cheaper calculator nearby – you will find the radio is blanked out by white noise. In fact, the radiations from TVs and radios (yes, they do transmit – how do you think the TV detector people find you?) come within the VOR and ILS regions as well. Cellular phones are dodgy, too, but when you're up in the air, you also log on to more than one cell, which screws up the system.

Passenger Briefing Procedures

Where you work for extended periods with particular passengers, say in a corporate environment, you can probably do away with a briefing for every single flight, and just use a briefing card as a reminder. On the other hand, in a remote bush camp, for example, you could get everyone together (including the cook) and do them all in one go. Naturally, some will complain that they don't need to do it then, but you could explain to them that the only way out at the end of their tour is by helicopter, and a briefing at that point will take more time, which is just what they need when they have a scheduled flight to catch.

Get everyone's names and have them sign something as an acknowledgement.

Anyway, as I said, you, as commander, are responsible for ensuring that all passengers are briefed, or have equipment demonstrated, as outlined below. One member of the flight or cabin crew should be responsible for cabin safety from the time the aircraft is accepted for flight, until all the passengers have been offloaded at the end of it.

Pre-flight

Whoever it is should confirm that the passenger compartment contains emergency equipment in its appropriate stowage(s), that seatbacks are in the upright position and lap straps and/or harnesses are ready for use (neatly arranged seatbelts always give a good impression, or, rather, untidy ones don't). Tables should be folded and stowed, and catering secured in its approved area or compartment. Unless the weight and balance allows random seating, passengers should be shown, or conducted to, their seats.

Once they are seated and you have their attention, give them a briefing in a calm and authoritative manner, and be as interesting and informative as possible, with a bit of humour if you can; some passengers may be experienced air travellers, others may not. The idea is to ensure they will retain enough to react sensibly in an emergency which, it should be emphasised, is unlikely to occur.

For helicopters, briefings can be done in the departure area of airports, heliports or oil-rigs by video, covering immersion suits, lifejackets, liferafts, radio beacons, emergency exits and windows, and jettisoning of doors. Before take-off and landing (and whenever you deem it necessary, e.g. during turbulence), they also need to be told (it's no good just showing them the card) about the dangers involved in various aspects of aircraft operation, in particular the following:

❏ Your authority as aircraft commander
❏ Methods of approaching the aircraft, in particular avoiding exhausts and tail rotors – if nearby aircraft have their engines running, it could mask the sound of a closer one. Propeller-driven aeroplanes must always be approached from behind the wing, unless it is unusual in configuration, in which case the engine(s) should be shut down. There's always the danger that someone may bang their head on a wing strut or something. Pitot tubes are especially sensitive (and hot!). Children should be kept under strict control. Long pieces of equipment should be dragged by one end
❏ Loading of baggage and hazardous items that must not be carried. Bear scares (pepper sprays) must not be in the cabin. No objects above shoulder height – carry equipment horizontally. Long pieces of equipment should be dragged by one end. Do not throw cargo
❏ Methods of opening and closing cabin doors (from inside and

outside) and their use as emergency exits. Not leaving seat belts outside. Where not to step and what to hold on to. Sharp objects must be handled carefully when working with float-equipped helicopters.

❏ Hazards of rotor blade sailing and walking uphill inside the rotor disc while rotors are running

❏ When they can smoke (not when oxygen is in use!)

❏ Avoidance of flying when ill or drunk – not only is this dangerous to themselves, but if they are incapable next to an emergency exit, others could suffer too (see Chapter 6)

❏ How to use the seat belts and when they must be fastened

❏ What not to touch in flight

❏ Loose articles, their stowage (tables, etc.) and the dangers of throwing anything out of the windows or towards any rotor blades (seat backs must be in the upright position)

❏ Use and location of safety equipment, including a practical demonstration (if you intend to reach a point more than thirty minutes away from the nearest land at overwater speed, you need to do this with the lifejacket, maybe in the terminal). When oxygen needs to be used in a hurry, adults should fit their masks before those of their children

❏ The reading of the passenger briefing card, which should be of at least Letter or A4 size, so that it doesn't get lost in a pocket. It should also be as brightly coloured as possible, so that it catches the eye. Particular things to place on this card that always seem to be forgotten include instructions not to inflate lifejackets in the cabin and full door-opening instructions (don't forget any little bolts that may be about)

❏ The brace position (including rear-facing seats). If you ever have to give the order to adopt it, by the way, don't do it too early, otherwise the passengers will get fed up waiting for something to happen and sit up just at the point of impact

❏ Location and use of floor proximity emergency escape path markings, where fitted

❏ Landing areas should be clear

❏ Nobody in the cabin when slinging – no riding on long-line

❏ How long the flight will be, and how high you will be flying, what the weather will be like

You might want to adapt the following sample brief:

'Welcome aboard this flight. I am the commander and I must ask you to take notice of any instructions you may be given by myself or my crew, and this includes any given by means of signs. If I have to land quickly or in an emergency, I will tell you in enough time for you to prepare properly. You will know it's an emergency, because you will hear me say something like "Oh sh*t"(Only joking). Emergency exits include the window there and the door by which you came in. Full instructions for each are on the briefing card, which I would like you to read thoroughly, as it gives further instructions for the lifejacket, should it be required, under your seat. Other emergency equipment includes fire extinguishers which are there and there, and the First Aid kit there. The Emergency Locator Transmitter is here, with the On switch clearly marked. For take-off and landing, please ensure that seat backs are upright and all loose articles are stowed away. You may not smoke during taxi, take-off and landing, and please do not throw anything out of the windows. Finally, the flight should take about one hour, and I hope you enjoy it.'

In-flight and pre-landing briefings may be given by a crew member, or with illuminated cabin warning signs. In an emergency during flight, passengers must be briefed on relevant emergency action.

Pre-board briefing concerning dangerous goods
Except as mentioned in Chapter 9, dangerous goods must not be carried in or as baggage, including security-type attaché cases.

Pre-take-off demonstration
The following items must be demonstrated:

- ❏ The use, fastening and unfastening of safety belts/harnesses
- ❏ Use of oxygen masks when cruising level will be above FL 250, or the minimum altitude is more than 14,000 feet
- ❏ Location and use of life-jackets, if any part of the take-off or approach path will be over water, or when any part of the flight will be more than 50 nm from the shore. This demonstration can take place before boarding

In flight
If by yourself, get a passenger to tighten lap straps and tidy things up for landing. Otherwise, a first officer or pilot's assistant may visit the cabin occasionally to check, while established cabin crew should automatically do it.

Post-flight

Passengers should remain seated with seat belts fastened until the aircraft has come to rest and the engines have been stopped. They should also refrain from smoking until they have entered a clearly defined smoking area. Normally a crew member opens the door(s) and remains with the passengers until an approved escort is available.

Refuelling

Refer to Fuelling Procedures earlier in this chapter.

All-Weather Operations

Non-Precision and Category I Operations

Operating minima

Described earlier – see Page 61.

Definitions

See Glossary.

Operating Procedures

Take-Off Briefing

There must be a clear division of responsibilities between handling and non-handling pilots, with special emphasis on the monitoring role of the latter, bringing to the former's attention any significant deviations. As I said before, every commander has a training role, to help the P2 gain experience; the P2 is trained to handle emergencies, and good CRM allows you to make use of that ability so that you can keep command; in other words, don't automatically take over in an emergency, but keep the big picture in mind – use the P2 as an autopilot.

In general, the PNH (Pilot Non-Handling) should select and identify aids, make radio calls, look out for other aircraft and the visual reference for landing, call deviations and heights on finals, loudly and clearly enough for the PH to hear them, until at least after climb power has been set.

Pre-departure briefing

With a fresh crew, a full briefing should be done each day with differences emphasised as the day goes on. Cover the following:

Operations Procedures

- Emergency procedures. Engine failure drills before and after V_r should be rehearsed for the abort and continue cases, the flight path for continued take-off after engine failure should be declared (e.g. fly the SID unless obstructions, etc.), together with the return alternate. Don't forget relanding procedures. On subsequent sectors, the P2 can be challenged on his knowledge of the game plan
- Runway state. Anti-icing precautions, etc.
- Wake turbulence
- Icing, airframe and engines
- Initial terrain
- Transition altitude
- SID
- Radio aids, OBS and compass settings
- Vital speeds

Example: Most of this can be completed before the engine starts and finished when you get your clearances.

'This is a left/right-hand seat take-off from _____(runway). The runway condition is _____, the wind is _____, and wake turbulence can/cannot be expected The take-off will require _____ amount of flap and anti-icing will/will not be required.

On this take-off, it will be my brakes, steering, throttle and flight controls. The departure aids are _____, which you will tune and identify before I need them. We shall follow the noise abatement procedures, or as specified by ATC.

I will handle engine controls and carry out drills from the checklists. You verify my actions and prompt or correct as necessary. During the take-off roll, you will monitor the engine instruments and call passing _____ kt; I will respond to this call.

At V_r, you will call "Rotate", and on reaching the blue line, call "V_2". I will retract the undercarriage and you will report when the cycle is complete. Flaps, yaw-dampers and other vital after take-off drills you will action at my command.

If we have any malfunction before _____ kt, shout "STOP". If we have any major malfunction or fire before V_r, shout "STOP". I will close the throttles, apply reverse thrust and bring the aircraft to a halt, and will call for any checks or drills to be completed to which you will respond. If anything happens after V_r, we will continue the take-off for a return landing or diversion to _____.

There is/is not a terrain problem and we will require/not require an emergency turn or route. I will ask you to do checks or drills after take-off.'

Pre-Take-off Brief

This should be the final item of the lineup or pre-take-off checks, and done by the handling pilot. It's an opportunity for reappraisal after changes.

Pilot Handling	Pilot Non-Handling
Take-off brief	Decision speeds, acknowledge departure clearance
Sets power, checks warning lights	Verifies and prompts, checks lights and instruments
Selects T/O power setting	Checks power and warning lights
Steers aircraft	Monitors engine instruments
Responds to speed calls	Call-speeds, V_r
Rotates or aborts	Identifies + re rate of climb. Call V_2 at Blue Line
Retracts undercarriage	Calls undercarriage retracted
Calls climb checks	Carries out same
Calls to set navaids	Sets and identifies
Calls any malfunction	Same (if P2 handling, hand back to commander)

After Take-off

The handling pilot should be mainly concerned with flying the aircraft. The PNH should monitor the flying, flight path, engine instruments and navaids.

Abandoned Take-off

Usually, only a major malfunction or fire warrants abandoning before V_r.

Pilot Handling	Pilot Non-Handling
Controls aircraft	Malfunction occurs – calls STOP
Selects full reverse thrust	Confirms and actions drills on command
Selects brakes as necessary	Informs ATC

Engine Failure After V_r

This drill should be carried out before 1,500 feet, unless you can either stop or land back on the runway and stop.

Pilot Handling	Pilot Non-Handling
Maintains pitch attitude	Monitors instruments on live engine
Calls for max power	Confirms set
Retracts undercarriage	Confirms
Retracts flaps	Confirms
Establishes positive ROC, identify	Confirms failed engine
Shuts down or feathers failed engine	Confirms initial drills
Maintains climb, carries out failure drills	Confirms drills complete. Inform ATC.
At safe ht, calls subsequent actions	Confirms

Approach Briefing

Before commencing the approach, the PH should brief the PNH on the following, who should note the details in the nav log:

- ❑ Approach procedure; routeing, runway, salient points of approach plate (MSA, intercepts, etc.), weather
- ❑ Alternate airfield
- ❑ MSA/transition level, timing of descent
- ❑ Tuning and identification of radio aids
- ❑ Cross-checking of instruments and procedures
- ❑ Handling (flap settings, speeds, etc.)
- ❑ Monitoring – specific warning if the ROD exceeds 1,000 f.p.m. or the ILS indicator exceeds half-scale deflection
- ❑ Height calls
  - ❑ 1,000 ft prior to cleared levels
  - ❑ Flags clear
  - ❑ 1,000 ft agl
  - ❑ 200 ft above DH
  - ❑ 100 ft above DH
  - ❑ DH
- ❑ Runway visual reference in sight
- ❑ Missed approach action, number of attempts
- ❑ Runway (wake turbulence, surface state)

Missed Approach (all engines operating)

If, at decision height, the visual reference has not been obtained, use this procedure:

Pilot Handling	Pilot Non-Handling
Applies full power	Monitors engine instruments
Rotates to climb attitude	Monitors flying
Retracts flaps	Confirms
Retracts undercarriage	Confirms
Identifies positive ROC	Monitors engine instruments
Checks speeds	Completes baulked landing checks
Reports go-around	Informs ATC
Missed approach checks	Reads from checklist

After Landing
Shutdown checks should be completed only when the aircraft has come to a final halt at the stand. Crashes have occurred because one of the crew has been doing the final paperwork instead of looking out of the window.

Monitoring of radio aids
Cross-Monitor Possible
That is, using one radio aid to cross check another. All should be identified by at least one pilot, and the primary aid by all crew.

No Cross-Monitor Possible
Only one aid, which must be identified by all crew members, and the call sign monitored or re-identified as follows, bearing in mind that the presence of a callsign does not necessarily mean a good signal.

- ❏ ILS. When established on the localiser, whenever warning flags have appeared and cleared, or whenever there is any doubt
- ❏ VOR. When established on the inbound radial, or on final approach, whenever warning flags have appeared and cleared (including passing an indicated overhead), or whenever there is any doubt
- ❏ NDB. The call sign must be monitored throughout the approaches

Even if you don't legally require it, stopwatch timing provides useful navigational information and is a good gross error check.

Missed approach
An approach must be discontinued with no visual reference, and:

- ❏ warning flags indicate a failure. Sometimes, these do not appear when the main signal is invalid, which is why cross-monitoring is important, together with being alert for abnormal headings, rates of descent, etc.

- ❏ the call sign of the primary aid ceases
- ❏ indications are in doubt
- ❏ you are displaced vertically or laterally beyond pre-determined limits
- ❏ on an SRA or PAR approach if communications cease

Descent for approach

You should not descend below the relevant safety altitude unless you are either using an approved approach procedure, you are under positive radar control (and are satisfied with the flight profile) or are in continuous visual contact with the ground and able to keep clear of all hard objects.

Note: if you are only using the ILS glideslope for vertical guidance, do not descend below safety altitude until you are established on the localiser within 10 nm of touchdown.

Approach and landing briefing

This must be given by the handling pilot or commander before initial descent for approach, and should cover at least the following items:

- ❏ initial descent point navigational fix
- ❏ any aerodrome special briefing
- ❏ safety altitudes, MOCA, MORA and Sector Safety Altitude (SSA) and Minimum Safe Altitude (MSA) from the approach plate
- ❏ STAR or arrival route including transition level, holding, minimum hold altitude and speed restrictions
- ❏ the Instrument Approach Plate (Chart) covering procedures, radio aids, and approach minima
- ❏ the chart covering touchdown elevation, QNH/QFE millibar/hectapascal difference, expected visual cues on contact, runway conditions and expected exit
- ❏ aircraft operation covering flap setting, anti-icing, approach speed and wind additives, continuous ignition, wipers, landing lights, reverse thrust and wheel brake settings
- ❏ planned alternate aerodrome and fuel requirement
- ❏ any additional items, and
- ❏ questions

All pre-landing checks should be completed before descending below 1,000 ft above the threshold, excepting only type-specific and/or late-phase items such as landing lights, windscreen wipers, etc., which are normally done late downwind. This is so that the final stages can be monitored properly, especially during non-precision approaches where altitude/height versus range/fix checks must be strictly observed. For aerodromes with no navaids or procedures, specific instructions will be in Part C of the ops manual.

International Operations

On the face of it, going abroad should be no harder than anything else, except you have longer stage lengths and sometimes nothing but water underneath (even single-engined aircraft go regularly across the Atlantic, albeit indirectly). The basic principles of navigation, accurate flying and fuel management are just the same and you could be forgiven for thinking there was nothing to it.

At one level this would be correct, especially when pottering around Europe, but real international operations require deeper planning and knowledge than you think. For instance, do you know to what accuracy your instruments need to work? Do you know what instruments you need? Is your knowledge of radio you learnt for your exams up to date? Can you still calculate a Point of No Return?

You certainly need the right avionics. If you intend to join the big boys and use the non-radar Organised Track System across the Atlantic, for instance, where separation is down to 60 nm between aircraft (and distance from track of 25 nm is a Gross Navigational Error), you will need approved long-range navigational equipment (INS, OMEGA, with LORAN-C OK in certain places only) and communications equipment (HF). The mere fact that you've got this stuff on board doesn't mean you can file a flight plan and launch off, however – you may find that the aircraft itself has to be certified to take the equipment.

You may also need to establish true mach numbers, because speed control is one method of separation, based on accurate position reporting (if your HF radio fails, there is a common VHF frequency, 131.8, which you can use to ask other aircraft to relay for you). The OTS tracks themselves are established twice daily and there is a one-way day and night track structure according to winds and demand.

ICAO and the CAA jointly publish an operations manual for this area, called the *MNPS Airspace Operations Manual*.

As far as general knowledge goes, knowing where to look is half the battle – it's the planning that's most important, the fine print especially. *Jeppesen* or *Aerad* will have details of the overflight and landing clearances you may need, together with entry requirements for you and your passengers. A little reading of the newspapers will give you an idea of any political restrictions. Some permissions may take thirty days or more to obtain – if you go without them, you'd better swot up on your interception signals as well (in Canada, they must be carried at all times).

You may not realise it, but you actually need permission to fly over any country. In most cases, this is taken for granted in the interests of commercial activity – after all, they have to fly to the UK. But a delay causing restrictions over a commonly used country may well cause you to go elsewhere, possibly somewhere hostile. You will have to pay your way, so don't forget credit cards or other financial instruments, particularly cash if you're going somewhere out of the way where you may need to bribe somebody to get what you need – the Mafia is alive and well in many places (Oops, I forgot – there's no such thing).

Naturally, you will need passports (including visas) and licences (with related certificates), but you may also want proof of immunisation for most things nasty you can think of. As well as the paperwork mentioned elsewhere, the aircraft itself should carry any flight authorisations, permits for overflight or landing rights, insurance details, maintenance information, Customs forms (e.g. permit for temporary export/import), if required, General Declarations (crew and passenger) and passenger /cargo manifests, tickets or waybills.

The flight plan system is very complex, and they get lost in the system sometimes, so if you have pre-filed across several stages, it's worth asking at every stop-off point while taxiing in whether the outbound plan is OK. If it isn't, and you're somewhere like Nice, you'll then have to walk a couple of miles round all the relevant offices, which is when you wish you had a handling agent.

If you're going very far away, do you need a survival kit? Flying north of a certain latitude in Canada requires a few items to be carried. Depending on circumstances, you may need a polar (or tropical) survival kit. If in doubt, check the ANO, Schedule 5.

MELs (see below) also need to be checked – for instance, some countries may require LORAN or HF/sideband as well as the normal ADF, VOR, etc. (certainly near the Azores). You can rent, if you're only on a one-off trip. Don't forget to take a few spares, if possible.

There is an *Airports and Handling Agents Manual* (published by Jane's) which, together with the *Official Airline Guide*, contains information on bank schedules and daily life in the country of your destination (you don't want to arrive during half-day closing). In these circumstances, handling agents, while having limited usefulness in UK because of their cost relative to the whole trip, can be worth their weight in gold when you're abroad. You can use their credit, for one thing, and they can do most of your work as you come down the ILS, because you will have contacted them by radio on the way in.

Although English is the language of aviation, it's not always so, and some nationalist controllers may insist in speaking their own language (a helicopter pilot I know got one out of this habit by reading back an imaginary clearance to proceed across Paris City Centre at 1,000 feet!). GMT, of course, is now UTC.

Just in case you've forgotten, here are some formulae:

Time to PNR

$$\frac{E \times H}{O + H}$$

where E = endurance, O = gspd out (kt) and H = gspd home (kt).

Time to CP

$$\frac{D \times H}{O + H}$$

where D = total distance. Others as above.

The CP can differ depending on the type of emergency. If it's a medical one, for instance, your aircraft will have no change in performance characteristics and you won't lose any airspeed. However, if you lose an engine, it will all change drastically, as you'll also find out if you lose pressurisation and have to descend. As most aircraft keep similar fuel flows with less airspeed when you lose an engine, this means your effective range will decrease by whatever percentage.

This is where carrying proper reserves becomes important, because that slower speed will eat into whatever you planned to have left over. What you need to do is calculate what fuel you estimate having left at the CP, and use the anticipated engine out airspeed against wind (you can obtain tables of statistical winds from Boeing) to get groundspeed and divide it into miles to go. If your endurance is less than this, you will not get to where you want, and if you're over the Atlantic, you will get your feet wet! (The shortfall in endurance divided by two gives you the time either side of the CP during which, if an engine fails, you are faced with such a situation, hence *wet footprint*. In practice, you can gain a little extra by drifting down, but don't bank on it).

Extended Range Twin Operations (ETOPS)

Essentially, this covers twins on routes more than one hour's flying time, at the approved one-engine cruise speed (under standard conditions) from a suitable aerodrome. It applies to public commercial air transport aeroplanes (turboprop and piston engine) over 8,618 kg max take-off weight and certified for more than nineteen passengers. Not relevant here, as it's quite specialised, but included for interest.

A twin-engined turbojet must be able to continue or divert where the flying time is no longer than 180 minutes. Higher maintenance standards are naturally needed for all this, and dispatch of an ETOPS aircraft must be carried out only by authorised people; for engineering, this means a licensed engineer. In the UK, there is no flight dispatcher's qualification as such, and the training is left to internal company procedures. Flight crews must be able to cope with changes to planned route, en route monitoring and diversion procedures, and must also demonstrate familiarity with the routes flown, in particular en route alternates.

A suitable aerodrome for ETOPS must allow you to stop within the landing distance available (inside normal limits). Services and facilities must also be adequate, as must operating minima for the expected runway. For an hour either side of ETA, the latest forecast weather conditions must equal or exceed the planning minima for alternates, and the forecast crosswind component, including gusts, must be less than the maximum for landing, with one engine out.

Carriage of Freight Overseas

Freight is easier to carry than passengers in the UK (mainly because it doesn't answer back), but considerably more complex when doing it overseas, although, having said that, as long as the paperwork is properly done, moving freight can be surprisingly speedy. And that's the problem. The paperwork. The best advice I can give you is never self-handle freight if you can possibly help it – always employ an agent, although for one box it can seem over the top – even assuming you find the right forms, they all require special computer codes which describe the goods, but the book on these alone is thicker than a telephone directory and has no intelligible index. Don't expect help from Customs, either – you might get it, but filling in your forms is not part of their job, as they will no doubt gleefully tell you.

Usually, therefore, all you'll be asked to do is simply transport the stuff from airfield to airfield with the formalities being taken care of by the client. However, it's difficult to claim you're only a carrier if anything goes wrong, as the vehicle used for conveyance is liable to forfeiture as well as the goods concerned, so you need to know a bit of what goes on to cover yourself. You should impress upon the client that you're not a properly qualified freight agent, and that you reserve the right to use such people at both ends of the journey. Naturally, he will have to pay. However, circumstances may lumber you with a parcel on your hands one day, so if you must do things yourself, try and do it through a major airport, even at the expense of greater landing fees. A part-time Customs officer at a small one who is waiting to go home will be no help at all.

Each carton must have a label with the consignor's and consignee's names and addresses on, covered by a cargo manifest which should have each item listed separately, numbered and described. There will also need to be an air waybill, which is the freight equivalent of a passenger ticket. You may need several copies of an invoice as well.

If you can, try and get sight of what's inside the boxes and check it doesn't tick! Be especially careful of people asking you to take wrapped 'presents' for others at your destination.

Minimum Equipment and Configuration Deviation Lists

The company will hold a permission for you to operate with some equipment unserviceable for a limited time, subject to the Minimum Equipment List (MEL), which is based on the master MEL produced by the aircraft manufacturer (there are none approved for aircraft less than 2,730 kg MTWA in UK). A master MEL will not necessarily apply to everyone, as circumstances will differ, so operators must prepare their own.

MELs are lists of systems and equipment installed on an aircraft, showing how many defects may be allowed for how long (older hands may remember the Acceptable Deferred Defects List, or Allowable Deficiency List). In some cases, additional restrictions are applied – for example, you may have to troubleshoot, inspect or secure items as conditions to be met before take-off.

As the MEL is an exhaustive list, it follows that any item not on it must be working at the time of dispatch. However, MELs are usually black-and-white and only address operation (or not), and not degraded performance, such as unusually slow landing gear or excessive fuel consumption, which means that not every possible combination is allowed for, or the additional workload from multiple defects. You still therefore need to exercise some judgement, but there are circumstances where operation is definitely not permitted and, although you are given the authority to operate with specified equipment unserviceable, you don't have to if you don't think it's safe. When in doubt, consult an engineer, but, although their signature in the log book is a maintenance release, the responsibility is still yours.

In general, defects such as buckling, cracks or extensive corrosion of the skin or structure beyond the safe limits established by the manufacturer will render that aircraft unfit for safe operation. Once a MEL has been approved, compliance is mandatory. MELs are not transferable between operators.

Note: The idea is to get you to a place where a defect can be fixed, or to fly while awaiting spares – it is not for skimping on maintenance.

Configuration Deviation Lists (CDLs) are the structural equivalent of MELs, permitting operation with certain minor bits missing, like fairings, access panels, vortex generators and static discharge wicks. They take no account of dents, distortion, cracks or corrosion.

A Deferred Defect (as it's sometimes called) is one which will not prejudice the safety of a flight, but should be rectified as soon as practicable after it. For example, the minimum navigational equipment for IFR operations in most areas is 2 VOR + 1 ADF or 1 VOR + 2 ADF, ILS, DME, Transponder, Marker and 2 720-channel VHF Comms (below FL100 in Amsterdam you can get away with 1 VOR and 1 ADF, but watch out for Germany). However, you can fly when one item of the above list is unserviceable if it isn't reasonably practical to effect repairs or replacements before taking off, especially as outside maintenance organisations should not be used without the approval of your own maintenance contractor, though the JAR system should help in this respect.

On the assumption that you, as commander, are satisfied that the forecast weather conditions, latest route information, regulations, etc. allow your flight to be safely made, you are allowed to complete one flight to a place where repairs may be effected. The ANO also allows you to fly to a place where a Certificate of Release to Service can be issued for any defect rectification when you are at a place where it is not reasonably practical to do so. In this case, you will have to submit a report to the CAA (FOD 7) within ten days, so to cover yourself, the flight must have been made to the nearest place at which certification can be made, and the aircraft must have been suitably equipped for the route, as well as taking into account any hazards to the liberty or health of persons on board.

As a general rule, a defect will only be allowed for a *return* to base; only under exceptional circumstances should you *depart* with one. Defective equipment should be isolated from the remainder of the relevant system by removing fuses, blanking pipelines, locking selectors, or anything else that will promote safety, including labelling the equipment as defective (on gauges, the label needs to be placed so that no readings can be taken).

Because you must be aware of the condition of an aircraft to exercise proper judgement, all defects should be entered in the relevant part of the tech log. The aircraft should not then fly until they are either cleared or deferred. Details of deferred defects should also be recorded on the deferred defects sheet, which is carried with the tech log. A new tech log page must then be started, but if, for any reason, the same page must be used (you might have run out), the defect(s) must be clearly identified by numbering. When a deferred defect is finally cleared, the entries are made on the *current* tech log page and DD sheet (not the originals), cross-referencing the original DD sheet number, rectification action and clearance certification.

For specific details of what is or isn't allowed, refer to the Minimum Equipment List in the flight manual, or part B of the ops manual.

Non-Revenue Flights

Passenger-Carrying

Non-commercial air transport flights with passengers (that is, company personnel) should be conducted as per the ops manual.

Non-Passenger

When no passengers are carried, as with training, air tests, delivery, demonstration or empty positioning flights, you must still follow the ops manual, except that you don't need to raise a mass and balance document if remaining within the appropriate limits, and neither do you need licensed aerodromes (in the UK, except for training), provided performance and minima requirements can be met.

Oxygen Requirements

Pure oxygen is a colourless, tasteless, odourless and non-combustible gas that takes up about 21 per cent of the air we breathe. Although it doesn't burn itself, it does support combustion, which is why we need it so much, because the body turns food into heat energy. As we can't store oxygen, we survive from breath to breath.

How much you use depends on your physical activity and/or mental stress – for example, you need four times more for walking than sitting quietly. The proportion of oxygen to air (21 per cent) actually remains constant for quite a long way up, but as the air gets less dense, each lungful contains less oxygen in proportion (that is, the *partial pressure* becomes less), which is why high-altitude flight requires extra supplies. Nothing more is required below 5,000 feet, as 95 per cent of what you would find on the ground can be expected there. However, at over 8,000 feet, you may find measurable changes in blood pressure and respiration, although healthy individuals should perform satisfactorily.

As you creep up to 10,000 feet, the symptoms of oxygen deficiency (otherwise known as hypoxia), that is, impairment of vision (especially at night), lassitude, drowsiness, fatigue, sharp headaches and a false feeling of well-being, can catch you unawares. The intensity varies from person to person according to altitude, the exposure and amount of exercise being undergone – the more energy expended, the more severe the symptoms. If they occur without obvious cause, suspect hypoxia (or hyperventilation, described below) and either descend or use sup-plemental oxygen. It's important to use it before the onset of hypoxia, because the condition itself makes you think you don't need it

Sometimes, however, unconsciousness may occur before symptoms occur, due to a high rate of ascent (or rapid decompression, which amounts to the same thing). You may get some symptoms as low as 8,000 feet, but these are considered acceptable. There's more about this in Chapter 18, *Crew Resource Management.*

As mentioned above, hypoxia means lack of oxygen, whether because there really is too little, or because you don't have enough blood to carry what you need around the body – you may have donated some, or have an ulcer. You might also be a smoker, with your haemoglobin blocked by carbon monoxide. A blockage of 5–8 per cent, typical for a heavy smoker, gives you the equivalent altitude of 5–7,000 feet before you start!

Hyperventilation is breathing too quickly, but the effect is not to increase the blood's oxygen content, but decrease the carbon dioxide level, making the blood more alkaline so that the blood vessels get con-stricted, hence less oxygen to the brain and maybe a headache.

The oxygen to be carried, and the people to whom masks should be made available, varies with altitude, rate of descent and MSA. The latter two are dependent on each other, in that it's no good having a good rate of descent if the MSA stops you. It may well be that, although you're flying at a level that requires fewer masks, the MSA may demand that you equip everybody.

Pre-flight stuff includes ensuring that oxygen masks are accessible for the crew, and that passengers are aware of where their own masks are. Check the security of the circular dilution valve filter (a foam disc) on all of them, together with the pressure. Beards will naturally reduce their efficiency. Briefings should include the importance of not smoking and monitoring the flow indicator. All NO SMOKING signs should be on when using it.

Non-pressurised Aeroplanes

Non-pressurised aeroplanes must not go above 10,000 feet without masks and supplies for:

❑ all the flight crew above 10,000 feet PA, for the whole time over thirty minutes between 10,000 and 13,000 feet

❑ the cabin crew when above 13,000 feet PA, and for the whole time over thirty minutes between 10,000 and 13,000 feet

❑ all passengers when above 13,000 feet PA, for one hour or the duration of the flight, whichever is greater

❑ 10 per cent of passengers (minimum one) after thirty minutes between 10,000 and 13,000 ft PA, for the whole time over thirty minutes

When cabin crew is required, you must also have a dedicated supply of therapeutic oxygen for 1 per cent of the passengers or one person, whichever is greater. In the USA, altitude limits appear to be between 12,500 and 14,000 feet. Above 15,000, each occupant must have oxygen.

Pressurised Aeroplanes

Defined as those operating above 10,000 feet PA, but maintaining cabin pressure altitudes below that.

Flight crew

Each member of the flight crew shall have:

❑ an oxygen mask within immediate reach, which may be the same one as above, excluding the portable apparatus. When above 25,000 feet, the mask must be a quick-donning type

❑ when cabin pressure fails, sufficient oxygen for the time cabin altitude exceeds 10,000 feet, with a minimum of thirty minutes for aircraft below 25,000 feet, and two hours for those above

❑ essential flight crew members must use oxygen continuously after thirty minutes at a cabin pressure altitude over 10,000 feet, and at all times over 13,000 feet

❑ when above FL 410, at least one pilot must wear an oxygen mask at all times, except on supersonic aeroplanes

Cabin crew

When they are required, enough for when you are over 13,000 feet, but at least thirty minutes between 10,000 and 13,000 feet, after the first thirty minutes.

Passengers

The following must be available below 25 000 feet:

- ❏ supply for all passengers for the time above 15,000 feet, or ten minutes, whichever is the greater
- ❏ supply for 30 per cent of the passengers for the time the cabin altitude is between 14,000 and 15,000 feet
- ❏ supply for 10 per cent of the passengers for the time the cabin altitude is between 10,000 and 14,000 feet

Crew Protective Breathing Equipment – Pressurised Aeroplanes

Flight crew

Equipment must protect eyes, nose and mouth and provide oxygen for at least fifteen minutes; if there is more than one person and a cabin crew member is not carried, a portable protective breathing apparatus for one member of the flight crew for at least fifteen minutes must also be available on the flight deck and be immediately accessible.

Cabin crew

Portable protective breathing equipment to protect the eyes, nose and mouth of each cabin crew member for at least fifteen minutes, next to each duty station. With a seating capacity of seven or more passengers, and if a hand fire extinguisher is required in the cabin, an additional portable protective breathing apparatus must be carried, and located at/or next to the fire extinguisher except inside a cargo compartment, when you can stick it next to the entrance.

Performance

The take-off and landing phases are the most critical, demanding the highest skills from crews and placing the most strain on the aircraft. Because of this, strict regulations govern the information used for calculating take-off or landing performance. Of course, in the old days (say during the war, or when the trains ran on time), having enough engines to lift the load was all that mattered and no priority was given to reserves of power and the like. Now it's different, and performance requirements will be worked out before a C of A is issued, over a wide range of conditions. They are subsequently incorporated in the flight manual, which actually forms part of the C of A. In addition, the ANO requires you to ensure that your aircraft has adequate performance for any proposed flight.

Aircraft are certified in one of several groups (A, A (Restricted), or B for helicopters, or A, B, C, D, E or F for aeroplanes); the higher the performance of the aircraft, the lower the alphabetical letter (a 737 comes under Performance A, for instance, while anything up to nine seats that may require a forced landing after engine failure will come under F). Well, at least, that's how the ANO works. JAR does it differently, as we have already seen.

The group in which an aircraft operates depends on its certification, max all-up weight and the number of passengers it carries. Within these limits you can choose which group to operate in, and come under the appropriate weather and weight limitations; it may be more acceptable commercially, for example, to operate in a lesser group if it enables you to take more payload, and make more money – all you might need is longer runways.

Individual aircraft of a given species will vary in performance due to such variables as the age of the airframe and engines, the standard of maintenance, or the skill and experience of the crews. What you can do on one day under a given set of circumstances may well be impossible another time. The original testing, of course, is done with new aircraft and highly experienced pilots. These results are *unfactored*, and not all performance data for foreign aircraft is are actually verified by the CAA, though they do carry out spot checks. In fact, any figures are a mixture of actual readings and calculated (or guesstimated) adjustments from them. The 'performance' of an aircraft is therefore a set of average values – particular machines may be better or worse.

There are fudge factors applied to unfactored figures to produce *net performance* (and *gross performance* when they're not). Occasionally, performance data (as amended by the CAA) in a flight manual will already be factored, but you will have to check the small print on the chart, in case they surprise you.

Figures and graphs are based on standard conditions which allow for fixed reductions in pressure and temperature with height. As we all know, the real world isn't like that, so these assumptions may not always be true and due allowance must therefore be made for them (if your aircraft is performing sluggishly, you may find it's not the machine, but the conditions it has to work under that are at fault).

Performance A aircraft must (with one engine out) clear all obstacles under the departure track within a defined area by a specified margin, without relying on seeing and avoiding them. All the relevant data will be in the graphs, but some groups have no information at all in some areas. For instance, an aircraft in Performance Group C is assumed to have all engines working until above 200 feet, under which height there is no data for landing or take-off (which is why the take-off minima will rarely be below this, because you must be visual to avoid any obstacles should an engine fail). Sometimes, there can be no specific provision for engine failure at all.

Each group requires certain conditions to be met, either in standards of power available, environment or special procedures. For example, take-off, landing and reject areas need to be prepared surfaces for Class A helicopters, which also have to achieve certain net gradients at particular points in the climb. Lower groups are more relaxed, but still have limitations – you need somewhere to land in emergency, but for these you only need to avoid risk to third parties while meeting certain weather limits.

Keeping to the helicopter theme, Class A (1) take-off procedures involve a vertical and backwards lift-off to a predetermined height before going forward, which is known as the Critical Decision Point (or CDP), and gives you a choice of action if an emergency happens (actually, ICAO now call it the Take-off Decision Point, or TDP). Having moved backwards, you still have the take-off spot in sight and it's therefore available for landing. At CDP (or TDP), if you elect to carry on to forward flight, you should be able to clear the landing spot during the steep dive you have to make to achieve flying speed (that's why the CDP is about forty feet high). Things happen in reverse on landing. This procedure is not without its critics, since prolonged hovering at high engine-power outputs is not good engine handling.

Anyhow, whatever you're flying, you will find the data needed to check your performance in the flight manual, which will have a UK supplement if your aircraft is foreign-made – these override any information in the standard manuals. General principles concerning distances for take-off and landing are similar for aeroplanes and helicopters; for example, take off distances for both will increase by 10 per cent for each 1,000-foot increase in pressure altitude.

Some factors affecting performance include:

Density Altitude

Your real altitude resulting from the effects of height, temperature and humidity, all mentioned below in various places, and the details you need will be in the flight manual. The idea is that the more the density of the air decreases for any of those reasons, the higher becomes your density altitude, with all the problems that that entails. The effects are found at sea level, as well as in mountainous areas, when temperatures are high – for example, 90 degrees (F) at sea level is really 1,900 feet as far as your aircraft is concerned. In extreme circumstances, you may have to restrict your operations to the early morning or late afternoon in some areas. Here is a handy chart:

Degs F/C	30/–1.1	40/4.4	50/10	60/15.6	70/21.1	80/26.7	90/32.2	100/37.8
1,000'	0	600	1,300	2,000	2,700	3,600	3,900	
2,000'	400	1,100	1,700	2,350	3,100	3,800	4,600	5,100
3,000'	1,600	2,250	3,000	3,600	4,300	5,000	5,700	6,250
4,000'	2,950	3,600	4,300	4,650	5,600	6,300	7,000	7,500
5,000'	4,350	5,000	5,600	6,350	6,900	7,600	8,250	8,650
6,000'	5,450	6,150	6,700	7,400	8,100	8,800	9,450	9,950
7,000'	6,700	7,350	8,000	8,600	9,300	10,000	10,600	11,250
8,000'	7,900	8,600	9,200	9,700	10,400	11,100	11,750	12,300
9,000'	9,200	9,800	10,350	11,000	11,600	12,400	13,200	13,600
10,000'	10,400	11,100	11,700	12,250	13,000	13,600	14,300	14,750
11,000'	11,800	12,500	13,100	13,600	14,300	15,000	15,650	16,150
12,000'	13,000	13,600	14,200	14,750	15,400	16,000	16,550	17,150

Runway Length

Details are declared by the airport authority and published in the AIP. This declared distance is either the Take-off Run Available (TORA) or Landing Distance Available (LDA). Any areas at the ends unsuitable to run on, but nevertheless clear of obstacles, are called clearways, which, with the TORA, form the Take-off Distance Available (TODA), which should not be more than 1.5 × TORA.

However, getting the wheels off the runway is only part of the story. You must also clear an imaginary screen (usually thirty-five feet, but fifty for piston aircraft) at the end of the TODA (TORA + clearway). The distance to do this is the Take-off Distance Required. If a single runway distance is given, it must be used for both TODA and TORA. The Take-off Run Required (factored TODA) is 92 per cent of the TODR.

Part of the clearway may be able to support an aircraft while stopping, although not under take-off conditions. This may be declared as Stopway which may be added to the TORA to form the Emergency Distance

Available (EDA). This is the ground run distance available for an aircraft to abort a take-off and come to rest safely – the essential point to note is that Stopway is ground-based. EDA is sometimes also referred to as the Emergency Distance or Accelerate-Stop Distance. The greater the EDA, the higher the speed you can accelerate to before the point at which you must decide to stop or go when an engine fails.

Obviously, the TODR must not be more than the TODA. If not already done in the flight manual, the TODR must be factored by 1.33, after the corrections below have been multiplied together and applied (factoring means that the distances are multiplied by those figures to provide a safety margin).

The Landing Distance Available must similarly not be less than the Landing Distance Required. If there's a choice of runways, the LDR is the greater of that on the longest one in zero wind or on the runway used due to forecast winds. Don't forget the LDR is from fifty feet. Unless the flight manual states otherwise, the LDR must be factored by 1.43 (giving 70 per cent of distance available), again, after applying the following corrections.

Airfield Altitude and Ambient Temperature

The higher you are, the less dense the air and the less the ability of the wings (rotating or otherwise) and engines to 'bite' into it, thus requiring more power and longer take-off runs to get airborne. Humidity has a similar effect, but is usually allowed for in the graphs.

TODR will increase by 10 per cent for each 1,000-foot increase in aerodrome altitude and 10 per cent per 10 °C increase in temperature (factor by 1.1).

LDR will increase by 5 per cent for each 1,000-foot increase in pressure altitude and 10 °C increase in temperature (factor by 1.05).

Aircraft Weight

Greater mass means slower acceleration/deceleration and longer distances. TODR will increase by 20 per cent for each 10 per cent increase in weight and LDR 10 per cent per 10 per cent increase in weight (factor by 1.2 and 1.1). Very few aircraft allow you to fill all the seats with full fuel.

Some manuals give take-off and landing weights that should not be exceeded at specific combinations of altitude and temperature, thus ensuring that climb performance is not compromised. These are known as WAT limits (Weight, Altitude and Temperature), and are mandatory for commercial air transport flights.

Sometimes rates of climb are given instead, so you need to be aware that a commercial air transport aeroplane must be able to maintain a rate of climb of 700 f.p.m. if it has retractable landing gear, and 500 f.p.m. otherwise. In a multi, if you can't visually avoid obstacles during climb or descent, you must be able to climb at 150 f.p.m. with one engine out at the relevant altitudes and temperatures (that's 500 feet in five miles!). This means *all* obstacles – you can't exclude frangible ones, so you may have to restrict take-off weight.

Runway Slope

Going uphill when taking off will delay acceleration and increase the distance required. The converse is true of downhill slopes, and a rule of thumb is that TODR will increase 10 per cent for each 2 per cent of uphill slope, and vice versa (factor both by 1.1). When landing, an uphill slope aids stopping, thereby reducing LDR. Any gains from landing upslope or taking off downslope should not be made use of but accepted as a bonus (that is, don't use them as part of your planning).

Surface Winds

Headwinds will reduce the distances required and improve the flight path after take-off. Tailwinds have reverse effects and crosswinds may even exceed the ability of the tyres to grip the runway. Aside from the handling problem, crosswinds may also increase the TODR if you need to use the brakes to keep you straight. Forecast winds must be factored by 50 per cent for a headwind and 150 per cent for a tailwind – this may already be allowed for in the charts.

TODR and LDR will increase by 20 per cent for each tailwind component of 10 per cent of the lift-off and landing speed (factor by 1.2).

Surface

Performance information is based on a dry, hard surface. The runway state can affect directional and braking ability, and has been discussed already. Meanwhile, for dry short grass (under 5 in.), the TODR will increase by 20 per cent, a factor of 1.2. When it's wet, 25 per cent – a factor of 1.25. For dry, long grass (5–10 in.), TODR will increase by 25 per cent, and 30 per cent when wet (it's not recommended that you operate when the grass is over 10 in. high).

For dry short grass (under 5 in.), the LDR will increase by 20 per cent, a factor of 1.2. When it's wet, 30 per cent – a factor of 1.3. For dry, long grass (5–10 in.), LDR will increase by 30 per cent, and 40 per cent when wet. For other soft ground or snow, the increase will be in the order of 25 per cent or more for take-off and landing.

Obstacles

Take-off requirements also need to consider obstacles further along the take-off path which cannot be avoided visually. The area concerned is a funnel extending up to 1,500 feet above the airfield elevation from the end of the TODR within 75 m either side of track (with all engines operating). The Net Flight Path is made up of segments covering various stages of flight (such as when undercarriage or flaps are raised) and is so called because NET (i.e. factored) performance data are used to assess it. The NFP commences from fifty feet above the end of the TODR, this being the imaginary screen the aircraft must clear.

If an obstacle (including a frangible one) intrudes on the Net Flight Path, then take-off weight must be reduced until it's cleared by a margin of thirty-five (or whatever) feet, so this may be a determining one in calculating Restricted Take-off Weight (see also Mass and Centre of Gravity, earlier in this chapter). You can make gentle turns to avoid obstacles, and not have to fiddle with take-off weights, and there will be graphs in the flight manual allowing you to calculate radii and procedures for it. However, you will need to be visual as well, so a minimum cloudbase is necessary.

If an engine fails in the climb-out, normal practice would be to return to the point of departure, but if you can't (maybe the weather) the NFP and MSA must be examined at the flight planning stage. It may even be necessary to climb overhead the airfield to get the height required before going for your return alternate.

You must use the *one-engine inoperative net flight path* data from the point at which full instrument flying commences, or is expected to commence.

Balked Approach Flight Path

This is similar to Net Flight Path, and commences at DH above the upwind end of the LDR. However, you may not be able to complete a balked landing or go around once you have entered a low-energy landing configuration, without touching the ground, because your flaps and gear would be set for landing, you would be below about fifty feet, in descent, with the throttle in the idle range and with decreasing airspeed. *Balked landings or go-arounds should be initiated before this point is reached* – if you put your aircraft in this state, the subsequent board of inquiry would only assume you thought it was safe to do so. As there will be no performance figures in the charts to cover it, this is a high-risk experiment – in fact, you are very likely to stall if you try to climb before your engines have spooled up.

Diversions

You must be capable of continuing the flight from any point of engine failure at or above MSA to 1,500 feet above a suitable airfield (within WAT and runway limits), where you must be able to maintain a positive rate of climb. Consideration must therefore be given to height loss, and the likely drift-down rate with engine(s) out is established from the flight manual. The charts will indicate how quickly you can expect to descend, based on aircraft weight, temperature, altitude, etc.

If the MSA is quite high (say over the Alps or the Rockies at 14,000 feet), you're obviously going to be pushed to get there in some aircraft with two engines, let alone one. If you have to go that way and suspect you may have performance problems, you could always work out your drift down with the help of an emergency turn, information about which will also be found in the flight manual. What you do is establish a point one side of which performance is OK and the other side of which, if you have an engine failure, you make an emergency turn to get yourself away from the area and (hopefully) out of trouble. Again, the charts will indicate the rate of descent in a turn, and all you need do then is ensure that your MSA reduces at a greater rate than your altitude! If you can't comply with any of this, you may have to reduce your weight until you can.

Speed

Peculiar to landing is speed – a higher one than specified naturally requires a longer distance, not only for slowing down, but the FAA have also determined that being five knots too fast over the threshold is the equivalent of being fifty feet too high.

Power Settings

These are important. Noise abatement sometimes means reduced thrust on take-off, which obviously tightens performance limits, so will increase all your distances. EPR gauges should not be used by themselves as an indication of engine power output, and should be cross-referenced with other instruments, especially when there is a chance of the probes icing up. The relevance of this becomes apparent with an engine failure after V_1, where some aircraft allow full throttle without exceeding performance limits (like those with automatic controls). Others need the levers to be set more accurately, and you should have a likely idea of what the limits will be before take-off. V_1 is a fixed speed based on weight and flap settings (nothing to do with runway length), and is supposed to give you a safe full stop or a successful engine-out take-off. However, high-speed rejects are among the top three causes of accidents. Unless you feel the aircraft will be uncontrollable, your chances may be better in the air.

Miscellaneous

Low tyre pressures increase distances required.

Summary

It's obviously not a good plan to operate to the limit of all the above factors all at once, as you would be arriving high and fast at a wet, downward sloping runway with a tailwind!

Checklists

Funny things, these. You need them, but if you let passengers see you using them, they wonder if you know how to fly the aircraft properly, though we all know that they are there to make sure you have done everything, and are not actually instructions. Psychologically, at least, it may be a good idea to use them as discreetly as possible. They are especially important in companies, where different pilots leave switches in strange positions, or when an aircraft comes out of servicing – using a checklist properly will ensure that an aircraft is in a standard position before any flight.

Checklists should be available for every crew member, and they will also be fully listed in the operations manual. They should be used on all relevant occasions. On single-crew flights, checks usually done in the air may be completed from memory, but is not recommended. Memorised drills must be strictly in accordance with company checklists, and emergency drills must be verified as soon as possible.

It may be helpful to have the vital actions placarded somewhere – either on the back of a sun visor or printed on the nav log.

It's worth considering leaving the navigation or anti-collision lights (or engine-out warnings) on when you leave an aircraft, despite what the checklist says about switching them off - then you know that you've left the master switch on as you walk away.

Daily Inspections

Each day, before the first flight of any aircraft, a daily (Check A) inspection is carried out. Although it's meant to be a specific maintenance inspection, as laid down in the Light Aircraft Maintenance Schedule (LAMS), it's sort of equivalent to a pilot's pre-flight inspection, which in turn is equivalent to the 'external walkround' in the flight manual, only more detailed. The Check A is similar to the status of the 'First Parade' given to every military vehicle at the start of each day, when the tyres and oil levels are checked.

On smaller aircraft, it may be carried out by a commander with the approval of the chief pilot, who will arrange for the necessary training with the company maintenance organisation. You will then be issued with a number to use against your signature on any paperwork. In keeping with General Aviation practice, the commander performing the first flight of the day normally performs the Check A, and is responsible for signing the tech log. You are responsible (as commander) for checking it is signed by the person who did it.

The term 'inspect' means that all items are examined externally and *in situ* and that their condition when so inspected is so as to preserve continued airworthiness. Throughout the inspection, a thorough examination should be made of all surfaces and parts for damage, corrosion, loose or missing rivets or bolts, distortion, cracking, dents, scores, chafing, kinking, leaks, excessive chipping of paintwork, overheating, fluid contamination and other signs of structural or mechanical damage.

All parts should also be checked for general security and cleanliness, and a particular inspection made of each drain and vent hole to ensure it is unblocked.

Radio Procedures

A radio listening watch should be kept at all times as a matter of airmanship, even though there are still vast areas of the UK where you can fly for hours without having to talk to anybody.

There are one or two points, though, that aren't often taught properly during training. The first is to wait a split second to speak after pressing the transmit button, which gives all the relays in the system a chance to switch over so your message can get through in full, that is, not clipping the first bit.

Secondly, whenever you get a frequency change en route, not only should you write it down on your nav log, but change to the new frequency *on the other box*, so that you alternate between radios. This way, you have something to go back to if you can't get through on the new one for whatever reason (although it is appreciated that this could create difficulties with two station boxes and you have to switch them both every time). Also, use the switches on the station box to silence radios, not the volume controls, otherwise you get endless embarrassing situations where you transmit, get no reply, wonder what-in-hell-is-happening and suddenly realise you've turned the volume down and have been blocking everybody else out. That's when the Standard Air Traffic Voice tells you he's been calling you for the past five minutes . . .

Transponders
The code your flight will use is allocated when the computer spits it out to the appropriate sector controller before you get airborne. Together with the callsign, it's also passed to the callsign distribution system for display on the radar screens of the relevant ATC units, after which the flight is activated automatically by the radar, in the case of London or Manchester, about a minute after take-off.

Reliability here is entirely dependent on you squawking the correct code, otherwise another flight could be activated.

Radio failure
Essentially, comply with the last clearance, which hopefully included permission to land or clear the area. If you don't need to enter controlled airspace, carry on with the plan, maintaining VFR as necessary; don't enter it even if you've been previously cleared. If you must do so, divert and telephone for permission first.

If you're already in controlled airspace, where clearance has been obtained to the boundary on leaving, or the field on entering, proceed as planned. If in doubt, clear the zone the most direct way as quickly as possible, avoiding airfields.

The military have a system of flying a left- or right-handed triangle pattern that can be seen on radar, although it's usually only used if you're lost as well as having a duff radio. Use it as a last resort, though, because ATC have other things to look out for than possible triangles. If they do recognise your problem, they will send up a shepherd aircraft to formate on you and bring you down, so remain VMC if you can, and as high as possible so that radar can see you better. If you can squawk Mode C, do so, because that will give a height readout to work with.

If you can only receive messages, fly in a right-handed pattern for a minute (if your airspeed is over 300 knots, make it two). Fly at best endurance speed and make each 120-degree turn as tight as possible. If you can't transmit either, do the same, but to the left.

RT Emergency Procedures

You should always declare an Emergency, even if you have to downgrade it later.

The distress call (or 'MAYDAY') is used when the aircraft is threatened by imminent danger and is in most urgent need of immediate assistance. If and when the threat of danger has been overcome, the distress call must be cancelled by notification on *all* frequencies on which the original message was sent.

The urgency call (or 'PAN') indicates that the aircraft has a very urgent message to transmit concerning the safety of a ship, aircraft or other vehicle, or of some person on board or in sight.

Flights Over Water

Except with permission from the CAA, no flight may exceed three minutes continuously over water, for which float gear must be fitted and serviceable (in a helicopter), and life jackets worn. For over three minutes, aircraft must be equipped as per Schedule 4.

Helicopters

Any flight beyond autorotative distance from land (twenty seconds) is an overwater flight. For any such flight, or when flying along the Thames in the London Control Zone, between Hammersmith Bridge and Chelsea Reach, approved life jackets for each person on board should be carried, as well as flotation gear.

For flights more than three minutes over water, the following conditions should apply:

- ❏ A dinghy and SARBE (Search And Rescue Beacon) must be carried
- ❏ No night flying (single-engined only)
- ❏ Two-way radio communication must be maintained with position reporting every ten minutes
- ❏ Flight plan to be filed
- ❏ SAR to be notified
- ❏ Immersion suits to be worn when practical
- ❏ A serviceable radio altimeter with voice must be fitted

❏ Passengers must be given a full briefing on the use of all emergency equipment

Aeroplanes

In an aeroplane, when over water for more than ninety minutes' flying time at the recommended over-water speed, an approved life jacket for each person on board must be carried as well as enough life rafts for everyone. If over thirty minutes, a demonstration must be given.

Also, when beyond gliding distance from shore, the life jackets need to be carried whenever it is reasonably possible that a landing may have to be made on water during take-off or landing, to cover for coastal airfields. If you're in a single-engined aircraft, and going beyond gliding distance from shore, make the passengers wear their life jackets from the start, and ensure they know how to use them. In a twin, it's enough just to point out their location and the instructions on the briefing card. However, if one of the engines stops, you become single-engined, so get your passengers to don them immediately.

Except due to the nature of the task, over-water routings should not be planned if alternative overland routes are available. No unplanned over-water flight may be conducted except in emergency. In any case, over-water time should be minimised.

Life Rafts

On any flight planned to coast out from the mainland or cross a tract of water more than three minutes flying time wide, a life raft must be carried, which must carry all occupants and be properly restrained so it's ready for use. Life rafts must be equipped with carbon dioxide inflation bottles and a secondary means of inflation, as well as having adequate protection for the occupants, bailing apparatus, leak stoppers, a maritime survival pack and a water-activated light.

Flares

On any flight carrying a life raft, the commander must have either a day/night distress flare or a miniflare gun and cartridges, which may be carried as part of the life raft equipment.

Personal locator beacon

On all flights carrying a life raft the commander must have an emergency locator beacon designed to transmit on 121.5 MHz and 243.00 MHz.

Immersion Suits

To be worn by all crew and passengers on all over-water flights when the water temperature is at or below 10 °C.

Sea State

Over-water flights must not take place where forecast wave height exceeds six feet.

Weather Minima

Six-hundred feet cloud base and horizontal visibility of 6,000 metres. Minimum wind 5 kt.

Ditching

A successful ditching depends on sea conditions, wind, type of aircraft and your skill. It's also a good idea to have a basic knowledge of sea evaluation, as getting the heading right may well determine the difference between survival and disaster.

Whereas waves arise from local winds, swells (which relate to larger bodies of water), rely on more distant and substantial disturbances. They move primarily up and down, and only give the illusion of movement, as the sea does not actually move much horizontally. This is more dominant than anything caused by the wind, so it doesn't depend on wind direction, although secondary swells may well do. It's extremely dangerous to land into wind without regard to sea conditions; the swell *must* be taken into consideration.

The vast majority of swells are lower than 12–15 feet, and the *swell face* is the side facing you, whereas the *backside* is away from you. This seems to apply regardless of the direction of swell movement.

You will need to transmit all your MAYDAY calls and squawks (7700) while still airborne, as well as turning on your ELT, or SARBE. If time permits, warn the passengers to don their life jackets (without inflating them, or the life rafts) and tighten seat belts, remove any headsets, stow any loose items (dentures, etc.) and pair off for mutual support, being ready to operate any emergency equipment that may be to hand (they should have been briefed on this before departure).

One passenger should be made the 'dinghy monitor', that is, be responsible for the life raft. If it's dark, turn on the cabin lights and ensure everyone braces before impact (the brace position helps to reduce the flailing of limbs, etc. as you hit the water; there are different ones for forward- and aft-facing seats). Consider opening the cabin door before impact, so that it doesn't get jammed in place.

If only one swell system exists, the problem is relatively simple – even if it's a high, fast one. Unfortunately, most cases involve two or more systems running in different directions, giving the sea a confused appearance. Always land either on the top, or on the backside of a swell in a trough (after the passage of a crest) as near as possible to any shipping, meaning you neither get the water suddenly falling away from you nor get swamped with water, and help is near.

Although you should normally land parallel to the primary swell, if the wind is strong, consider landing across if it helps minimise groundspeed (although in most cases drift from crosswind can be ignored, being only a secondary consideration to the forces contacted on touchdown). Thus, with a big swell, you should accept more crosswind to avoid landing directly into it. The simplest method of estimating the wind is to examine the wind streaks on the water which appear as long white streaks up- and downwind. Whichever way the foam appears to be sliding backwards is the wind direction (in other words, it's the opposite of what you think), and the relative speed is determined from the activity of the streaks themselves. Shadows and whitecaps are signs of large seas, and if they're close together, the sea will be short and rough. Avoid these areas as far as possible – you only need about 500 ft or so to play with.

The behaviour of the aircraft when it hits the water will vary according to the state of the sea; the more confused and heavy the swell, the greater the deceleration forces and risks of breaking up. In an aeroplane, you should aim to have as high a nose-up attitude as possible consistent with safe handling, as there will be little control once you're on the water; trim for the sea surface rather than the horizon, and you will need a lot of power (if your engines are working) at this stage. Reduce thrust a little earlier than you would on a normal landing to lessen the chance of overshooting what may be the only clear area for miles – it will also help to stop you skipping over the water several times. The use of power is so important that it's best to ditch before your fuel is exhausted (if the engine's working), especially at night. If you have less than full power, or none at all, use a higher than normal approach speed, to give you more inertia in hand at the flare-out, so you can feel for the surface and avoid stalling high or hitting the water unexpectedly.

Landing is less hazardous in a helicopter because you can minimise forward speed. In fact, if you are intentionally ditching, you should come to a hover about five feet above the water first, then throw out the kit and the passengers. Having moved away from them, settle on the surface.

Once in the water, hold the machine upright and level using all the cyclic control there is, and use the rotor brake (if you've got one). Then roll to the right, if your blades rotate anticlockwise, to ensure that the advancing blade is aft of the fuselage.

The way out of a submerged cabin is to place a hand on an open window or door, and follow your hand out. You will thus have a better idea of which way is up. Otherwise, whatever you're in, instruct passengers not to leave until everything has quietened down. When you do, take the flotation and survival gear, but keep everyone together (remember that even seat cushions float). Attach the raft to the aircraft until you need to inflate it, as it will sail away downwind quite easily.

If your aircraft is floating comfortably on the water and with no danger of fire, consider remaining on board (but able to get out quickly). Don't be tempted to leave a relatively safe vessel, but have life rafts ready for a quick exit if need be. This way, you will be more conspicuous, and warmer. Alternatively, you could always get into the raft and stay nearby. Make safe everything you can, then retransmit the MAYDAY call. Splash, use flares or mirrors to attract attention, but let the rescuers come to you. Don't leave the security of the raft or aircraft unless you're actually being rescued, as the downwash or wind will blow them away from you.

Apart from drowning, the real threat is hypothermia, described later in this chapter, so, once you're in the water, keep moving – don't attempt to swim unless land is less than a mile or so away, but DON'T DRINK SEAWATER – it absorbs liquid, and body fluids are used to try and get rid of it, so it gets you twice. Cold makes you give up, so try and keep a positive mental attitude. Except in mid-ocean, SAR will be operational very soon after the distress call, so switch on the SARBE or ELT as soon as convenient, which will also assist a SAR satellite to get a fix on you. Try not to point the aerial directly at rescue aircraft as this may put them in a null zone.

Don't worry if the rescue helicopter disappears for ten minutes after finding you. It will be making an automatic letdown to your exact position after locating your overhead at height. This is where the temptation to use speech is very strong, but should be resisted because this is when your homing signal is most needed. Speech should only be used as a last resort, as not only will it wear your batteries down, but it will also take priority over the homing signal used to fix your position. If you feel the need to do something, fire off a few mini-flares instead. Or scream.

Finally, once in the winch strop, don't grasp the hook, because of the possibility of shocks from static electricity.

Operations and Forced Landings in Remote Areas

Because of the difficulties of communication in remote areas, Ops, or someone responsible, must know where you are. If you have to make a forced landing, you must ensure that the company is notified together with the appropriate ATC, so that overdue action is not set in motion unnecessarily. In the Sparsely Settled Area of Canada you must be able to communicate with a ground station from any point along your route, which means using SSB HF (5680 kHz), unless within 25 nm of your base or an airport.

When operating a helicopter in out-of-the-way places, keep in mind the recovery problems should the engines fail to start after a shutdown; always position as close as possible to a track or road to save trouble later (engineers like being near a pub as well, if you can manage it).

Don't let your fuel reserves get too low – fuel caches are usually delivered to accurate GPS co-ordinates, which may be on top of a frozen lake, so they will sink in spring and not be there when you want them. Either that or the ops clerk may have written them down wrongly. My point is that the added stress of looking for fuel that isn't there when you're short anyway is not what you need.

Assuming your passengers don't carry too much baggage, you should be able to carry a few comforts, such as a tent, a stove that runs on aircraft fuel, high-calorie food and a sleeping bag rated for the temperatures you expect to meet. Keep it out of the aircraft when refuelling, so you don't get left with nothing if it catches fire.

If you're forced down, the same principles of passenger preparation for landing apply as for ditching (see above). Having arrived on the ground, the first task (if necessary) is to assist survivors and apply first aid, after turning on the ELT or SARBE if you have one, and the second to provide shelter (once the ELT is on, leave it on, as that will make best use of the batteries). The absence of food and water should not become a problem for some time – even in the Arctic, in summer, there's plenty of water around, and you won't get any much fresher. Try not to eat or drink at all for the first few hours, and divide whatever you have into equal parts. When you do eat, do it slowly and eat small amounts of food. Consider using the aircraft for shelter if it hasn't burned away, and has actually stopped bouncing. In the Arctic, move the wreckage if you can to the highest point around, so you can be seen more easily. Don't wander too far away from it, and ensure that everyone stays within sight of each other at all times. Use remaining fuel for light and heat as necessary (fuel must be warm before it will light) and maintain a positive mental attitude.

The best cure for hypothermia, when your body loses more heat than it produces, and your organs lose their ability to function, is to use blankets and lukewarm sweet drinks. Direct heating, such as hot water bottles, will only serve to open up the surface blood vessels and take heat away from the core organs, where it's most needed. Victims may also vomit, so give them nil by mouth, even when they are alert. They may have an altered level of consciousness, so handle them carefully.

Hypothermia happens quite slowly, and arises from cold and wind, poorly insulated or wet clothing, prolonged immersion in even warm water, and fatigue (in water, heat is conducted away 25 per cent faster than in cold air). Shivering and grogginess are among the early symptoms, allied with poor judgement and muddled thinking. As it gets worse, the shivering may stop and the attention span will reduce, together with shallow breathing and a slow, weak pulse. Unconsciousness and little or no breathing, with dilated pupils, signifies the full thing.

You can communicate with SAR aircraft visually by making the following signals on the ground, which are only a selection of the full range available (see the UKAP). They should be at least eight feet high with as large a contrast as possible being obtained between the materials used and the background.

Require Doctor, Serious Injuries	I
Require Medical Supplies	II
Require Food and Water	F
Require Fuel and Oil	L
Require Engineer	W
All Well	LL
Negative	N
Unable to Proceed	X
Affirmative	Y
Proceeding This Direction	->

Leave about 10 feet between them. Rocking of the rescue aircraft's wings during daylight and flashing of the landing or navigation lights twice at night indicates that your signals are understood.

Wait before operating the SARBE or ELT until it's likely that SAR services are in your area (an hour past ETA in Canada), and once it's on, leave it on, as that will make best use of the batteries. Otherwise, follow the instructions in Ditching, previously in this chapter.

A typical job done in a remote area is Site Support, described elsewhere.

Use and Location of Emergency Equipment

Every aircraft carries a first aid kit that conforms to the ANO (and is certified by an engineer). Life jackets are commonly stored under the relevant seats when carried, and life rafts should be securely stowed but easily accessible.

ELTs are supposed to come on automatically, and they generally do if they are attached to fixed-wing aircraft, assuming the batteries are kept up to scratch and they're checked regularly, but with helicopters, there are fewer guarantees that this will happen. For a start, there's a lot more vibration, and there are fewer places to attach them, as they should be fitted as far aft as possible, aligned fore-and-aft so that the shock forces activate the G switch properly. Where it's fitted in the cabin, it's often switched off so that it doesn't get kicked or bashed and set off accidentally, which is why it's a good idea to include switching the thing on as part of your emergency checklist on the way down. Not all military helicopters monitor 121.5, as it's primarily a civilian emergency channel, so get one with 243 Mhz as well, which is where they mainly hang out.

Make sure the survival kit can be easily opened one-handed with cold fingers! Talking of which, this item should also be inspected regularly, as you don't want any nasty surprises when you come to use it, and find that someone's pinched the chocolate, or the matches. As space is limited, food should be of a lesser priority than fire-making and signalling devices, and drinking water, and anything specially required for the area you are in. Try to carry it in your pockets, or in a place you can get it in a crash, because Murphy's Law will dictate that the luggage compartment is underneath the hull when the aircraft stops bouncing.

9

Dangerous Goods
And Weapons

Dangerous goods include anything that poses a risk to life, property or the environment, such as aerosols, solvents, paints, chainsaws, matches, stoves, car batteries, gas tanks and even perfume under the right circumstances – in other words, mostly stuff that anyone may have at home. *Single packaging* includes things like oil drums or propane cylinders. *Combination packaging* covers batteries or bottles, etc. in boxes. For transport purposes, there are nine classes, described below, which should have a diamond-shaped label on their packaging to identify them.

In the UK, the legislation concerning this is in the Air Navigation (Dangerous Goods) Regulations 1985, made pursuant to the ANO, where it says that dangerous goods must not be carried unless a Permission has been granted by the CAA (and all States concerned). In Canada, try the Transportation of Dangerous Goods Act, but you will find that most countries base their legislation on the ICAO Technical Instructions for the Safe Transport of Dangerous Goods by Air, or at least allow them to be used as a working document (this is an A4-sized book, with a pretty, coloured cover and lots of adverts in). However, they were written for major air carriers, and can therefore be very restrictive for small operations, particularly when spraying or on fire suppression, so some exemptions are allowed in certain areas, for which you should check your national legislation. Most of them are based on common sense, in that your aircraft may be too small to separate goods that require it, or you may not even have a cargo hold.

You don't need approval if the stuff is needed for the job in hand, or extras for the health of passengers and crew, like fire extinguishers, first-aid kits, insecticides, air fresheners, life-saving appliances and portable oxygen, or anything to do with catering or cabin service. Neither do you need it for veterinary aids or humane killers for animals.

Common sense applies with exempt goods, in that the containers must be properly constructed, staff must be trained, and the items stowed properly. If spraying, the aircraft must be properly ventilated, and you can even carry medical goods after patients have been offloaded, if it's impractical to offload them as well.

Some dangerous goods (for personal use only) can also be carried without an approval, which include:

❏ Receptacles with less than five litres of less than 70% alcohol

❏ Not more than 0.5 litre or 0.5 kg per item of aerosols, hair sprays, etc. (i.e. medicinal or toilet articles). The total is two litres or 2 kg

❏ Safety matches or lighters, for your own use when personally carried. 'Strike anywhere' matches, lighters with unabsorbed liquid fuel (other than liquefied gas), lighter fuel and lighter refills are not permitted

❏ Hydrocarbon-gas-powered hair curlers, if the safety cover is securely fitted over the heating element. No gas refills

❏ Small CO_2 cylinders for mechanical limbs, etc., and spares

❏ Pacemakers or other devices implanted for medical purposes

❏ Small mercury thermometers, but cased

❏ Dry ice, for perishable items, not above 2 kg

❏ Small oxygen or air cylinders for medical use

❏ Small CO_2 cylinders in self-inflating life-jackets, and spares

❏ Wheelchairs or other battery-powered mobility aids with non-spillable batteries, as checked baggage. When the equipment can always be upright, the battery must be securely attached and disconnected, with the terminals insulated against short circuits. Otherwise, it must be removed and carried upright in strong, rigid, leak-proof packaging. The package itself must have on it 'Battery wet, with wheelchair' or 'Battery wet, with mobility aid', bear a 'Corrosives' label and be marked for correct orientation

❏ Not more than 5 kg of cartridges for sporting weapons, providing they are in Division 1.4S (see below), are for that person's own use, are securely boxed and in checked baggage. Cartridges with explosive or incendiary projectiles are not permitted. Division 1.4S is assigned to an explosive, in this case cartridges packed or designed so that dangerous effects are confined within the package, unless it has been degraded by fire, and which do not hinder fire fighting. Mercurial barometers in the cabin baggage of representatives of government weather bureaux or similar official agencies must be packed in strong packaging with a sealed inner liner, or bag of strong leak-proof and puncture-resistant material impervious to mercury, closed to prevent its escape whichever way up it is

Heat-producing articles, like underwater torches or soldering equipment, in cabin baggage must be disabled. Chemically based oxygen generators are not allowed on passenger aircraft.

Bear Scare canisters should not be carried in the cabin, as they consist of pepper spray that will cause extreme discomfort if they go off. They should be gathered together by the leading hand of the group to be carried, inspected to make sure the pressure release screw is secure and placed in a bag which will go in the cargo hold. Batteries should be carried in a container, or at least have their terminals secure against shorting, either against themselves or the airframe. Fuel containers must not be leaking.

Explosives should not be carried together, except in a long line which must be at least 30 m in length with a static drain line attached which will touch the ground before the load. Their packaging must be separate. The hook must be of the carousel type with separate release mechanisms. When carrying detonators, radios should be switched off. The machine should be shut down when loading and unloading explosives.

Packages with dangerous goods in them must have diamond-shaped labels that indicate their hazard by class or division. These are:

Class 1   Explosives
            Division 1.4   Usually permitted
                             Black on Orange
            Division 1.5   Usually not permitted
                             Black on Orange
            Division 1.6   Usually not permitted
                             Black on Orange
Class 2   Gases
            Division 2.1   Flammable (e.g. Propane)
                             White on Red
            Division 2.2   Non-flammable, non-toxic
                             White on Green
            Division 2.3   Toxic (e.g. Chlorine)
                             Black on White
Class 3   Flammable liquids – White on Red
Class 4   Division 4.1   Flammable solids (matches)
                             Black on Red/White stripes
            Division 4.2   Spontaneously combustible
                             Black on White, Red lower
            Division 4.3   Water reactive
                             White on Blue
Class 5   Division 5.1   Oxidising substances (bleach)
                             Black on Yellow

	Division 5.2	Organic peroxides
		Black on Yellow
Class 6	Division 6.1	Toxic substances (poisons)
		Black on White
	Division 6.2	Infectious substances
		Black on White

Class 7   Radioactive materials — Black on White, or Black on Yellow
with White lower half

Class 8   Corrosives – Black on White

Class 9   Miscellaneous – Black on White

Depending on the danger, goods can be further classified into Packing Groups:

Group	Danger
I	Great
II	Medium
III	Minor

There is an alphabetical list of dangerous goods (the IATA book, section 4.2), where goods have their class and packing group determined for you, with maximum quantities, type of label, etc. Packing instructions are in Section 5. Be aware that you might need specific containers for certain items. Where more than one hazard is involved, a label must be used for each one.

Guidance for Acceptance, Handling and Stowage

In practice a ground handling agent may sort it all out for you, and it's the shipper's responsibility to ensure that all is correct. Some companies have a checklist of dangerous goods that are commonly carried. Before any goods are accepted, though, an acceptance check ensures that packages, overpacks and containers are not damaged or leaking, are correctly marked and labelled, and documents are correct, according to the technical instructions. Unless you loaded it yourself, you must be informed of any dangerous goods on your flight with a form that includes:

❑   the Air Waybill number
❑   the proper shipping name and UN number (when assigned, such as Acetone UN1090)

- [ ] the class or division, any identified subsidiary risks and, for explosives, the compatibility group
- [ ] the packing group (when assigned)
- [ ] number of packages, net quantity or gross mass per package
- [ ] loading location
- [ ] confirmation of no evidence of damaged or leaking packages

You should keep one copy with the shipment, and another must be retained by the company for anything up to two years. The consignee should get a copy, too. Packages must carry the appropriate labels, that is, the hazard label (diamond-shaped) and the labels, including 'This Way Up' if combination packaging has been used for liquids.

Dangerous goods must not be carried in the cabin, except as provided for in the technical instructions, including those suitable only for cargo aircraft. In this context 'passenger' excludes a crew member, an operator's employee (see below), an authorised representative of an authority and anyone with duties in respect of a particular shipment of dangerous goods or other cargo on board.

Neither must dangerous goods, especially toxics, be loaded, stowed or secured anywhere near foodstuffs, people or live animals (including the crew). Those that react with each other should be separated as required by the technical instructions. This includes segregating incompatible packages, securing them the right way up and ensuring they are accessible in flight in a cargo aircraft.

Explosives and detonators must be in their original packaging, and separate from each other. Damaged goods must not be carried at all.

Responding to Emergencies

You must inform the appropriate Air Traffic Services Unit of any dangerous goods on board, especially the proper shipping name, class/division and identified subsidiary risks, the compatibility group for explosives, the quantity and the location on board.

More information is in the *Emergency Response Guidance for Aircraft Incidents Involving Dangerous Goods*, which is published by ICAO.

Duties of all Personnel Involved

Everyone must ensure that:

- [ ] dangerous goods are correctly identified, with approvals
- [ ] inspection, acceptance and loading procedures are carried out as

required by the technical instructions, especially with regard to passengers
❏ action is taken if packages of dangerous goods are found damaged or leaking during processing for transport
❏ if there is an aircraft incident or accident, information is passed to the State where the incident or accident occurred, as required by the technical instructions
❏ if there is a dangerous goods incident or accident, a report is made to the appropriate authority

Carriage of Employees of the Operator

When carrying dangerous goods which can only be carried on a cargo aircraft, company employees can also be carried in an official capacity, that is, having duties concerned with the preparation or undertaking of a flight or on the ground once the aircraft has landed.

Weapons, Munitions of War and Sporting Weapons

Weapons of war and munitions of war need an approval from all States concerned before a flight. They must normally be inaccessible to passengers and unloaded, but you can get approval otherwise, for policemen, etc., or if you can prove it is impractical.

Sporting weapons and ammunition may be carried without an approval, if they are inaccessible to passengers and unloaded.

If you ever need it, permission to carry munitions of war is provided through the usual channels, which basically commence with an application to your flight ops inspector at least ten days before the permission is required, who will then contact the Home Office, after which you'll be visited by a gentleman in a trilby hat. If the journey also involves going abroad, the Foreign Office will also become interested, making diplomatic moves, etc. on your behalf. Actually, the whole process has the potential for being rather messy and is best left alone anyway.

Carriage of Livestock

You can carry guide dogs or police dogs on special operations only if they're restrained with a leash, but be very careful with wet ones; not only will the extra moisture mist up the windscreen, but the first thing they will want to do is shake themselves dry once inside the cabin, and soak everyone in sight!

Otherwise, carriage of animals is forbidden unless they're in a suitable carrying case (try that with a horse!) and are accompanied by a responsible person, preferably their owners. The carriage of livestock is covered by the Transit of Animals (General) Order 1973, but IATA also have Live Animals Regulations which should tell you all you need to know about labelling, hygiene, feeding, etc.

You may also need to carry animal first aid and emergency kits, with drugs and humane killers being kept under lock and key by you, the commander. Any attendants must also have been trained in their use.

Horses are somewhat of a special case, perhaps needing a groom to stand by them on take-off and landing, a special exemption, together with a large aircraft and lots of sugar cubes. They like apples, too.

Don't forget there are stringent regulations regarding the carriage of animals across international boundaries.

10

Security

You must be aware of the National Security Programme, for which you will either get trained in-house or packed off to an airline for a course. Otherwise general advice and guidance can be obtained from:

Transport Security Inspectorate
Hampton House
Albert Embankment
London SE1 7TJ

0207 228 5214

The company security officer has overall responsibility for security matters, reporting directly to the ops manager.

The senior operations officer on duty should keep people informed of all security related matters.

Training

Training will help you prevent acts of unlawful interference (e.g. sabotage or hijack) or to minimise their consequences (see below).

Search Procedures

Expect to use a checklist when searching for concealed weapons, explosives or other dangerous items.

Flight Crew Security

Lockable flight deck doors should be closed and locked.

Carriage of Authorised Persons

In addition to those listed in the ANO, an Authorised Person (as far as the company is concerned) is normally a fare-paying passenger on a properly arranged trip or a non-fare-paying passenger flying with the permission of management or Operations – however, when going foreign, nobody is authorised until they have passed through Customs (see below).

Under the ANO, you can refuse to carry anyone who seems unfit for any reason (see also Refusal of Embarkation in Chapter 8).

All flight ops inspectors are Authorised Persons and will occasionally wish to fly in company aircraft to check on operational procedures, unless you think the safety of the flight will be compromised. Arrangements will normally be made in advance, but the right is reserved for them to turn up without prior notice. Inspectors carry authority/identity cards which will be produced on request.

Carriage of Unauthorised Persons

No person is authorised on a foreign trip without first passing through Customs, depending on local arrangements. For flights within Europe, for example, UK Customs just need notification so that they can turn out if they want to (say, four hours), assuming everyone is an EEC passport holder. Aside from people mentioned below, there are certain types of passenger who are excluded from flying anyway, including those under the influence of drugs or alcohol, infected with a contagious disease, of unsound mind and a danger to the aircraft in general. They should only be carried with special safeguards and prior arrangements.

Unlawful Interference

Terrorists apparently belong to three categories. The first is ideologically motivated, believing that the higher cause represented is superior to anything else and is morally correct, even if it does mean killing. The only fear he will have is of failure and he is likely to belong to a well-organised group, with others somewhere in the pipeline. A loner, on the other hand, may either be craving attention or striking back at the organisation that owns the aircraft; in other words, the motivation will be more personal. Such a person will be unpredictable as well as dangerous, but will also have no specific plan. Perhaps just pandering to his ego will help you.

Lastly, there's the psychopath who is actually sick and doesn't understand what's going on anyway (no, not part of the management!). In addition to the previous characteristics, he will also be very volatile.

Of course, if your luck's anything like mine, you will get a combination of all three. However, the point is that each one must be treated individually – you can't cater for them all.

Having said that, you must stay calm – you'll be no good to anybody otherwise; resistance will almost certainly cause trouble. If you can, make yourself as inconspicuous as possible. It may be difficult to grasp, but you must realise that (temporarily at least) you are no longer in control. Pilots by nature tend to have larger than average egos, but, if there is a clash, you would be wise to subdue yours and wait for your turn later. If possible, tell ATC every small detail which could be helpful to someone storming the plane later, should it become necessary. You must also tell the truth and not try any funny stories. Terrorists have *no* sense of humour. If it comes to that, neither do security guards.

If you have a weapon, it's time, like the equivalent of 'working to rule' and abandoning the short cuts that normally make the wheels of aviation run smoothly (!?). Any excuse will do: you need more maps, fuel, staff, servicing, oxygen or whatever.

The idea is to keep the aircraft on the ground, as once you're flying rescue becomes more unlikely. Make them do a bit of work – it will help as a distraction. Also, don't make eye contact – nervous people become more so if you do. Don't resist; and don't volunteer, either. Try to remain invisible.

Company policy is normally that pilots should not attempt to frustrate the hijackers' plans, particularly if there is any risk to passengers. You should try to appease the persons involved and carry out any reasonable orders or demands, simply doing your best to ensure the safety of your passengers. And you, of course.

Reporting

You must report unlawful interference to the local authority, company security officer and:

> Director and Co-ordinator of Transport Security
> Room 58/14
> 2 Marsham Street
> London SW1P 3EB

Bomb Threats

Essentially, don't take off if you receive one, and, if you are flying already, land as soon as you can, then evacuate the aircraft in a remote, yet accessible place.

Security of Information

The nature of General Aviation frequently involves you being party to confidential information which shouldn't be discussed or relayed to third parties. When passengers freely discuss business, it's tactful to make use of the intercom cutoff switch. Documents, maps or written instructions should also be regarded as confidential.

11

Accidents/Occurrences

Accident

An accident occurs when anyone is killed or injured, or the aircraft (or other property) sustains damage or structural failure, or is missing, between the time *any person* boards it with the intention of flight, and *all persons* have disembarked. Stowaways and deaths not associated with the aircraft are not included (not in Canada), and neither are underslung loads (on a helicopter) that do not affect third parties. The definition may also include exposure to jet blast or rotor downwash.

'Damage' does not include anything limited to the engine, its cowling or accessories, or propellers, wing tips, antennae, tyres, brakes, fairings, small dents or punctured holes in the aircraft skin. Doesn't leave much, does it? *Significant damage* in this context means anything that may involve an insurance claim.

Serious Injury

A fatal injury is one that involves death within 30 days. A serious injury involves:

- ❑ more than forty-eight hours in hospital within seven days
- ❑ more than simple fractures of fingers, toes and nose.
- ❑ lacerations causing nerve or muscle damage or severe haemorrhage.
- ❑ injury to any internal organ
- ❑ second- or third-degree burns or any over 5 per cent of the body
- ❑ exposure to infectious substances or radiation

Pilot Post-Accident Procedures

When a notifiable accident occurs, the pilot or senior survivor, company or aerodrome authority (in that order, if practical) should take as much as possible of the following action after evacuating passengers to either a sheltered location upwind of the aircraft, or into the life raft:

❏   Prevent tampering with the wreckage by ANYBODY except to save life, avoid danger to other persons or prevent damage by fire, for which turn the fuel and battery OFF – disconnect the battery if there is no risk of a spark, but the Accident Investigation people won't like you to touch too much, so only remove emergency equipment, such as first-aid kits or survival packs, recording their positions. In the Arctic, however, those parts of the wreckage that can be lifted should be moved to the highest point in the area so that you can be seen

❏   Account for all persons on board. Attend the injured and cover (decently) any bodies

❏   Activate the distress beacon and maybe use aircraft radio equipment. Prepare pyrotechnics, select and prepare a helicopter landing site or lay out search and rescue signals

❏   If people or communications facilities are close, consider sending for assistance

❏   If rescue is likely to be delayed because of distance or failing daylight, prepare suitable shelters, distribute necessary rations of food and water. If necessary, find fresh water

❏   Inform the company (ops manager, chief pilot) by the quickest means of:
   ❏   Aircraft and registration number
   ❏   Time and position of accident
   ❏   Details of survivors
   ❏   Nature of occurrence/other details

❏   Notify Police, Fire, Ambulance, ATC, Gas/Electricity

❏   Note weather details

❏   Make sketches and take photographs. Preserve and protect documents and any flight data recorders

❏   Refer all media enquiries to the company

Aircraft Accident Reporting

All phone calls and actions taken should be recorded by the person receiving the initial notification – continuous watch should be kept for at least 48 hours or the duration of the process, whichever is longer. Callers should be identified, to ensure it is not a false alarm and to ensure it is indeed a company aircraft. No information should be released without company authority, mainly for liability problems.

You should complete the company Accident Report form, in addition to complying with the laws and regulations of the country of registration and the country in which the accident or incident occurred. If there is any doubt, the occurrence should be reported as an Accident; it can be re-classified later.

The company should form an Accident Board, consisting of people with varying qualifications as deemed necessary. This won't be done on the spot there should be a permanent list somewhere.

Accident Reporting Procedures

Check the Civil Aviation (Investigation of Accidents) Regulations 1989 and the Air Navigation (Investigation of Air Accidents involving Civil and Military Aircraft or Installations) Regulations 1986.

Complete and despatch the company Accident Report form as soon as possible but in any case within seventy-two hours. Where items cannot be completed, they should be marked as such and the missing bits forwarded later, rather than delaying the report. A second copy should be sent to the managing pilot. The message should be as follows:

	Reference
	ACCIDENT
AA	Date
BB	Aircraft registration
CC	Pilot's name
DD	Other crew members
EE	Number of passengers
FF	Location of accident
GG	Time of accident (local)
HH	Brief description of pilot's injuries
II	Brief description of crew/passenger injuries
JJ	Brief description of accident
KK	Brief description of extent of damage
LL	Post-accident procedures carried out
MM	Action taken on site to notify authorities
NN	Immediate action requested by company

Where communications are difficult or liable to delays, and if there are no fatalities or serious injuries, the message may be held back for up to six hours if more information is likely to become available.

Flying After an Accident

Crew members should remain on site, unless medical treatment or examination is required, and may not be scheduled for flying duties until authorised by the chief pilot in consultation with the medical examiner. No comments should be made until either they feel fit to do so, or a night's rest has passed since the accident, whichever is sooner.

Incident

Definition

Any happening other than an accident which hazards or, if not corrected, would hazard any aircraft, its occupants or anyone else, not resulting in substantial damage to the aircraft or third parties, crew or passengers. In Canada, this refers to aeroplanes over 5,700 kg MAUW and helicopters over 2,250 kg.

Examples

Precautionary or forced landings, due to engine failure, tail rotor control failure, an external part of the aircraft becoming detached in flight, instances of contaminated fuel, a forced, unscheduled, change of flight plan caused by the failure of aircraft instruments, navigation aids or other technical failure, obstructions on rig landing platforms or other landing sites, loss of an external load, with no third party claim, bird strikes, Airprox, in-flight icing, crew incapacitation.

Serious Incidents

These are nearly accidents, or have serious potential technical or operational implications, or may result in formal disciplinary action against aircrew or engineers. The 'Serious' classification is normally made by the senior person on the operation as soon as possible after the event and before the crew or aircraft fly again, mainly to preserve their recollection of the incident or to ensure their fitness for duty rather than for disciplinary reasons. Away from base, you should load a replacement CVR or CVDR and return the others to base. Both should be disabled after shutdown to prevent data being overwritten when power is re-applied.

Incident Reporting Procedures

A serious incident must be notified to the Chief Inspector of Air Accidents, and is not a reportable occurrence under the ANO. The pilot involved should complete the Incident Report form within three days.

The chief pilot and chief engineer should add the results of their own investigation, with comments and recommendations stating any immediate preventative action which may have been taken, not forgetting Page 7 of the Accident Report, Details Required for Insurance Purposes. The completed Incident Report should be despatched to Ops (Flight Safety) within five days.

Supporting Information

These documents and information should accompany Accident or Incident Reports:

- ❏ Photographs of the aircraft and area
- ❏ Position of cockpit controls and switches
- ❏ Sketch map of the area
- ❏ Passenger/eye witness report
- ❏ Post-accident medical reports for crew and passengers
- ❏ Copy of the standard or multiple sector loadsheet
- ❏ Any relevant extracts from local legislation and/or base instructions
- ❏ Weather report
- ❏ Passenger seat plan in the aircraft
- ❏ Extract from radio log
- ❏ Engine power checking data for the thirty days preceding the accident or incident
- ❏ Post-accident procedures carried out

Accident and Incident Report Distribution

All should be addressed to the Operations Department (Flight Safety) with a copy held at the unit and supplied to the area manager or managing pilot. The report must be kept intact and not separately posted to the respective department heads. Likewise, supporting information should be attached and sent under the same cover, if possible. A receipt will be returned to the unit by the Flight Safety Department, giving a reference number to the accident or incident, which should be used in any further correspondence.

The reports will be subject to immediate internal distribution and distributed to all on a monthly basis. Monthly summaries should be made available to all pilots and engineers, but not copied or shown to non-company personnel, and should be treated as confidential.

An accident file can only be closed by the operations director.

Mandatory Occurrence Reporting Scheme

The CAA Mandatory Occurrence Reporting Scheme (MORS) relates to all British-registered public transport aircraft heavier than 2,300 kg, but reports should be submitted for *all* aircraft. The overall objective is to improve flight safety and not to attribute blame. Occurrences should be reported to the flight safety officer, who will forward the MOR to:

> The Research and Analysis Department
> Civil Aviation Authority
> Aviation House
> Gatwick Airport South
> West Sussex RH6 0YR
>
> 01293 573744

Objectives of the Scheme

- ❑ To ensure that the CAA is advised of hazardous or potentially hazardous incidents and defects, referred to as 'occurrences'
- ❑ To ensure that knowledge of occurrences is disseminated so that other persons and organisations may learn from them
- ❑ To enable an assessment to be made by those concerned, of the safety implications of each occurrence, both in itself and in relation to previous similar occurrences, so they may take or initiate any necessary action

Definition of a Reportable Occurrence

A reportable occurrence is:

- ❑ Any incident (not a notifiable Accident under Section 5 of the Civil Aviation (Investigation of Accidents) Regulations 1989)
- ❑ Any defect in or malfunctioning of any part of the aircraft or its equipment, being an incident, malfunctioning or defect endangering, or which if not corrected would have endangered, the aircraft, its occupants, or any other person
- ❑ Failure or inadequacy of facilities on the ground, used, or intended to be used for, or in connection with, the operation of the aircraft
- ❑ Any incident arising from the loading or the carriage of passengers, cargo or fuel

Informing Base of Occurrences

The first point of contact should be the duty ops officer. Generally, unless the aircraft is up to public transport standards it should not be ferried back to base until the problem has been fully researched, in which case it follows that a return to base without passengers will only be undertaken when specifically authorised with the concurrence of the commander, who will always have the final say.

Because of possible misunderstandings due to poor communications, crews stranded away from base should arrange to discuss their problem by a radio/telephone link call if possible, having alerted the relevant base personnel to stand by through HF radio.

In-flight unserviceabilities which in your opinion can be rectified at base must still be reported on VHF or HF so that the engineering department can get ready for when the aircraft lands. Crews must inform base of birdstrikes, minor illnesses, etc., as well as technical defects before continuing, or as soon as possible after take-off.

Airprox, Birdstrike and Lightning Strike Reports

Because of the specialist and detailed nature of the information required, Airprox, birdstrike and lightning strike reports should be made on the specialised report forms CA 1094 and CA 1282, or the Lightning Strike Report form, each of which should contain the address to which they should be sent. For birdstrikes, damage photographs should be submitted, if possible, with a duplicate copy sent to Ops (Flight Safety) attached to a Company Incident Report. All these come under the MORS.

Certain information following an Airprox should immediately be reported by radio to the ATS unit being used at the time, or immediately after landing by telephone to any UK ATCC. A telephone report to the LATCC, West Drayton will start tracing action. Tel: 01895 445566.

The initial report should be confirmed within seven days on Form CA 1094. The CAA is obliged to issue a press statement following any Airprox involving a commercial air transport aircraft, which is initiated by the first report to ATS. If you decide not to proceed, the ATS unit to which the initial call was made must be informed as soon as possible.

Birdstrikes

Prevention is better than cure, and you may like to avoid birds as much as possible, although some stroppy pheasants have been known to attack aircraft lining up on the runway. Notification of permanent or seasonal concentrations of birds are sometimes issued in NOTAMs.

Otherwise, keep away from bird sanctuaries or other areas where they may be expected, such as along shorelines or rivers in autumn or spring – migrating birds use line features for navigation as well, but they don't necessarily keep 300 m to the right. Gulls seem to be struck the most often, and they hang around the seaside or rubbish tips.

Noticeably fewer birdstrikes occur at height, so try to fly as high as possible, certainly above 1,500 ft; also, the lower you go, the slower you should be. Avoid high-speed descent and approach – half the speed means a quarter of the impact energy. A short delay on the approach could mean the clearance of a group of birds, as they do move in waves.

Groups of birds will usually break away downwards from anything hazardous, so try to fly upwards if possible. You could also use landing lights to make yourself more visible. Avoid freshly ploughed or harvested fields, and beware of updraughts in mountainous areas, where the birds will be trying to get some free lift.

At 100 kt, the impact from a 1 lb bird can exceed 1,200 p.s.i. (the force is actually determined by the square of your speed multiplied by the mass of the bird). The problem is that, below a certain weight of aircraft, the windshield will only be designed to keep out rain and insects. However, a hot windshield is more pliable and less susceptible to shattering if it gets hit – some aircraft require these to be on for take-off and landing, but if there is nothing in the flight manual about the optimum warm-up time, use fifteen minutes. Overheating is as bad as underheating, so be wary if your aircraft has been left in the sun a long time.

If a birdstrike does occur, stop and inspect the damage immediately. If you can't, make sure you have controllability before trying to land again – fly the aircraft first.

In the report, you will be asked what the species is (or was), and if unsure, you're invited to parcel up the remains and send them to the Aviation Bird Unit, whose telephone number is (01483) 232581, but what the Post Office think of that idea, I don't know (talking of which, I'm told that at one time you used to be able to send game birds with just a label, provided they weren't leaking).

Wake Turbulence

Reports should be sent to the Wake Vortex Incident Scientific Group at the Air Traffic Control Evaluation Unit at Bournemouth International Airport. Tel: 01202 472340 Fax: 01202 472236.

Confidential Human Factors Incident Reports (CHIRPS)

Reports of incidents or occurrences involving human factors and/or errors which should remain confidential should be sent to the Defence Research Agency (DRA) Centre for Human Studies at Farnborough. Tel: 01252 392654 or 394375.

Investigation/Rectification away from Base

You may carry out an investigation or minor rectification under base engineers, such as examination and cleaning of a magnetic plug following a chip warning. In such cases the ANO requires details to be given to the CAA within ten days, namely:

- ❑ Date and time of occurrence
- ❑ Type and registration of aircraft
- ❑ Name of aircraft commander
- ❑ Location at which inspection/rectification was carried out
- ❑ Brief details of defect and action carried out
- ❑ Brief details of engineering action following flight to base

Notification of Dangerous Goods Accidents or Occurrences

Information must be sent to the State authorities where the accident occurred as soon as possible, or when requested for an incident.

Report

Within seventy-two hours, covering:

- ❑ The date, location, flight number and date
- ❑ The air waybill number, pouch, baggage tag, ticket, etc.
- ❑ A description of the goods, including the proper shipping name and UN number (when applicable), class/division and any subsidiary risk
- ❑ The type of packaging, its specification marking and quantity
- ❑ The name and address of the shipper, passenger, etc.
- ❑ The suspected cause of the accident or incident

❏   The action taken, if any
❏   Any other reporting action taken
❏   Any other relevant details and
❏   The details of the person making the report

Copies of the relevant documents and photographs must be attached.

In-flight Emergency

If the situation permits, you must inform the appropriate ATS unit of any dangerous goods on board, using the information above.

Confidentiality

You must not discuss any accident or occurrence with anyone outside the company, other than authorised investigators.

Aircraft Overdue Action

An aircraft is overdue thirty minutes after its last known ETA. The last known point of departure and next planned destination should be contacted as well as en route ATC, before escalating the situation to initiate SAR and accident procedures. Naturally, should the aircraft be found, cancel this action.

Assistance to Others in Distress

You should, at your discretion and with due regard for the safety of your own aircraft, render any assistance that is practical and possible for the saving of life in any event demanding such assistance.

The prime function of a non-SAR-equipped aircraft at a scene of distress is to act as a communications relay, assuming properly equipped rescue units are coming. If not, then rendering first aid has priority, provided you can land.

If you are first on the scene:

❏   **A** ssess nature of emergency and survivor details
❏   **B** roadcast position and details:
    ❏   Type of aircraft involved
    ❏   Position
    ❏   Time
    ❏   No. of passengers

- ❏   Their activities (e.g. remaining or abandoning)
- ❏   Your endurance and proposed actions
- ❏   **C** alculate endurance and alternates
- ❏   **D** irect other aircraft and hand over to rescue commander
- ❏   **E** nsure constant visual contact
- ❏   **F** loat life raft to survivors (helicopter)
- ❏   **G** ive survivors a wide berth to avoid downwash (helicopter)
- ❏   **H** over high – fifty feet or so (helicopters)

If you are *not* first on the scene, inform the controlling aircraft of your endurance and what assistance you can give. If you're not required, clear the area. If you're there with the media, keep well out of the way!

12

Special Use of Aircraft

Of necessity, most of this chapter will concern helicopters, because they are used most often for weird operations – you can't do much with aeroplanes except cart passengers and freight about, take photographs and spray crops (or fires). Where both types could be used, though, many techniques will have much in common.

Passenger handling itself is a specialised task. As I've said before, in General Aviation you're very much involved with your passengers, who will usually get quite excited and engage you in conversation about all manner of things. Of course, a frequent business traveller may not get this familiar, but you might still be asked to join them for lunch; not only out of courtesy, but also as cheap entertainment – if you're not a good conversationalist when you start your career, you'll very soon learn! Other little things are good for customer relations, too, such as helping them with their belts, checking they're OK and settled down just before take-off and during the flight, and generally looking after their well-being. All this is pure salesmanship. A lot of repeat business comes from a company's pilots' relationships with passengers, and if you're not naturally gregarious (a good mixer), think twice about charter work as a long-term way of earning a living.

Otherwise, some of the more exotic things you can do with helicopters include bombing avalanches, rapelling (that is, dropping off people to fight forest fires, otherwise known as dope-on-a-rope), wildlife capture, aerial ignition, water sampling, where you hover very low over a body of water and a scientist dips the equivalent of a jamjar into it, or frost control, where a large barrel of oil is lit to provide smoke that will indicate the level of an inversion. You then fly with your rotors just above the smoke to bring the warm air down and prevent frost on crops. So, unlike Chapter 3, this chapter won't be boring!

External Slung Loads

A helicopter can go where a crane is impractical or more expensive, or you might not be able to get a particular load inside the machine (maybe you wouldn't want it there anyway, if it's a dead animal or explosives). There may also be no other way of getting there.

In theory, you can lift anything, provided the payload is available; I've even been asked to quote for lowering 800 feet of unrolled telephone cable down a mine shaft, because the drum it was rolled on wouldn't take the weight. However, more common tasks are logging, placing air conditioning or ventilation equipment on the roofs of tall buildings, pulling cows out of bogs, picking up water to put out forest fires (water bucketing), dropping solution over forests (top dressing) or moving seismic equipment about. In fact, many tasks done with a helicopter are really extensions of load slinging, and, in remote areas, this will be a major part of your bread and butter – really specialised stuff will be found as subheadings below. A typical length is 75–100 feet, or even 200, so don't forget to include the line as part of the payload – it will be heavy. Long-lining (or vertical reference) proficiency to some customers involves putting a small load at the end of a 100 ft line onto a 4 × 8 ft sheet of plywood three times from different approach angles, but there's more about this later.

Logging, officially, is removing felled and bucked logs from areas where all trees have been felled. It is very fast, with lots happening at once, and there will be a smaller helicopter to carry the used chokers every 75 minutes or so (chokers are lanyards with the equivalent of a slip knot which tightens as the load is taken up, making it more secure). It is not an operation based on finesse, as the machines are continually using full power cycles and undergo a lot of twisting, etc.

Selective logging is removing wood from where trees are standing, and is considerably more dangerous, at least to workers on the ground, because the downwash could dislodge all sorts of things. *Cedar salvage* involves moving loads of cut cedar blocks, which should all be of a similar length for best stability. Logs will be taken from high ground first so that there is less risk of anything falling on workers below and you can see what's going on better. They will be delivered to holding points on land or in water.

In the UK, you will find it useful to check out the following:

CAP 426	Helicopter external load operations
ANO Art 35	Public transport aircraft and suspended loads
Rule 47	Marshalling signals
ANO Art 55	Picking up and raising of persons and articles
ANO Art 56	Dropping of articles and animals

In Canada, external loads come in four classes, A, B, C and D. A Class A load does not extend below the landing gear and is usually bolted to the aircraft, such as a stretcher, spray kit or fuel tank. A Class B load can be jettisoned and is not in contact with land, water or any other surface. A Class C load is similar, but remains in contact with the surface (as when towing), and a Class D includes a person or is anything that doesn't come inside the other classifications, for which you need two methods of release and must use a multi-engined helicopter that can hover on one engine in the prevailing conditions, with appropriate engine isolation. However, most loads you come across will be Class B. If you do all this over a built-up area, you will need to submit an Aerial Work Zone Plan to Transport Canada at least five days in advance.

You should only get involved in load slinging if you have the proper experience, and you get that by being trained properly and supervised. Ex-military pilots will have done it as part of their original flying course, but in some companies, 'training' is once around the circuit. If you're 'experienced' with some slinging in the past year you can probably get by with a full briefing from the chief pilot. If you're not current, expect no fewer than two observed sectors if loading permits, or at least some training circuits. There'll be a bit more for long-lining, where you need to hover with your head out of the door so that you can see the load properly, which has obvious problems when it comes to checking your Ts & Ps (Temperatures and Pressures) and losing your baseball hat if it's not nailed on. Some pilots fly from the left-hand seat (not in an AS 350) to help with this.

In this case, you might have people on the ground to help you when you pick the load up (see below), but you will more often than not be dropping it by yourself. The best way to do so, when you can't look out or see much in the mirror, is to pick the landing spot, then extend your view forwards and sideways till you reach something you can see, and use them as markers for a vertical descent.

With external load work, the C of A changes from Public Transport to Aerial Work, so passengers should not be carried. You would be forgiven for thinking that you'd also get away with duty hours, but you're still regarded as being on commercial air transport, even though the helicopter isn't – in fact, you may even need an official exemption from the full equipment scales required.

There may be a little paperwork to do before you start – your customers will probably need to be made aware that cargo insurance is available, if your company provides it, and authorise the flight by signing a damage and injury waiver agreement. A couple of other points: Your C of G will be fairly near its ideal position with a load on, but maybe not when you release it, especially if you're low on fuel to lift it. Also, loads that must be guided into place or even secured while still attached to the helicopter must be given special consideration, especially when you are briefing passengers – they must NOT go anywhere underneath the load or any similar position that would be dangerous if the load gets released.

Don't do any long-lining near high-voltage lines or thunderstorms.

Oh, yes, one more thing – the maximum hook load has nothing to do with payload, but is merely the weight the hook can stand as a structural limit. If you try to lift the max hook load in a 206, there'll be no room for you!

Ground Crews

When you haven't got a mirror, the ideal team on the ground consists of at least three handlers at every point of pick-up or deposit, so, in a simple lift from A to B, you need six, although this could be reduced when you've got decent communications. All procedures given here are based on the assumption that communications are not decent, but things will go so much better if they are – just make sure that any instructions given don't require acknowledgement, as not only will you have your hands full, but it's also easy to hit the load release button when moving your hand to transmit. Actually, that goes both ways; very often both hands are needed by the loaders, so they put their radios in their pockets, and can't hear them, which is why having them in helmets is recommended.

One person would be for marshalling and the remainder for hooking up, etc. – marshalling signals are in the Rules of the Air (47–48). However, in remote areas, you will probably be operating by yourself, including picking up the load, which may mean continual shutting down, etc. Expense is not actually the reason; in the Arctic, for example, you don't leave somebody by himself in case you can't get back, but, in general, you are dropping stuff off where you can't put people anyway. It's not as hazardous as it sounds – you just need to be far enough behind the load to stretch the line properly, with no kinks, and make sure it's straight, so that it's away from the landing gear when you lift into the hover. However, don't attempt anything by yourself without a mirror.

Ground crews should dress appropriately – downwash will cause severe chill factors.

Equipment

There should be as many ropes, strops, nets and hooks as can be made available, as more will always be required than you think. Steel slings are best, although ordinary rope will do, provided it doesn't have a tendency to stretch or bounce up if it breaks (for this reason, don't use nylon lanyards). At the very least, you need one set of slings at each drop-off point, so while the first load is being undone you can be on your way back with one and not waste flying time (when logging, a smaller helicopter is used for this job). All equipment should be able to withstand six times the anticipated load because flight conditions may increase its weight artificially. You can work out a rule of thumb SWL (Safe Working Load) for wire ropes in tons with this formula:

$$SWL = Rope\ Diameter^2 \times 8$$

This figure may change if you do strange things to the line, like bend it, or use a choker hitch. The sharper the bend, the greater the reduction. Once you've bent a line, don't use it for slinging again.

Ground equipment should include VHF radios and whistles (for communications), weighing scales, accurate to at least 25 lb, and capable of weighing more than the maximum payload. Emergency equipment should be similar to that for pleasure flying sites.

Ground crew should have hard hats (maybe different colours for different groups, but not essential) with chin straps, goggles or safety glasses, protective gloves and a metal probe for discharging static electricity. As mentioned above, radios in the helmets are most useful.

Static Electricity

This comes from a number of sources, the main ones being engine and precipitation charging from friction between the aircraft's surfaces and airborne particles. There is also a risk from thunderstorms and airborne snow particles.

Although the capacitance associated with this is small, voltages as high as tens of kilovolts can throw people to the ground, as well as being dangerous near a potentially explosive cargo or fuel tank, or even short-circuiting the hook electrics. It's for this reason that a *static discharge probe*, which is earthed to the ground, is applied to the hook before any other contact takes place and the procedure kept up as much as possible. If you can't get one, make sure the guys wear thick rubber gloves.

Setting Up

Before doing anything else, you should check the following carefully:

Helicopter Condition

Check your HOGE performance and use the standard lapse rate if you don't know what the temperature is at the drop-off point. Remember your fuel consumption will be higher than normal, due to using high power in the hover and flying at slower speeds. Leaving the heavier loads till last will help with your planning.

The rear doors need to be removed so that used harnesses can be placed inside quickly from either side – very often drop-off points are in places where you can't land but only come to a very low hover. Also, there is a little less weight for the machine to carry. If you're doing vertical reference, you will need your door off as well so that you can stick your head out of the side. However, taking any door off will mean checking weight and balance and performance figures, and your V_{ne} – going too fast may pressurise the cabin and blow the windscreen out (this is particularly serious in the AS 350). You will also have higher fuel consumption and slower flight times.

You need a mirror so that you can see the behaviour of the hook and the load. The hook mechanism must be checked for consistent electrical (and mechanical) operation, as must all standby release methods. All hooks must be enclosed, that is, there must be no opportunity for the load to come out of the mouth of the hook when flying.

Check both manual and electric releases, and don't accept the fact that the solenoid clicks as evidence of it working. If there's no-one else around, put a rope in and pull on it when you operate the mechanism. After you operate the manual release, check that the Bowden cable between the hook and the body of the helicopter doesn't bind and stop the hook from rearming. All witness marks should be aligned on the knurled knob or lever and the hook body, and make sure the hook moves over its full range of travel and that the bungee cord keeps it tight against the bottom of the fuselage, so that you don't land on a vertically extended hook.

Be aware that garbage on the landing site has been known to pull the manual release enough to allow the load to work itself free.

Condition of sling equipment

Because of the direct connection to the aircraft and the potential for damage, it should only be used on helicopter operations, and any worn or frayed items should be discarded (you're generally allowed up to ten randomly distributed frayed wires on a steel sling, or five in one strand). Nylon deteriorates when exposed to petroleum, and wire rope rusts and doesn't like being mistreated, so protect them from moisture and heat, and inspect them regularly. Cables without their internal grease will snap readily. The maximum length for nylon or poly rope should be 6 feet.

Long lines made of Spectron or Kevlar are strong, but light, so will trail after you longer than a steel line – that is why there is a maximum external load speed. These lines also get longer when new, so, if you can't pre-stretch them, allow a good length of extra electrical cable.

There must be an eye in each end of a sling, preferably reinforced with steel, to protect the rope, and the shackle that goes inside the eye must be the right size for the hook, otherwise it may come out by itself, or not come out when it's supposed to (as a guide, the shackle should be the same thickness as the rope – DON'T use a bolt instead; it will bend). Using a swivel will stop the load from spinning and un-ravelling the line.

Loading and unloading areas
Non-involved personnel should be absent, and there should be no loose articles to be blown around by the downwash and cause damage. Approach and departure lanes should be into wind.

Performance planning
Check your Hover performance Out of Ground Effect (HOGE), in case it places a ceiling on your Max All-Up Weight, although most heli-copters have a higher gross weight for external loads. Here are charts of suggested payloads for various types according to pressure altitude:

Typical hook loads at MAUW HOGE
Assuming 1.2 hours' fuel, pilot at 185 lb and slings, etc., at 100 lb.
These guidelines will vary with the APS weight!

2,000 ft

Degs C	–15	–10	–5	0	5	10	15	20	25
SA315	1,748	1,748	1,748	1,748	1,748	1,748	1,748	1,748	1,748
AS350B2	2,097	2,097	2,097	2,097	2,097	2,097	2,097	2,097	2,097
AS350B1	1,846	1,846	1,846	1,846	1,846	1,846	1,844	1,734	1,624
AS350BA	1,652	1,652	1,652	1,652	1,652	1,652	1,652	1,539	1,424
AS350B	1,400	1,400	1,400	1,400	1,400	1,400	1,400	1,400	1,300
500D	1,134	1,119	1,104	1,089	1,074	1,054	1,034	1,004	974
Bell 206B	1,002	987	972	957	942	927	912	897	882

3,000 ft

Degs C	-15	-10	-5	0	5	10	15	20	25
SA315	1,748	1,748	1,748	1,748	1,748	1,748	1,748	1,748	1,748
AS350B2	2,097	2,097	2,097	2,097	2,097	2,097	2,097	1,990	1,885
AS350B1	1,846	1,846	1,846	1,846	1,846	1,746	1,654	1,544	1,434
AS350BA	1,652	1,652	1,652	1,652	1,652	1,589	1,474	1,359	1,244
AS350B	1,400	1,400	1,400	1,400	1,400	1,400	1,375	1,250	1,125
500D	1,099	1,069	1,039	1,009	979	949	919	889	854
Bell 206B	977	962	947	932	917	902	887	872	857

4,000 ft

Degs C	-15	-10	-5	0	5	10	15	20	25
SA315	1,748	1,748	1,748	1,748	1,748	1,748	1,748	1,738	1,728
AS350B2	2,097	2,097	2,097	2,097	2,097	2,000	1,895	1,790	1,685
AS350B1	1,846	1,846	1,846	1,794	1,684	1,574	1,464	1,354	1,244
AS350BA	1,652	1,652	1,652	1,652	1,544	1,424	1,304	1,184	1,064
AS350B	1,400	1,400	1,400	1,400	1,400	1,400	1,250	1,100	950
500D	1,064	1,024	984	944	904	964	824	779	734
Bell 206B	952	937	922	907	892	877	862	832	737

5,000 ft

Degs C	-15	-10	-5	0	5	10	15	20	25
SA315	1,748	1,748	1,748	1,748	1,728	1,708	1,688	1,668	1,648
AS350B2	2,097	2,097	2,097	2,080	1,945	1,830	1,715	1,600	1,485
AS350B1	1,846	1,824	1,714	1,604	1,494	1,384	1,274	1,164	1,054
AS350BA	1,652	1,652	1,634	1,509	1,384	1,259	1,134	1,009	884
AS350B	1,400	1,400	1,400	1,400	1,275	1,150	1,025	900	775
500D	1,024	974	924	874	824	774	724	669	614
Bell 206B	927	912	897	882	857	827	757	687	617

6,000 ft

Degs C	−15	−10	−5	0	5	10	15	20	25
SA315	1,748	1,748	1,748	1,718	1,688	1,658	1,628	1,598	1,568
AS350B2	2,097	2,085	1,975	1,860	1,745	1,530	1,515	1,400	1,285
AS350B1	1,744	1,634	1,524	1,414	1,304	1,194	1,084	974	864
AS350BA	1,652	1,652	1,484	1,354	1,224	1,094	954	834	704
AS350B	1,400	1,400	1,400	1,275	1,140	1,005	870	735	600
500D	984	924	864	804	744	684	624	569	494
Bell 206B	902	882	862	842	822	742	662	582	497

Preparation of loads

There are four basic types of load – rectangular, cylindrical, heavy compact and nets, and five ways of lifting them, starting with nets and ending up with a four-point sling (through 1-, 2- and 3-point). **Nets** are used for loads consisting of many small pieces. On a 206, one about 10–12 feet square with a 2 in. square mesh is quite suitable. Items should be carefully and evenly stacked in the centre, with the net stretched round the load on the ground before pick-up. Individual light loads, such as jerry cans or containers, ought to be lashed together, since the net may not completely enclose them at the top. If there are many small items, consider a tarpaulin as a liner, which will stop them falling out. Be aware that lifting points already attached to anything may have been designed for cranes, which don't, as a rule, fly sideways or get caught in updraughts, etc.

The weight of each load should be known, with sand and stuff being kept dry and, if possible, weighed immediately before loading, as a good soaking will increase the weight dramatically and give you a surprise when you lift it. What happens most often, however, is that the guys just bundle stuff into a net, and as long as you don't overtorque the machine you're OK.

Although convenient, a **single-point hook-up** is not the best plan, and should only be used on loads designed for it, with a swivel, to stop the line unravelling, although it works well with a net. You also need to be particularly careful about the load's C of G, or it may tip and start rocking. For a single pole or log, wrap the rope or chain twice around the end of it and carry it vertically. (Fig 1)

A **2-point sling** with a 60 degree angle to the hook or tag line is a common method for most loads, especially long ones, such as drill collars, pipe stems, etc. The angle at the hook should, in any case, always be less than 90 degrees. (Fig 2)

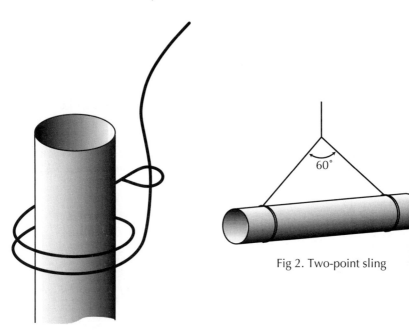

Fig 2. Two-point sling

Fig 1. Single pole or log

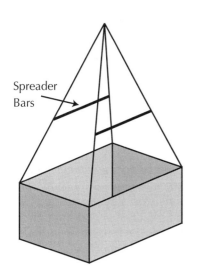

Spreader
Bars

Fig 3.
Four-point sling

Double-wrap the cables, and maybe slip some wood between them and the load to stop them slipping.

Three-point hook-ups are not common, and usually reserved for loads designed for the purpose. **Four-point slings**, on the other hand, are quite common and used for box-like loads, attached to each corner – where the sling may catch or damage the load, use spreader bars to keep the rope away, as well as for stability. Beware of loads with a high C of G, as they may tip over. (Fig 3)

Tag lines (short lines underneath a load) are for loaders to grab on the setdown. They should have a safety latch and weigh at least 5 kg to stop them waving about.

Personnel briefing

All concerned should be aware of:

- ❏ The hook-up
- ❏ The setdown
- ❏ Hand signals
- ❏ Proper use of radios (i.e. don't hog the airwaves)
- ❏ Direction to move in case of engine failure
- ❏ Don't stand under the load
- ❏ Number of trips between refuelling stops
- ❏ Manner of retrieving slings and nets
- ❏ Use of protective equipment
- ❏ Accident procedure

Hooking Up

The marshaller should be positioned at least 25 m from the load with his back to the wind so that you can see him from your high position. If he needs to change places, he should cease marshalling first, so that he doesn't move backwards into unseen obstructions. Using standard marshalling signals, you will be positioned over the load, where the loaders apply the static discharge probe to the hook and place the eye of the net or sling inside it.

The loaders then give an affirmative signal to the marshaller, who subsequently gives you the 'move upwards' signal until all the slack has been taken up. You will increase hover height slowly, until the strain is taken, with the loaders guiding the strops as necessary, taking care to be free to move away quickly should the need arise. At all times in the event of engine failure, the ground staff must move in the opposite direction that the helicopter would go, e.g. JetRanger to the right, staff to the left, or the opposite for a Squirrel (it depends which way the blades rotate). They should not turn their back on the load, or get directly underneath it. Neither should they wrap lines directly around their wrists or bodies. When finished, they should clear the area as soon as possible.

As you take up the weight and the rope stretches, the difference in performance will immediately become obvious – it will feel as if you're attached to a large rubber band. Once you're hovering, and the marshaller is sure that the load is clear of the ground (and you are sure you can lift safely, flashing the landing lamp once to indicate this), the marshaller should check behind you for other aircraft and give the affirmative signal, as you will find it difficult to do a half-turn to check for yourself. Keep a close eye on your Ts and Ps at this point.

The machine will feel quite sluggish, as if it's tied to the ground. Move forward slowly, giving due regard to the load's inertia, not alternately slowing down and speeding up, or you will confuse it. Rather, move forward and keep going to allow the load to follow, which sometimes takes a bit of courage, to see how it flies. Make all control movements smoothly and evenly. Don't allow the load to sink, as if it hits the ground it will trip you. The torque used at this point will give you a good idea of what is needed for landing, so be careful if you are going to a higher altitude.

One technique used in New Zealand, when you are near all-up weight and lifting the load into the hover would be difficult, is to stretch the long-line out behind, attach it to the helicopter and, keeping it taut, build up some speed in a parabola-like manoeuvre before lifting the load (I'm told that this requires some practice). However, if a log lifted this way starts spinning, it will undo the rope, so another way is to get a 300-foot line, get up into the hover as far back as possible with a taut line and take off straight ahead so that you get some translational lift before pulling the load off. This tends to crack the blades, though.

Once in flight, keep away from anything underneath that could be damaged (well, try anyway!). Only with imminent danger to the aircraft should a load be jettisoned, usually from excessive swinging (commercially, dropping loads is definitely regarded as a non-macho thing to do, but it's your backside the helicopter is strapped to). As a point of interest, ten gallons of fuel from 500 feet will go straight to the basement of a three-storey house. If you drop fertiliser in water, expect your company to pay for the clean-up and testing for the next five years.

If you get an engine failure in the mountains with a load attached, consider not jettisoning it. This may sound daft, but it may stop you from falling down a crevice or something – just try to keep the line taut so that you don't get a nasty jerk.

Load behaviour

Every load has its own V_{ne}, unfortunately usually only found by experiment, which is why you should always start off slowly and build up to a point where it starts to give trouble, then back off. Most helicopters will carry loads at quite high speeds, but the load itself might not be able to handle it – a sudden input of drag when something falls off could become quite a problem. Although customers don't like to pay for unnecessary flying, there's no rush. Take it easy.

External loads increase the frontal area of the whole aircraft, which naturally increases drag, so you will need more power overall. A load may be easy to lift, but may present enough drag in flight to cause severe difficulties, particularly where you may reach power limits too quickly to maintain forward flight, and have a situation where the load overtakes you and pulls you along. A long-line needs more anticipation, so you need a high degree of co-ordination and patience. It's not the sort of thing that can be learnt in any other way than by having lots of practice.

There is no sure way to predict how each load will fly, but those with an uneven shape will tend to spin and, if they're slung without reference to their centre of gravity, could tip over. A drogue chute can stabilise it, but use a windsock type rather than a pure parachute, which will oscillate to spill the air being forced into it. Naturally, these must be kept well away from the tail rotor. Logs or cut timber usually fly poorly unless a tail is installed, which can be made out of a bough or piece of plywood, so that it sticks out of the back.

Oscillation or excessive vibration can come from a number of places, usually a combination of the stability characteristics of the load and forward speed. Heavy or dense loads, such as bags of cement or drums of kerosene, will not usually present problems due to their mass, but large-volume loads of low density can oscillate at a certain critical speed, again usually only found by trial and error.

You can dampen oscillation by reducing your airspeed to at least 10 per cent below this critical one, going slower if necessary while increasing power. Turning could provide enough centrifugal force to stop it as well, which is also the usual remedy when the load starts to swing, but this will increase its effective weight, possibly to more than your lifting capabilities (a good reason for not being too tight on payload), so applying centrifugal force in these cases could make things worse.

Load swing is proportional to speed and the length of the sling – the faster you go, the more it occurs because of the load's own lift and drag. As it takes as long to swing through fifteen degrees as it does through forty-five, like any pendulum, if you move the opposite way, as is natural, you just make the load swing faster. Going with the swing, that is, load to the left, helicopter to the left, will stop it quickest. You can do the same with a fore and aft swing, but watch out! Very often, a load can suddenly produce more drag, if something breaks off, for instance, which puts the nose down, which you correct with aft cyclic that simply puts the tail rotor nearer the line. If the load starts forward again, pulling the nose further up, correcting with forward cyclic may set you nicely up for mast bumping. The correct thing to do here is to apply collective, which will also add an upward force. Using a longer line will slow any swing down.

Special precautions must be taken for bulky loads with a tendency to float, such as empty containers. In these cases, leaving doors or panels open reduces drag and can help keep the load facing in one direction.

Scaffolding and planking are prone to swinging violently with only a few knots change in airspeed. Items with an aerofoil shape could even have a tendency to generate their own flying characteristics.

Setting Down

Approach into wind as much as possible, coming into the hover high enough not to drag the load, so you might be slightly steeper than normal. It's best to undershoot rather than overshoot, as it's easier to creep up to a target than go round again if you miss it. If the load hits the ground, stop moving forward. Because of inertia, all manoeuvres should be anticipated well in advance and made smoothly (not suddenly) *with reference to the speed of the load over the ground.* In a confined area, the load will tend to pull you down as the wind effect is lost, so a couple of knots in hand under these circumstances may be desirable, even if it's not what you would normally expect to do. Keep a constant scan going, because you need all the information you can get, especially when it comes to depth perception. If everything goes pear-shaped, it's because your scan has stopped, as it might if you get fixated and suddenly tense up on the controls. Relax and start looking around again, it will soon get better.

Once in the hover, you again come under the guidance of a marshaller, who signals descent until the load touches the ground and the cables become slack (if you haven't got a marshaller, you can judge your height from whether the ground crew are looking up or down). Release the cables after moving to one side so they do not foul the load or hit someone on the head. Don't drop cables from anything more than normal hover height, and especially not under tension, or you'll get somebody in the eye. A manual release is provided if the electrical one doesn't operate, and, once it has done so, you should see a 'load released' signal from the marshaller, whereupon you hover by the side of the load while the replacement sling is placed inside the cabin, *having moved away vertically first.*

You should behave at all times as if the load has not been released. Especially, do not release the load when the line is under tension, because whatever is in the hook will shoot downwards at a fast rate, and the hook itself will be opened violently and may be damaged.

If you can't hover, just keep max power in and let the aircraft settle by itself, without overtorquing – you will only be pulled down as far as it takes for the load to reach the ground, so just try and give it a gentle arrival. If you are delivering the load by yourself, land behind it, as far back as possible so that you don't get the sling under the skid, and to provide a little tension for the hook mechanism to work.

There is a phenomenon called *Collective Bounce* that occurs when a sudden vertical force is placed on the helicopter, making you think the load has reached the ground. Although really relevant to larger machines, it can occur on smaller ones, and arises when blade resonance matches that of a vibrating rope. The collective movements to correct this get out of phase, due to the response lag, and the answer is simply to stop moving the collective or go into autorotation, as the machine will self-destruct about the fifth bounce. A little extra friction will help.

If a load starts spinning in flight, and continues to do so in the hover (or your downwash sets it going), you could gently put it on the ground and pick it up again.

If you have to hold a load while it is being secured to something else, you must take particular care to ensure that ground crews don't get themselves into positions that could be dangerous if you have to release it. It is particularly important to be conservative with the allowable sidewinds.

Vertical Reference (Long-lining)

As we said before, there is some skill attached to this, but it isn't too hard to learn. Many pilots actually prefer it, if only because any problems with the load occur further away from the aircraft, and therefore produce less hassle with the controls, and you're that bit further away from mechanical turbulence, although you are almost always out of ground effect and in the avoid curve, and a prime candidate for vortex ring.

The line itself is made of two strands of wire rope, wound around each other, to help prevent spinning. At the bottom you might find one or more electrical hooks, surrounded by a metal cage, both for protection and to stop the line flapping around when the hook is empty. There will also be an electrical cable so that you can operate the hook, and this will usually be taped directly to it. You need to be particularly careful not to kink the line, which means not driving over it, landing on it, dragging it along the ground, or dropping it from too great a height.

When actually looking out of the door, there is a tendency to pull the cyclic the same way as you are leaning, and back, so this is something you need to practise first, keeping the hook directly over the load and keeping the line is sight, which is more difficult in the AS 350, as compared to the 206. Be as gentle as possible when it's time for the load to leave the ground.

In mountains, keep in mind the principle of ignoring the slope, and be aware that your downwash may well bounce off it and push the load away from where it should be, that is, underneath you.

Aerial Application

Aerial application (of insecticides or fertilisers) means either crop spraying or top dressing, the latter being used in forestry. Top dressing is more akin to load slinging, except that you use engine-driven devices like buckets to spread solutions over forests. Unlike crop spraying, it can be done in strongish wind conditions, but, otherwise, it's characterised by always being in, or very near, the avoid curve and many other situations that you're taught to avoid normally. You can tell with forests that have been sprayed in the early stages of their growth whether the pilots were successful or not – you very often see trees shorter than others, which is where they missed.

Crop spraying, like slinging, is very satisfying when a good rhythm is obtained with an efficient team that keeps you in the air as much as possible. Unlike it, however, you will be operating a heavy machine with unwieldy spray booms attached to it at some speed in fairly confined areas, and the low-level manoeuvres will require a high degree of co-ordination. There's usually very little wind to help you, either, because of the legal restrictions on wind speeds and the possibilities of *spray drift* (see later) – spraying cotton in Australia is actually done at night. It therefore becomes very demanding halfway up a mountain at 3,000 feet with high temperatures and an airspeed of about five knots!

The idea with a helicopter is to fly between 35 and 45 kt at about ten feet along the 'grain' of the crop, at the end of the run pulling up and pivoting around to face the other direction on the end of the boom that is pointing into wind, so that you resume where you left off. Thus, you turn into wind at the end of each run, all the while progressing along the crop towards the wind direction.

To make money out of it, you must apply about 10,000 acres' worth inside about fifty miles over a season (about four months). Set prices are usually charged for an area, which means the quicker the job is done, the quicker another can be started – about the only way to maximise income; as a general rule, expect to spray between 300 and 600 acres per working day. The aircraft should be placed centrally, and its production (in acres per hour) will depend on payload available, endurance, dead time between sites, volume of work at each site, terrain, pilot's experience, time spent on the ground reloading, rate of application and weather (I think that's all). Organisation, however, is most important. If you keep changing chemicals, the whole pattern of work will be disrupted, so grouping crops that require the same cover on a regular basis can get rid of not only dead ferrying time, but also unnecessary cleaning of tanks. Very often, you can expect to top up with fuel after every delivery, to get the maximum spread.

Aerial application in UK takes place under a 'Certificate', which is broadly comparable to an Air Operator's Certificate (see Chapter 15, *Setting Up A Company*). Under the terms of this, a ground operations manager must always be present, who must have certain minimum qualifications. There should also be a field support engineer, who monitors aircraft performance and attends to routine servicing. The same person could combine both jobs, since they cannot take place at the same time (you can't fix it when it's flying!).

There may also be a flagman, who marks out the areas to be sprayed and the routes to be followed. Although an experienced pilot could do without markers in an emergency, it isn't recommended for prolonged operations. Other ground staff include loaders, who mix and load the solution, which usually requires fast action to keep things going as much as possible, but, when things are happening quickly, there is more danger of spillage and subsequent contamination.

To minimise weight, liquid solutions will be more concentrated than normal, and exposing yourself and ground staff to the spray must be regarded as a possibility. Minimise skin contamination with rubber gloves and boots, and clean clothing which includes long trousers and sleeves, which is just what you need on a hot day. It's not essential to use anything waterproof unless you actually expect to get drenched. Flaggers can avoid exposure to whatever is being sprayed by simply keeping out of the way of each pass.

Spray drift is the movement of whatever you're spraying to areas it was not intended for. It's undesirable, not only because it reduces the chemical used on the job, but it also causes damage in non-target areas due to concentrated amounts accumulating downwind, sometimes more than that applied to the target (it's also trespassing). Spray drift is affected by greater wind velocity at height, volatility of the solution, temperature inversions combined with spray pressure, nozzle spray angle and air movement around the aircraft. You can reduce the chances of it by releasing large droplets close to the target, by:

❑   Flying as low as possible
❑   Locating nozzles away from wing or rotor tips
❑   Placing the spray boom well below the wing of aeroplanes or as far forward as possible on helicopters
❑   Orienting nozzles backward and spacing for uniform patterns
❑   Using low nozzle pressures
❑   Using larger orifices in the nozzles
❑   Spraying when winds are light and the air is cool. In the UK, this generally means between about four and ten in the morning, which must be the most unsociable hours in aviation
❑   Using herbicides that do not produce damaging vapours

You can also modify the solution with additives that produce more viscosity, or with an invert emulsion system, which will apply a mayonnaise-like material. They both have disadvantages, in needing either specialised equipment or mixing techniques.

If you're trying to increase the volume of solution over a particular area, you're better off tinkering with the nozzles than reducing speed or raising spray pressure. This will help to avoid small droplets, or 'fines', that are more likely to drift. There are some crops, however, that require good coverage and small droplets, which is the opposite. This is where you need to be a bit of a chemist as well as a pilot to satisfy the customer.

Accurate records are essential, not only as aids to the business but also for later complaints of drifting. It's helpful to note such items as nozzle size and spacing, wind velocity and weather conditions, rate of application and time on task, together with a diagram (which you should have made anyway, for planning purposes).

Seeding

When a pipeline, or similar, has been laid, the countryside has to be made to look attractive again as soon as possible. A large hopper full of grass seed is used to do this, and you will do a series of runs over the pipeline to spread it.

The hopper is basically a large fibreglass bucket that weighs about 300 lb. It has a large petrol motor on the bottom, about the size of the average lawnmower engine, with a gate that is opened and closed from the cabin, and the important thing to remember is to positively switch off after a run, otherwise you will drop the seed everywhere. In other words, just letting go of the On button doesn't automatically stop the flow.

The other thing to remember is that it is attached to the helicopter in two places, that is, the hook and the electrical cable, and the latter has to be pulled out by ground staff or you will strip the cables from it when the hook is released.

If you have a lot of ground to cover, think about placing the seed on a truck and operating from various points around the countryside, which will save a lot of dead flying time. Lastly, depending on the machine and how far you have to fly, it's not uncommon to top up with fuel after every delivery.

Fire Suppression

This is subject to the normal restrictions, such as weather or night, although fixed-wing fire-bombing operations do take place in darkness. You may be asked to help fight the fire itself, contain it, or simply channel it in a specified direction, perhaps towards a natural barrier like a cliff top. If you're not part of the operation, you should not be within 5 nm and below 3,000 feet agl of the fire's limits.

The most obvious use of an aircraft is as a water bomber, but this will tend to be restricted to large aeroplanes, although some ways of using helicopters (in similar fashion to top dressing or by using an internal tank in a Chinook) are gaining in popularity – helicopters are at least able to make use of handier sources of water, like swimming pools or small rivers, but these are really combinations of load slinging and top dressing, as mentioned previously. The Bambi Fire Bucket is one popular tool for this. Mind you, other people could be affected by your activities . . .

And you thought it was a bad day (*California Examiner*, 20 March 1998):

> Fire Authorities in California found a corpse in a burnt out section of forest while assessing the damage done by a forest fire. The deceased male was dressed in a full wet suit, complete with a dive tank, flippers, and facemask. A post-mortem examination revealed that the person died not from burns but from massive internal injuries. Dental records provided a positive identification. Investigators then set about determining how a fully clad diver ended up in the middle of forest fire. It was revealed that, on the day of the fire, the person went for a diving trip off the coast – some 20 miles away from the forest. The firefighters, seeking to control the fire as quickly as possible, called in a fleet of helicopters with large water buckets. The buckets were dropped into the ocean for rapid filling, then flown to the forest fire and emptied. You guessed it.
>
> One minute our diver was making like Flipper in the Pacific, and next he

was doing a breaststroke in a fire bucket 300 feet in the air. Apparently, he extinguished exactly 5'10" of the fire. Some days it doesn't pay to get out of bed.

Anyhow, picking up water in single-engined helicopters beyond gliding distance from shore has the usual problems, plus possible disorientation if you go too far in. Fast-moving streams don't help, making you feel as if you were moving the wrong way, so it's best to find a calm area in these, because otherwise you will have to move the helicopter to keep up with the water, ending up in a fast taxi unawares – always face the flow of the stream. Approach the water with some forward speed so that it tips over and starts to fill as you move forward, close the gates and apply power in one smooth movement. In valleys, be aware of the extra power required to get you out of the 'hole' with a load on. Lines can also catch on skids, which, if you have a full bucket on the end, will cause you to exceed lateral C of G.

Checks for your bucket include the cargo arming switch, bucket open and close switch and electrical and mechanical jettison, and the capacity level to fit your performance. Don't forget the mirror and cables, as you would with any slung load. When flying with an empty bucket, do so with the dump gates open to prevent swinging or oscillation.

Fighting forest and moorland fires also requires a considerable work-force, who are usually tired by the time they get to the fire from the long walk to get there, so you may be used as transport for fire-fighters and their equipment, as well as for observation, where your passengers will have some rank and experience, since they will be directing ground forces from the air. Slinging expertise on your behalf is essential as portable equipment will also need to be moved.

One development of this is rapelling, which is the rapid deployment of fire crews by rope from a helicopter (and back in emergency) until the regular crews arrive. This saves them the trek to the fire in the first place and ensures they are not exhausted when they start. They can survive for up to forty-eight hours in the bush, and a command spotter will stay in the helicopter. All this will typically be for fires started by lightning, which are often in remote locations, down to weather conditions roughly equivalent to Special VFR. Rapelling shouldn't be done when it's too windy, or when it's raining, as the special rope used will swell up in the pulleys and stop working (just for interest, lightning can be up to 50,000 degrees in temperature – when it hits a tree, the sap boils and the heat can be held internally for days until fire actually breaks out).

Another task is flying round a fire with digital mapping equipment so the firemaster can see the extent of it. A small fire is one that takes five hours to fly round! So, transporting men and materials is just as useful here as at any other time.

Your accuracy will need to be considerably sharper than usual for several reasons; one is that there will be no marshallers to guide you in the target areas (a bit hot, there), and another is that chemical fire retardant (highly concentrated foam detergent) is often used and not welcome when sprayed over already tired firemen by mistake, although retardant tends to be dropped in an indirect manner as a holding tactic. A third is that evaporation will take its toll on whatever is dropped, ensuring that only so much of it is actually effective. Also, you will very likely not be the only aircraft about. The combination of lots of smoke (and poor visibility), coupled with heat turbulence and other machines buzzing about could prove to be extremely dangerous – many people report it's just like being in a war zone. Constant communications between machines (on the same frequency) are essential, especially if you are picking up from the same swimming pool. One pilot reported that the distance from a pond to the fire was so small as to only require a fast hover taxi between them both, which meant that oil temperatures began to redline, as there wasn't enough airflow to cool things down. You will be tired, as well, after a couple of days' continuous flying from dawn to dusk, though you probably won't notice till afterwards, as adrenalin does a lot. Landing sites near burnt areas may blow up ash and produce a similar effect to white-out.

Hover drops are not recommended, as your downwash may fan the fire. Upslope drops should be avoided as much as possible, and should only be attempted by experienced crews, especially on low targets, as you will need more airspeed than normal to create a pull-up to clear the area *with the load* if necessary, without using extra power. Aside from trying to do a 180-degree pedal turn in a high hover out of ground effect, the resulting high power setting will probably fan the flames, as with a hover drop.

With downslope drops, you will not necessarily see the target until you clear the ridge, so you will need targets to line up on beforehand. For very steep slopes, try reducing speed before diving off the ridge, so that you don't end up with excessive speed. Cross-slope drops are OK, provided you remember where your rotor disc is.

In order not to make embarrassing mistakes, like dropping water in the wrong place, you need to be aware that some fires are deliberately set, to make use of the pecularities of airflow, as in 'backfiring'. The idea is to remove fuel in the path of a rapidly moving fire, where the head creates a powerful convective column which pulls air in from all sides, including downwind. When this flow is steady, a fire is started ahead of the main fire from a natural barrier, such as a road or river, which is sucked in and creates a wider firebreak.

For ground support, as well as load-slinging gear, you will also need mobile fuel and provision for fire brigade radio equipment, not to mention a few aircraft spares. The fire service will have their own trained ground staff, but take your own just in case. After the fire, you may be asked to lift an unrolled hose to drain it. This saves exhausted firemen from having to under-run miles of hose before they roll it for stowage on their appliances. That alone should be good for a few beers.

Casualty Evacuation/Air Ambulance

Patients just being moved from one hospital to another do not qualify for any exemptions for saving life, although special provisions may apply for duty hours (see Chapter 7).

A *Helicopter Emergency Medical Service* (HEMS) flight is for immediate and rapid transportation of medical personnel, supplies (equipment, blood, organs, drugs) or ill or injured persons and anyone else directly involved. An approval is required. The purpose of a *casevac* is to give immediate assistance to sick or injured people in life-threatening circumstances, typically from the scene of an accident.

Otherwise, there are two types of ambulance flight, *Intensive Care Transport* (ICT) and *Ambulance Taxi Transport* (ATT). Both are usually planned in advance, meaning that there's not so much of a rush. Any police observers or medical attendants should be able to monitor and assist the patient during the flight and inform you of any problems.

Whatever you get involved in, the following should generally be avoided:

❑   Anyone with previous or present signs or symptoms suggesting epilepsy or any other form of fit
❑   Unconscious patients, unless in-flight attention is available
❑   Patients with severe haemorrhagic types of injury, unless in-flight attention is available
❑   Abdominal or chest injuries if altitude changes of up to 1,500 feet are likely to be involved
❑   Those under the affluence of incohol or drugs, unless prescribed by a qualified doctor
❑   Persons of unsound mind or who may be a potential danger to the aircraft or persons therein

'Walking Wounded', that is, passengers who are infirm due to age, ill health or otherwise, may be carried subject to the approval of the qualified medical personnel who should accompany and be responsible for

215

them. No patients should be placed near emergency exits, and wheel-chairs, etc. should not impede escape paths. If your company does a lot of medical work, it may be worth retaining a doctor to advise on certain cases, especially where infectious diseases are concerned. Routes should be planned to take into account changes of altitude and rates of descent, and you will need to accelerate or decelerate with care.

Aside from the patient's condition, the consent of both referring and receiving hospitals is required, together with confirmed arrangements for road transport at the departure and destination airports. You also need to make sure that the type of aircraft is what is wanted, together with the details of staff and equipment.

Specialised equipment should be properly installed, and instructions must be available to all attendants. Some of it could actually be classed as Dangerous Goods (say, large quantities of aeromedical oxygen), so you may need an exemption to carry it. Anything that needs to be fixed to the aircraft (e.g. stretchers), or connected to its systems, must be through an airworthiness/manufacturers' approved system, as it must be compatible with the aircraft environment (for instance, that used in road ambulances may be unsuitable for flight).

Oxygen (if used) must cover the duration of loading, flight, technical stops and unloading, plus about 1.5 hours' reserve for eventualities.

Patients who can sit should occupy a seat and use a seat belt, which may be a little looser than normally required, except for take-off, landing, flight in turbulence or during manoeuvres. Stretcher patients should be secured by belts or a harness as per the flight manual. Other passengers must be limited to whatever seats are left after stretcher equipment has been fitted.

Accompanying flight attendants must have proper medical experience, and doctors must be qualified and registered in the states concerned in the move. In fact, a doctor is always required on ICT flights and on ATT flights which are other than simple escort cases.

Nurses must also be registered in the relevant states and work under direct instructions of an accompanying doctor (or apply those given before flight by one). Nurses must not be used on their own on ICT flights or with any possibility of the patient's condition changing. Paramedics may be employed with the agreement of the patient's doctor. Their training may not be valid in some states.

Pleasure Flying

The aim of pleasure flying is to carry groups of people, generally members of the public who have never flown before, for a short period in a company aircraft for a fee. It can be very lucrative if the operation is slick and smoothly controlled, and it's also an ideal opportunity to promote aviation in general, so everyone should take care to ensure that the customer's association with aircraft (and the company) is a happy one. The machine must therefore be handled smoothly with no sharp manoeuvres, unless they're specifically asked for, with *all* passengers being in agreement. The only types of flying generally recommended are spot turns and sideways movement in the hover and normal climb, descent and cruise. Oddly enough, hovering manoeuvres are quite popular, but not good commercially, as you need to be about three minutes in the air to give them their money's worth, so you should keep the rhythm going.

Because ground idle isn't officially counted, your turnaround time does not affect the revenue per flying hour, but, obviously, the quicker you are, the more cash you have in your pocket at the end of the day. The duration of the trip itself is what determines productivity – the shorter it is, the more you get, but regard 2½–3 minutes as the minimum before you get complaints.

On top of the public actually flying, there will also be those attending the associated event, so don't forget the exemption to fly nearer than 3,000 feet to assemblies of over 1,000 people. Any site must be organised and staffed to afford the maximum safety for all concerned.

The size and location of the site, the type of event and anticipated numbers need to be noted and a site inspection arranged before you start. This *must* be done by someone who knows the requirements; if possible, a qualified pilot, because the positioning of the aircraft must be paid for as well, and if the site turns out to be unsuitable and is rejected on the day, you've all wasted your time.

A site's physical characteristics and position relative to areas available for emergency vehicles must be taken into account, together with those for the aircraft. For instance, it may be acceptable for downwind take-offs (provided performance is OK) if emergency vehicle access is better in that direction.

You are allowed some discretion if an otherwise perfect location is spoiled by one or two major obstacles which can simply be avoided by curving the flight path (there might be a tree in the middle), but an airfield should be all right on this point.

The CAA Flight Operations department must be notified at least seven days beforehand on a special form that they provide (it should be in the ops manual). Local emergency services must also be notified.

Running the Site

All this is geared to helicopters in particular, but may be adapted for aeroplanes.

On the day, you should check that your area is roped off properly, and is the same as was agreed originally – beware of tents and marquees creeping up on you. If you don't use the agreed area, then (by arrangement) you will have to inform the your inspector within seven days as he will have been informed of the original proposals.

Next, find the organiser and check for other activities affecting you, like aerobatics, balloons or parachuting. Give him an idea of what you want the announcements to sound like (preferably every half hour) about your activities. He will also need to know your start time, and may have been given some free seats, and run a competition to get rid of them, or possibly have just given them to his friends, so you will need a positive means of identifying the freebies. You may be plagued by people claiming they're from the organisers or the local papers asking for free flights, but unless you can identify them, politely refer them back to the organiser.

Meanwhile, back at the operational area, set out the safety equipment just inside the ropes and carry out whatever checks you need on the fuelling equipment – this will save time later when the pressure's on. Show the marshallers around all the equipment. It's a good idea to keep the emergency equipment accessible, but out of sight, as the public tends to be put off by the sight of anything designed to help in emergencies (like checklists). If local fire engines are on site, rescue equipment is not necessary, but take it anyway, because they will either be swamped with children sounding the sirens or be called away and you will have to stop flying until they come back.

Standard rescue equipment consists of the following:

❏　A vehicle capable of carrying everything – not a wheeled trolley, but something self-propelled. A car or van will do, but it must be able to go over all relevant surfaces. The ultimate is a long-wheelbase Land Rover, as you will discover when you try and pull a trailer with all the stuff mentioned below with it, not to mention fuel barrels

❏　11 kg dry chemical fire-extinguishing agent, 1×7.5 kg CO_2 or 1×3.5 kg BCF extinguisher and 1×20 gal premixed AFFF foam unit with a minimum discharge rate of 16 gallons per minute. Although the BCF extinguisher is as good as the first two combined, the chemical is difficult to get hold of. Fire extinguishers have to be serviced every year and tested every ten, according to the BSI

❏　For each marshaller, helmets with visors, flame-resistant gloves, fire

218

tunics or donkey-type jackets and stout boots. Most local fire brigades have a surplus equipment office where you can buy them

❑ Release tools as follows:
  ❑ 1 axe (rescue, small, non-wedging or aircraft)
  ❑ 1 × 24-inch bolt cropper
  ❑ 1 × 40-inch crowbar
  ❑ 1 harness knife
  ❑ 1 flame-resistant blanket

❑ Medical equipment as follows:
  ❑ 6 BPC9 dressings or equivalent
  ❑ 6 BPC12 dressings or equivalent
  ❑ 6 triangular bandages
  ❑ 6 foil blankets
  ❑ 1 pair scissors
  ❑ 1 basic first-aid kit
  ❑ 2 stretchers

BPC9 and 12 are now officially out of date, but still about, so try and get the right ones, as insurance companies will do their best to weasel out of any claim they can, and you don't want to give them an excuse. Scissors are in the average first-aid kit, anyway.

There should be only one entry and exit to the operational area, usually under the control of the cashier, but there's a danger of the money being taken if an emergency crops up and it's left unattended, so you need a hefty table with a very large metal box screwed down to it, padlocked, with a slot in the top into which the money goes.

The minimum personnel to run the site effectively will be three, one to collect money and brief passengers (the cashier) and the remaining two to marshal passengers in and out and operate seat belts, etc. If, for any reason, such as last minute sickness, you can't get enough people, you can get away with one marshaller on passenger movement, if all embarkation and disembarkation is done from one side of the aircraft, one door at a time. It's not recommended, however, as it takes longer and passengers *en masse* must be regarded as thick as two planks – they will take every opportunity to walk into a tail rotor or a propeller, regardless of how many warnings you give them. A large version of the briefing card is recommended as a sort of briefing board they can read in the queue, on top of the ones you hand out anyway. It'll be a waste of time, but you ought to make the effort.

While marshallers can also be the rescue crew, they're not expected to wear firemen's uniforms all the time, but should still be dressed well and in a good enough substitute if something happens quickly (so no shorts and T-shirts). A good source is Air Cadets, who not only look smart in their uniforms, but are also keen to be near aircraft, and will do a day's work for free flights, which is where you can use up any positioning flights, as you can't sell them to the public. That's not to say that you should abuse the privilege, though. Give them their money's worth.

Place the sign with the company identification (and the price) on about ten metres or so from the cashier's desk, so if people are put off by the charge, you don't give the wrong impression by having lots of them turning away at the last minute. It also saves the cashier answering the same questions all day. You will need plenty of other signs around the event as, unless you're careful, regulations will ensure that you're far enough away for people to think you're nothing to do with it. *Potential passengers will not walk more than about 100 metres.* As with any customer, the sales process must be made as brainless as possible, as pleasure flying is done on impulse 99 per cent of the time. If you make it difficult for them, they will not do it, so make sure you can take all major credit cards, so that they don't feel as if they're spending real money.

Next, brief the loaders, ensuring they know that people should always approach and leave the helicopter from the front and that nobody should be allowed further aft than the rear skid support (or forward of a similar point on an aeroplane). They also need to know about the opening and closing of doors and the operation of seat belts, all of which should be covered anyway in the passenger brief.

The most dangerous time is when the passengers change over, so that's when marshallers must be most wary. When you land, outgoing passengers should be out of the area (or at least the edge of the rotor disc) before the others are ushered in, although you can tighten the operation by shepherding the new ones to the edge of the disc while the others are getting out. Never close the throttle to ground idle during this, so that you can lift into the air and get out of the way of anyone you see about to run round the back end – believe me, they will! The tail rotor is dangerous at whatever speed it's going.

With reference to refuelling, it's very tempting to carry on till the last minute when you've got a long queue, but be careful about your fuel reserves. Not only is it good airmanship to land with a reasonable amount on board (don't trust those gauges!), but you must have a thirty-minute break every three hours anyway. Passengers (and employers) understand a helicopter stopping for fuel, but not for you sliding off for a hamburger somewhere. There's another safety point as well. In a way, helicopters are regarded in the same sense as a fire engine – the public make no distinction between an old one on show and a new one actually on duty. If there's a fire, they will turn to anything for help. The same goes for a helicopter. If an accident happens, you could be asked to ferry someone to hospital. Do you know where the nearest one with a helipad is, and will you have enough fuel to get there?

For maximum revenue, fill the machine up on every lift. If it takes four passengers, don't fly with fewer than three. If only two turn up, they should wait, or come back later when others have arrived. Children less than two years old on an adult's knee should have an approved seat belt extender provided for them – don't expect to carry more than one, or preferably none at all, because they're too young to appreciate it and you stand a real chance of putting them off flying for life, aside from having sick down the back of your neck.

Don't sell more than two loads in advance in case something happens and you have to return all the money. Also, don't strap one passenger in whilst waiting for more custom. This is for two reasons; firstly if nobody else comes along you're obliged to go up with just one person (un-economical) and, secondly, you will have to make conversation by shouting while the customer is waiting, because usually you're the only one with a headset. Talking of economical flying, and the subject of freebies, if the show organisers send along more than one, allow them up one at a time, so the costs are covered by the other revenue passengers on each trip; if you take all the freebies up at once, you lose money on the whole lift.

You must identify those who have paid as well, which is usually done by sticking labels on them, date-stamping their hands, or whatever. If someone asks how long the flight is (they will), say six miles or so – it sounds better than three minutes. While the aircraft is flying, ground staff can brief the next load something like this:

'When the helicopter lands, please stay here until you are called forward, as we have to unload the other passengers first. You and you go to the right-hand side as you look at it, one to the front and one to the back door. The other two please go to the left-hand side, you to the front and you to the back door.

[Don't mention 'the back' by itself or they will take it literally.]

When you get in, please do not step on the floats, but use the foot rests on the skids which will be pointed out to you. Once you are in, we will do up the seat belts and close the doors. After you land, we'll get you out, so just sit tight and wait for us.

Some very important safety points – please don't touch the door handles in flight, don't throw anything out of the windows, and keep away from the tail rotor – always move to the front where the pilot can see you. Any questions?'

Again, this sort of stuff should be on the standard passenger briefing leaflet – you could hand out a few to keep people in the queue occupied, as they won't listen to you properly, anyway. Have one enlarged and pinned to a large board so that it can be read from a distance. The cashier will need a small pile of change, but you could keep the price at a round figure so that you don't need it all at once (multiples of five are best). If in doubt as to what constitutes an infant – charge. When it's closing time and obvious that not everyone will get a trip, stop selling in good time.

Keep an eye out for your inspector! He will be lurking behind a tree with a notebook.

The Technical Bits
Operational Area
This area, which is under positive control of the company, encompasses the landing site, the taxiways, HAAs and IAAs (see below for definitions) and take-off, climb and approach slopes. It has side surfaces rising upwards and outwards to 100 feet at a gradient of 1:1 from its edges, unpenetrated by obstacles, and will be fenced, roped off or otherwise protected from intrusion by unauthorised persons – therefore it should not include a public right-of way. Rope and stakes used for demarcation and public control are not considered obstacles for this purpose, though they may for performance planning.

Final Approach and Take-off Area (FATO)
This is inside the *Safety Area* (see below), where the final phase of the approach to hover or landing is completed, and from which take-off is commenced. It may be square or circular and the minimum size is 1.5 × the rotor diameter (for dimensions of popular helicopters see later).

Safety Area (SA)
Surrounds the FATO, for reducing damage to helicopters accidentally diverging from it. It is also square or circular, according to the FATO, and the minimum size is 3 m or one quarter of the rotor diameter, whichever is the greater. It must be free from obstacles. The combined size of the FATO and SA should be at least twice the overall length, including rotors, of the helicopter and, where it contains the TLOF (see below), the surface should be firm and not blow away with downwash.

Touch-down and Lift-off Area (TLOF)
A load-bearing area on which the helicopter may safely touch down and lift off; it should be free from slopes, to ease passenger embarkation and disembarkation, and not have them walking uphill into tail rotors. The

TLOF has a diameter of at least twice the length of the helicopter, including rotors, and is normally contained within the FATO (it's the same minimum size), but may be separate.

Taxiways
Used where the TLOF is remote from the FATO, with a minimum clearance of one rotor diameter from obstructions either side of the rotor disc (that is, a minimum overall width of three rotor diameters, or 33.9 m for the Bell 47).

Helicopter Acceleration Area (HAA)
Should have a minimum width of 30 m or twice the overall length of the helicopter, whichever is the greater, obstacle-free and long enough to accommodate one third of the 'take-off distance to 100 feet' (168 m – Bell 47) given in the flight manual (therefore 56 m). The surface should be substantially level so that a helicopter can land safely if an engine fails, without risk of injury to the occupants or third parties.

Take-off Area (TA)
At the upwind end of the HAA, with the same width and at least twice the length, and free from significant obstacles. The minimum Take-off Distance Available (Helicopters) (TODAH) should be greater than the Take-off Distance Required to achieve a height of 100 feet, e.g. more than the HAA and TA combined. The total length of the TODAH is therefore about 168 m.

Note: Performance figures here are for the Bell 206B for +20 °C and 1,000 feet PA at max AUW (hot Bank Holidays).

The take-off area and downwind two-thirds of the IAA may contain insignificant or frangible obstacles only. The remainder should be obstacle-free (rope and stakes used for demarcation and public control are not considered to be obstacles).

Inner Approach Area (IAA)
For each direction of landing, has the same width as the HAA and accommodates the Landing Distance Required from 100 feet as detailed in the flight manual. The upwind third of the IAA should be completely free from obstacles. The minimum Landing Distance Available (Helicopters) (LDAH) should exceed the Landing Distance Required from 100 feet.

Note: The TODAH and the IAA are essentially the same patch of ground, except that the TODA is slightly longer. As both the HAA and the upwind third of the IAA must be obstacle-free and are at opposite ends of this area, the whole TODA should be obstacle-free in the first place.

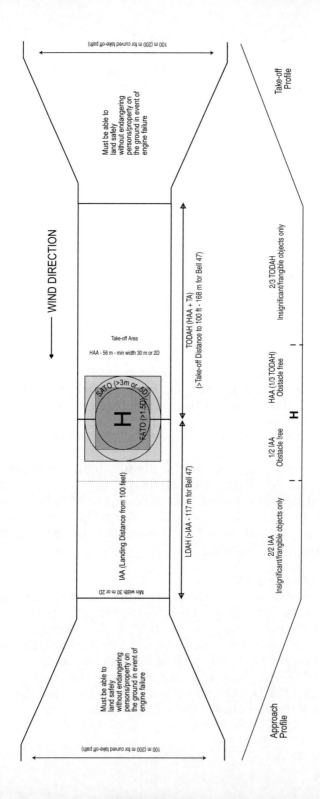

Pleasure Flying and Feeder Site Criteria

Side Surfaces and Slopes

The operational area will have side surfaces rising upwards and outwards to 100 feet at a gradient of 1:1 from the edges of the HAA, take-off area or IAA which will not be penetrated by any obstacle, fixed or transient. It will also be fenced, roped off or otherwise protected from intrusion by unauthorised persons, and therefore should not include an unguarded right-of-way.

Take-off, climb and approach slopes (which may be curved) must not be over large areas of water unless you can land safely on it in emergency. They should be obstruction-free with a gradient of not less than 1:8 and be 1,000 m long, possessing areas suitable for emergency landing.

Helicopter Dimensions

Type	Wt (kg)	HAA (m)	TOD to 100' (m)	ELD fm 100' (m)	Rotor Dia	Length inc Rotors
AS 350 Squirrel	1,950	200	500	460	10.7	12.94
206L	1,882	95	285	232	11.3	12.94
206B JetRanger	1,452	95	263	229	10.1	11.92
Hiller 12E	1,405	56	168	117	10.8	12.41
Hughes 500	1,361	77	230	189	8.1	8.97
Bell 47G	1,338	56	168	117	11.3	13.5
Enstrom F280	1,066	58	168	151	9.8	8.95
Gazelle 341G	1,800	102	305	140	10.5	11.97
Robinson R22	1,300	122	366	110	8.18	8.74

Special Events

Vast numbers of people being moved into a major sporting event (such as the British Grand Prix at Silverstone) make the feeder sites used for their lifting and dropping-off liable for special treatment. These events are good for business – one good day at Silverstone keeps some companies in profit for the year. As for pleasure flying sites, Flight Operations need to be notified (in this case at least twenty-eight days before), but other considerations arise as well.

First of all, if you sell single seats to the public, rather than the whole capacity of the aircraft on a 'sole use' charter basis, you will either need a full Air Transport Licence, or an exemption (pleasure flying is a special case). It also needs to be done in your own right; you can't do it on the back of someone else, as you can with an AOC sometimes. Whoever holds the AOC must apply for these exemptions from Branch 2 (ATL) of the CAA, nominating the positions of the intended aerodromes. They will consult Flight Ops as to the suitability of said aerodromes who will apply pleasure flying site criteria (as found in the ops manual) to support their judgments. Again, there is a special form to fill in which will cut out most of the lack of communication over this subject, and you should find a copy in Ops.

Secondly, you need arrival and departure slots, which are usually at a premium. Because of the numbers of aircraft involved (usually over 126 H1 types alone at the Grand Prix), there will be a briefing for all concerned well before the event, at which all companies are expected to send a representative. At the very least a NOTAM will be issued. H1 helicopters, by the way, are less than 15 m long, and H2s between 15 and 24 m; they therefore require different treatment at their feeder sites.

A feeder site is one where more than five movements take place in any one day in connection with an event, as a result of which they require special facilities (a movement is a take-off *or* a landing). If using H1s you can get away with normal equipment as used for pleasure flying, but H2s need something a bit more macho. Actually, it's basically the same, but the vehicle must have four-wheel drive and there must be a minimum of sixty gallons of water and five gallons of foam concentrate, with equipment able to deliver it at forty gallons per minute. A minimum of 100 lb of CO_2 or 50 lb of dry powder or BCF is also required.

The rescue and medical equipment requirements are also more comprehensive, needing transfusion and resuscitator gear to be readily available in addition to:

- ❏ large non-wedging axe
- ❏ small non-wedging axe
- ❏ grab or salving hook
- ❏ 1" cold chisel
- ❏ 4 lb hammer
- ❏ fire-resisting blanket
- ❏ heavy-duty hacksaw with six spare blades
- ❏ suitably large ladder
- ❏ feet of 2" line
- ❏ one pair 7" side-cutting pliers
- ❏ 24" saw
- ❏ large slotted screwdriver
- ❏ large Philips screwdriver

❏   one pair tin snippers
❏   pneumatic rescue chisel with spare cylinder
❏   chisel and retaining spring
❏   quick-release knife with a sheath
❏   enough pairs of flame-resistant gloves
❏   24" bolt cropper
❏   3' 6" crowbar

Line Patrol Flying

Electricity companies carry out their line inspections generally with a helicopter, but a (very) light aeroplane could be used if no hovering is required. However, anything fixed wing will largely be useless.

Observers from the companies will be carried and the sorties flown in line with their normal procedures, which are pretty exhaustive. All their staff are fully and professionally trained to exacting standards. They need to be, as following and inspecting tower lines calls for a high degree of proficiency and concentration from everyone. The very nature of the exercise (flying close to the lines inspected) means that for most of the time you will be very near the avoid area of the height/velocity envelope (or *Dead Man's Curve* – see the Glossary). This needs to be studied and will be found in the flight manual.

For normal wooden poles, being one and a half rotor spans laterally and flying at about 40 kt is the ideal, although 11 kV ring circuits in a clover leaf pattern could make this difficult. At the very least, you need a positive airspeed, that is, one showing on the ASI.

The CAA assumes the flight won't take place in the avoid area, so exemptions from Rule 5, etc. are geared towards looking after third parties on the ground not directly connected with your activities. However, the flights are still Commercial Air Transport, and entering the avoid curve is therefore prohibited. If prolonged incursions are likely, consider using a twin.

Even where a single-engined machine could be used, it's usually over areas that aren't suitable for forced landings or are unable to afford safety (hostile environments). There should be a full restraint harness for each occupant, together with a protective helmet and flameproof overalls, or clothing with suitable shoes.

Before patrolling takes place, a low-flying exemption (from Rule 5 (1)(e)), must be obtained from the CAA in writing, which will say that no flights are to be made at night, over fuel installations or over the congested areas of any city, town or settlement. Dispensations will be required to fly near nuclear installations and HM prisons, which should also be notified by telephone (the latter get twitchy, in case you're part of an escape plan).

Flights must also be confined to within 300 feet of the lines concerned (but no closer than one and a half rotor diameters to the lines when level, or one diameter plus thirty feet when above their level). In addition, lines should be crossed vertically at least 100 feet above them (common sense dictates that you should do this over a tower rather than the lines themselves). You will not be allowed closer than 100 feet to any people or vehicles directly concerned with line operations, and 200 feet to any other structures than those to do with the lines themselves. You shouldn't, but if you have to go under a wire for any reason, get your skids on the ground as near to a tower as possible.

As well as the proper permissions, other problems include insurance. Ensure that whatever you get also covers you for frightened animals bolting and causing havoc – this usually happens with sharply changing noise levels caused by rapid manoeuvres. If you can't help flying over animals, at least try not to chase them through the fence!

Line patrol should not normally happen if the visibility is less than about one mile, and two if raining (one mile is approximately six towers or poles ahead). These limits are higher than usual because moisture will stick to the windscreen at slower speeds, and things are further complicated if you have no windscreen wipers, as precipitation won't blow away either. Under those conditions, speeding up to get rid of water is not what you want to be doing! Give serious consideration to aborting if rain is anything near heavy, although really heavy stuff will tend to run off better than the light variety. Also, line patrol should not normally be attempted if the wind is above twenty-five knots, and the cloudbase below 400 feet.

Lines are patrolled at twenty or so knots, a little above pole height and to one side. Observers will normally be on the opposite side to you with the lines closest to them. They make commentaries on tape which are later transcribed into useful information.

Always try to follow the line as near into wind as possible or, if not, in trim at least, which will help if you lose tail rotor authority. If it's in the order of ten knots or so, being downwind generally will only ensure the transit time along the wire is too fast, with the consequent danger of you trying to slow down and having no airspeed – if any more it's likely to be rough as well, especially in the mountains.

Monitor vital instruments and be particularly aware of overtorquing or overtemping. Don't forget the possibilities of tail rotor and wire strikes, and other lines (especially tower lines) crossing – the observers will be too busy to assist your lookout. If a closer inspection is called for, *do not* try to come to the hover and backtrack, but gain height and speed, positively identify the area and make a conventional circuit and approach to come to the hover alongside the line into wind.

A constant lookout must be maintained at all times, especially for fast, low-flying military aircraft, so High Intensity Strobe Lights (HISLs), nav lights, landing lights and anti-collision beacons must be on at all times. HISLs should be at least 2,000 candela in power (so don't drop one or you'll have to pick them all up). If they become unserviceable, patrol above 500 feet. Don't plan on doing more than two to three hours per day due to the high workload.

Power Line Cleaning

Done in Canada, when the Electricity people can't get to them by road. There is a platform on your helicopter, maybe with a boom sticking out, and a water pressure system powered by a small gasoline engine. As you can imagine, a lot of training is required for this.

Civil Aviation Notification Procedure (CANP)

Powerline survey, sporting activities, aerial photography, crop spraying, underslung loads and anything else low level (i.e. below 1,000 feet) that will affect military operations should be notified on 0800 515544. The relevant (RAF and ATC) authorities will be informed by the duty airman of the details of your flight. Naturally, try to give them as much notice as possible.

Pipeline Flying

This is very similar to line patrol, so most of what is said there will apply here. Gas pipelines (or whatever) are not very far below the surface of the ground, and potential hazards include building works, ditch construction, drainage, flooding, leakage and falling trees.

1/250,000-scale maps will be provided, on which the pipeline route will be marked. Observers will be using 1/50,000-scale maps supplied by their companies.

The normal patrol height is 300 feet, with an associated speed of 50–80 kt, taking into account the efficiency of inspection, terrain, wind direction and helicopter operation (avoid curves, etc.). However, between 500 and 700 feet is recommended to avoid low flying military aircraft. No helicopter should approach closer than 300 feet to any person, vessel, or structure, and only closer than 500 feet within a horizontal distance of 300 feet from the pipelines to be inspected.

The cloudbase must be at least 200 feet above inspection height, with a minimum visibility of 1,500 feet.

Police Operations

A police force will either own its own aircraft or charter from operators as and when required, in which case the only things you can get away with are low flying (closer than 500 feet, etc) and going in bad weather. Even then, a helicopter may not get closer than 50 feet, or 1.5 rotor diameters, whichever is greater. In fact, to take full advantage of any restrictions, your passenger needs to be either a police officer, an employee of the police authority, a medical attendant, a pilot under training, an inspector, a fire officer, a customs officer on a joint operation, or any other agreed in writing by the authorities. However, there will always be a police observer on board, and the job involves a lot of cross-controlling when on observation, not to mention short-notice tasking.

As they may need to recover their costs from time to time, they also need a Police AOC and Ops Manual (PAOM), although, in Canada, they come under Private Operator legislation.

Prisoners

Prisoners are passengers and qualify for all the normal safety considerations, although their movement is definitely not routine. Handcuffing should always be done to the front, so that seat belts can be released in emergencies.

Potentially violent prisoners should be carried one at a time and have enough escorts to restrain them if necessary. In any case, at least two should be used, ensuring that neither the pilot nor any of the flight controls or exits can be reached.

If a prisoner does become violent, land as soon as practicable and have them continue the journey by surface means.

Persons Under the Influence of Drugs or Alcohol

These should be avoided, but sometimes it can't be helped. First of all, you will need to decide whether they are fit for a normal seat or need a stretcher. You will need at least two escorts for both restraint and emergency evacuation, and a suitable receptacle for vomit.

As with prisoners, you should land as soon as practicable if there are any signs of violence. Further movement should be undertaken by surface means.

Bodies and Remains

Their carriage is affected by how inaccessible they are, that is, precluding other methods of transport. The main considerations are the health and hygiene of the aircraft occupants, which means they might have to be carried outside if they are a bit ripe, so you need to be current on winching or slung loads. Whatever you choose, bodies and remains should be secured in body bags or coffins.

If there is any spillage of body fluids, or any part of the body has come into contact with the aircraft, a thorough wash down is needed as soon as possible.

Police Dogs

Should be embarked or disembarked with the aircraft shut down, but if this is not possible, the observer should meet the handler and dog clear of the aircraft for the briefing. The dog should be on a short lead, so that it doesn't interfere with anything.

Fly smoothly, but be prepared to land if the dog becomes unwell, although you will find that they mostly like travelling and prefer to look out of the window rather than being made to lie down.

If the dog breaks free and moves towards the tail rotor or propeller(s), the handler must not attempt to follow, but give you a signal to close down.

Weapons and Munitions

The overriding consideration is the elimination of danger to the aircraft, its occupants and persons and property on the ground. Munitions include gas/smoke canisters, stun grenades, shotgun cartridges and ammunition for rifles and sidearms.

These weapons should not be carried in a loaded state:

- ❏ double-barrelled shotgun
- ❏ single-barrelled shotgun (unless automatic or pump action)
- ❏ baton gun
- ❏ CS discharger
- ❏ dartgun

Loading, unloading or firing of weapons on aircraft is not permitted.

Where all passengers are securely seated, loaded weapons must be in a safe condition, weapons and munitions should be carried in holds, compartments, or other areas that are inaccessible in flight, and secured normally. Weapons or munitions must not be distributed among passengers until the aircraft has landed.

Weapon	Safe Condition
Self-loading pistol. self-loading rifle, carbine, automatic shotgun or pump-action shotgun, bolt-action rifle, automatic rifle.	Working parts forward and trigger released, safety catch applied where possible, magazine charged with ammunition and fitted to the weapon. NO ROUND IN THE BREACH.
Revolver	Cylinder loaded with ammunition; weapon in a secure holster, to prevent accidental discharge.

When passengers on a special operation need their weapons to hand, hand weapons and spare ammunition for them may be carried in readily accessible boxes or holsters, with the ammunition in pockets. Rifles and shotguns may be stowed securely within the cabin, with spare ammunition in body belts or readily accessible boxes. Gas/smoke canisters must be in boxes but these may be readily accessible. Boxes must be strongly constructed, fire resistant and have an 'explosives' label.

Hover Emplaning and Deplaning

Done where you can't land properly. There should be no danger to third parties and minimal risk to the aircraft, crew, seated passengers and those carrying out the activity. The major consideration is engine failure.

You should be able to hover at least at 4 ft, although the actual height should be less than that – 2 feet is best for boarding, with one skid or wheel in contact with the ground to get rid of static. One passenger should be seated before the next gets on board. To give you a decent power margin, the maximum weight should not greater than 95 per cent of the maximum.

Make sure the time in the hover is not more than the time limit for take-off power.

If you intend to do this at night, a twin-engined machine is better.

Formation Flying

Used when chasing another aircraft, but not at night, in cloud, or when the cloud base is below 500 ft or visibility below 3 km. As the pilot of the other machine may not be aware of your intentions, and might not even wish to be identified, you shouldn't do this too closely. In other words, spend the shortest possible time at the minimum permitted distance from the other machine. Conduct shadowing from the maximum range consistent with obtaining photographic, or other evidence, and maintaining visual contact.

Do not endanger the other machine or attempt to force it to alter height or heading, or to land. You need to be able to take safe avoiding action if the other machine attempts to endanger you.

If you cannot establish RT contact, approach while the target is in straight flight, which may be level, or climbing, or descending. Establish a stand-off position behind, between 4 and 8 o'clock, not closer than 200 m. Reduce the range slowly and progressively to at least 100 m, moving back out once the required evidence of registration, type and other features have been noted.

Landing Helicopters on Roads

The area must first be secured (but see below), with radio or verbal communication having taken place to confirm that you have authority to land there. Unaffected carriageways should be closed at all times.

Normally, you can only land at an unsecured site (i.e. where the police are not in attendance) in remote rural areas outside congested areas, but you may do so on dual carriageways (divided highways) or motorways (turnpikes) in daylight, where no traffic is moving – no landings should be made by night.

In any case, there must be no threat to persons or vehicles on the ground from the helicopter, or vice versa. Always be aware of the effects of your downwash, which may blow away crucial evidence, not to mention dislodging broken glass and other loose debris, particularly from damaged buildings, at bomb scenes.

Try not to land in school or other playgrounds, or areas where children might be confined or suddenly emerge. Don't use the aircraft presence or public address system to clear children from a site.

Parachute Dropping

In the UK no parachute dropping should be undertaken unless (as a pilot) you've been approved by the British Parachute Association and the parachutists themselves are in possession of an operations manual authorised by them. You get your certificate by passing a check ride with a TRE, who in turn has been approved by the BPA. The normal regulations for the dropping of articles from aircraft also apply.

In addition, the flight manual should include a supplement to cover the situation. For some strange reason, parachutists do not seem to be classed as passengers or freight, so it's a good question as to whether a parachute trip is actually commercial air transport or not. Check your insurance cover, even though on the way down they are not in the aircraft, and on the way up they are normal passengers.

Parachutists should be strapped in at all times except just before dropping, and before take-off they should be shown how to secure seatbelts so that they don't flap around in flight, as part of a proper briefing. There should be no loose articles in the cabin, and seats must be removed, as must be dual controls if one intends to drop from the front seat (of a helicopter). There should be no other passengers.

Don't use static lines from a helicopter, and remove the doors (check the flight manual for limitations on flight without them).

A typical freefall drop needs one pass over the drop site into wind at approximately 2,000 feet, where the jumpmaster will drop weighted paper markers. You then commence climbing to the drop height, turning downwind and keeping the markers in view all the time. When at drop height, come over the site again at about sixty knots into wind, where the jumpmaster will guide you to where he wants to be.

When dropping, use both sides of the aircraft if possible, so the lateral centre of gravity limits are not exceeded – this is one of those times when you might want to calculate it for take-off *and* landing. The helicopter should be level, above 2,000 agl with an airspeed between 20 and 70 kt IAS.

Mountain Flying

Mountainous areas are strange – in them, general principles common to other areas will be vastly different. You must be prepared to adapt your flying techniques as the need arises, for the peculiarities of the region and the type of aircraft. In other words, have not only Plan A, but Plan B, C, etc. up your sleeve, because, very often, once you've looked at a site and gone round for finals, you will find a cloud has got there before you! You cannot afford to assume that a particular situation is the same as, or similar to, any other you might have encountered previously. You can also expect fog, especially in the early morning, which will often stick to the sides of valleys.

In the UK, mountainous areas include Scotland and Wales, the Lake and Peak Districts, and generally any hilly country above 1,500 feet amsl, although a geologist would probably expect to see 2,000 feet. In many other parts of the world, these would be considered as just foothills. In Canada, look out for *Designated Mountain Areas*, which naturally include the Rockies, which extend into the USA.

Performance changes drastically when both temperature and height increase – just the opposite to flying in cold weather, but you knew that anyway. As far as altitude is concerned, low-level operations (below about 5,000 feet) probably won't need you to get too concerned, apart from taking notice of airspeed placards and power limitations, because some of the power lost with altitude is regained with cooler temperatures. You will find that at least 75 per cent power is available to a fair height, but be careful.

Power available is reduced with height (and temperature), and propellers and rotors turn at the same speed, so, as you increase altitude, higher pitch and power settings will be required (in some helicopters, like the 500C, the rotor blades will stall before you reach engine limits). The dynamic pressure applied to the ASI is also reduced, so IAS will read less in relation to TAS, so, if you maintain a particular airspeed, your ground-speed will increase accordingly, and you will be going faster than you think. Landing and take-off distances will therefore increase, as will circuit patterns.

Larger control movements will be needed, with more lag, so controls must be moved smoothly and gradually, or the effects may cancel each other out – in a helicopter, you may find yourself on the ground well before that large handful of collective pitch even takes effect! Rotor r.p.m. will rise very quickly with the least excuse.

Your maximum weight for a given altitude (and vice versa), as well as cruising speed in relation to them both, should be known, at least approximately, in advance. You also need to know the Hover ceiling In and Out of Ground Effect (HIGE/HOGE) for any weight, so you know you can come to a low hover properly, however briefly, and recover from an unsuitable landing site (hovering should actually be minimised, partly because you can't rely on ground effect, and you have less power anyway, but also because you need to keep a little up your sleeve if the wind shifts, or you begin to lose tail rotor authority. Having said that, no-hover landings are not recommended, because of the chances of snagging the skids on something). Check the performance charts in the back of the flight manual, and start practising hovers about 1–2 feet off the ground, bearing in mind, of course, that the said charts were established by test pilots, in controlled situations.

If you allow for these effects as part of your flight planning, fine, but it's easy to get used to a particular place with a particular air density and a corresponding take-off run, base leg, etc., and you may get caught out one day when things change.

Mountain flying involves a bit of psychology, as it requires a good deal of self-control, because you will have to overcome a certain amount of fear and tension, which is not good when you really need to be relaxed on the controls, and some optical illusions.

Almost the first thing you will notice is the lack of a natural horizon, and maybe want to use the mountain tops or sides as a substitute. This, however, will probably cause a climb, or other exaggerated attitudes, and make it difficult to estimate the height of distant ground, either from a cockpit or on the ground itself, so you will find it best to superimpose a horizon of your own below the peaks. This is where using your instruments will help, both to keep attitude and give you a good idea of your height and speed (however, you're not supposed to be instrument flying!).

Close to the ground, you will get an impression of increased speed, especially near to a ridge. For example, climbing along a long shallow slope is often coupled with an unconscious attempt to maintain height without increasing power so, unless you keep an eye on the ASI, you will be in danger of gradually reducing speed – if your airspeed is reducing, then either the nose has been lifted or you're in a downdraught (downdraughts will be associated with a loss of height or airspeed for the same power).

The strength of downdraughts can frequently exceed your climbing capabilities. Strong updraughts can suspend you in mid-air with zero power – if it subsides suddenly, you will be going down faster than you

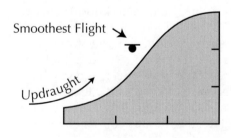

can apply it (sometimes, waggling the cyclic gently will spill the lift for you). A lack of cloud above, i.e. descending air, is a possible indication of a downdraught. Do not fight it, but guide the aircraft towards a lifting slope. A helicopter might get help from the ground cushion, but the effect will be less on a slope or grass. When valley flying, upslopes or slopes exposed to the sun can produce updraughts, so place yourself on a converging course to the line of the ridge and positioned to obtain a straight flight path two-thirds up the slope and one across, which is generally the area of smoothest flight. However, local conditions could vary this.

It's quite possible to climb on a lee slope (that is, the other side from where the wind is coming from), taking advantage of the updraught formed by stronger wind returning on itself (i.e. a backlash, which tends to occur with abrupt surfaces), but beware of exceeding power limitations as your speed is reduced.

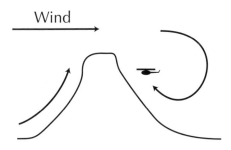

Wind

Also, there is so little room to manoeuvre if something goes wrong, or you meet someone coming the other way. If you find you have to do this, converging on the ridge line at 45° gives you the best chance of an escape route.

Similarly, try and avoid flight along lee slopes, but if you need to (because life's sometimes like that), smoothest flight will be obtained by flying as close as possible to the ground, say about six inches, so you're in the boundary layer, which is a steady movement of air close to the surface, with a vertical element. This gives even less room for error, though. If the relative humidity is high, you could watch for rotor clouds, which will indicate wind currents and turbulence. When cruising downwind, along a lee slope or not, sudden wind reversals could make the aircraft exceed V_{ne} or even take away your airspeed completely.

If bad visibility and rain are likely to be a problem, choose a more mountainous route even if the winds are a little stronger – Fohn effect will often provide a clear passage.

Winds are very important – they can increase your operational ceiling, payload, rate of climb, range and cruise speed, but they can also do the opposite, and be very difficult to predict, with formidable up- and down-draughts associated with them. There are several types of wind, which can loosely be grouped into *prevailing* or *local*, with the latter classification subdivided into other types, such as anabatic, katabatic, etc., and infinitely variable. The former is steady and fairly reliable, and start to affect you from about 6,000 feet upwards. Smoke from local fires may be used to detect wind direction, as can water, but this may only give half the story. For instance, it's not uncommon for the windsocks at each end of Banff airstrip in the Rockies to be 180 degrees at variance with each other! Indeed, upper winds can come in many directions at different levels, and are usually the opposite of lower winds. Where mountains are concerned, they also acquire a vertical element, which is actually where the boundary layer comes from.

Whitecaps on water foam at 10 m.p.h. Dark depressed puddles on water are called Bearpaws and are caused by downbursts. The most important thing to watch out for is the funnelling of wind as it progresses down a valley, so although the mean windspeed may be reported as five knots or so, you may find it as high as thirty in some places, and not necessarily coming from the expected direction.

In fact, understanding how air moves around terrain is one of the keys to good mountain flying, particularly the demarcation lines between smooth and turbulent air (in general, that moving up is smooth, and that moving down is turbulent. You can visualise the difference if you think of a waterfall, and the state of the water before and after dropping over the edge). Close to the ground, the air moves in laminar fashion, but the depth of the laminar section and the gust spread will vary considerably, depending on the nature of the surface and its heating. The laminar flow will become broken if the ground becomes rough, or there are trees, and the wind is strong. Turbulence will occur on both sides, resulting in an updraught close to the leeward side and a downdraught close to the windward side as the air is made to curl. The movement of air over a crest line has a Venturi effect, giving an increased windspeed over the summit and a corresponding reduction of pressure, which could cause your altimeter to over-read. On passing over or round an obstacle, the air may become turbulent or have formed into rolls which have a vertical or horizontal axis. Updraughts would be on the windward side and downdraughts to the leeward.

The general effect of a series of ridges is to form rolls between the crest

Wind

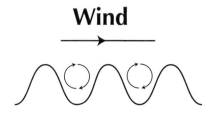

lines, possibly causing a dangerous situation where a downdraught can exist on an upslope where an updraught would normally be expected. As a result, on top of steep ridges there may be an area of nil or reverse winds which is difficult to locate on the first recce.

The vertical distance to which a mountain chain will influence the movement of air is about 3–5 times its height, changing with the windspeed. Horizontally, the effect is variable and most noticeable in stable conditions with more than twenty knots of wind, when standing waves will form, as mentioned in Chapter 8. As you know, you can recognise the existence of these by lenticular clouds, but you will also see ragged cloud around the peak. These should be avoided at all costs due to the turbulence associated with them, especially at the wind speeds that lead to their creation. In addition to shockloading, momentary loss of control may occur, not to mention coffee all over the place.

A couple of thoughts for when you're very high up: how much time it takes to get down if you have a problem, and meeting anyone else at that height on an airway who doesn't expect you.

Landing Sites

Those on peaks or crests usually present you with more escape routes than any on flanks or valley bottoms, so, wherever possible, landings should be made on ground higher than the immediate surroundings, so that you can vary the approach direction according to the wind and have a clear overshoot path.

If landing on the sides of a slope, use the windward sides; leeward sides should only be used in operational necessity – this is because wind flowing down the slope can increase its apparent angle (you need more lateral cyclic to hold the helicopter in place, and you could run out when you reduce power to lower the downwind skid). Don't forget you will not have the full effects of a ground cushion, if at all.

Where conditions allow, go as far to the windward edge as possible, to avoid suddenly finding yourself in dead or reversed airflow (as if on a lee slope) and make overshooting easier. The wind coming over the peak will have increased in speed, due to Venturi effects (remember them?) – a fifteen knot wind can easily become double that.

Finding the wind direction can be interesting if the site is bare and gives you no information, and it doesn't help that mountain flying tends to take place in high-pressure conditions, that is, where the winds are light and variable. We are now talking about local winds, caused by convection, for instance, or katabatic effects, combined with the prevailing wind influenced by the ground, or even a mixture of them all. Even a cloud shadow can increase the speed of a downflowing wind from a cold surface. You could judge its effects on the machine itself, flying round the site with a constant speed and power setting, or a constant altitude. Look at your power settings, whether the air is turbulent, your groundspeed varies or whether you drift. How much pedal you use to keep the thing straight is a good help – a lot of right pedal means the wind is from the left, for example, and a fair amount of vibration means it is behind you, but it may be a good idea, if you can't have it at the front, to get the wind off to the side that requires the use of the power pedal (the left one, in a 206), just in case tail rotor authority becomes a problem. A lot of aft cyclic would indicate a tailwind as well.

So, with constant power and airspeed (say 40–50 kt), when you rise, you will be on the windward side, and vice versa. On the other hand, you would use less power on the windward side if you kept a constant height. However, use turbulence as a guide only in lighter winds – any found in updraughts will be from mechanical effects, such as trees. Smoke grenades are often used if there's nothing else.

Aside from picking a speed which will be slow enough to detect changes and yet give enough for a margin of safety (and cope with any turbulence), when testing for wind, you should also fly about 50–100 feet below the top of the peak you want to land on, to keep yourself away from the demarcation line and reduce the chances of getting the rotors in an updraught on the leeward side. Also, keep tight in to the side, to stay inside the boundary layer.

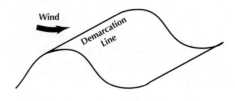

The demarcation line is where smooth air is separated from turbulent air around a peak, rather similar to that over an aerofoil. It can be horizontal as well as vertical. Above or to the side of the line, air is relatively smooth and upflowing – below, it is downflowing. It steepens as wind velocity increases (and the severity of the slope), as does the area of downflow, and moves towards the top of the hill.

Having decided on wind direction in general, you now need to look more closely at your proposed landing site. In strong wind conditions, you won't need the contour crawl at all, because it's obvious where the main body of wind is coming from, but it may have very little influence over your final approach anyway.

The basic manoeuvre is a figure-of-eight type inspection, making all turns *away* from rising ground (returning towards the site) to give you a good view all the time. You could go round in a circle, but the landing point would be out of sight most of the time.

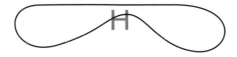

As with any other potentially dodgy landing site, you need to check for Size, Shape, Surroundings, Slope, Surface and Sun (you don't want it in your eyes). The most important, however, in this case, is Slope, as there's no point in trying at all if you can't land. You will get little idea of ground conditions if you overfly the site, so what you must do is have a look at eye-level, which results in the aptly named Eye-Level Pass (assuming it isn't surrounded by trees).

The most economical way is to start with a downwind pass, turn round and land, which is entirely possible if you know the wind direction before you start. Sometimes, though, this is not obvious at all, so just make an educated guess and fly at about 40 kt in the direction you think is down wind, very close to the site *level with your eyes*. This point is crucial. As you do so, note the reading on the altimeter (those people used to QFE may want to set it to zero), and climb up an extra hundred feet as you increase speed to about 60 kt, using the collective.

At 100 feet, turn round for another approach and repeat the process, taking note of the new groundspeed and deciding which way the wind is coming now you are closer. If there is no real difference in speed, check for vibration through the pedals, aft cyclic, etc, or anything that might indicate the wind is coming from behind.

The next step is an initial approach and overshoot, but if you have to make a circuit, you may as well do another eye-level pass and get as much information as you can.

Turn in at around 50–60 kt, taking particular note of escape routes, up and down draughts and turbulent areas. Maintain a constant angle, aiming directly for the point you wish to land on, *controlling your speed with collective* and avoiding any last-minute corrections. The idea is to keep the fuselage as level as possible, so don't move the cyclic at all, if you can help it. One reason for using the collective in this way is to minimise large control movements in the final stages, as this is a shallow approach.

Approaches

There are several schools of thought about these, but no real standard – as with many other activities involving helicopters, there is more than one 'right' answer to this one. A fairly flat, disc-loaded (shallow) one will (in theory, anyway) minimise collective for the hover, and give you the most control as you keep translational lift as long as possible, but there's very little up your sleeve at the end, and you need to be very aware of your winds, as forward speed will mask the effects right to the last minute, although it does give you a good idea of the level of your site. This assumes you remember your training and keep going forward and down, so the cyclic is ahead of the game and operating in the cleaner air in front of the machine that helps with translation. In other words, keep the rotor disc forward, so the flow of air is from front to back, especially where snow is concerned, but you shouldn't use the shallow approach with powdered snow, because you will lose sight of your landing point at the critical moment in the resulting white cloud.

You could, on the other hand, use a steeper angle, particularly if you're going into a clearing surrounded by tall trees, increasing with the wind strength, but this requires large handfuls of power and attitude changes in the final stages if you don't get ground effect, so you wouldn't try this in an underpowered piston-engined machine that really shouldn't be there in the first place – the engine may be able to cope with it, but can your tail rotor? (Leading with the pedals will help.) Anyway, since ground effect reduces your torque requirement for the hover by up to 15 per cent, if you approach in such a way that you need no more than that amount to stop, you should find your descent stopping nicely in the right place, assuming the surface is conducive to it, and depending on whether you have high skids or not. You also have some potential energy available for an escape.

Use whatever works – I generally turn in steep around 60 kt with the disc loaded as much as possible, consistent with descending at about 250 fpm – if the blades have some tension on them, they are less likely to be overstressed. Not only that, the controls are more responsive. The power used will give you a good idea of what you need in the hover, so you have an early chance to abort if you are using too much (you get to know with experience). This works, because you are using nearly the same air as at your landing point (it's a steep approach, remember), and 250 fpm reduces the thrust required to transition into the hover by about 15 per cent, i.e. much the same as for ground effect. Flare the disc without moving the fuselage if you can. 250 fpm is about 20 feet every 5 seconds, if you haven't got a VSI (altimeters usually have 20-foot segments).

Whichever you choose, if the machine wants to weather cock, let it – there's no point in using power or making a lot of effort to keep straight if you're going in the right direction anyway.

When you eventually make a final approach to land, remember that you may not be able to hover when you get there. If you do manage it, make it low, somewhere between 1 and 2 feet, and brief, one or two seconds. No-hover landings are not recommended.

In a confined area, there will be a point beyond which you're committed, so don't go beyond it until you're sure. Pick a point to aim for where you know your tail will be clear, not too far towards the end, and fly the machine in, in as smooth a movement as possible, going over the lip to the clearing at around walking pace. As for power checks, you will know very early on if you're running out (keep an eye on the torque). The size of any surrounding trees will give you a false impression of the size of the clearing, in that big trees will make it look smaller and *vice versa*. A typical clearing will have stumps and slash all over the surface – if you don't have logs to land on (and these present their own problems when they are slippery), take off as cleanly as possible, to avoid your skids getting caught in something (also be aware that tall trees will sway from your downwash). With reference to the idea of not using pedals too much, you will be able to use the cyclic to turn the machine if need be. It is always a good idea to do a clearing turn before taking off, but often you cannot, so exercise extra caution if you think someone may be behind you.

Always be prepared to break off at any time, even if you are only seconds from success. Never commit yourself till the very last moment. Short cuts don't exist with mountains -- they've been around a lot longer than you have!

Landing sites on the bottoms of valleys often have difficult access, and frequently leave no escape route once an approach has started. In this case, it's important to have safe power reserves before committing yourself. In any case, placing the aircraft downwind near to ground should be avoided, but if you have to, go low and slow when approaching downwind with a last-minute turn into wind.

In snow, try landing with the sun behind you, as the aircraft shadow will give you a useful guide to the ground slope and surface, and provide a focus for a sight picture approach. Some people use the landing light. For take-off, try not to hover too much. A jump take-off is useful if little power is available, where you get light on the skids, proceed to the edge with full r.p.m. and tip yourself over the edge. Good fun, but you should be able to hover at least for a moment, just in case your C of G is out. In a confined area, for a JetRanger, at least, you need about 15 per cent torque in hand to do a proper vertical take-off, so you're probably OK if you're hovering at about 80 per cent.

Log Pads and Platforms

Log pads are used when slopes are steep, on rough ground. The quick and easy one is a single log across the slope for your rear skid to a solid mat of smaller ones. They can be slippery! Platforms are still made from logs, but are much more refined. The problem with them all is, you can only land one way, and there may be no room to turn once you get there, so approaching with the wind in totally the wrong direction is often the only choice. In such cases, you need much more anticipation than normal, and the willingness to throw things away much earlier. Of course, you don't actually have to land, but it's often worth a try.

A typical log arrangement (note the larger one at the back).

A typical forestry landing site (look at the slash on the ground).

Summary

- ❏ Mountains take no sh*t from nobody
- ❏ Make all turns away from rising ground
- ❏ Use the eye-level pass as much as possible
- ❏ Get used to using controls for different functions, such as the collective for controlling speed and the cyclic to help with pedals
- ❏ Take off as cleanly as possible to avoid getting snagged

Night Flying

Night flying can be pleasant – there's less traffic, you tend not to go in bad weather and the air is denser, so the engine and flying controls are more responsive. However, the tendency is not to allow single-engined night flying on commercial air transport, but occasionally positioning may take place with the pilot only on board. This doesn't make it any safer, but at least reduces the number of questions in the House. Don't forget there is no VFR at night.

Searching for an overdue aircraft in low light conditions causes lots of problems, and route planning should take account of this. Otherwise, planning is much the same as for day, though there are some aspects that demand some thought. Plot your route on the chart in the normal way, but navigate with electronic aids or features that are prominent at night, such as town lighting, lighted masts or chimneys, large stretches of water (big black holes), aerodromes, motorways, etc.

One of the optical illusions you might come across is the apparent motion of a stationary object, which isn't helped by rain on the windscreen. Apart from reducing visibility, it's a particular threat when fixing your position by a single light source. When little or no light is on the surface and a prominent one comes into view, it may seem that the light is above the horizon, which could lead you to pitch into a steep attitude in keeping with the resulting false horizon.

Sometimes the effect is not much more than an uncomfortable climbing sensation even when you're straight and level, but an obscured windscreen could make objects appear lower than they really are. This will be more apparent with high-intensity runway lighting, which may also give you the same effect that actors have on stage, where they can't see the audience through the bright lighting.

The lack of normal contrast will also upset your altitude perception, making you feel further away and higher than you are. As a result, on a final approach you could find yourself too low and fast. The solution is to use every piece of sensory information you can, including landing lights and instruments. Problems will arise if several of the above factors affect you at once, especially if the landing point is sloping – this is where more frequent cross-referencing of altimeters is important.

Helicopter landing sites must be checked out in daylight on the same day as they are to be used at night. Pre-flight checks should allow for night flying – a torch must be carried and two landing lights are preferred.

Permission to enter the rotor disc is given by flashing landing lights.

In a helicopter, hovertaxi higher and slower than by day, making no sideways or backwards movements. Great care should be exercised in pointing the Schermuly flares to a safe place at all times (which is admittedly a bit difficult when they're fitted and the fuelling truck pulls up right alongside them). The flares should not be armed at this stage, but at the holding point immediately before take-off and disarmed at the same place after final approach. They should also be disarmed after reaching cruising altitude, if this is high enough.

The maximum useful height for discharging a flare is approximately 1,800 feet. Its burn time is eighty seconds, during which time it will fall about 1,500 feet. Therefore, having established autorotation after an engine failure at night, the first flare should be discharged immediately, or on passing through 1,800 feet, whichever is later. Don't bother doing it before this, as they will be useless. Due to the way the switches work, and depending on the height at which your engine stops, you may not be able to set off more than one flare before landing, but, if possible, the second should be discharged between 800 and 1,000 feet agl.

In all autorotations at night, a constant attitude approach should be used, at whatever speed you feel is comfortable, which will keep the beam from the landing light in the same position on the ground, because otherwise it will shine up into the air when you flare, from which position it's no good to you at all.

Winter Operations

(See also Adverse and Hazardous Atmospheric Conditions, in Chapter 8).

There are some benefits to flying in cold weather. The denser air means that the engine works better, so there's less danger of exceeding temperature limits, but there are hazards too, including freezing precipitation, low ceilings and cold temperatures. Rapid changes in these are typical, and it's possible to get weathered in for days at a time.

The Weather

In the Frozen North, the best conditions are in late winter or early spring, with one of the major problems being darkness. Once the snow is down, the air is quite dry and it can stay clear and cold for long periods, so you can ignore fog and the rest until it gets a bit warmer.

Above the sixtieth parallel, don't expect the weather to behave rationally at all. For example, further south, the east wind is responsible for bad flying conditions, but up there the west wind is the one to look out for, as well as large swings between low and high pressure which will often bear no relation to what the weather is doing (so don't rely on cloud shadow movement over the ground as an indicator of surface wind speed). Aside from barometric changes, look out for wind shifts, which will bring changes in wind speed and amounts of blowing snow and less visibility. Temperature changes often mean bad weather is approaching from the north – if it drops, expect ice-crystal fog, which is the low-level equivalent of contrails made at high altitude, and created by air disturbance, which could actually be from the aircraft itself (usually a helicopter). Rising temperatures will produce melting and poor visibility.

The chill factor from propellers or rotors can reduce the ambient temperature by several degrees. When it gets to below –20 °C or so, contact gloves will prevent your skin freezing when it comes in contact with cold metal, which is a more efficient conductor of heat than air is. You may also need sunglasses.

247

Always dress accordingly – in a forced landing it could be that the clothes you wear will be the only protection you have. Also, being cold when you are actually flying is a flight safety hazard – metal foot pedals will conduct heat away from your boots very quickly. Extra time for planning should always be allowed, and the pre-flight inspection should include you – being improperly dressed and making a series of short exposures will fatigue you more quickly, especially when the clothes you are wearing are bulky and awkward to move in. Maintain blood sugar levels as more calories are consumed in the cold (you need 3,000 calories a day in Norway). If the air is very dry (as in the Arctic), you will lose fluids more quickly through the usual ways, but especially breathing. Losing 10 per cent causes delirium, and a 20 per cent loss is fatal. You could try and eat snow, but the conversion to water takes more energy, so melt it first.

Preserve your machine's heat as much as possible on the ground, by covering vital areas as soon as possible after landing, not opening and closing doors too much, etc. It's very important that the machine does not get so cold that it won't start again, so you might consider starting it every couple of hours or so, which will use both fuel and battery capacity – certainly, in the average car, it takes about half an hour's driving to replace the energy taken by one start, and I'm sure it's worse with a helicopter – a depleted battery will sooner or later result in an expensive hot start. At the very least, remove the battery and keep it warm.

Special attention should also be paid to the following:

❏   That correct oil and grease is used and special equipment (like winter cooling restrictors) is fitted to keep engines warm. For Bell 206s, at least, below –40 °C, your oil must meet MIL L7808 specifications, and you will need fuel additives in all fuels other than JP4 below –18 °C. **Note:** It has been found that when visible water is present in jet fuel containing anti-icing additive, the additive will separate from the fuel and be attracted to the water. After a certain amount, thought to be about 15 per cent, the density of the new liquid changes so much that it is not identified as water, and will therefore pass through water filters, and will also not be detected by water-finding paste, which is not, in any case, intended to detect water in suspension. Where the ratio becomes 50 per cent, as much as 10 per cent of whatever is going through the filter could actually be water, which is very likely to get to the engine, since the filters on the airframe itself are not as restrictive (thanks to Northern Mountain Helicopters for that little snippet)

❏   That you use de-icing fluid if possible – scrapers do not leave pretty results. Fluid, if it's thick enough, helps prevent further ice forming (see the tables in Chapter 6). Don't forget to fit engine blanks, etc.

before using them. Bear in mind that de-icing fluids are also efficient degreasers, particularly alcohol-based ones

❏ That windscreens are defrosted (if you use a mechanical heater, keep moving it around, or it might melt the Perspex). Don't forget to have a cloth handy for wiping the windscreen from the inside when it mists up

❏ That you have proper tie-downs and pitot/engine covers, static vent plugs, etc.

❏ That the heating systems are working properly and don't allow exhaust into the cabin (if you get regular headaches, check for carbon monoxide poisoning)

❏ That de-icing and anti-icing equipment is working properly and that all breather pipes, etc. are clear of anything that could freeze

❏ That the aircraft has not been cold soaked below minimum operating temperatures. If so, there are particular (and tedious) ways of starting the machine again, which essentially involve preserving the heat from repeated attempted starts so that the engine compartment can warm up, with a ten-minute gap between each, removing and replacing engine blankets every time. Just in case you were wondering, cold soaking occurs when the aircraft, and fuel, becomes much colder than the ambient temperature, which can happen over a cold night or at high altitudes, and it becomes a problem because heat is conducted more quickly away from precipitation, making ice formation easier

❏ That all frost, ice and snow has been removed, particularly on lift-producing surfaces. If you leave hoar frost on the fuselage (only if it can be seen through), beware of flying into cloud where more will stick. It *must* be removed from places where its dislodgement could cause ingestion, e.g. engine cowlings

❏ That you check any particle separators, as water seepage may have frozen inside the engine, resulting in abnormally high N_1 and TOT readings (in a turbine).

❏ That the skids of a helicopter are not frozen to the ground. On a solid surface, you might be able to rock it using the tail. Otherwise, use the pedals with a little collective just before take-off

❏ That you unstick windscreen wipers and moving parts (including rotors and propellers) by hand, otherwise you will strain the motors

❏ That control linkages and movement are checked

❏ That pitot heat is checked by hand – don't accept a flicker on the ammeter

❏ That water drains are not frozen

❏ That carb heat operation is checked

Static becomes a problem when it's cold, as snow and air can be very dry and therefore good electrical insulators – a helicopter can retain its normal static charge quite efficiently when landing on snow (before re-fuelling, remove your survival kit, so that if it blows up you've got something to wear after you've warmed your hands in the fire).

When possible, the first start of the day should be external. With a turbine in cold weather you can expect a lower achieved N_1 before light up with abnormally high TOT peaks, eventually settling down lower than normal. Oil pressure will be slow to rise, but high after starting – do not go above ground idle until pressures are in the green and will stay there as you increase the throttle. Temperature, on the other hand, will be very slow to rise at all, and you want the transmission to be at least indicating something, which will mean the engine oil is OK as well, as it gets hot more quickly. Allow the electrics to warm up as well – even the knobs can get brittle.

In a helicopter, don't wind up too quickly in case you spin or yaw on the pad (the cyclic should be central), especially if there's an engineer on a ladder doing a leak check (be careful with rotor brakes as well). If the machine has been frozen to the ground, one skid may come free first and cause dynamic rollover. If it has not already been freed, pull collective until ready to lift and crack it free with a little controlled pedal movement, though on a big machine you might want to use engine torque for the same effect, otherwise you might bend the tail boom. You could also try gently circulating the cyclic.

Taxi slowly with caution if the taxiways are clear of snow. If not, in a helicopter, taxi higher and slightly faster then normal to keep out of the resulting snow cloud. In an aeroplane, act as if you have no brakes.

Marshallers should be well clear and move slowly themselves. If the heater is required to be off in the hover, ensure the blower is on, to help clear the windscreen.

White-out
Defined by the American Meteorological Society as 'an atmospheric optical phenomenon of the polar regions in which the observer appears to be engulfed in a uniformly white glow'. That is, you can only see dark nearby objects – no shadows, horizon or clouds, and you lose your depth perception. It occurs over unbroken snow cover beneath a uniformly overcast sky, when the light from both is about the same. Blowing snow doesn't help. Once you suspect white-out, you should immediately climb or level off towards an area where you can see things properly.

Taking off

In snow, the accepted take-off method in a helicopter is the towering type, because a normal one may produce a large snow cloud to blind air and ground crews, and a failed engine (you may be able to blow a lot of loose snow away with a little application of collective before the take-off proper). If a white-out does happen, apply maximum collective for an immediate climb and forward cyclic (i.e. no hover), keeping the ball centred and using the A/H if necessary.

After getting airborne, exercise any gear once or twice to dislodge any slush, etc. that may have stuck to the legs, to stop it freezing later. With any piston engine, use carb heat regularly and check instrument readings frequently for carb icing. Have carb heat fully on or off, but not on for prolonged periods – it increases fuel consumption markedly (see also Engine Handling, in Chapter 13 – page 270).

The Cruise

Icing itself can be experienced from sea level up to 44,000 feet, but you can expect it between 3,000 and 24,000. There are two types of icing cloud, stratus and cumulus, the most likely altitude for which will be 10,000 and 5,000 feet, respectively. The most probable icing temperatures in relation to altitude will be –3 °C at sea level, decreasing to –24 °C at 20,000 feet, but mountain wave clouds can be loaded with heavy ice at remarkably low temperatures (remember that low pressures coupled with low temperatures will cause your altimeter to read high).

The instant answer is to change altitude. If you're in freezing rain, the warm air will be above you; if in sleet, stay where you are, as you may get freezing rain above and below. Going higher may also take you out of the cloud tops, but more ice may accumulate en route underneath the wing as more of the lower side is exposed to the airflow.

When using anti-icing, take into account the inaccuracy of the temperature gauges, so if you must turn it on at four degrees, and the temperature gauge is only accurate to within two degrees, start thinking about it at six degrees.

Navigation

Sun tables are used for resetting your DI in the Arctic, with true Sun bearings taken every twenty minutes or so (assuming you can see it), based on the fact that we know where the sun will be with reference to True North for a given time, date, latitude and longitude. Having obtained the local time, look in the tables for the Sun's bearing, point the nose towards it and set the DI to True North. The two types of navigation used are *True North* and *Grid North* (to find Grid North, add your longitude to True North, and vice versa).

In True North navigation, headings have to be measured from your point of departure, using the longitude of your departure point as a base line. Every time you cross a longitude, you add a degree going east, and subtract going west, so if you cross ten longitudes en route on a heading of 090 °T, your return heading will be 280 °T, not 270 °.

Many pilots drop dye balloons en route so that they can find their way back. Others fly low enough to create a disturbance in the snow surface with their downwash, with the obvious dangers.

Landing

Helicopter landing sites should be selected with a view to pulling out of a resulting snow cloud (refer to Page 125 for fixed wing).

Carry out a normal approach, using a constant attitude with minimum changes, losing translational lift at the last minute. Aim to keep going forward and downward until a few inches above the snow, so that the downwash is always behind you, using the aircraft shadow, a smoke grenade or the landing light to provide texture to the surface. Another good trick is to use a dark-painted stake with a flag attached to it – the flag makes the stake behave like a dart, so the point goes into the snow, and acts as a wind indicator afterwards. Do not hover, and don't go beyond the marker. Try to land just as the snow cloud develops.

When you commit yourself, you will need to check the firmness of the surface, not usually a problem at a camp or something similar, as the ground crew will have done this for you. The danger lies when you're going to an unchecked site for the first time. Touch down lightly without delay, treating it as a sloping ground landing – the vibration of the heli-copter itself can cause ice to crack. Any form of load spreading is a good idea if you can take advantage of it, like landing on a log pad, although your landing gear will largely determine what you can use. As an example, a fully loaded JetRanger on floats weighs 133 pounds per square foot, whilst one on skids and bearpaws is nearer 400. Whatever you choose, it needs to be twice as thick if you intend staying overnight.

The colour of ice can be a good clue as to its suitability. White or blue is the thickest, and therefore safest, whereas black ice may have running water underneath and will be quite thin (for this reason, avoid inflows or outflows of streams or rivers). Granular, dirty-looking ice is melting. Large puddles or sheets of water are also a dead giveaway.

On snow, bounce the skids a little to see if there's a crust, but don't forget to keep your r.p.m. to flying levels until you're sure you're on firm ground. Always keep the helicopter light on the skids until passengers are clear, regardless of the surface. Don't let anyone out till you're happy.

Shut down carefully on an icy surface, anticipating ground spin. After final shutdown, fill fuel tanks to prevent condensation, always being aware of your next payload. Remove batteries if temperatures are forecast to be below –10 °C. Ensure that propellers are aligned so that water can drain out of the spinners, then you won't get a nasty surprise from lumps of ice inside causing imbalance and vibration. Try to park the machine facing the sunrise, so the Sun's warmth can help with de-icing.

Also see that the battery is fully charged before departing from base, and consider taking a spare, together with an external start cable – if the ship's battery runs down completely, the plates will become sulphated and won't actually hold a charge, so, even if you start from an external source, you won't be able to start again without one if you shut down. A good ploy is to use the external battery for operating electric fuel pumps, etc. Check that heaters, blowers, etc. work and that snow deflectors are fitted. Also, note whether tie-downs and covers are serviceable. De-icing fluid cans should always be carried, as should a small amount of food. If all this becomes too much, consider a support vehicle.

Aerial Filming and Photography

Flights should be planned so that emergencies don't put structures or persons in the vicinity at risk – you must observe the low-flying rules unless an exemption has been granted; in practice, with a helicopter, you can get one down to 200 feet for photography, but you will need to keep a record of when it was taken advantage of, as you would with any other.

If a door needs to be removed, loose articles and surplus seat belts should naturally be secured and manoeuvres carried out where possible so that the side of the aircraft without the door is uppermost; people near the open door should wear a bit more than the seat belt supplied. This point is controversial – very often a photographer will expect the door to be off, not have a mount and just use a normal seat belt. No way, José! In this case, I would insist on at least a rope around his middle loosely attached to an anchor point as well, but a professional outfit – which includes your company – will have its own dispatcher's harness. Think about it – the photographer needs to shift to get a better position, so he undoes the seat belt to help him get it! Then falls out!

A camera mount will normally be fitted by the company supplying it, but you should oversee the work and annotate the loadsheet accordingly (it should not be fitted unless there is a supplement to the flight manual covering its installation). When the mount is in place, the C of A changes to Aerial Work, therefore no passengers should be carried without an exemption, or unless they are essential to the operation, which includes the photographer. The C of G requirements will change as well. If you get a choice, sit the cameraman on your side – keeping the target inside an area in the top front part of your side window will give him the field of view required. It's important to get what's wanted first time, not only for economy, but also noise nuisance. Camera crews are famous for wanting 'just one more shot' and going 'a little lower', but don't push yourself or the machine.

Bear in mind the helicopter's height/velocity curve – the JetRanger must have at least 450 feet to regain the sixty knots it needs for a good engine-off landing (having said that, I have seen a successful one from a fifty-foot hover, which is not to suggest that you should try it).

Operations should inform local emergency services of your activities.

Aerial Survey

This is the process of photographing areas of land from varying heights, the results generally used for map making. As a result, this takes place at great heights, but it may get exciting and bring you down to 300 feet, depending on the results required. Aerial survey can give good job satisfaction, especially when you can see the results, and the target appears in every frame as requested by the surveyor.

When doing low-level work, you will be given a large-scale map with flight patterns marked on it, and you do everything by pure map reading. The pattern can be star-shaped, with sets of two or three parallel runs at angles to each other over the target. The equipment used is something like the Zeiss trilens, which will take one flat and two oblique photographs at the same time. You can work at higher levels with a 35 mm, but you will need a navigation aid, like Decca Navigator, or GPS, as close map-reading is not so easy up there.

With 35 mm at least, as the focal length decreases, depth perception increases, and required altitude decreases. Your camera can be aligned either transversely (i.e. in landscape mode), or longitudinally; the former makes for easier navigation, and should be used for overlapping strips, but the latter is more flexible. As to the results, a 28-times enlargement is used for display purposes, otherwise a contact strip with a 7x stereoscope is good enough for most work except map revision, which needs to be blown up around 6.3 times. A larger scale makes the results easier to read, but you need to fly lower and take more photos.

You need to know such things to use certain tables that give you altitudes to fly to get proper coverage, from 500 to 11,000 feet, that is, the lowest for low flying and the highest without oxygen. They also give you the speeds to be flown and the intervals between pictures, which will ultimately tell you how long you will be flying and how much to charge the customer. The book with all these in is called *Parameters and Intervals for 35 mm Aerial Photography*.

Normally use a shutter speed of 1/500 second, or 1/250 if the light is bad. Make sure the camera is set to the ASA rating of the film. Use a 28 mm lens above 4,000 feet and 35 mm for lower, and focus to infinity. A yellow filter is needed for winter black-and-white photography.

Air Testing

If you're a junior pilot, you may find yourself doing quite a bit of this, anything from just engine running to full C of A air tests, although many engineers are cleared for engine runs. The reason why junior pilots tend do them is because they're boring and regarded as a waste of time by anyone except engineers. Nevertheless, air testing demands your full concentration, and everyone due to fly in the aircraft later deserves it as well. One point to bear in mind is that the aircraft is only technically serviceable for the air test – if in doubt, insist that an engineer goes with you; if he won't fly, then don't you bother either.

The least taxing are straight engine runs. When a sliver of metal is detected in oil, there can follow an engine run for anything up to two hours or so (I have known one for five) to see if it happens again.

Then there are compass swings where you place the aircraft on a series of headings on an isolated spot well away from large hangars and other machines, while someone with a landing compass stands outside in the cold and rain taking readings. Comparison of your readings with his, adjusted with certain formulae, give the corrections.

The shorter air tests tend to concern themselves with the proper rigging of flying controls. The longer ones creep into the full-blown C of A air tests which are Extremely Official and done under strict procedures. For these, you must be on the maintenance contractor's approved list of test pilots (approved by the CAA, that is), which means having some experience of type and flying accurately.

The basic idea is to perform a series of prescribed manoeuvres (timed climbs, for instance) while an engineer takes notes of temperatures and pressures, etc. The results are plotted on performance graphs (by you) so that they can be compared against the standard figures in the flight manual, which is where you see how accurate your flying really is, when the plotted points end up all over the place instead of being in a straight line. Before you start, though, be sure that the props or rotors are as clean as you can get them, because their state will make a surprising difference on the climb figures.

Mail Flights

Newspaper flights come under this heading as well, and both involve much night flying in 'orrible weather. The main thing to watch is that the cargo is loaded properly, as it's a great temptation just to pack the thing and go, as everything is done in a hurry – there will often be a penalty clause imposed on the company if things are delayed, so you may well find commercial pressure to depart on time, even if the payload calculations aren't done and the load isn't secured properly. With reference to the load, if your aircraft weighs less than 5,700 kg, *actual* weights must be used, and, regarding security, bags must be lashed down leaving you an emergency exit *after* the load has shifted!

One last thing – you don't know what's in mailbags, so consider lining the aircraft floor with plastic, in case something nasty leaks out.

Site Support

An oil or seismic company operating out in the field needs a helicopter for various reasons. First of all, there are not likely to be any roads, or, at least, no more than forest access roads to the staging area, and people (such as slasher teams and drillers) will need to be moved, as well as their supplies, which will be anything from fuel for the drills to explosives. This will mean a lot of slinging into tiny areas at the end of a very long line – in the latter stages, you might have a carousel at the end holding six bags which you must drop carefully in precise locations, as they hold about $6,000 worth of equipment each. The expected rate for 'production long-lining', as it's called, is between 35 and 45 bags per hour. Sometimes, you will have a Dynanav machine to help, which produces a series of squares on a screen, and when they all line up, you will be on target. With this taking the strain, the slashers only have to clear a couple of trees here and there. You will be expected to do it all yourself, as manpower is short, but unless you have had specialist training in hovering out of ground effect with your head out of the side of the machine, with the doors off, or at least a bubble window, you will need help on the ground both to guide you in and to hook up the load (in practice, they won't let you near the place without it).

In the early stages, the slashers (big guys with chainsaws) will create the helipads so that you can position them in every morning for the rest of the week while they cut lines a metre wide for the surveyors to mark out for drillers, who make holes for explosive charges. When the whole lot is blown up, the vibrations are recorded and analysed in the hope of finding oil or gas. You will need to know how to work a GPS, as there is some precision involved, although, except in winter, decent map-reading skills are good enough once you know where the pads are. However, when required to fly the lines so that the surveyors can check on how the slashers are doing, you want a GPS that can pictorially show you the lines to be flown.

There will be a truck acting as a flight watch station and you will be expected to report in every time you land and take off at any helipad. The person in the truck (usually the medic) will be keeping a log of all movements and radio calls and will therefore have the most information to hand if an incident occurs. Expect also to be given an Emergency Response Plan, which is a bit of paper telling you what action to take in emergencies, together with the following information:

- ❏ Your location (Lat/Long)
- ❏ Who's in charge
- ❏ Any radio frequencies
- ❏ Police, Fire, Ambulance, Hospital
- ❏ Other helicopter companies
- ❏ Medic
- ❏ Safety, etc.

All this concerns your second job of aerial ambulance. You will have to juggle fuel loads to have enough to get to the nearest hospital, but not so much that you can't lift the patients, who, typically, will be the heaviest guys in the camp coming out of the tightest clearing with the tallest trees.

A couple of tips. Try to get fuel in the staging area, to save both dead flying time and unnecessary starting of the engine. This is not always practical, but as it saves them a lot of money, you should find them more than interested. More importantly, it stops you being away when an accident happens. A handheld radio is also useful, for keeping in touch with the ground crews when the helicopter is shut down, and for you to call for help with when you see a bear tying a large bib round its neck.

Finally, bear in mind that all your passengers will be competent professionals in their own field and will be used to helicopters, probably flying with several companies aside from yours. All they will be interested in is safe transport, so give them a smooth flight and a good briefing. Word gets around.

Aerial Ignition

The waste product from the activities of slashers, who cut down trees and undergrowth is, not surprisingly, called slash. The forestry people would normally like this to rot naturally, but many farmers disagree and burn it instead. Because it is both extensive and inaccessible, helicopters are used to set the whole lot on fire, but only in temperatures above freezing, and below 45 kt, from somewhere between 150 and 300 feet. You might carry a drip torch beneath your machine and become an instant pyromaniac. Another method is to use polystyrene balls about an inch across, full of potassium permanganate, and injected with ethylene glycol (anti-freeze) in a special dispenser and ejected from the aircraft. For maximum safety, the balls should not ignite inside ten seconds.

The Heli-Torch uses propane and fuel, and your maximum speed is whatever you can control, after flight manual limitations, so that burning fuel reaches the ground at about 15 kt. If you go too fast, say, over 20 kt, the mixture will be too lean and the fuel will all be used up before reaching the ground. If you fly greater than translation, the fuel will recirculate and you will get a poor pattern, aside from damaging the equipment.

Aerial ignition is also used in fire suppression.

Aerial Harvesting

Removing tree crowns or cones from standing trees with a helicopter, for monitoring the progress of growth, insect or disease infestation, and pesticide or fertiliser trials. There are two ways of doing it. The first involves an unmanned device underneath the machine which uses the downwash to separate foliage from the tree, which ends up in the device. A *Branch Collector* cuts branches from the main stem, a *Rake* collects cones by stripping them from the foliage with stationary or moving tines, and a *Top Collector* takes away the upper portion of the tree crown.

The second is really aerial clipping, since it is done by someone from the rear door with a battery-powered electric chainsaw while you hover near the top of the tree. Whatever is cut ends up in the helicopter, so there will be a barrier between the two parts of the cabin so that you don't get a bump on the head. Believe it or not, this was originally done with a steel box with retractable doors, the edges of which cut the tree as the box was lifted up from it, but it proved to be slow and cumbersome, and strained the equipment too much.

As well as the clipper, there will be a navigator on board to tell you where to fly, since you will be quite busy enough at that level. Don't expect to fly more than 6 hours in a day, or in wind over 15 kt. The aircraft itself must be on low skids, with no bearpaws, or items that can get caught. You yourself must be an ace at long-lining, with at least 1,000 hours on type.

Start with a hover somewhere between 25 and 50 feet above the trees concerned, using up to 85 per cent torque, so that you've got a reserve. Keep them between your right shoulder and just forward of the front edge of the front door. Then descend to within eye level of the target, always being aware that trees sway in the wind and you can either get hit by another or hit something else as you try and keep up with the tree you are working with (your downwash won't be helping). Its top should be level with your eyes or the cabin roof, slightly forward of your right shoulder. Don't fixate on the tree top, but on something else that isn't moving. Slide the skid in between the branches until the stem of the tree is against it, using a little collective just before contact. Then lower the collective so that the skid rests against the lower branches to keep it steady for the clipper, who shouldn't take more than a minute to do what's required. Before you move away, check that the skid isn't caught on anything, then increase collective and use left cyclic to pull you away gently. Don't move directly sideways, as upwards slanting branches near the tops of trees could snag you.

A couple of points to watch. If you bend a tree beyond the cyclic stops, when it rebounds you will be out of limits as you try to correct things. You will do best to keep level and use left cyclic with the rebound. Don't go straight up or you might get dynamic rollover. Trees with bent tops indicate heavy crops and should be avoided, because they will have too much momentum. If you have to work round a tree top, hover away and assume a new position every time rather than spinning round it.

Avalanche Control

This involves applying explosive charges to selected places in an avalanche start zone, so you need permission to carry Dangerous Goods. There is some precision involved, and there will be a qualified blaster (bombardier) on board to dispense the explosives, who will have a body harness secured to the helicopter in two places – it must not have a quick-release mechanism. The doors will be off, so you need to dress properly and watch your speeds and C of G, especially lateral. In fact, the weight of explosives and people required for the job must not be more than 75 per cent of the useful payload. Ski baskets, or any other restrictions to dropping, must be removed beforehand.

The area should naturally be closed. Primers must be prepared before entering the aircraft and pull-wires carried separately – no primers are to be adjusted inside, and they are to remain in the same container at all times. Only the explosives to be used on a particular sector should be carried, and they must be pushed away from the bombardier's seat position where you can see them, not above, behind or below. You have 90 seconds after dropping the first bomb to do the rest before you must pull away to a safe area for observation. If there is no assistant, that is, just you and the bombardier are on board, you can only drop three charges anyway.

Wildlife Capture

Normally done with a pilot and gunner (who has a net gun), but there may also be an assistant (called a mugger) as well. If there isn't, and you have to do the job instead, you should only handle the head of the animal, so that you don't get injured unnecessarily. Your briefing should include getting in and out of the helicopter whilst in the hover.

A slightly forward C of G is preferable. Keeping the rotor disc as flat as possible, and avoiding tight turns, you should approach the animal from behind, slightly away from the skid and forward of the gunner, almost definitely with a sideslip. Don't fixate on the animal, but keep it in view with your peripheral vision – you must maintain situational awareness. The reason for the flat disc is to keep it out of the line of fire, and high-G turns will upset the gunner's aim.

Sometimes the wildlife will be seals, so you have to wear life jackets and dodge the waves when they get a bit big (actually, sometimes you have to use the waves to get you back up in the air again).

Helicopter Instrument Flying

This is much the same as for fixed wing, but there are a couple of differences worth noting. Firstly, thrust and lift come from the same source, that is, the main rotors, so you can have different attitudes from what you expect when climbing, descending, or in level flight, so you need to learn particular power settings for particular stages of flight to do it correctly. These, of course, are controlled by the collective and displayed on the torquemeter. *The AI indicates fuselage and not disc attitude*, so does not always tell you what the aircraft is actually doing – you could be nose-up and still descending at 60 kt, so more cross-checking with other instruments is required than with a fixed-wing aircraft. Put another way, while it is still important, the AI loses a little of its distinction.

Also, the ability to fly at low speed, say, below 60 kt, means that the pitot-static instruments become less reliable. You also get reduced stability, which is why there is a minimum IMC control speed (V_{mini}), below which you shouldn't go into cloud, as well as minimum speeds with one engine out, should you have two.

Having said all that, the *attitude + power = performance* equation is still valid.

13

Techie Stuff

An ops manual, despite the adoption of the flight manual as part of its structure, will need a technical section dealing with aspects peculiar to the company's types of aircraft (that is, Part B). You may feel you've been taught enough of it already, but things like oil and fuel requirements and specimen performance data will still need to be emphasised. Also, the checklists in the usual standard of owner's manual are nowhere near good enough for Commercial Air Transport, so these will need to be expanded, too (they never seem to grasp the idea of battery saving, as the master switch is often the first thing to be switched on and left on for the next ten minutes while you check everything before starting an engine).

Whilst not too much information should be duplicated between the flight and operations manuals, enough ought to be included that may be relevant in flight, with anything of a detailed descriptive nature left in the flight manual. This is important in smaller aircraft with no room for a complete library up front.

Topics to be covered include crosswind take-offs on ice-covered runways, action not included in checklists or drills, special handling techniques and other stuff that needs to be brought to your attention. Try placing emergency drills on different-coloured pages.

If you haven't thought of it already (because most pilots tend to be mechanically minded), it will be well worth your while digging a little deeper into engineering principles and practice in general. Not only will it help you stay alive, but you get more out of engineers when you speak their language. Having said that, engineers speak in a very precise manner – to give you a flavour, try reducing the description of a piston to just three words (one suggestion is a *sliding, gastight plug*).

Just for fun, here is a selection of replies to pilots' comments on returning from test flights in the USA. They are known as SQUARKS and are left for maintenance crews to sort out before the next flight.

Test flight OK, except auto-land a bit rough
Auto-land not installed on this aircraft

DME volume unbelievably loud
Volume set to a more believable level

Friction locks cause throttle levers to stick
That's what they are there for

Number 3 engine missing
Engine found on right wing after brief search

Target radar hums
Reprogrammed target radar with the words

Aircraft handles funny
Aircraft warned to straighten up and be serious

Left inside main tyre almost needs changing
Almost replaced left inside main tyre

Evidences of leak on right main landing gear
Evidence removed

IFF inoperative
IFF always inoperative in OFF mode

Something loose in cockpit
Something tightened in cockpit.

Leading Edge Protective Tape

Protective tape is used on leading edges of rotor blades (and some propellers) to protect against wear and tear from dust or precipitation. A partial loss of it can dramatically affect aerodynamic efficiency, resulting in substantial increases in power when hovering. It will also cause a slight loss in r.p.m. during autorotation.

The most likely time for the stuff to come off is during or after flight through rain, which is just when it's needed, so check it before take-off. If it looks like wearing out, remove or repair it before the next flight, removing an equivalent amount from each blade, as it may have also been used for balancing. It will be put on in short strips of anything between 6 and 18 inches (so you're not flying with a great length of it hanging off) which should be removed as a whole – don't just cut bits away.

If tape comes off in flight (with a distinctive 'chuffing' sound, sometimes accompanied by vertical bounce), reduce power and speed and make gentle manoeuvres while landing. If it comes off before landing, just carry on.

Propeller Overspeed

If engine control is lost and r.p.m. rise above the maximum, reduce power, raise the nose and hope reduced airspeed gets things under control. If the CSU is not working, feathering immediately may leave you with a shutdown engine in fully-fine pitch, though it does depend on the aircraft (Doves, apparently, have a separate feathering motor).

If you're not quick enough, damage could be caused from over-revving, and the feathering system may not cope with the extreme r.p.m. *Do not* attempt to unfeather the engine but land as soon as possible.

Failure of Feathering System

Most feathering systems don't function below a certain low r.p.m. (typically 700–1,000), so you don't start with the blades feathered. However, there are further implications – if your engine fails through a major mechanical fault, you may not be able to catch the propeller quickly enough. The usual reaction is to close the throttle of the dead engine first, so opening it a little may increase the r.p.m. for feathering to take place properly. Keeping your speed up may help as well.

If the propeller fails to feather, reduce your airspeed to a minimum (but not below scheduled engine-out climb speed) and allow the r.p.m. to stabilise as low as possible. Try again. If feathering still fails, try to reduce speed so that the rotation ceases, which will cause less of a drag penalty than a windmilling prop, even if it has stopped in fine pitch.

Not only will your single-engined climb-out performance be affected, directional controllability will be, too, though you should be OK down to V_{mca}.

Engine Failure/Autorotations in Helicopters

Engine failure in a helicopter is detected by a noticeable decrease in engine noise (!), yaw in the same direction as blade rotation, loss in height/speed and ENGINE OUT audio/visual warnings (if fitted), because there's so much noise you can't tell whether the engine's still going anyway. While speed is of the essence, there is usually time enough to verify actual engine failure by looking at the instruments while you're reducing to autorotation speed to maintain height, certainly in a Bell, unless you're very heavy in a high-hover situation, such as long-lining, where you have no time to do anything other than dump the pole.

For all practical purposes, your gliding distance is about equal to your height, or, put simply, what you can see slightly above the bottom of the windscreen. If you keep your landing spot in the same place in that area, your speed watch needn't be so critical (remember sight picture approaches?). Loss of revolutions at the entry into autorotation is more important – a higher angle of attack from the new relative airflow as air rushes up through the rotors will cause enough drag to slow the rotors drastically, especially if your weight is high or air density low, meaning that your blades will be at a higher pitch angle anyway.

Reducing pitch to compensate will, of course, increase the rate of descent, at which point the inner 25 per cent of each blade is stalled, and the outer 30 per cent is providing a small drag force. The best lift/drag ratio in autorotation is obtained at best endurance speed, whatever that is (check the manual, but most helicopters are designed for a speed of about 45 kt).

Try to establish the cause of engine failure – if it's fire, close the throttle immediately, but, if not, consider initially closing it only to idle speed (or not closing it at all), as the engine may be able to provide enough power to enable you to downgrade the incident from catastrophe to mere disaster. The discussion that follows will consider it as being fully closed.

Several factors may affect your rate of descent, such as gross weight, air density, airspeed and rotor r.p.m. Changing airspeed, though, is about the only one you have direct control over that gives any flexibility, as the r.p.m. must remain in a small band to be effective – remember that only the portions of the blades between 25 and 70 per cent of their length provide any lift. In any case, every 1 per cent reduction in rotor r.p.m. results in a 2 per cent loss of thrust, which will be the same as if somebody threw that weight in the back of your machine. The other significant point about keeping your r.p.m. up concerns the tail rotor, which runs at a fixed speed relative to the main rotors – if they go slower, the tail rotor does too, and loses some of its effectiveness.

Changes in airspeed can have dramatic effects on the rate of descent. If the recommended IAS is 60 knots (fairly common), for instance, speeds of either 30 or 100 could increase RoD to as much as 3,000 f.p.m., because the lift vector is reduced when you alter a relatively horizontal rotor disc, so if you want to change your angle of approach, don't forget to use the collective to compensate. Turns will have a similar effect, but the results will be worse if pedals are used. Steep turns are good ways of losing height if you find yourself overshooting – if you are seated on the right, turn right first, then go left, so that you have the best possible view through the windscreen, and you don't get the instrument bulkhead in the way on finals. If you are on the left, go the other way.

Each helicopter will have an optimum rate of descent for the longest range. Best endurance speed will give the best lift in autorotation (i.e. minimum sink). Where winds or density altitudes are high, expect to increase speed a little, but decrease it when winds are calm or density altitudes are low. If you deliberately decrease the r.p.m. to increase range (and possibly lessen the rate of descent), don't forget to build them up again for landing.

Don't worry about the avoid curve in autorotation, either – this is only a function of the pitch angle of the blades, so if you're in flat pitch it doesn't exist.

Having entered autorotation:

- ❏ Select landing spot
- ❏ Transmit MAYDAY
- ❏ Warn passengers
- ❏ Turn off electrics, but *not* battery or radio (for the intercom)
- ❏ Close throttle if required

Plan to slightly overshoot your landing spot, and when about seventy feet from the ground, use rearward cyclic to slow down vertically and horizontally. The amount of flare is proportional to your speed and increases the total lift reaction (which stops the sink) and shifts it to the rear (which stops forward movement). Continue the flare progressively, to be at the correct speed for landing at ten feet, applying collective as flare effect decreases to check the descent more positively. As the flare ends, and the kinetic energy of the rotors is used when the collective is raised, the airflow through the rotors is reversed, assisting you to level, (not in an AS350 – it levels itself), ready to cushion the landing as you apply collective pitch. Try and stop any drift or yaw until the aircraft has stopped. This is where correct use of airspeed during the descent will have had the most beneficial effects: as the kinetic energy stored in the blades is what slows you down, it follows that any you have to use to slow an unnecessarily fast rate of descent is not available for the final stages of touching down.

If you are in a vertical autorotation, there is a phenomenon known as dynamic stall that will help, where an aerofoil that is rapidly stalled can produce double the normal lift, just for a moment, because the breakup of the boundary layer on top is delayed for a short while, if indeed you don't actually create a little vortex along it that improves lift even further. Do not try to gain speed, as you will split the lift vector and increase your rate of descent, just pull max collective very quickly.

Anyway, try not to let the rotor revolutions drop below about 70 per cent, as head resonance in some helicopters may cause ripples in the tail boom – but protect yourself before the aircraft. With high skids, land more slowly because of the couple between the body and the skids when they contact the ground – but again, you are more important than the machinery.

After landing:

- ❏ Close throttle
- ❏ Close fuel valve
- ❏ Turn off battery
- ❏ Evacuate aircraft
- ❏ Follow the accident procedure in Chapter 11

Ground Resonance

In flight, most parts of a helicopter vibrate at their own natural frequency. On the ground, these vibrations collect through the landing gear. If the gear's natural vibration matches that of the main rotor, every time a blade rotates, the present vibrations receive another reflected pulse to increase their amplitude, which can cause the aircraft to tip over and be destroyed. Peculiar to some helicopters, with fully articulated rotors, this is indicated by an uncontrollable lateral oscillation increasing rapidly in sympathy with rotor revolutions. It could be caused by blades not being in balance, unequal tyre pressures or finger trouble, but will only occur if the gear is in contact with the ground.

It's best avoided by landing or taking off as cleanly as possible, but, if it does occur, the helicopter must either be lifted off or the collective lowered fully with throttle closed.

Dynamic Rollover

This occurs when your helicopter has a tilted thrust vector with respect to the C of G, commonly encountered with some side drift when you have one skid or wheel on the ground acting as a pivot point, but you can also get a problem when your lateral C of G falls outside the width of the skids or wheels – every object has a static rollover angle, to which it must be tilted for the C of G to be over the roll point, for most helicopters being 30–35 degrees. As your lateral cyclic control at that point is a lot less effective than if you were actually hovering, because it is rotating, not around the C of G, but around the rollover point, you have less of a chance to get out of trouble, and the only effective control is through the collective.

Dynamic rollover is at its worst with the right skid on the ground (with a counter-clockwise main rotor) and with a crosswind from the left, with left pedal applied and with thrust about equal to the weight (i.e. hovering). It is possible for the machine to roll upslope if you apply too much cyclic into the slope, or downslope if you apply too much collective, enough to make the upslope skid rise too much for the cyclic to control.

The best way not to get into trouble is avoid tail winds, and land and take off vertically.

Tail Rotor Failure

When the tail rotor fails, it will be in varying degrees of positive, neutral or negative pitch, depending on what you were doing at the time. Unless it's a drive failure, the chances are that you won't discover the problem until you change your power setting, as it's very unlikely you'll be flying along in the cruise, for instance, and find a pedal forcing itself completely over to one side, as simulated by instructors on test flights, unless you have a motoring servo or similar, in which case your problem is hydraulics, and not the tail rotor, although the effect might be the same. More typically, you will be in a descent, climb, cruise or hover, with the pedals where they should be and won't move when you want to do something else. When descending, for example, in the AS350, you will have more left pedal (more right in the Bell 206), both of which will aid the natural movement of the fuselage against the main rotors. The pedals would be in a neutral position if you were flying at medium to high speeds, and the power pedal would be forward in high-power situations, like hovering. In any case, the spread between the pedals is not likely to be more than a couple of inches either way, certainly in a 206 – try an autorotation properly trimmed out to see what I mean. You will notice the same in the hover.

In fact, landing with a power pedal jammed forward should be easier to control, since the tail rotor will already be in a position to accept high-power settings. If the pedals jam the other way, look for more speed because there will not be enough anti-torque thrust available.

A *drive failure*, on the other hand, will cause an uncontrollable yaw, and a possible engine overspeed, so the immediate reaction should be to enter autorotation, keeping up forward speed to maintain some directional control, which is difficult in the hover, if you have time. As speed is reduced towards touchdown, you will yaw progressively with less control available in proportion, so it may be worth trying to strike the ground with the tailwheel or skid first (if you've got one), which will help you to keep straight. According to the JetRanger flight manual, you should touch-down with the throttle fully closed, as you would if the failure occurs in the hover. This is to stop further yaw when pitch is pulled to cushion the landing.

However, in other circumstances, such sudden movements may not be best. If you can reduce the throttle and increase collective, this would reduce the effect of the tail rotor at the same time as keeping the lift from the main rotors, as does beeping down to the bottom of the governor range (difficult in most AS350s or Gazelles, where the throttle is not on the collective). Remember, the tail rotor's function is to counteract torque, so if you give it less work you will be more successful.

Otherwise, you might find a power and speed combination that will maintain height until you find a suitable landing area, then you've got as much time as your fuel lasts to solve the problem. In the hover, try a combination of closing the throttle and pulling collective, and don't forget that the cyclic can be useful, enabling you to fly sideways to create drag from the tail boom and vertical stabiliser, for example. It's the sort of situation where it pays to be creative sometimes. After all, the aim is to walk away, not necessarily to preserve the machine.

If you want to run-on for landing, get the wind off to the opposite side of whatever pedal is jammed, so that the fuselage is crabbing, and control your descent with a combination of throttle and collective, applying more of the latter as the throttle is closed just before touchdown, so that you run on straight. This is not always best, as applying power to an already overstressed tail rotor may make this worse, and some helicopters (such as twins) won't let you use the throttle as precisely as that. Not only that, you may well be so busy that worrying about minor details like the wind's exact quarter will be the last thing on your mind.

Loss of Tail Rotor Effectiveness

Sometimes known as *tail rotor breakaway*, or a stall, which is not strictly correct, as thrust is still being produced – it's just not enough for the task in hand. It shows up as a sudden, uncommanded right yaw (with North American rotation), and has amongst its causes high density altitudes and power settings, low airspeeds and altitudes and vortex ring. Your helicopter will be more susceptible to it if the tail rotor is masked by a tail surface, like a vertical fin, and it can be especially triggered by tail and side winds (this is actually a significant reason for maintaining main rotor revolutions – as the tail rotor runs at a fixed speed in relation to it, lower NR will reduce tail rotor effectiveness in proportion). Recovery in this case comes from a combination of full power pedal, forward cyclic and reduction in collective, or autorotation. Prevention lies in keeping into wind and always using the power pedal (left in a 206 or one with similar blade rotation). If you use the other one, not only will the fuel governor ensure that the aircraft will settle after a short time (using the power pedal by itself makes it climb), but a large bootful of the power pedal in a fast turn the other way will create a large torque spike.

Hydraulic Boost Failure

Indicated by feedback forces in the controls, which will be negligible when they are held in a fixed position. Hopefully, your failure will be just from fluid leakage, but it could be a hydraulic pump drive failure – in a JetRanger, this will be confirmed by looking at the NR gauge, as the pump is driven from the transmission. Note that the hydraulic CB sometimes relates to the *switch* and not the system. Reduce forward speed and control inputs to a minimum, making necessary movements at a rate of travel not faster than one full displacement, stop to stop, per second.

Overpitching

In a helicopter, overpitching is where the rotor revolutions are too low to maintain flight, giving the impression of 'labouring'. It's the nearest equivalent to stalling and is commonly caused by being overweight for the particular conditions. Reduce power to maintain r.p.m.

Mast Bumping

This happens on helicopters with teetering rotor heads where cyclic input occurs with a low G-loading on the head, causing it to exceed flapping limits and strike the mast, with disastrous consequences (like the head falling off). Reduced or zero-G conditions should be avoided.

Engine Handling

Pulling full power just because it's there is not always a good idea. The limits in the flight manual may be there for other reasons – for example, the transmission might not be designed to take that much, which is why you can't go faster than 80 kt in a JetRanger when pulling more than 85 per cent torque (actually, in this case, the transmission ends up in a strange attitude). Excessive use of power will therefore ruin your gearbox well before the engine (and will show up as metal particles in the oil).

Maximum Continuous Power is the setting that may be used indefinitely, but any between that and maximum power (usually shown as a yellow arc on the instrument) will only be available for a set time limit.

While I'm not suggesting for a moment that you should, piston engines will accept their limits being slightly exceeded from time to time with no great harm being done. Having said that, the speed at which the average Lycoming engine disintegrates is about 3,450 r.p.m., which doesn't leave you an awful lot of room when it runs normally at 3,300! Turbines, however, are less forgiving than pistons and give fewer warnings of trouble because of the closer tolerances to which they are made. This is why regular power checks (once a week) are carried out on them to keep an eye on their health. The other difference is that damage to a piston engine caused by mishandling tends to affect you, straight away, whereas that in a turbine tends to affect others down the line.

In a turbine-engined helicopter, power used is indicated by the torquemeter, which, in a twin, means mast torque, or the drag of the rotor multiplied by the distance from the rotor hub, so a torquemeter measures drag on the rotor blades. In this respect, power is regarded as the output of the engine (loosely equivalent to fuel flow, if you ignore inefficiencies), which itself is the product of torque multiplied by rotor revolutions and a constant for each helicopter type. If power is fixed, therefore, and the rotor slows down, torque measured will increase because of the extra drag from the higher angle of attack.

In a piston, you get this from manifold pressure combined with r.p.m. Too much manifold pressure relative to r.p.m. will cause overboosting (the same as labouring a car engine by being in too high a gear), which will cause detonation, or pre-ignition. This in turn will unnecessarily increase the operating temperature, but the real harm to the engine is caused by the shock waves that result from the piston getting the effects of the power stroke when it doesn't expect it. Prevention of pre-ignition (or 'pinking' in a car, the same thing) is done by adding substances to the fuel.

The 'LL' in 100LL stands for low lead, but there is still about four times more than is needed. As well as the lead (in the form of TEL – tetra-ethyl lead), a scavenging agent (ethylene dibromide, or EDB) is also added to ensure that the lead is as far as possible in a vaporised form, ready to be expelled from the cylinder with other exhaust gases. Unfortunately, this is not totally successful, but the results are best at high temperatures and worst at low ones.

These unwanted extras result in fouling of spark plugs, heavy deposits in the combustion chamber, erosion of valve seats and stems, sticking valves and piston rings and general accumulation of sludge and restriction of flow through fine oil passages (come to think of it, expensive fuel may well be just as bad as the cheap stuff in your car).

You obviously need less priming to start a warm piston engine than a cold one, but you may still need a little even where you would not expect to, especially with fuel-injected types, where the feed pipes lie across the top of the engine and consequently get warm, with the fuel inside them evaporating nicely, so you need a short burst of pressure to ensure the presence of fuel in the first place.

Leaning makes the engine run hotter and give more power for less fuel; it also improves scavenging and hence wears the engine less. Engines originally designed for 80.87 and now using 100LL will benefit from leaning on the ground to avoid lead build-up. A 112 h.p. aircraft cruising at 4,000 feet and 85 knots will burn 5 gallons an hour when rich, but only 4.5 when leaned, giving a range of 116 miles as opposed to 100 – a saving, or an increase, of 16 per cent. Not only that: at height, the engine will not work at all if the ratio of fuel to air is not correct.

Apart from sympathetic handling, the greatest factor in preserving engine life is temperature and its rate of change. Over- and under-leaning are detrimental to engine life, and sudden cooling is as bad as overheating – chopping the throttle at height causes the cylinder head to shrink and squeeze the piston with the obvious results, the thermal shock and extra lead is worth about £100 in terms of lost engine life. In other words, don't let the plane drive the engine, but rather cut power to the point where it's doing a little work. This is because the reduced power lowers the pressure that keeps piston rings against the wall of the cylinder, so oil leaks past and glazes on the hot surfaces, degrading any sealing obtained by compression. The only way to get rid of the glaze is by honing, which means a top-end overhaul. For the same reasons, a new (or rebuilt) engine should be run in hard, not less than 65 per cent power, but preferably 70–75 per cent, according to Textron Lycoming, so that the rings are forced to seat in properly. This means not flying above 8,000 feet density altitude for non-turbocharged engines. Richer mixtures are important as well. You should open the engine compartment after shutting down on a hot day, as many external components will have suddenly lost their cooling. With some turbine engines (like on the AStar), you have to keep track of the number of times you fluctuate between a range of power settings because of the heat stress.

For better economy, lean-off slightly in the climb, but never take off with reduced power or too lean a mixture. It may save fuel, but the extra is needed to cool the engine at low speeds. When levelling in the cruise, the combination of increased IAS and throttling back cools the engine rapidly, so close the cowl flaps beforehand. Don't use the cowl flaps as airbrakes, either, but to warm the engine after starting and to cool it after landing (allow the temperatures to stabilise before shutting down, especially on turbocharged aircraft).

In the cruise, better fuel consumption may be obtained at slower speeds and lower power settings, at the cost of extended running time, so you might not really save that much. For example, leaning to ten degrees lean-of-peak exhaust gas temperature (EGT), without exceeding the maximum, loses about five knots. Typically, EGT probes are fitted to one cylinder of the engine, which is not necessarily the one that reaches peak temperature first, even though it may end up as the hottest, so a margin of twenty-five degrees rich of peak may still not be enough to stop another cylinder from getting too close to peak for comfort, or even lean of peak.

Don't forget to enrich mixtures before increasing power when at peak EGT or when increasing to more than 75 per cent power. Move the engine controls slowly and smoothly, particularly with a turbocharged engine. Harsh movements that (on older engines) will result in a cough and splutter and having no power can be embarrassing.

Jets, of course, need different handling from propellers, which are only efficient up to certain speeds, below which jets use too much fuel relative to the work done – the airstream provided by a propeller is of a large diameter and moves at approximately the same speed as the aircraft it relates to. The output from a jet engine, on the other hand, is hot and thin, and very much faster, which is why it's fuel-inefficient (it's also noisy, and like driving a car in permanent high gear). At higher speeds, say above 350 kt, jets are best only because propellers don't work at all. Of course, you could have a fast airframe, like Concorde, but that just introduces complexity.

Turbo-props are a good solution, but your top speed is still limited, hence the fanjet, which is simply a propeller (with lots of blades) enclosed in a duct, so that you don't waste power in the shape of air that spills centrifugally out of the sides. This not only gives better thrust (actually, more than double), but also provides cooling. They are called 'bypass' engines because the bulk of the air bypasses the core of the engine. The end result is a large, relatively slow-moving column of cold air enclosing a thin, hot and fast exhaust, which reduces noise. The back end of the engine, unfortunately, runs a lot hotter, even white-hot in the early days.

Although many flight manuals state that as soon as an engine is running without stuttering it's safe to use it to its fullest extent, try warming up for a few minutes before applying any load, at least until you get a positive indication on the oil temperature (and pressure) gauges. Even better, warm it before start-up, particularly when it's cold.

Similarly, many engines have a rundown period which must be strictly observed if you want to keep them for any length of time. As engines get smaller relative to power output, they have to work harder. Also, in turbines, there are no heavy areas to act as heat sinks, like the fins on a motorcycle, which results in localised hotspots which may deform, but are safe if cooled properly, with the help of circulating oil inside the engine (75 per cent of the air taken into a turbine is for cooling purposes).

If you shut down too quickly, the oil no longer circulates, which means that it may carbonise on the still-hot surfaces, and build up enough to prevent the relevant parts from turning. This coking up could seize the engine within fifty hours or less. Aside from cooling, oil keeps parts from grinding against each other, and cleanses them. As many engines don't have oil filters, it makes sense to change it at the recommended periods, or even more frequently – every twenty-five hours has been suggested.

While on the subject of oil, an engine that is not used enough develops corrosion very quickly on the inside, and rust flakes, which are very abrasive, will circulate when the engine is started, which is why you have to change the oil even when you don't fly a lot. Another reason is an increased water content, which will have an acidic effect once it mixes with the byproducts of combustion, which is why you should just pull the propeller through several rotations if you cannot fly. The most wear takes place in the first seconds of a cold start, after the oil has been allowed to settle. Priming will wash whatever is left off the cylinder walls, so don't do too much, and maintain the minimum revolutions to let it circulate.

Synthetic oils have come from turbine oil development, but they have one drawback, in that the sludge tends to centrifuge out inside the dome of a constant-speed propeller and make cycling a bit difficult. They also hold contaminants longer.

Many flight manuals recommend not changing brands of oil (I'm thinking of the JetRanger), but if you check with the engine manufacturer's manual (in this case Allison), you may find that it is permitted on a top-up basis: that is, if you already have one brand in there, just start using the new stuff until eventually the contents change completely. Do not drain your present oil and replace it in one go, because oils have different cleaning characteristics – your new brand may be more efficient and leave bits of coke and carbon floating around that could cause a seizure. However, this is something you should discuss with your maintenance people.

Carb Icing

Even on a warm day, if it's humid, carburettor icing is always a danger, especially at small throttle openings where there's less area for the ice to block off in the first place. The difference between the OAT and the temperature in the Venturi can be anywhere between 20 and 30 °C, so icing (in an R22, anyway) can be expected even when the OAT is as high as 21 °C (70 °F). Icing could even come from water in the fuel precipitating out, and impact icing. However, it usually arises from the action of the Venturi in the throat, just before the butterfly valve, which regulates the amount of fuel into the engine. You will remember the Venturi's purpose is to accelerate airflow by restricting the size of the passageway, which has the effect of reducing the pressure and pulling the fuel in. Unfortunately, this process also reduces the temperature, as does the fuel vaporisation, hence the problem. In fact, the vaporisation (and cooling) can carry on most of the way to the engine cylinders, causing the problem to persist. With smaller engines, use full settings for every application – that is, carb heat on or off, avoiding the continuous use of hot air, because it not only reduces air density (less power), but keeps the fuel consumption down. OGE hover performance charts usually assume the carb air is cold.

If ice is present, rough running may increase as melted ice goes through the engine. Also be careful you don't get an overboost or too many r.p.m. when you reselect cold. Of course, aeroplanes have some advantage if the engine stops from carb icing, as the propeller keeps the engine turning, giving you a chance to do something about it. In a helicopter, because of the freewheel drive which allows the machine to autorotate, the practice of only selecting hot air when you actually get carb ice is not such a good idea – usually, a gauge is used with a yellow arc on it, signifying the danger range. Use carb heat as necessary to keep out of it. The other peculiarity with regard to helicopters is that they tend to use power as required on take-off, whereas aeroplanes use full throttle. This makes them more vulnerable, as the butterfly opening is smaller, and is particularly apparent on the first take-off of the day, when the engine and induction system are still cold. If it is filtered, your carb heat may be used to preheat the induction system during the engine warm-up.

Most of these problems are avoided with fuel injection, where the fuel is metered to the engine according to its power requirements, automatically taking air density into account. Ice is not formed because there is no Venturi to cause temperature drops. The only control you have (apart from the throttle) is idle cut-off (ICO). In fact, the biggest problem with fuel-injected engines is blocked jets.

Aircraft Husbandry

A company can tell how well its pilots look after their aircraft by the amount it spends on servicing – the lower the costs, the better they are. Aircraft should not be parked on soft or sloping ground, and suitable chocks should be placed under the main gear wheels of aeroplanes. They should be parked into wind whenever possible, with the nosewheel in line with the fore and aft axis. Control locks and covers should be used whenever convenient (especially when wind speeds are expected to be high, in which case consider picketing as well), and all doors, hatches and windows should be closed when the aircraft is left unattended.

Anti-collision lights should be switched on immediately before starting engines, but it is suggested (like the military) that this be done immediately the aircraft is occupied, always having due regard for the capabilities of your battery. Speaking of which, always leave the anti-col light switches on when leaving the aircraft, because that lets you know you've left the master switch on.

Engine ground runs and taxiing should only be carried out by authorised pilots or engineers, who must ensure there is adequate clearance when taxiing near obstructions. Where space is limited, a marshaller should be used, but remember you are still responsible if you hit anything.

Don't forget the usual taxiing procedures, such as not using the brakes too much, or using aircraft momentum when turning corners to save using the engine. Engine runups (e.g. on power checks) should be done into wind for better engine cooling and least strain on the prop, and away from loose items on the ground, to protect both people behind and the prop itself, as the airflow around the tips will tend to pull bits of gravel, etc. towards it, and cause damage.

Lastly, let me mention oil cans, which come sealed so that you need a special implement to open them. Actually, you can use a screwdriver, but whatever you use, don't bang it down on the lid to get your way in, but gently prise it open. This stops you getting slivers of metal in the oil, which may disagree with your engine.

Maintenance

There are two types of maintenance, *Scheduled* and *Unscheduled*, which basically speak for themselves. Both are supposed to ensure that an aircraft is kept at an acceptable standard of airworthiness. Depending on the performance category and its maximum authorised weight, there will be different schemes covering this, but the nature of General Aviation means that aircraft are very often not seen by an engineer from one scheduled check to the next. Aircraft below 2,730 kg come under the general umbrella of the Light Aircraft Maintenance Schedule (LAMS). Those exceeding this weight must comply with an approved maintenance schedule.

The maintenance schedule (which is only valid for a given period, and is not usually transferable) contains the name and address of the owner or operator, and notes the type of aircraft and equipment fitted. It lays down the periods when every part of the machine will be inspected (including the Check A), together with the type and degree of the inspection, including the periods of cleaning, lubricating and adjustment. Maintenance schedules are written specially for each aircraft (although they can share the same one), so it can be awkward to change maintenance contractors as the equivalent of an annual check may have be carried out before an aircraft is accepted by the new one.

Types of check include 50-hour, 100-hour and annual, the last being where the C of A is renewed as well (unless the MAUW is below 2,730 kg). There are variations, but regular checks (such as 50- and 100-hour checks) can be extended by 5 or 10 per cent, respectively, for scheduling, but this should not be used as part of normal operations (lack of planning on your part doesn't justify an emergency on an engineer's part).

Checks are also valid for a period of time, sixty-two days for public transport, so the servicing will still have to be carried out, even if no flying has taken place (this can also be extended for a short time at the engineers' discretion). Some maintenance companies submit schedules for checks at 75 or 150 hours, and vary other aspects of their operation. In between these checks, there will also be times when components need to be changed, on either a planned or emergency basis.

A Certificate of Maintenance Review is issued after every annual check, and a Certificate of Release to Service after a regular service (or sixty-two-day inspection). Both documents should be current at all times. A Certificate of Release to Service is not valid by itself – it must be backed up by a Certificate of Maintenance Review.

When a company applies for an Air Operator's Certificate (see Chapter 15, *Setting Up a Company*), Flight Ops 7 of the CAA will want to ensure that this aspect of your operations is satisfactory. It's not so much a problem if the maintenance is done in house, but if your company has sub-contracted this out, a written agreement needs to be in force between the two parties, detailing exactly who does what and the general divisions of responsibility. You would be forgiven for thinking there are certain things an engineering outfit gets up to that can be taken for granted, but such is not the case. For example, you would expect them to supply tools, spares and suitably trained personnel as a matter of course, but your contract needs to spell this out in detail.

Engineering companies have engineering manuals and expositions, which are equivalent to ops manuals, and their standard procedures will also be laid out in these, so between the two of you, you should be able to cross-reference everything quite satisfactorily. Just in case this is difficult, here's a small sample of what you may need to include:

- Operator's name and AOC number, and equivalent details of the engineering support organisation
- Title and reference number of the exposition or engineering manual concerned
- Any sub-contracts arranged for either party for anything specialised, such as avionics
- Specific responsibilities for compliance with statutory requirements, service bulletins, mandatory modifications, provision of spares, tools, personnel and the compilation of and amendment to any technical publications that may be about, including the completion of log books
- Control of deferred and repetitive defects; somebody needs to keep an eye on the tech logs as they are returned from each flight to make sure that the same faults don't keep recurring

The agreement should also include termination or expiry arrangements (not financial) and any action that may be taken without the company's approval, or which needs agreement.

Type Certification

This happens at the end of an aircraft's certification process, when the aircraft is proved to have met minimum design requirements. A Type Certificate Data Sheet (TCDS) will detail the equipment needed for the aircraft to continue meeting the requirements, which is where the MEL and CDL are derived, since pilots will not normally have access to it. The C of A will require that the aircraft be operated under the TCDS.

If equipment used is not cargo, is used during flight and interacts with controls or systems, or affects performance, aerodynamics or handling, you need a Supplemental Type Certificate (STC) for it, which may also be included in the flight manual if pilot attention is required.

Busbars

Most multi-engined aircraft have left and right main buses, and a battery master bus, but there the similarity ends. There are so many variations on a theme that it's quite difficult to keep track of them all, and getting acquainted with a new type of aeroplane can be quite difficult, especially when the flight manual is less than perfect. It helps in these cases to understand the philosophy behind buses (which are notoriously complicated).

The lighter an aircraft is, the better, so it's impractical (if only for weight saving) to run a wire from the battery to every component used on it. A better solution is to run a single (big) wire to a collection of electrical appliances and serve all of them from the end of that line, which is what a busbar is all about. Physically, an electrical busbar (bus for short) is a metal bar with provisions to make electrical contact with a number of devices that use electricity. There's nothing to stop you having main buses supplying secondary ones.

Essential things to know about buses are what they power, how to reroute power to them and how to isolate them, a bit like fuel tank arrangements. All aircraft must have standby electrical power systems, in case the normal one goes down. For small aircraft, this is usually the main battery, which is oversized for this reason. The problem is, it's time-limited and, although there is a theoretical minimum, it's not always safe to rely on more than about ten minutes.

It's helpful to know which equipment (on which buses) uses the least power, which will be listed in the flight manual. It's perfectly possible to navigate successfully by only turning the VOR (or whatever) on every five minutes and off after a minute, having fixed your position. The same principles apply to everything else, and will go a long way towards conserving battery life.

Fire

Fire has three elements – fuel, oxygen and the heat. Take one away and it stops. With dangerous goods, you can get fire from the chemical reaction of flammable materials with an oxidising agent – you don't necessarily need a source of ignition.

A Class A fire is an ordinary one, that is, of normal combustible material on which water is most effective. A Class B fire is in a flammable liquid, such as oil or grease, where you would probably use a blanket. A Class C fire is electrical, for which you need a non-conducting extinguishing agent. For the latter two, you could use either carbon dioxide or dry powder (which ruins the avionics), but the fumes may be toxic, so you will need plenty of ventilation afterwards. A Class D covers other materials, such as metals, that may burn if persuaded.

To help you identify the source, smoke associated with electrical fires is usually grey or tan and very irritating to the nose or eyes (it doesn't smell too good, either). Anything else (say from the heater) tends to be white, but you may get some black from upholstery.

If you think you have an electrical fire, it's no good just using the extinguisher, because you may just be treating the symptom and not the cause, although there is a school of thought that advocates not using an extinguisher at all if you can possibly help it, due to the fumes and stuff you have to breathe in till you land. Whatever you do, transmit a Mayday before it's too late – you can always downgrade it afterwards. Bear in mind also that your first strike with your extinguisher is the best, because the contents and pressure decrease from then on.

Next, put an oxygen or smoke mask on, if you have one, then bring on *essential* electrics one at a time until the smoke appears again.

On the ground, engine fire drills may vary considerably between different types, and these will have to be memorised, but there are some general points that can be made. One is, before evacuating the aircraft, make sure the parking brake is off, so it can be moved somewhere safer if things get out of hand, always being aware that it could run off by itself, as well!

If the fire has been caused by spilt fuel, has spread to the ground under the wing and the other engine has been started, taxi clear of the area (or more specifically, the fuel on the ground) before evacuation, keeping the fire on the downwind side. If the other engine has not been started, evacuate first, carrying out what drills you can.

If you can, use the radio to summon help, and don't forget to take the extinguisher. Remember that human beings *en masse* need very different handling from when they are encountered singly.

In the air, initial shut-down actions are similar everywhere – after performing vital actions from memory (e.g. identifying the source and all that), refer to the checklist to see if you have forgotten anything.

If the engine has been secured promptly, the fire should go out quickly after the fuel supply has been cut off. You will find, however, that structural failure of the wing will be imminent after about two minutes if the fire is uncontrolled, which is a sobering enough thought to make you commence emergency descent *immediately*, no matter how good it looks.

If you've got fire extinguishers in the engine bays, delay actuating them until the engine has been secured and you've no reason to suspect a false alarm; that is, unless you can actually see signs of a fire. In the cabin, whether in the air or on the ground, the priority is to get out, and as soon as possible, because if the flames don't get you, the fumes will. The only difference between the two situations is how quickly this can be done, and what you can do about it.

14

Legal Stuff

The first point to bear in mind is that this chapter applies mainly to the UK, though there are enough hints for people elsewhere to benefit, especially in Canada, where the legal systems are similar, and a lot of it is international anyway. The second is quite simple – I am not a lawyer. I have had some training in it as part of wider Transport examinations, but I cannot lay claim to any great theoretical knowledge. However, in much the same way that you don't have to be a doctor to diagnose a headache, a layman can have views on what is usually regarded as the province of experts. And that is what this chapter contains; my views, that may very well have suffered from the attempt to translate laws into plain English. So if you need it, get proper legal advice. In other words, sticking to the medical theme, a headache may be a symptom of something worse.

Digression: The proper legal advice can often be wrong, which is really helpful when your legal insurance insists that you must do what their appointed lawyer says when you claim against it.

Law in General

You probably feel by now that you've had enough law to last you a lifetime! The trouble is that aviation is affected by a lot more about normal commercial life that needs to be known to protect your interests, which, when you think we all started off with Ten Commandments, makes you wonder. The background to some of them is international, but most come about in the way that UK law is usually created, the most distinguishing feature of which is that not all of it is written down. Luckily, most of what concerns you is.

Very briefly, but accurately enough for our purposes, UK law commences with the common law, which derives its power from having been around from 'time immemorial', a phrase which technically means from before 1189, and from not having been put into abeyance by Act of Parliament.

Common law is not written down, but its principles are regarded as common knowledge among the population, based on the idea that people have certain rights as a result of being created by God (who is supreme). During medieval times, when people went off on Crusades, etc., they would return to find the King had declared their lands vacant and taken them for himself, which would include towns, animals, serfs, and the rest; so, on 15 June 1215, various lords forced King John to sign the Magna Carta at Runnymede, which guaranteed the common man his rights, hence common law.

One of these was the right to enter into contracts, and be bound by them, which becomes relevant with Public Transport, mentioned later, but what's more important right now is the common law right of silence, which means you're not obliged to say anything to *anyone* on the very reasonable premise of not being expected to incriminate yourself. New legal developments do not propose to take this away, but allow juries to take your silence, and reasons for it, into account, which may be commercial, or otherwise (but see also Statements, below). Common law cannot be altered by Parliament or any other authority. It can, however, be put into abeyance, but comes back into effect when that provision is repealed or replaced. The common law applies unless it is expressly or necessarily implied that it has been properly put into abeyance by plain words in an Act of Parliament.

In the US, common law was replaced with merchant law in 1938, at least at the federal level, because there were two systems running at once (i.e. civil and common), and it needed to be sorted out. In fact, in some states, such as Ohio, common law activities are no longer legal, including marriage.

Administrative Law

Parliament often makes laws about subjects it knows nothing about, or cannot keep up with, or which are strictly for a local area (i.e. bye-laws), so it may grant a suitably qualified authority the power to make laws on its behalf, which saves a lot of time. This is known as *subordinate* legislation (or more commonly, and wrongly, as *delegated* legislation).

It is brought to the notice of the public mostly by Statutory Instruments (in this context, an 'instrument' is another name for a document), which is where we come in, because that is how the Air Navigation Order, and most other laws that affect your professional life, have been made (the ANO is both a Statutory Instrument *and* an Order in Council). In contrast, CAA Charges Schemes are subordinate legislation but not Statutory Instruments, in the same position as the appointment documents of an Authorised Person, discussed later.

The major point concerning this type of law is that it can be invalid under certain circumstances, whereas an Act of Parliament cannot. When this happens, it is known as being *ultra vires* when it purports to deal with subjects outside its terms of reference (*ultra vires* is Latin for 'outside the powers').

This could be where some conditions concerning its existence are not fulfilled, such as the print size in the SI document being not the same as specified. You may think this is a technicality, but this method of law-making must have strict controls, for obvious reasons, and every effort is made to give the citizen the benefit of the doubt, as it's not on to deprive anyone of their rights because somebody got the procedures wrong. For example, there was a gentleman who escaped a parking ticket because the yellow lines he was parked on were two inches thinner than the size specified. In this way, Parliament is supposed to keep a tight control on any authority that may be created by Act of Parliament, because the end result could be that civil servants end up making unauthorised laws, and they aren't elected.

In Canada, the Aeronautics Act confers upon the Governor-in-Council (i.e. the Cabinet) the authority to make regulations which are then part of the Act, i.e. CARs. The Governor-in-Council in turn makes regulations authorising the Minister of Transport. Enforcement provisions thus become part of the Act. As long as the Act and Regulations are not found unconstitutional, as an Act of Parliament they are valid and enforceable. Ordinary rules of legal procedure apply and a person aggrieved by a charge has the right to seek legal representation to overturn the charge (having said that, you need to wary of the enforcement division's tendency to impose sanctions without benefit of a hearing).

To be properly enforceable, subordinate legislation must also be given *judicial notice*, so it can be admissible evidence in a court of law. It's worth noting that the Civil Aviation Act 1982 does not appear to grant this to its subordinate legislation, which has the effect of shifting the burden of proof of being *intra vires* (or within its terms of reference) to the maker of the law, rather than to you to prove the opposite, that is, that it may be *ultra vires*. In the absence of provisions requiring judicial notice to be taken of it, subordinate legislation must be pleaded (and proved by) the party seeking to rely on it, but this virtually never happens.

Although subordinate legislation need not necessarily be brought to Parliament's notice (because there's so much of it), the Act behind it usually requires submission to *affirmative* or *negative resolution* procedure. The difference is simple; where affirmative procedure is used, SIs do not become law unless actually approved by Parliament – in other words, a vote of approval is specifically given. Negative procedure means they are law unless rejected by Parliament within forty days. In the case of the Civil Aviation Act 1982, as to whether a particular procedure is used or not depends on Schedule 13, which expressly provides that negative resolution procedure is to be used, except for noise certification, which uses the affirmative.

The process is overseen by a committee, which unfortunately only has jurisdiction while the Instrument lies before Parliament. It meets every fourteen days, so it is possible, with judicious timing, for Instruments to get the minimum time for scrutiny, as there is no pre-publicity – it just arrives on the table, so to speak, at the same time as in the shops and both Houses. As there are not many members on the committee, and they may need to look at over 100 at a sitting, for all practical purposes Instruments are not read.

There is no general rule as to when an Instrument may be unenforceable because the wrong procedure was used, because each case turns on its own circumstances. A *penal* statute (that is, one which involves penalties for its contravention), however, must be strictly observed, a classic case being that of Ronald Biggs, who could not be extradited from Trinidad because the extradition treaty between Trinidad and the UK had not been laid before the Trinidad Parliament. Since Civil Aviation subordinate legislation purports to be enforceable by criminal proceedings (that is, you get punished if you break it), it occupies the same position.

In a *remedial* case, though, some latitude would be allowed, such as where a person was being refused a licence which would enable a living to be earned because the law had not gone through the proper procedure – righting a wrong, in other words.

Interpretation

Expressions in subordinate legislation have the same meanings as those in the Act behind it, unless there is a clear statement otherwise, so you can't use 'ordinary meanings' as with normal statute. In fact, interpretation must be done in terms of:

❑   a combination of the common law rules for interpretation of statute
❑   the particular enabling Acts, and
❑   the context of the regulation concerned

using the *Interpretation Act 1978* as a guide, not the circumstances of the case. This is because legislation cannot necessarily be taken to mean what it says because it may be badly drafted, leaving the law open to interpretations the enabling Acts do not permit, from which injustice could result (*Commissioners' Decision 1/74*).

As far as we are concerned, the first interpretation is made in the cockpit. You (as commander) have the final authority as to the disposition of your aircraft (Chicago Convention Annex 2 Chapter 2, as embodied in the Civil Aviation Act 1982), while you are in command, therefore your word is law until overturned by judicial review on an application made within three months by a person with a lawful interest.

In the case of any dispute, the question of interpretation is always primarily a matter for the High Court, because a magistrate's court tends to concern itself with fact and not law (that is, as to whether a case should be brought in the first place), with the above methods of guidance being used as support in case of ambiguity. Any judgements resolving this would probably take place in accordance with the *spirit* of the law, that is, what, in the judge's opinion, was the presumed intention of those who made it. Provided a literal interpretation isn't absurd, then it applies regardless of any inconvenience it may cause (subject to the doctrine of precedent).

Law arises from these judicial interpretations as well, because notice is taken of them in later proceedings, depending on the status of the court in which they were made. Interpretations made in the House of Lords (which is the highest court in the land) are binding on any lower courts, but not the other way round – what a Crown Court may think has no bearing on the House, although it does in magistrate's courts, which are lower in status. This is known as *judicial precedent*, which, naturally, must be written down somewhere, otherwise decisions would get forgotten, hence the expression *case law*.

In short, regulations under Civil Aviation subordinate legislation are subject to the same Parliamentary control as the enabling powers and must be interpreted and applied in accordance with them.

Summary

So, to summarise, whether a law affects you or not depends on:

- ❏ The validity of the law itself
- ❏ If it's valid, whether it's enforceable
- ❏ Whether it's been interpreted correctly in the circumstances, and
- ❏ Whether the court actually has jurisdiction

With reference to jurisdiction, Section 99 (3) of the 1982 Act says that (for the purposes of conferring jurisdiction) any alleged offences under the

ANO or Section 81 do not take place in an actual place, but only in a deemed place, which means that cases can be heard at selected places, to give some flexibility where a British-registered aircraft acts dangerously towards a Dutch ship in international waters, where the jurisdiction can therefore be given to the place where the offender is caught – the best example of this was the Lockerbie trial, where a Scottish Court was convened abroad. This point is also useful to you, in that it means you may not have to go to the court nearest to the place you're supposed to have committed the offence, but could choose by manoeuvre somewhere more convenient, such as where your solicitor lives, or where the juries are more friendly.

Talking of Scottish Courts, be aware that Scottish Law is based on Roman Law (as is the law in France, which affects the law in Quebec) and is therefore different in many ways from the rest of the UK.

Negligence

The common law imposes on every citizen a duty of care to other people. Unfortunately, there is no standard as to how much care is reasonable, but, in aviation cases, you may find that your duty is absolute and anything, however remote, will be judged as foreseeable. Also, juries generally consist of people who haven't a clue what aviation is all about, and probably think that planes or helicopters are a pain anyway, so behave accordingly – (they will certainly be aware that aviation companies are required to carry lots of insurance, even though its existence is not strictly relevant to a court).

UK Air Transport Law

Although you are usually concerned with law that affects you as a pilot, Air Transport Law in the UK is made in the same way as any other, by a mixture of common law, Acts of Parliament and subordinate legislation which sometimes implement international agreements (see later). Where the question of interpretation arises, reference is sometimes made to Road Transport in comparison, especially for production of licences.

The Civil Aviation Authority was created as a statutory body corporate by section 1 (1) of the Civil Aviation Act 1971, which is now Section 2(1) of the Civil Aviation Act 1982. Under this Act, which received Royal Assent on 5 August 1971, the Aerospace Minister for the time being in office was made responsible for the organisation and development of Civil Aviation in its many and varied aspects.

Thus, the CAA actually came into being in early 1972, combining under one authority functions previously carried out by various organisations such as the Board of Trade, the Air Registration Board and the Air Transport Licensing Board. In fact, up till the mid-thirties, civil aviation was controlled by the Air Ministry, which naturally concentrated on military needs. In 1936, the ARB was formed from various interested parties – it was actually a limited company which had permission to drop the word from its title. The ARB subsequently became the Airworthiness Division of the CAA.

As a corporate body (which as an entity only consists of its board members, or the equivalent of shareholders in a limited company, acting collectively), the functions of the CAA are specified in the statute creating it. The 1971 Act was repealed and replaced by the Civil Aviation Act 1982, which was a Consolidation Act, not debated in Parliament (actual changes to the 1971 Act would have been done by a Civil Aviation (Amendment) Act 1982, a subtle difference).

The manner in which the CAA is to perform its functions is given in Section 4. The regulation of the carriage of passengers for reward takes place under Section 64. Section 60 authorises things to be done by Air Navigation Order, which may pass functions on to the CAA, but this is not mandatory. Section 2 (4) points out that the CAA is not to be regarded as a servant or agent of the Crown, but section 20 (2) allows it to act on behalf of the Crown in clearly specified cases.

There was an oversight in establishing the CAA, in that the ARB (a company limited by guarantee, which carried out many of its functions previously) was subject to the jurisdiction of the Parliamentary Commissioner, whereas the CAA is not. This increases the difficulties of getting redress for wrongs committed.

Here is a list of functions that may be conferred on the CAA by (or under) an Air Navigation Order, from Section 3 (c):

- ❏ Registration of aircraft
- ❏ Safety of air navigation and aircraft (including airworthiness)
- ❏ Control of air traffic
- ❏ Certification of operators of aircraft
- ❏ Personnel licensing
- ❏ Noise certification
- ❏ Certification of airworthiness of aircraft
- ❏ Licensing of aerodromes
- ❏ Approval of persons and equipment
- ❏ Approval of schemes for the regulation of flight times
- ❏ Validation of any certificate or licence

Other functions were later added, such as receiving of MORs. However, there seems to be nothing that permits an ANO to specify who enforces it (the ANO could authorise any government department to do flight crew licensing, for instance, but not a non-government one, other than the CAA). As the above functions are specified by subordinate legislation, it has no power to concern itself with anything not mentioned. There are two reasons for this.

The first is that those activities would be *ultra vires* anyway, and the second concerns the CAA being funded by *charges schemes*, that is, other peoples' money. Funds utilised for anything not authorised are improperly used, technically being *misappropriation of funds*. At first sight, it might seem that the CAA could use its funds to bring prosecutions, but the problem is that prosecutions (criminal ones, anyway) are brought by the Crown (*R v Fred Bloggs*, for instance), so these activities would have to be specifically allowed under the terms of Section 20 (2) of the Civil Aviation Act 1982. The bringing of criminal prosecutions has not been conferred on the CAA by ANO, and it cannot be because it is not listed in Section 3 of the Civil Aviation Act 1982 as a conferrable function (see above). Anyway, Section 2 (4) declares that the CAA is not to be regarded as an agent of the Crown.

Close inspection of Section 2 also discloses that the CAA is a *juristic person* (e.g. artificially created, as opposed to a 'natural' one), meaning that it is very definitely subject to the *ultra vires* doctrine This means that the burden of proof falls upon that person to prove its right to do anything, the reverse position to the case of a natural person, who is innocent until proved guilty – the end result of this is that an offence must be proved *beyond reasonable doubt* in every respect before a prosecution brought by a juristic person can be upheld against a natural one (i.e. you).

Any natural person (say an investigator) laying information before a court on behalf of a juristic one (say, the CAA) must be duly authorised. This is Rule 4 (1) of the Magistrates' Courts Rules 1981, which is in fact an instruction to officers of those courts to ensure that such is the case. If he's found out then (or later) not to be authorised for any reason, then the person who laid the information could actually be considered to be the prosecutor, which means the wrong person is described on the charge sheet and possibly without proper authority to bring charges in the first place.

The ANO consists of Articles and Schedules, the latter being amplifications of the former, so where an Article would require an aircraft to carry markings, the related Schedule would spell out how they are to be made and positioned.

Authorised Persons

An Authorised Person is one who has been given authority by the CAA to perform certain functions on its behalf. Paragraph 15 of Schedule 1 to the Civil Aviation Act 1982 permits the CAA to authorise any member or employee of it to do so. Because of the constraints of subordinate legislation, the activities of Authorised Persons must necessarily be restricted to those within the CAA's responsibility, that is, those in Section 3 of the enabling Act.

CAA Resolution 21, dated 5 June 1975, notes that a quorum for authorising anyone to perform functions on its behalf is one member (a quorum is a minimum number of people). Therefore, a minimum of one member of the Board of the CAA must form a board meeting to do this.

Thus, the appointment of an Authorised Person must be made by at least one person authorised to authorise, so to speak, be it a board member or somebody duly delegated. If the card carried by the AP does not carry any proper indication that the authoriser was in fact so authorised, then it may not be valid (this may sound like a cheap point, but as the CAA is not a natural person in its own right, its range of action is limited without proper procedures).

To enable it to be produced in court as part of a case, that is, to be *admissible evidence*, a document must be properly authenticated. Paragraphs 16 and 17 of Schedule 1 (of the 1982 Act) provide that a document received in evidence should have the seal of the CAA on it, and that the seal itself is not valid unless authenticated by the signature of the Secretary of the CAA (or somebody duly authorised by the board). In the light of this, unless a document carried by an alleged AP has such a seal and signature on it, and is dated because it is subordinate legislation, there may be no proof (acceptable to a court, anyway) that he is in fact an AP, and therefore probably should not have wasted your time asking all those questions in the beginning.

A constable is an Authorised Person, but don't forget to ask for his warrant card or note his collar number (*every* policeman has one, including detectives, so don't let them tell you otherwise). A policeman *in full uniform* is properly appointed, but if he's not wearing a hat, or his buttons are undone, his authority is in question (a motorist was stopped by two policemen without hats, and the charges were thrown out). He may be from plain clothes, of course, but 'constable' in the normal sense doesn't usually mean 'detective'.

Statements

Statements (made by you) can cause a problem, especially with reference to your common law right of silence. If given, a statement should contain all relevant points, not just answers to the investigator's questions, which may only reflect what he wants to hear. What is actually relevant is naturally open to argument, which is why you should either have expert assistance or stay silent. Where a jury is allowed to take notice of your silence, you could explain that you were not convinced that such points were being covered.

As nothing generally happens except by agreement (which means a contract is formed), there is an implication of confidentiality between you and the interviewer, essentially meaning that all that is discussed by yourselves should not be relayed to third parties – this includes within the CAA, as they make copies of everything.

Interviews

Interviews are statutory inquiries to which certain rules of procedure will apply, on top of natural justice. 'Statutory Inquiry' is actually defined (in the Tribunals and Inquiries Act 1971) as 'an inquiry or hearing held or to be held in pursuance of a duty imposed by a provision contained in, or having any effect under, any enactment'.

According to Sections 7 (2) and 7 (3)(c) of the 1982 Act, the CAA is in all civil proceedings a Tribunal supervised by the Council on Tribunals. Where the CAA requests an interview, which is a civil proceeding, Regulation 25 (2) of the CAA regulations imposes upon them a duty to disclose certain information relevant to those proceedings beforehand, which could include copies of the evidence to which the inquiry relates. Under Section 12 (1)(a) of the Tribunals and Inquiries Act, it is the CAA's duty to furnish a written statement of its reasons for an inquiry if so requested at the time notice of the inquiry is given.

Production of Licences

The ANO says that you must produce your licence to an Authorised Person within a reasonable time after such a request from them. This request must obviously be made personally, because you will need to check their credentials, and because a request to send your licence somewhere is actually one to 'surrender', which is not the same thing according to the 1982 Act. The Act itself specifically mentions 'custody', 'production' and 'surrender' as three separate things, so the intention clearly is to regard them as such.

A 'reasonable time' is as long as it takes to reach inside your navbag in an immediate post- or pre-flight situation, or within five days of the original request, as for driving licences.

As the Civil Aviation Act only allows provision by the ANO for access to *aerodromes* and *places where aircraft have landed* for the inspection of documents, it's arguable that requests for production are invalid if made at your home, for example. A constable, of course, can go anywhere within the limits settled by the Act and the ANO. In practice, anyone wanting to see your licences will actually come and visit you if you are willing to allow it, but you may be entitled to payment for your time, like any consultant, provided you give advance notice that there will be a charge.

Logbooks

A logbook is your personal and private property, not having been issued to you under the ANO. Also, according to the relevant Article, only two classes of people are required to keep a personal flying logbook:

❏   Every member of the *flight crew* of a UK-registered aircraft
❏   Regardless of registration, those qualifying for licence purposes

The Civil Aviation Act itself doesn't mention logbooks, except to mention fleetingly that an Air Navigation Order is allowed to make provision for things to be done to 'documents' other than licences, which presumably includes them. However, since the word 'issue' is mentioned in the same breath, and logbooks aren't issued to you, maybe it doesn't. In any case, filling in logbooks is not within the ordinary meaning of 'air navigation'.

Actually, the question of logbooks can provide another useful illustration of how interpretations of the law can vary. The ANO says that everyone required to keep one needs to produce a personal flying logbook if requested to do so within two years of the last entry. Simple enough, at first sight. But . . .

One of the defined classes of person is 'every member of the flight crew of *an* (not *any*, italics mine) aircraft registered in the UK'. The definition of 'Flight Crew' (Art 129) includes: '. . . those members of the crew of *the* aircraft [emphasis mine] who respectively undertake to act as pilot, flight navigator, flight engineer and flight radiotelephony operator of the aircraft.'

It could follow, therefore, that to be flight crew (and therefore subject to the requirement to produce a logbook, or maybe anything else for that matter) there must be an undertaking at the moment of the request for production to act as such on a particular aircraft.

So, even leaving aside that point, once you've finished flying and are off duty there is no longer an undertaking to act as flight crew, therefore there's no requirement to produce a logbook when requested (in any case, there doesn't seem to be a requirement to carry a log book in flight). In other words, as you're only flight crew between chocks away and chocks on (or rotor start and rotor rundown) that's when the requirement exists – the request to produce should be made between those times (note that, in some countries, the timings are between boarding an aircraft with the intention of flight and when the engines stop).

Looked at this way, the logbook referred to could be merely a record of undertakings to act as flight crew of a particular aircraft which is closed after each one and must be produceable for two years. If so, a copy of the tech log for each flight will do, provided it has your name and address on it, as required by the ANO.

It just goes to show how much care must be taken both in setting up laws and reading them – that's why it's a specialised job to draft Acts of Parliament.

Prohibited Airspace

This may only be created by the ANO itself; the 1982 Act permits aircraft to be stopped from flying over such areas as may be specified in the Order. It also allows the ANO to provide for exemptions, so, unless specified in the ANO, or exempt under the terms given in it, prohibited airspace does not exist. Mere 'notification' of its existence may not be enough.

Commercial Air Transport or Not?

WARNING! This subject is complicated and causes acute brainfade!

Public, or Commercial, Air Transport is defined in the ANO as being where valuable consideration is given (or promised) for the *carriage of passengers or cargo* on a flight (it actually says *in the aircraft on that flight*, but you know what I mean). Aerial work is anything else for which valuable consideration is given.

In addition, it covers anyone or anything that may be carried free on that flight, not being employees of any air transport undertaking that may be operating it (although it looks as if it's worded otherwise, company directors and anyone working on behalf of the CAA, such as Authorised Persons and TREs, are employees for this purpose).

Thus, if you carry a passenger (say, a friend) on a check flight who is not an employee or a director of your company, it will be regarded as Public, or Commercial, Air Transport, even though valuable consideration is not promised or given. In the USA, even if you do a job for charity that only gives you a tax break, and even if you don't take advantage of it, that tax break is considered to be the equivalent.

If the valuable consideration allows a particular person to fly an aircraft, then that is also Public Transport (unless it's being bought on HP or a conditional sale agreement). Presumably this is meant to cover self-fly hire, or maybe trial lessons, since the phrase used is 'fly the aircraft' rather than 'fly in the aircraft'. Although that person may not be an employee of the operating organisation, crews are not passengers (although they may be for insurance purposes, so I don't quite see where this one fits in, as CAT only exists when passengers or cargo are carried for valuable consideration).

However, these clauses are the only ones to affect the average professional. Otherwise, in broad terms, you are allowed to win prizes in air races (up to certain limits) and recover direct costs and a pro rata contribution to the amount of hours flown every year if you go to air shows and the like. If a payment is made to a (registered) charity (with CAA permission) that allows someone (maybe a prizewinner) to fly, that is a private flight.

Equal contributions to the direct costs of a flight borne by the pilot if up to four persons (including the pilot) fly in an aircraft are exempt, but direct costs do not mean HP payments, insurance, hangarage . . .

There must also have been no advertising for that flight, except in the confines of a flying club, in which case all passengers (over eighteen) must be members. It also helps if the pilot is seen not to be employed as such (this situation is what anyone else would call 'cost-sharing'). A similar situation exists where a pilot reclaims direct expenses paid out on behalf of an employer. There are other exemptions, such as jointly or company-owned aircraft. Remunerated parachute dropping (and positioning for it) is regarded as aerial work.

In Canada, a *Commercial Air Service* means any use of aircraft for hire or reward, and different regulations apply for aerial work, air taxi, commuter or airline operations. An *Air Transport Service* means a commercial air service operated for the purpose of transporting persons, their belongings, baggage, goods or cargo in an aircraft between two points (does this mean that if you take off and land from the same place you're not an Air Transport Service?).

Let's have a closer look at the words 'valuable consideration' as an example of not-so-good drafting. The word 'consideration' means money or something of money's worth that is more than merely nominal. It is legal expression referring to something that is used to bind a contract, even the chocolate wrappers sent in to a manufacturer to obtain a free gift.

The word 'consideration' by itself would have been enough, but somebody saw fit to add 'valuable' in front of it, which changes the position somewhat, because now everybody has to rush around trying to decide what that particular word means and subsequently how valuable should consideration be to qualify for inclusion in the ANO?

The actual definition there comes from the nineteenth century, which reads: 'any right, interest, profit or benefit, forbearance, detriment, loss or responsibility accruing, given, suffered or undertaken pursuant to an agreement, which is of more than a nominal nature'.

Try instead: 'money or money's worth, which is more than merely nominal [i.e. chocolate wrappers], including the release of debts, meaning money or anything capable of being turned into money, possibly including some services which cannot'.

The real problem with this, though, lies with insurance. You may (or may not) know that there is no such thing as a 'contract' of insurance, because you are betting: in this case, that you crash your aircraft before a certain date. The insurance people, of course, are betting that you don't (or is it the other way round?).

The trouble is that insurance companies are well known not to pay if they can get away with it, so if they can prove that you were doing illegal Public Transport, you may well find that your insurance is invalid as well, not to mention being caught for third-party liability in some cases.

Anyway, back to the subject. The ANO (Art 6) says that an Air Operator's Certificate is needed for all flights that may come under the definition of Public Transport: 'an aircraft registered in the United Kingdom shall not fly on any flight for the purpose of public transport, otherwise than under and in accordance with the terms of an air operator's certificate granted to the operator . . .'.

Article 6 was originally Article 3A of the ANO 1960, and was inserted as an afterthought to it to cover AOCs that would be unenforceable during the time gap until section 1 (2) (a) of the coming Civil Aviation (Licensing) Act 1960 came into force on 30 March 1961. This section was later repealed by the 1972 Act, so from that time the ANO could no longer legally make provisions for an AOC with enforceable terms.

The 1982 Act says that only Statutory Instruments can establish enforceable terms; in other words, no enforceable law (that is, by criminal proceedings) can be made below the level of a Statutory Instrument, which of course an AOC is not. AOC terms are laid down by the CAA, which cannot issue SIs.

By the way, the term 'operator' above has been held by leading counsel to include the pilot (any person with the management for the time being of an aircraft is regarded as being the operator). Reference to Road Transport Acts shows that if it had been intended that a 'driver' was not to be an 'operator', then the proper wording was available for aviation.

Actually, the imposition of Public Transport conditions is only permitted by the enabling Act (of the ANO) where the aircraft is used for a commercial, industrial or gainful purpose (specifically Sect 60 (3) (f)). What it says is that: 'An Air Navigation Order may contain provision as to the conditions under which passengers and goods may be carried by air and under which aircraft may be used for other commercial, industrial or gainful purposes'.

Quite a mouthful, but the use of the word 'other' in conjunction with the Rules of Interpretation of Statute infers that 'conditions' may only be imposed when aircraft are being used for gainful, etc. purposes (notice the absence of the words 'valuable consideration'). As these rules are meant to be enforceable by criminal proceedings, they become penal situations, and as such must be strictly construed in accordance with the enabling statute.

So what may be relevant as to what is or is not Commercial Air Transport is not the presence of any consideration, but, if there is, whether the aircraft is being used for a commercial, industrial or gainful purpose. Therefore, all you really have to do is pin down who the user is and see what his use of the aircraft is to see whether Commercial Air Transport or Aerial Work conditions might apply.

Since, in most circumstances, light aircraft are chartered to a sole user, most 'charter' flights could in fact be called private flights (if it were not for the ANO) unless the aircraft is actually being used *during flight* for commercial, industrial or gainful purposes.

The user (that is, the hirer) is using the aircraft for his own purposes (unless buying and selling is going on in the back) and the 'operator' is the pilot. Whoever hires out the aircraft to the user could be held to be their agent in respect of maintenance and all the other things needed to keep the aircraft flying.

If passengers are being carried for separate fares, on the other hand, then the aircraft is being used in that way by the person with the right to the money collected.

But beware! The terms of an AOC could be enforceable if made as the terms of an Air Transport Licence. If an aircraft is being used for the carriage for reward of passengers or cargo, the CAA may apply air transport licensing even if the aircraft is not being used for anything resembling Commercial Air Transport or commercial or other gainful purposes.

All that being said, what about the situation where you're asked to do a job and you're not sure what's going on? Do you feel up to actually asking for a certificate to say a flight is not Commercial Air Transport?

This is plainly impractical, so you need to know a few ins and outs to protect yourself (please note the intention is not to enable you to do anything illegal!).

A workable CAT flight (ANO definition) must have the following:

- ❏ An Air Operator's Certificate issued to 'the operator'
- ❏ The crew must have current licences (e.g. CPL/ATPL) and be type rated, base/line checked, etc. in accordance with the operator's operations manual (indeed, the whole flight must be conducted in accordance with it)
- ❏ The aircraft must have a (current) Transport Category C of A, Certificates of Maintenance Review and Release to Service, Technical Log (with Deferred Defect Sheet), Passenger Briefing Leaflets and all legally required equipment (fire extinguishers, placards, etc.)

You may be able to get around these requirements by ensuring that the person hiring the aircraft does so with a contract separate from the one he hires you with, and you'll be better off if you can also prove that you weren't paid, or at least you were an employee of the hirer's organisation (if you do this, you may have to show that the enabling Act only permits an Air Navigation Order to make different pilot licensing provisions according to whether the person concerned is actually employed or merely engaged in a flight crew capacity). You could also get base and line checked by a proper company and put it through their books, but don't forget you must use their ops manual and other documentation.

Finally, you could resort to drastic measures and form a company for a short time with nothing in its memorandum and articles of association about gainful use of aircraft or hiring them out by the hour.

There is a common law rule that you cannot buy or hire from yourself – this is the basis upon which co-ownership groups and non-profit members' clubs are run in every walk of life. However, the ANO says that any agreement between any such organisations, or members of them (this also means within the same group), in respect of a situation where valuable consideration would normally be expected, would be considered as if it had been given anyway. This is notwithstanding any rule of law as to such transactions; in other words, the common law purports to be specifically overridden, yet it is not clear from the enabling Act that the ANO is permitted to do this, that is, put common law into abeyance.

An unincorporated non-profit members' club can be created for a specific purpose or occasion and exist for one flight or a day only, being dissolved once it has served its purpose. They should pay for their own operating costs to avoid the inference of valuable consideration. For instance, it should not be too difficult for a group of parachutists to form a club for the day for the purposes of hiring an aircraft. However, the paperwork must be sound and, as I said, these are drastic measures, so try and get legal advice here.

Legally, there's nothing to stop you (as a pilot) obtaining your own Air Transport Licence or AOC should you feel the need.

International Air Law

The idea is to reduce the possibility of a phenomenon known as *conflict of laws*, and the resulting confusion that could arise where, say, a claim for damages is brought in a French court in respect of injury to a Dane whilst travelling on a ticket bought in Holland for a journey from Germany to England on an Italian plane.

International Law (Public or Private) consists of internationally agreed rules that courts of participating states apply to cases with a foreign connection, the private side of things affecting individuals and the public side affecting states. Public International Law takes precedence over Private, which in turn is superior to State Law, although ultimately (short of war) International Law is unenforceable where the original consent disappears.

Air Law has mainly evolved through agreements between 'high contracting parties', through various international conventions or treaties, too numerous to mention here. These form the basis of Public International Law which in turn can be incorporated into the law of individual states, an example in the UK being the UK Carriage by Air Act 1961 in relation to the Chicago Convention of 1944 (in fact, the Chicago Convention and its annexes are also embodied into Section 60 (2)(a) of the Civil Aviation Act, 1982).

A *Convention* is an agreement that many nations are at liberty to enter into, and the word *Treaty* is used to indicate agreements between two (or more) states that bind only themselves. The Tokyo Convention 1963, for instance, relates to offences committed on board aircraft (but not to offences committed by aircraft, as such). Thus, conventions can cover many subjects, including the agreement of standards for navigational equipment and documentation, but they can also establish governing bodies, such as the International Civil Aviation Organisation (ICAO).

ICAO is a worldwide body convened by governments, while the International Air Transport Association (IATA) is an equivalent body established by the airlines. Although IATA is a private organisation comprising virtually all the scheduled airlines of the world, it nevertheless has strong links with ICAO and governments, and is often used by many airlines as an agent for inter-airline co-operation.

IATA has many committees, but the most significant is *Traffic*, which negotiates many arrangements between states and airlines. Other airline organisations exist, particularly within Europe, which operate on a similar basis. As well as certain freedoms granted by conventions over the years (such as flying over certain territories, taking tech stops and collecting or discharging passengers), other rights of commercial entry are established by bilateral agreements, which provide for route(s) to be flown, estimate traffic capacity and frequencies of service and establish other precise rules under which operator and crew licensing are accepted by the respective parties to the agreement.

Employment

As soon as you start working, a contract of employment is deemed to have started. There are reams of papers on the ins and outs of contracts, but basically once a contract is formed there are rights and duties on either side, made the more binding if something called *consideration* (remember that?) is given by anyone to seal the bargain. This consideration need not be money, nor need it be adequate.

Unless you're a freelance, you will normally enter a contract of service where you have a master/servant relationship with your employer. If you're self-employed, you will be regarded as an *independent contractor*, and in a different legal position if a passenger decides to sue for any reason (your 'employer' may be able to drop you right in it).

If a passenger does want to sue, you're more protected if you're actually an employee, because the come-back is then on your employer, as you're a part of his business, although there is a let-out if he can prove you were acting *outside the terms of your employment*, but as long as you haven't done anything totally stupid, you should be OK (this also applies in Canada).

Aside from whether your tax is deducted at source, you can identify the essential difference between the two in the way that you're treated. An independent contractor is outside the employer's business and is told merely what has to be done, and not how.

In Canada, there is a four-part test as to whether you are an independent contractor or not, but, unless you actually own the air service or have income from other business pursuits, it is very difficult to meet (deductions at source are not part of it).

Most contracts are free and easy, it being up to both parties as to what they want out of any situation. However, contracts of employment (and sales of goods, incidentally) are regulated by law, so there is less freedom of movement, although the bias is on your side, helping to protect you and allow more collective bargaining (this last only applies if you're in a union, of course, but there are none for General Aviation).

Although any contract may be made verbally (which could override a written contract, by the way, subject to provability), the law lays a duty on the employer to give you a written statement within thirteen weeks of starting work detailing conditions about such things as pay, hours, holidays, pensions, sick pay, notice, disciplinary rules and any other procedures which may affect you. If you don't get a written statement, you may be able to use what actually goes on between you as evidence of the presence of a contract.

Employer's Duties

❏   To pay wages as agreed. You are entitled to a written itemised pay statement, regardless of the method of payment. It must contain certain minimum items

❏   To indemnify against liability and loss (as a result of doing his work)

❏   To provide a safe system of work (including premises and appliances – and aircraft)

❏   References are subject to the law of defamation (libel is written, or, rather, permanent – slander is spoken). Be careful, though, to distinguish between a false statement and an expression of opinion made without malice

Your Duties

❏   Obedience. It's your duty to obey a lawful order, but there are proper procedures for your dismissal if you don't

❏   To show good faith, that is, work in your employer's best interests

Like any contract, one for employment will take place according to agreed terms and conditions, but if there is a dispute, it will be judged according to what is reasonable. In the case of termination, there may be damages on either side, provided it could be proved that damages were suffered as a result of the action.

The usual problem is unfair dismissal on the employer's part, though, and there are strict procedures that enable you to go to an Industrial Tribunal should such an event happen. I suggest you check out your local Citizen's Advice Bureau for the latest information. In Canada, you would have to apply to the Human Resources Development people, as aviation is a federally regulated business.

There is an Equal Pay Act which allows women to receive the same pay as men for performance of equivalent work. It also makes it illegal (with certain exceptions) for discrimination on grounds of sex, and it applies both ways.

Neither is an employer allowed to discriminate on race grounds.

In Canada, employees have rights under the Canada Labour Code Part II, or Occupational Safety and Health Regulations.

Health And Safety At Work

This applies to Aviation as well, and there is actually a common law duty of care laid on whoever you work for to ensure that the aircraft flown are airworthy and fit for Commercial Air Transport in every respect. You are required to do a pre-flight check to be sure, but, not being a qualified engineer, there are some things about an aircraft's condition for flight you just have to take on trust, which become the operator's responsibility. If something turns out to be wrong, then despite the adherence to authorised maintenance schedules, there could be negligence involved.

Recent amendments to the ANO mean there are cases in which crews cease to be passengers carried under the terms of Commercial Air Transport. Under these circumstances, there is a lowering of safety standards applicable to working conditions, as they are obviously no longer protected by those conditions.

Reference

As you will recall from your licence studies, law can be quite a turgid subject at the best of times. If you haven't fallen asleep already, here is a useful selection of reference books:

Shawcross and Beaumont: *Air Law* (Butterworth)
Archbold: *Criminal Pleading, Evidence and Practice*, 39th edition 1976 (Sweet and Maxwell)

Brian Harris: *Criminal Jurisdiction of Magistrates*, 9th edition 1984 (Barry Rose)

Wade: *Administrative Law*, 5th edition 1982 (Oxford University Press)

The preliminary notes on Statutes contained in Halsbury's Statutes (Butterworth)

Wade and Philips: *Constitutional Law*, 7th edition 1965 (Longman)

Josling and Alexander: *Law of Clubs*, 5th edition 1984 (Oyez-Longman)

The Concise Dictionary of Law, 1986 (OUP)

Kiralfy: *The English Legal System*, 3rd edition 1960 (Sweet and Maxwell)

Francis Bennion: *Statute Law*, 2nd edition 1983 (Oyez-Longman)

A C D Mitchell: *Guide to Operational Aviation Law 1986* (The Avrisk Group) currently under revision.

15

Setting up a Company

Most pilots are quite happy working their way up the career ladder, graduating to larger and larger types as their experience grows, and don't concern themselves with the possibilities of operating their own aircraft.

One day, though, there will be an opportunity to set up your own company and obtain your own AOC, typically where you come across somebody with an aircraft who would like to offset the costs of operating it against some income. Or it may be that you come into some money yourself and feel able to go it alone. More common is where you fly somebody on a charter who is new to flying, they become impressed and decide to buy their own aircraft, and because you were their first pilot you get made an offer you can't understand.

There's nothing wrong with this, but think seriously before leaving employment with relative security for something that may only last a few months. One rule of thumb (which works very well) is that the more attractive the package offered, the less stable the job. Another is to subtract twenty-five from the physical age of anyone who's keen on aviation for its own sake, and wants to make a business out of it, to get their mental age. If you can, find out something about the company your prospective employer runs. Have they got credibility? Are they well established, or is the man you're talking to just an idiot with access to other people's money rather than his own? (See how many of his cheques bounce, and how much of what he says will happen actually comes true.)

Signs that a company won't last long include excessive flamboyance on the part of the boss, who naturally pays for everything, treating all and sundry to lunches, drinks, etc. (if it was really his money, he wouldn't be doing that). Statements to the press that are less than complimentary to other companies around should also be noted, as should excessive hype and illogical spending on non-essentials, where the basics aren't being looked after – that is, they spend money on smart new offices rather than servicing the aircraft.

I don't mean to put you off from anything that could lead to greater things, but a little scepticism in the early stages could save you and a lot of other people plenty of aggravation later on. There are several ways to protect yourself. One is, don't move at all – bide your time and see what actually materialises out of what your prospective employer promises. Many people say a lot, but not much actually happens – they give the illusion of movement without actually progressing anywhere (like 're-organisation' in a large company). The more urgency projected, the more sceptical you should be.

Another way of protecting yourself is to have somewhere to go to if things fail to materialise; an even better way is to estimate the amount of work you can expect to do for a year and insist on payment of the whole lot in advance. If they want you enough, they'll produce the goods. In fact, to work in aviation at any level (as opposed to playing in it) needs a more businesslike approach than most people think, at least as far as mental attitude is concerned. The whole idea of doing the job is to earn money; if you happen to enjoy it, you're lucky, but you are doing your-self and other pilots a disservice by underselling yourself just because you're keen to fly. You suffer the same fate as companies who undercut – in the end, the waters just get stirred up, nobody makes any money at all and very few survive.

Financial Matters

If, despite all that gloom, you still want to carry on, please let me add one more word of warning – you will need much, much more money than you anticipate. Not for nothing is it said that to end up with a small fortune in aviation, you need to start with a large one! But it needn't be that bad, provided things are done properly from the start.

First of all, if you need to borrow money, you'll need as much slack as you can get to cover cash flow while you're waiting for customers to pay, and emergencies – if you only ask for just enough money, it will be patently obvious you don't know what you're doing and will be shown the door. When running an airline, you will find that major travel agencies can take up to six months (or more) to pay their bills, if they pay at all, which will cause major cash flow problems. Once the fuel companies don't give you any more credit, you don't have long to go, because people who owe you money definitely won't pay if they can get away with it.

Also, in aviation, things only work out cheaper if you can afford to fork out the money from the start. Buying your own bowser, for instance, instead of positioning your helicopter to the local airfield for fuel, will probably cover all the empty flying and unnecessary landing fees inside three months, but you have to have the money in the first place – paying as you go along should be avoided as much as possible, as it will usually kill any project stone dead.

Don't depend purely on loans. In fact, you probably won't get one till the lender sees some input from another source (preferably yours), so you may need to find a venture capitalist who would be willing to invest in your project. These sorts of people supply money in return for stock (shares in the company), typically expecting to be free of their obligation in about four years or so with a handsome profit (although they could make a loss). The major benefit to you is that they provide ready cash and a bit of stability without your spending power being drained continually by interest payments. Although a business plan is important, you will find that your personality, or those of others in the plot, will account for at least half of the decision.

Use accountants, by all means (you will need one on board for the business plan), but never, ever let them run your business, unless they've either been there themselves or have gone to business school. The problem is, their training makes them very narrowly focused, and they often fail to see the big picture. Mind you, pilots running businesses have limitations, too, since they're programmed to fly and don't always realise you can make more money by not flying sometimes.

Business Plan

This is needed to raise capital – it is a brief sketch of your proposals, detailing how you mean to repay the money, together with how things will be run (this includes details of the management team). Like a CV, it should be short and to the point, somewhere between a quarter and a half inch thick, and, provided it is well thought out, need not be too polished, though it should still look neat, tidy and professional. Here are some suggested headings to get you started:

❑ Introductory letter. Why you are writing the plan (to raise money for expansion? An aircraft?)
❑ Title page. Name, phone, date completed
❑ Table of contents
❑ Summary of proposed venture. Description of business
❑ How much needed, and how it will be used
❑ Amount already invested; equipment, market testing, etc.
❑ Security. Property, stock and other assets
❑ Background info. Limited company? plc? Sole proprietorship?
❑ Mission statement. Key activities
❑ The industry. Niche available. Competition

- ❏ Management. Organisation, CVs, proposed benefits
- ❏ Target markets. Individuals or corporate
- ❏ Advertising
- ❏ Land, buildings and equipment
- ❏ Operations. Work flow, personnel
- ❏ References
- ❏ Financial plan. Capital requirements and sources to data, profit/loss – cash flow for at least one year; projected income for at least one year; proforma balance sheet, showing projected current and fixed assets, and liabilities. Break-even calculations
- ❏ Risks and problems. Worst-case scenario. What if demand falls, or you get more competitors, or more overheads? What's left if you don't succeed? Avoidance of risks. Impact of risks you can't avoid

The magic figure to survive in the small charter world is 500 hours per aircraft per year – that's revenue hours, ten a week, which doesn't include training, etc. Remember, the object of the company is not to fly, but to make a profit so that you can live, or to provide the investor with a return on his capital (not profit necessarily, although sometimes they can coincide). Far too many people forget this, set themselves up in an airfield having done no research, don't market their product and then expect the world to beat a path to their door just because they have an aircraft.

Even if work does come, more often than not by accident, the same people undercut everybody else around, thinking to put the opposition out of business, then put the prices up again. Unfortunately, it doesn't happen like that – they're the ones to go out of business first because they have no cash flow, left with debts and wondering what went wrong.

A lot of aviation companies owe their existence to a larger parent company that bought an aircraft as a way of spending excess money that can't otherwise be used (there is such a thing), but it's not impossible to survive purely on aviation without assistance from a Big Brother. Whether it is or not depends on the existence of competition, how big you expect your company to be and the availability of the work itself (if there's no competition, have you thought of the fact that there might not be any work?).

Purchasing an Aircraft

Whatever happens, you will have to get your hands on a machine. Expensive stuff like that (while being an asset in itself) will create massive debt which will require servicing, which in turn means interest. Which company will take care of that? If the aviation company itself buys the machine then it will have that much more to worry about.

What is more likely is that an outside company will own the aircraft and lease it to your company, giving the additional benefit of the equipment being one step removed in case of disasters. Outside aviation it's common practice to place all valuable assets into a holding company that trades only with associated ones, thus insulating them from unplanned contingencies. Where aviation is concerned, it also legally separates the registered owner from the user.

The leasing cost to you will be a total of maintenance costs, spares or engine replacement costs, insurance costs plus a bit on top for contingencies (the spares or engine replacement costs are similar to depreciation, which is an accountant's way of establishing a fund for future replacement of machinery).

There are two types of lease, *wet* or *dry*. The former will include fuel, which is useful, because there's less squabbling over who put what fuel in what aircraft. It's easier just to let the owner pick up the tab, provided he's not overcharging. Leasing costs are charged hourly and the total cost is variable, that is, dependent on the number of hours flown.

There is a chance that the anticipated costs above turn out to be less expensive than you anticipate, but that will be the lessor's good fortune, not yours. Of course, things could go the other way and it will cost him more – this will happen if he buys a bad machine in the first place and/or it's flown badly. Leasing means that you have no asset to fall back on, which you would have if you raised a mortgage and bought it. If you ever end up leasing an aircraft to somebody else, you will make the most money by stumping up at least 50 per cent yourself and financing the rest.

One creative solution is to raise a loan on something else, say, a house, and use that money to buy the aircraft – you will then get lower interest rates and longer terms.

The aircraft doesn't just cost, say, two million pounds. It will also cost what you can't do with the money having spent it – what economists call the *opportunity cost*. In other words, you lose the opportunity to do something else with it, even if only to sit in a bank account and gain interest. Sometimes it's better not to buy outright but to do it on a mortgage and let the interest gained from whatever you do with the rest pay the interest on the mortgage. With a little shopping around for interest rates (abroad as well) this is entirely possible.

Imagine you have the choice of two aircraft – one relatively expensive to buy, but cheap to operate, and the other cheap to buy, but expensive to run. Both do the job you want – well, near enough, anyway. The difference in purchase price between the two may well, if placed on deposit somewhere, more than pay for the increased running costs if you buy the cheaper one. However, in the UK, which is not an aviation-minded country in general, this may be low on the list of priorities, as often the purchasing of an aircraft will tend to be a personal decision on behalf of the chairman.

So, when evaluating an aircraft, first establish what you want it to do – in many cases, a simpler, cheaper aircraft will suit. For example, if you want a helicopter for corporate transport, use a 206B-III, but for training or pleasure flying, a 206A would be not only cheaper, but more efficient, as its C18 engine is not cycle-limited.

What's the maximum range, and where is the nearest airfield to the factory? What's its optimum cruise height and will you get a 'wet foot-print' if you have to go lower over water if an engine stops? Do you want an aeroplane, or would a helicopter be better, where you might spend longer in the air, but have a shorter time between offices and not need ground transport from airfields? How many passengers will you normally carry, and will they want to hold meetings in the back? The bigger and faster it is, the more money it will cost. True cost-effectiveness lies not in fulfilling all your needs, but compromising on some, so that you're not in a situation where your most demanding tasks (which are 5 per cent of the requirement) take up 95 per cent of the facilities offered.

However, having the most cost-effective aircraft ever won't help if you can't afford even that. Your budget may stop you dead and restrict you further – you have to run it as well.

If you get professional help, it will cost you money, so what you need to do is aim your money at the best target. The proportion of the cost to the actual purchase price will be larger with smaller aircraft because there's just as much work involved in selling them as there is with larger ones, and the total price is substantially less.

A *broker* will be selling somebody else's plane on their behalf, essentially taking money for the introduction and the paperwork, so you will probably never meet the seller. A *dealer*, on the other hand, will have bought the aircraft into stock and will be the owner. There is also the private advertiser, who is just selling his own ship, or maybe a bank or financial institution who are repossession agents.

Once you let it be known that you're after an aircraft of any description, you will get every man and his dog ringing you up with what they have to offer. On the one hand, this could save you a lot of work, but it could also be a pain in the neck, so here's another tip: get the registration number of what they're trying to sell – it could be the same machine several times over. If they won't give it to you, then treat them with the appropriate suspicion. They will have registered with the seller and will try and get a cut of the deal as an 'introduction fee'. Nice work if you can get it.

As with a car, look beneath the shiny paint. There's nothing wrong with sprucing something up for sale, it's common practice, but make a thorough examination anyway. Do not do what one buyer of my acquaintance did – looked at a helicopter and took it away to lunch, leaving the engineer that he'd taken along (at great expense) alone to look at the books which were written in German! Yes, he bought the wrong aircraft; and deserved it! It looked nice, though.

The problem now is finding a trustworthy dealer, but could you do your own purchasing? You've already done most of the work by establishing the tasks you need to perform and what you can afford. Yet another tip is, don't believe brochures or salesmen. Take time to talk to pilots and engineers who actually work with the type of machine you're after – you may find that what you're looking at is OK until the turbocharger goes, which then takes at least three days to repair because it's hidden behind the engine which has to come out completely. On the other hand, another ship could have similar work done in less than half a day and doesn't go wrong in the first place because the turbocharger is not in such a stupid place. Similarly, a particular helicopter could be cheaper to run on paper, but its shorter range on full tanks means that you're paying out for landing fees and dead flying more often, thereby bringing the total operating cost nearly equal to something more comfortable with more endurance.

You need to take account of the data for propeller, rotor or engine Times Between Overhaul (TBO), the Mean Times Between Failures (MTBF) on avionics equipment, amongst other things. Certainly, buy from a company that can provide support, particularly an engineering-based one, and have an independent survey by a competent engineer.

Aircraft Valuation

Actually, when it was built is largely irrelevant; what counts is the time remaining on its components, since they must all be inspected and replaced at specified times. Equally important is documentation supporting it– it can take longer to verify paperwork than physically survey the aircraft. In this respect, be especially careful when buying from the USA. There are many apparently 'cheap' aircraft available, mostly confiscated from smugglers or drug dealers – with no acceptable documentation, their only value is scrap. Also, the regulations for privately owned or agricultural aircraft are less stringent than in Europe, and you may need expensive engineering and/or major components replaced before they will get a C of A. So:

❏ There is no such thing as a cheap aircraft
❏ Especially, there is no such thing as a cheap helicopter

Which applies to maintenance as well; if you save money one year, expect to spend it the next. Remember that as well as shipping charges, you may have local taxes and costs of dismantling, packing and erecting when you get it to wherever you are. Shipping is normally All Charges Forward, and you will be responsible for insurance.

Depreciation

Because inspection, overhaul and replacement can ensure that a ten-year-old aircraft can be as efficient as a new machine, you can't apply this in the same way as a car, or other industrial machinery.

However, accountants like it, and it's useful for calculating operating costs, so take the purchase price and give it a one-third residual value, then write down the difference over ten years. Market prices, though, may vary this. If you have a new engine, or something equally as expensive, the machine's value could well exceed the new cost.

Direct Operating Costs

All manufacturers publish estimates of the cost of operating their machines, in amounts per flying hour, which naturally bear very little relation to reality.

❏ Fuel and oil. The shorter the average sector length, the higher the average fuel consumption. Fuel flow for budgetary purposes tends to be within 5 per cent of max cruise fuel flow for fixed wing aircraft and 10 per cent for helicopters. For oil, only bother with consumption; scheduled oil changes come under maintenance

❏ Scheduled maintenance (normal inspection cycles, divided by the hours between them). This is sometimes the second largest direct operating cost after fuel and varies with the flying. Much depends on the cycles incurred by an airframe or engine rather than the hours flown. Wear and tear is felt primarily on take-offs and landings, when engines run at high power settings and landing-gear and flaps are cycled. Some jet engines (particularly helicopter ones) are therefore restricted to the number of start cycles in addition to flying hours, because of the enormous spread of temperatures incurred in the start sequence. Thus, if your aircraft does relatively short trips your main-tenance costs per hour will increase as a result.

Whether maintenance is major or minor usually depends on the

cost of the item, and the cut-off point is usually left to company discretion. For avionics, 4 per cent of retail price should reserved for
maintenance (assuming 400 hours per year). Add 0.5 per cent for
every 200 additional hours flown, or subtract if need be

❏ Unscheduled maintenance, like snags and defects, special inspections
required by manufactures and authorities

❏ Aircraft overhaul – removing, overhauling, and replacing components at proper intervals, divided by the interval hours

❏ Engine overhaul – as above

❏ Lifed items – replacing when time expired, divided by life hours

❏ Engine lifed items – as above

❏ Labour rates

❏ Fuel costs

Fixed Costs

These cost the same per year regardless of the work, so the more you do,
the less per hour they become.

❏ Purchase/debt servicing, described more fully elsewhere. The figures
for your annual budget would be the amount of the purchase price
paid in the current financial year, whether borrowed or not

❏ Trade in/resale. This (hopefully) is a plus item, just resale income for
aircraft offered in part-exchange for your new one. However, the real
value of this will be degraded by inflation

❏ Depreciation

❏ Hull insurance, covers accidental damage to the aircraft, providing
for repair or replacement at the insurer's option. If the policy is
agreed or stated value, the insurers must pay a predetermined amount
in case of total loss and cannot offer a substitute or replacement hull.
This is normal, if the hull value is reasonable. Otherwise, you will get
the market value. There is usually no legal requirement for hull insurance (but there will be for liability; see below), but whoever
finances your purchase will likely insist on it.

The cost is expressed as a percentage of aircraft value, and varies
according to:

    ❏ Aircraft type
    ❏ Company claims record
    ❏ Type of operations
    ❏ Area of operations
    ❏ Market competition

❏ Liability insurance. The insurers agree to indemnify and defend you in respect of against claims made you by third parties and arising out of bodily injury or property damage caused by the aircraft, or articles falling from it

❏ Passenger and passenger baggage legal liability. Covers claims made against you by passengers for accidents resulting in death or injury as well as lost or damaged baggage – the policy cover is geared to the Warsaw System limits of liability (the Warsaw Convention dates from 1929 and limits the carrier's liability). The actual liability depends on the countries of departure and destination and whether or not they are signatories to the Convention, or one or more of the various amending conventions or protocols that have been introduced since 1929.

Cost varies according to:

❏ Aircraft type
❏ Number of crew and passengers
❏ Area of operations
❏ Company claims record
❏ Amount of insurance cover
❏ Market competition

In the UK, as in some other European countries, Air Transport Operators are now required to adopt a limit of SDR (Special Drawing Rights), £100,000 in respect of any one person.

In return for the benefit of limited liability, the onus of proof of negligence is transferred from the injured party to the airline, who must prove that there was no negligence if a claim is to be avoided. To benefit from this, certain requirements must be observed by the carrier. As far as insurance is concerned, the most important of these is the passenger ticket, which must conform to a laid down standard and be issued correctly to each passenger.

The carrier's liability in respect of passenger baggage is also covered by the Warsaw System. Liability is calculated by weight. Insurers normally impose deductibles in respect of baggage losses which effectively excludes coverage for losses falling within the limit. The insurance will therefore only pay for and defend claims which are likely to exceed the limit of liability. It is therefore necessary for the carrier to have a system for dealing with these small claims

❏ Other insurance, which may include:
  ❏ *Cargo Legal Liability* – an airline carrying cargo of any description has a legal liability to the consignor for damage to the goods in transit, which liability is also subject to the Warsaw Convention; the limit is calculated by weight alone

❏ *War and Allied Perils* – which includes riot, malicious damage and hijacking (excluded by Hull and Liability policies)

❏ *Deductible* – a compulsory 'Deductible' or 'Excess' is standard, and agreed by insurers worldwide, ranging from $25,000 for a small turboprop to $1,000,000 for a 747. This can also be insured against

❏ *Aero Engine Breakdown* – for repairs following an electrical or mechanical failure in the engine. Most operators include scheduled and unscheduled engine maintenance in their operating costs, which can be reduced or eliminated with this type of insurance (does not cover ingestion or external impact damage normally covered under the Hull or Deductible policies)

❏ *Loss of Use/Delay Insurance* – for strikes, riots or industrial action, adverse weather conditions, crew incapacity, accidental damage, mechanical breakdown, type-grounding by manufacturer or government agencies and political risks

❏ *Total Loss Only* – completely separate from Hull All Risks, designed to pay an agreed amount on top of the Hull Agreed Value in the event of a Total Loss of an aircraft.
  This aspect is often overlooked, but when you're leasing, the owner gets all the money if something happens, and you've got to fork out to get another

❏ *Spares* – spare parts holdings and engines can be insured while in store or in transit

❏ *Breach of Warranty* – under the terms of lease or finance, it's common for the lessor or finance house to seek to protect their asset, over which they have no operational control, by way of Breach of Warranty Insurance which must be purchased by the operators. This insurance indemnifies the owner to the extent of his financial interest in the event of a breach of insurance conditions resulting in the denial of a claim

❏ Coverage is arranged as an extension to Hull insurance

Note: All policies above are known as *contracts of indemnity*, meaning the insurer must restore your position as it was before the loss.

❏ Salaries. If you're an owner-pilot, you might be able to ignore this, but you may have management, operations, mechanics and pilots to pay

❏ Storage. Outdoor storage is less expensive than hangarage, but storms and damage do happen, as do vandals. The average annual costs of hangarage to be allowed should be roughly one per cent of the equipped price of the new cost of your aircraft

❏ Training, such as anti-terrorist training, if your company is so disposed

❏ Services. Manuals, trade subscriptions, airways manuals and maps. Association memberships

❏ Tax. Best left to the experts, this, but there are ways of obtaining an asset on a mortgage offsetting Corporation Tax

A corporate machine will average 200–300 hours per year, so the total of fixed costs divided by that will give you an amount per hour.

Incidental Costs

Hotels, taxis, landing, hangarage, handling, tips, oxygen, uniforms, cleaning, office costs (computers, telephone, fax) and freelancers.

Twenty-five per cent of the sum of Direct Operating Costs, Fixed Costs and Crew Costs is normally added on top as a contribution to running the business. The total will give the Cost Per Flying Hour. Divide that by seats available to get the Cost Per Seat. Further dividing Seat Cost by the speed will give you the Cost per Seat/Mile.

Obtaining an AOC

Now if you still think you'll be some sort of success, you will need your Air Operator's Certificate, which is required by all operators engaged in Commercial Air Transport (but watch for crop spraying, where a similar scheme is in force).

It's applied for on a form together with a CLM (Cheque for Lots of Money) made payable to the CAA, which will cover all types you wish to include initially. However, subsequent additions will cost the same again, so if you know you'll be adding a new machine later, it makes sense to try and include it from the start. Unfortunately, this will cause its own trouble in the form of additions to the ops manual and further training costs, as pilots must be qualified on the new type as well. Beware of having too many types in different performance groups.

You can only hold one AOC in one state, and your office and aircraft must also be registered there.

The application form itself is quite easy to fill out. If the operator is an incorporated body, you will need to know the directors' names, addresses and nationalities, and, if not, the same information with regard to the partners. If there is a trading name separate from the company name, that will need to be given as well. This bit is quite important, because the AOC is issued to the parent organisation trading as whatever they care to call themselves. The CAA will want to know exactly which trading names are to be adopted.

Otherwise, the only other thing that may need a bit of research is the maintenance schedule reference for each aircraft that you propose to use. This will be found in the aircraft logbook, and will look something like CAA/LAMS/FW/1978 Issue 2, if you're using an aircraft below 2,730 kg (check with maintenance, it's easier).

The application form and the fee should be sent to the Flight Operations Inspectorate at the CAA in Gatport Airwick at least six weeks before operations are planned to commence. Together with all that, you will need a copy of your proposed operations manual . . .

The Operations Manual (again)

Although you don't have to send the ops manual with the application form, things will happen considerably quicker if you do, because the CAA reserve themselves a minimum of six weeks to read it. If it's ready when you apply, some parts of the aforementioned form need not be filled in; you can just refer them to the manual.

Production of the operations manual, which is your way of indicating to the CAA how you intend to operate, is (to use the CAA's words) 'an onerous task'. The quick way is to buy one ready made (from me, if you have my phone number), but there is a pitfall in that, just because a manual has been approved once, there is no guarantee it will be so again (and that goes for the contents of this book, although the relevant parts have been in an ops manual at some stage or other).

This is because each company is assigned a different inspector who will have risen through the industry in his own way, having different experiences to fall back on. His job is to advise you in the light of that experience (more than being a 'policeman', although that is another function) and assist in the formation of the company. What one inspector thinks is OK is not necessarily what another will accept (they use that word rather than 'approve', as the latter has legal implications).

A typical inspector will have several companies under his wing, and will therefore have to guard against giving away confidential information (the CAA must not be seen to give commercial advantage). He will normally be the only routine contact a company will have with the CAA, and his main function when you're up and running is to inspect, report and make recommendations on your performance. On routine visits to the company, he is empowered to examine any documents or records which must be kept (by law), discussing and resolving any problems that may have arisen during your operations. Your AOC is reviewed annually by the Flight Operations Inspectorate on the basis of his reports, and is non-expiring, provided that the annual charges are paid up to date (based on the throughput of traffic that a company has) and you keep your nose clean.

Only specific parts of the manual are actually 'approved', namely certain documentation (such as the tech log) and the Flight Time and Duty Hours Limitations Schemes. All the rest is an indication to the authority of how your company intends to operate, which naturally varies according to circumstances, and they grant or withhold an AOC taking due note of the contents. Despite the apparent flexibility, however, there are definite indications as to what is and isn't allowed, most of it in JAR Ops 1 or 3 and the ANO.

The CAA requires a copy of your ops manual for its own records and for instant reference in case of queries. As it is the primary indication (to them) of your operating standards, it makes sense to produce the manual in the best possible way. This is psychological – if the Flight Ops Department see a well-presented manual on the shelves, then they're likely to be more convinced that the rest of the company is likewise (well, wouldn't you?). So you are doing yourself down if you skimp on the ops manual, no matter how boring it may be to produce it, but that's been discussed already.

Back to the AOC

Having submitted the application form and the manual, you sit and wait for the CAA to respond, during which time the chief inspector allocates whichever one he thinks will suit you. Your inspector then reads everything and produces a long list of things that need comment. They're quite efficient, so any delays are usually caused by you, but they still have to fit you in around their other duties.

For instance, there's no system of handovers – if your inspector goes on leave for three weeks, there's no procedure for another to take over. The same goes when your man is detached to the outback somewhere. In some cases, the grant of an AOC may take as much as five months through no fault of yours. It's no good delivering a finished manual as fast as you can if there's nobody in the office to read it!

There is naturally a conflict of interests here, in that an aircraft owner is forking out money while an aircraft is sitting idle, so obviously he's keen to get on. He's also paying you for what he thinks is idleness (generally, if you're not flying, you're thought not to be working, which you and I know is wrong). Your job here is to (tactfully) slow him down and speed the CAA up, but they've been there well before you have and know the problems. Also, they do like an empty desk, so the sooner they get you off the ground, the quicker they can relax.

While the manual is being read you can get your pilots checked out by your training captains and the system streamlined for the proving ride. For setting out the office, etc., see Running Things, later in this chapter.

Eventually you will get a standard letter from the Approvals Section of the Airworthiness Division requesting proposed Technical Log and Deferred Defect forms (don't forget the instructions). They will also need to see the maintenance schedule for the nominated aircraft and the contract between your company and the maintenance contractor. The maintenance schedule is produced separately for each machine by whatever maintenance contractor is used (several aircraft can share the same schedule).

Also appearing through the post will be the books mentioned earlier, so that you can write your ops manual. The ANO will also be needed, but you don't get that free.

Your inspector meanwhile will visit your proposed offices to ensure that they meet certain requirements (such as the chief pilot having his own office and being able to see the aircraft operate, the numbers of clerical staff and machinery relative to management). They need not be on an airport, but being away from one does cause problems, certainly for keeping track of fuel states (so that you can calculate your payload instantly if you get a quick charter).

Hopefully by then he will have produced some proposed amendments to the manual, but it could actually be read through for the first time in front of you just before lunch on the first visit. When he is happy with that, and your offices, he will want a proving ride (preferably with a line pilot) on your aircraft.

The ride itself is not a check of the pilot's ability, at least not in the sense of a Base or Proficiency Check, but more a check of the company procedures, which is why it should be done with a line pilot, to see if the system works. It's meant to be a simulation of a complete line operation and will be about an hour or so long. The inspector will pretend to be a passenger and will expect to be weighed, briefed and otherwise treated exactly as per the operations manual. Almost the first thing he will make a beeline for on arrival at the office is the ANO, to see if it's up to date! The same goes for maps and other documents. You don't have to have full copies of the *UK Air Pilot* or NOTAMs, provided you can prove you have adequate access to any flight planning information you may need, including weather.

After the ride, assuming all is well, the AOC should be granted in due course, possibly after a few more changes to the manual. The issue of the certificate signifies only that you are considered 'competent to secure the safe operation' of your aircraft – it doesn't relieve you from any other legal responsibilities that you may have, whatever they are.

Once you have your certificate, your inspector will pop round within a month and thereafter about every six months or so to ensure the continued competence of the company, including any outstations or agents that you may employ.

It's worth checking if you need an Air Transport Licence as well (see Special Events in Chapter 12).

Running Things

Any company operating aircraft must achieve as high a utilisation as possible for maximum cost-effectiveness – an aircraft on the ground is not earning money. While corporate flight departments do not make a profit as such, the comments here apply equally to them, as efficiency still helps the bottom line. Also, if you are operating an aircraft by yourself and have no commercial air transport experience to fall back on, you ought to realise that a good office environment back at base is very important to the overall operation. The following pages will give you some idea of what's required to run things properly, with a little information on the corporate scene that should be read as well because it's all relevant (and it saves me typing it twice).

The various functions to be filled include planning, day-to-day operation and administration. The bigger the company, the larger the departments handling these will be. You may find you need none of these, but it's still worth knowing what they get up to.

Planning covers everything from long-term management decisions to scheduling flights, minimising dead flying and taking care of maintenance requirements, although some of this could be regarded as day-to-day operations.

Administration is the only part likely to be really separate, but even here there is likely to be a lot of blurring between departments, as staff wear several hats.

In practice, you will find all the above activities (with the exception of top management matters) more than adequately looked after by the Operations Department in the average small company, and this is what we will mainly be dealing with in this chapter.

The Operations Department

Operations is in immediate control of all day-to-day business, the focal point of its activities being the ops room where, depending on the extent of your activities, will be found the operations staff, secretaries and the rest (if they can all fit in).

The role of the ops room (including staff) is to ensure that the right aircraft is in the right place at the right time and that everyone concerned is aware of what is happening, being pre-warned of any problems which may be expected.

If this cannot be achieved for any reason, Operations must initiate remedial action and minimise inconvenience to passengers, who are (after all) the source of the company's income.

One of the ways Operations keep track of events is with movements boards (boards are quite useful, and you will find that several will be required for AOC operations, including pilot qualifications, NOTAMs, and everything else you may think of). These boards should be kept well away from prying eyes who may pinch your business if they see destinations and customer names, so don't put them near windows.

Movements boards should be constantly updated as they're a major reference point. What goes on them is up to you – just use whatever information you think will be needed. The biggest movement board of the lot is the map, which will usually have a string-and-weight arrangement with a nav ruler that makes it easy to calculate complicated distances.

Linked to movement boards is the diary. There will be a scruffy one that's used daily, but there should also be a backup filled in after the day's work. In it should go all the scheduled work, upcoming pilot and aircraft checks (a week or so before they're actually due). Some people use files in which go royal flights, etc.

As mentioned before, there will be a quotes file. It is suggested that this be looseleaf, each page being filled in at the time of each query. If a trip looks as if it's going to happen, then that page should be put into a pending file until confirmed, when it's put into a diary file.

The diary file is simply thirty-two file holders, not necessarily in one book, representing each day of the month plus one, and all prepared documentation for a flight is placed in the file for the relevant day. The benefit of this system is that royal flight information (and anything else that's only valid for a day) can be put in there as well, which makes it easy to bring it to the attention of the staff concerned.

You can see that communications are beginning to be of vital importance. A good communications network is an essential part of modern aviation. Without knowing as quickly as possible what's going on, it's very difficult to plan ahead and foresee problems that might arise. Many methods are used, VHF radio, telex, AFTN, fax and even HF single-side-band radio for those longer distances, and you should encourage your pilots to use it often, because it helps with scheduling if you know where they are, aside from allowing quick responses to incidents.

The most common, however, is the telephone, and the correct use of it saves many problems. The first problem is that there is no record of what's been said, so important messages and decisions made on the telephone must be followed up immediately by telex or fax, since these are commonly accepted in business as a substitute for official correspondence on company notepaper. When taking down a message, always ensure you have the correct information and names, so that you know whom to blame later.

The telephone should be answered as soon as possible, and, before answering, be sure you have a fair chance of helping the caller. When answered, they should not be left holding. If they have to be left for any reason, ensure that nothing can be overheard that shouldn't be! A definite reason linked to holding is essential, and regular assurance that the problem is being dealt with is helpful as well.

Don't use jargon or be familiar with people you do not know; refer again to previous comments on being an ambassador of the company. Always terminate a phone call leaving a positive impression.

Corporate Flight Departments

Here you may well find yourself actually in charge of a Flight Department in the proper sense of the word. A charter company in fact, without the necessity of bothering with charges, although if they are offset between companies within the same group (known as *chargebacks*), they will normally be handled by Accounts.

Chargebacks are one way of allocating time between users in large companies, paying for the machine on paper, but if the rates are too high, the end result is that the departments who need it most can't afford it and therefore can't use it, which seems a bit pointless. A side-effect is that it opens the door to small charter operators who can do the job more cheaply, and then money flows outside the company instead of staying in it. Another is that Accounts have a chance to do a bit of empire-building, as they are the only ones who get any work out of it, namely chasing money round in a circle.

If you're employed as a full-time pilot, your company will probably already have an aircraft, so it's unlikely that they will charter-in except for times when they've lent their aircraft out.

It could even be worth considering leasing (self-drive) as a halfway house between chartering and owning. The cut-off point where owning an aircraft makes more financial sense than leasing is about 200 hours a year, so the average flying rate for corporate aircraft is at least 200–300 hours per year, but some get up to 600 or 700.

Your company may do things the other way round and lease their aircraft out to commercial operators. This causes problems, especially where allocating priorities are concerned, and if this is done extensively, management will have to get used to the idea of either going without their aircraft or hiring another. Sometimes trying for extra money on the side defeats the object of getting an aircraft in the first place, but that's not really your problem. Avoid aircraft management companies, by the way.

Despite chargebacks, company policy may dictate that the costs of operating the aircraft are not actually charged against the Flight Department (for instance, in one or two companies they come under Sales). Whoever looks after it, management will (naturally) want to know where the money is going and how much will be wanted next year so they can budget properly. This means getting involved in statistics and finance because as a company employee you're being paid anyway and you have nothing else to do, right?

If you do get lumbered with all that, you may find it easiest to add some columns to your tech log to fill in as you go along. Who is flying is often more important than just noting how many, so possibly you may like to account for corporate, divisional or production employees. Don't forget marketing, freight and sales.

Some useful tools for making impressive reports (especially in comparison with other forms of transport) include:

- ❏ Average speed. The number of miles flown divided by the number of hours airborne
- ❏ Average fuel consumption. Fuel burned divided by hours airborne (chock to chock), including ground runs, etc.
- ❏ Load factor. The total number of passengers divided by the total number of sectors, a sector in this case being a nonstop flight from A to B regardless of the ultimate destination. Non-revenue or non-productive sectors (positioning, training, air tests) if included will adversely affect the load factor, but will give a better picture of operational efficiency
- ❏ A/c miles travelled. Total miles travelled by the aircraft
- ❏ Pax miles travelled. Aircraft miles travelled multiplied by the load factor (if you're wondering why these need to be calculated, it gives a quick indication of productivity)
- ❏ Cost per hour. Total cost divided by number of hours flown

- ❏ Cost per aircraft-mile. Total cost divided by the number of miles flown
- ❏ Cost per passenger-mile. Total cost divided by passenger miles (obtained by dividing aircraft miles by the load factor)

Being a Chief Pilot

First of all, you should not be on the duty roster. The job requires so much management that you become ineffective on both sides if you try and do too much – there's simply not enough time (you can see the responsibilities in Chapter 1). Any flying you do should be strictly to keep current and step in when there's a shortage.

As mentioned before, you will be the main point of reference for officialdom, because you dictate the flying policy of the company – take something like not taking off until you reach Blue Line speed in an aeroplane (best single-engined rate of climb speed); most take-offs occur between stalling speed and Blue Line, but you could argue that if you don't get airborne until the latter, you already have speed in hand if one engine fails. However, if the nosewheel gets damaged because it wasn't built to take the strain, then it would be regarded as ultimately your fault as you directed your pilots to fly like that.

Another plus point about being a chief pilot is that you can also argue with management when they want to put commercial pressure on. Very often you will find yourself in a position where you're made to seem very unreasonable:

> 'Oh, go on, it's just a little snag. You've got another one and if you don't use this aeroplane I've got to get one all the way from up north. So what if none of the gauges work?'

or (and this is a true one):

> 'It's only a small crack in the fuel tank, and it's at the top, so if you don't fill it all the way up, it won't leak out.'

are common conversations between a managing director and a chief pilot. Come to think of it, it's more common between MD and pilot, so the chief pilot doesn't know anything about it. If a pilot comes to you with a problem like that, you must back him to the hilt, even if you think he's wrong. You can always sort that out in the pub later.

All this involves your personal integrity and credibility – referring to previous comments about money management, very often if you need to lease a plane, the lessor will take your word for it (as holding a position of responsibility) that they will get paid. In fact, less-than-honest management have been known to hide behind the reputation of members of their staff, with the resulting loss of several people's good names when the money wasn't forthcoming. You have been warned!

Being a Boss

Money is not a motivator. If people are unhappy, they will be just the same very soon after a pay rise – watch what happens to your engineers if you don't give them enough spare parts. You will find that, left to themselves, most people do the job well enough without supervision, and want to do well at what they do. You will get the best out of your staff if their goals align with those of your company, and that happens when you give them the ability to make decisions, or assume responsibilities. Any problems are 99 per cent because of bad leadership. Lastly, remember that you're not as concerned with what people get up to when you're there, but with what they do when you're not there!

In short, if you want your staff to look after you, you have to look after them.

16

Going for a Job

And you thought you were the unlucky department: In the USA, when pilots are leaving regional carriers after only a very short time in the saddle for higher things, their replacements are being asked not only for money up front to pay for their training, but a fee to submit an application for employment in the first place.

For low-timers, and anyone else for that matter, visiting as many companies as possible is about the only way to get yourself known. Just sending a résumé (see below) is not good enough when they haven't seen you before. When you do visit, make sure your car is clean, you are well-dressed and presentable, etc. and prepared to camp out on the doorstep – bringing the doughnuts for the coffee every day is definitely a good ploy! Believe it or not, someone with relatively low experience and who gets on with customers is actually in a better position to get hired than if it were the other way round, as experience and flying techniques can be taught – personality can't.

Remember also that loyalty goes both ways. Companies such as those mentioned above deserve all they get when their pilots disappear in a shortage – with no staff, they can't trade, and they go out of business. It's happened before and will happen again. On that basis, if you're a low-time helicopter pilot, for example, doing the traditional two years as a hangar rat before you get your hands on a machine, be prepared to move on if it seems as if the company is more interested in your cheap labour than training you.

In my opinion, in with your normal windscreen-washing, you should be doing the air tests and non-revenue flying, which will not only give you an incentive, but make your subsequent training cheaper by keeping you current. It is entirely possible to get upwards of 700 free hours a year in a busy company, if you're prepared to end up in strange places for days at a time.

You will have to do a bit of research about every company you target – you will certainly need the name of whoever does the hiring, and the head of the department you want, if they are different (in most cases, it will be the chief pilot or base manager, or, in other words, someone with local knowledge). Only go to the Personnel Department as a last resort, and even then just to ask for the right name(s). You need to know the sort of work they do, the type of customers they have, where they operate, and tailor your initial conversation around it, emphasising the benefits you can bring which cause them the least amount of work. For example, in Canada, one of the first questions you will be asked is if your PPC (Base Check) is current, because it's transferable between companies (it isn't in Europe), and they won't have to spend money sorting you out. It's almost guaranteed that the next question will concern either a mountain course or long-lining experience, so be prepared. The point is that their requirement for a pilot is to solve a problem, and you need to be the one with the solution, so get their attention, then create the desire to employ you and, more importantly, do something about it. In fact, the sort of telephone conversation a busy chief pilot up to the ears in paperwork would like to hear is something like:

> 'Hi, I'm an Astar pilot with mountain and long-lining experience, available now.'

or:

> 'I can fly a KingAir and I've got over 1,000 hours' turbine time.'

Music to the ears. Just adjust it for your own situation, but only get detailed after you start fishing for what they want. If you get asked any question at all, you've got what is known as a 'buying signal', but the question will probably come after a short period of silence, which you shouldn't break. Answering apparent brush-offs with further questions should keep the conversation going. If you can introduce the name of somebody already known to them, so much the better.

The Advert

This is usually the last resort for companies who need staff – apart from being outdated anyway, the best jobs are almost always filled by word of mouth, and the ad is placed merely to satisfy legal requirements. In fact, the way an advert is worded can tell you much about the company you may be working for.

Treat as highly suspicious the one that is obviously from a small company offering an extremely good package or reads something like: 'Aztec pilot required – Gulfstream II experience an advantage'. There probably isn't a Gulfstream anywhere near the place; they're just trying to wind up the opposition. Similarly, one company may advertise that, due to expansion, they want lots of pilots. This will be followed hotly by another one the following week from another company which, not to be outdone, forecasts even more expansion. Of course, they may be genuine, but my point is that you can save a lot of wasted interviews and postage by being selective right from the start.

Another way of not wasting time is reading what the advert actually says. If it states definitely something like 'must have 500 hours' jet experience', it means your application will go straight into File 13 (the waste bin) if you don't. On the other hand, another might say that such experience 'is desirable' or 'is an advantage'; if you score six out of eight on the requirements, then go ahead. In this case, circumstances will determine what happens to your application, for instance whether there is a pilot shortage or not, or whether the chief pilot or the Personnel Department actually wrote the advert (Personnel won't haven't a clue as to what's really required and may have just copied it from somewhere else).

However, your face may fit better than many suitably qualified people, and it's a favourite hobby of some pilots to keep applying for jobs anyway, so to help you get on where you may be at some sort of disadvantage (whether you're one of many applicants or you haven't quite got the qualifications required), you may need to employ a few tactics. The best known is through your CV, or *curriculum vitae* for short, or even *résumé* if you're in North America.

Tip: One tactic that works more often than not, when answering an ad, is to apply relatively late, say a week after it appears, ensuring that the bulk of them are out of the way and whoever has become cross-eyed looking at them will get yours when he's back to normal, possibly all by itself so that you are noticed more. You also (theoretically) go to the top of the pile. Another one is to always make a follow-up call, including after an interview. In some companies, the process is very long and you can easily get forgotten.

Your CV (résumé)

Applying for a job involves selling yourself, by which I mean that you are the product to be marketed, and the process starts even with the envelope in which you send your details. It's surprising how many people fail to use the CV and covering letter (they are, after all, a first introduction) as properly as they should. I have seen very badly handwritten CVs with no idea of spacing on ragged paper that would disgrace a fish and chip shop. This type of introduction says little for your self-image and is likely to go straight into the bin – if it doesn't, it will be a permanent reminder of what you were like long after the interview. You have to realise that, in a large company, as well as the hiring process being long and tedious, decisions are made because people are frightened of making mistakes, not because they might be the right ones, and people higher up in the food chain than your interviewer will be rubber-stamping their choice without ever having met you, so you've got to make the paperwork look right (this, of course, explains why people don't work so hard in large companies – those who make the least mistakes get promoted, and those who work the least make the fewest mistakes).

Having said all that, in a lot of aviation companies the atmosphere is relatively informal, and, although you need a résumé, hardly anyone ever reads it, at least not till you make them do so by turning up on their doorstep, so take the following remarks with as large a pinch of salt as you feel able. You may only be required to fill in an application form, which will also involve a breakdown of hours – usually first pilot and grand totals. The initial contact could well be a faxed one-page CV, with a full one later when asked for more details.

Tip: Keep a running breakdown of your hours, separate from your logbook and updated monthly, say, in a spreadsheet, which will help you extract these figures when required. It will also be a backup should the original get lost, but a logbook must fulfil certain requirements – see Chapter 14, *Legal Stuff*.

However, a large company with a Personnel Department (which therefore deals with several other professions) will expect to get the full treatment. Like flying, the more preparation that goes into your CV, the better the results you will get. Remember, you're trying to beat the opposition.

There should always be a covering letter which doesn't duplicate information in the CV itself, but may include reasons for wanting to join the company, or, more to the point (salesmanship again), how useful you will be to them, because that's what they're bothered about. You could, for example, cover specific points mentioned in the advert.

It is recognised that you may wish to include a breakdown of hours, so a little length in your case is acceptable, but still try to get the information in as short a space as you can without leaving anything out; if you're only going for a flying job, the tendency to include irrelevant information should be avoided, and everyone knows what a pilot does, so your résumé will be on the technical side, that is, short, competent and to the point. Management qualifications (if you have them) are not important to somebody who just wants a line pilot (all the advice here should be read in this light – you don't have to include everything). As with all salesmanship, you're trying to make it as easy as possible for the customer, in this case your potential employer, or at least the poor clerk in the personnel office who has to go through all the paperwork before the interviews. Jargon is acceptable, provided it's commonly used, but the problem is, if you don't use it, you may appear to be an outsider, so it's worth mentioning that the clerk's job is to *screen you out*, or to discover whom *not* to interview, so don't bore them too early, or put things in that might make them feel uncomfortable and give them an excuse. If you feel the need to be more specific, use the covering letter to get your details to the right person.

You need to use quality paper – a minimum standard would be Conqueror. It should be A4 (or letter size) and white, and therefore in-offensive, but this requirement is really for scanning. By all means hand write (neatly!) the accompanying letter, but the CV must be typed on one side of the paper only, with the script centralised, with no underlining or too many strange typefaces. Leave at least a one-inch border at the top and bottom of the page with a good-sized margin on either side. It will cost a minimal amount to get a two-page CV typed or word-processed properly, and not much more to get a reasonable number photocopied, preferably on to the same paper. *Use a spellchecker*, and don't fax it unless asked.

It should include your career history, commencing with your present position and working back about five years in detail, the remainder in brief. The name and town is enough to identify employers, with a brief description of their activities, if needed.

You may include reasons for leaving your current position. When people read a CV they almost always do it with a highlighter in one hand to mark relevant passages for later inquisition. It's a fair bet that this will be a prime target, so prepare it very carefully.

You will need to know something about the company you wish to join for the interview, so include a little about specific experience relevant to the post applied for as well.

In summary, the layout must be neat, as short as possible, well spaced and easy to read, with a positive attitude being conveyed throughout.

The Interview

Let us first of all establish what the interview is not. It has nothing to do with your competence as a professional, except for the simulator ride (if one is required). The mere fact that you've been put on any list at all, let alone shortlisted, indicates that your flying abilities are recognised (one of my employers didn't even look at my logbooks or licences).

On their side, the interview is really to see if your face will fit. They are about to let your personality loose on their customers and they want to see if you will help solve the problem or become part of it. In other words, you, as an employee, must create value beyond the cost of employing you. As far as you are concerned, it's a chance to see if you will like the company, in which case you may find it useful to write down what you want from them.

Note: With reference to value, mentioned above, the cost of employing you is not just your wages – you may have training or health insurance thrown in, plus other benefits, not to mention the staff employed to look after you, or any office you might have. In the first year, you may well cost much more than your salary.

Interviewing techniques are very sophisticated these days. You may be lucky and get away with a quick half-hour with someone who is just as nervous as you are, but the full-blown two-day affair with personality and IQ/psychometric testing is becoming increasingly common. Certainly, it is used by one electricity company in the UK, and almost every airline. The full nine yards might include written maths, intelligence and psychological tests (with over 600 questions), a simulator ride, an interview and a medical (don't forget the briefing for the sim ride).

Whatever it is, you must regard it as having started whenever you walk through the main door of the building or meet any company person. You are definitely under observation at lunch (why do you think so many people join you?), and the receptionist has been on the team on more than one occasion.

Note: The problem with lunch (for you, anyway) is that it's an opportunity for many questions that cannot be asked elsewhere, so be even more on your guard.

So, the interview is even more part of your sales technique. Naturally, you will be smartly dressed and presentable, and you must convince them that they are buying not so much a pilot as peace of mind.

Although unlikely in a pure aviation company, there may be questions or situations designed to put you well and truly on the spot by trying to destroy your composure. To combat this, there are ways of behaving that will give you the most confidence. Don't talk too much, don't be pushy or negative and don't break silences. The answers to awkward questions are not important, they are actually asked to see how you handle stress and whether you can be intimidated (by passengers, maybe), and the only weapon you have is to practise beforehand, though it's best to pre-handle certain types of question rather than specific ones (you might be asked how your life will change if you are successful, or even whether you would be happier elsewhere). It's certainly not on to slate other companies or be too eager to leave your present one – if you can do either, you can do it to the one you're going for. Do not sit until invited, and if you are not, at least wait until the interviewer sits down. Do not smoke without permission, don't swear, interrupt or 'interview' the interviewer, even if he is inept. Nor is it a good idea to argue, be familiar or apologise for yourself. The best tactic is to avoid extremes and place you and your opinions firmly in the middle – be the ideal 'Company Person', in fact.

Going back to the CV and the highlighter pen, you will more than likely be asked why you're going for that particular company and the reasons for leaving any previous employment. In the first case, you don't want to say that you have a mortgage, kids, etc. (those are personal problems), and in the second, try not to give money or better opportunities as a reason for moving on – well, not more than once early on in your career, anyway. Don't even think of mentioning personality clashes or 'philosophical differences' as they are more politely known (unless you want to be a trial lawyer!). Oh yes, and *do not tell lies.*

17

Training and Testing

Your training doesn't stop once you've passed all those exams. It will be there for the rest of your career, if only to maintain your licences. Of course, there may be some to increase your qualifications in the offing, but that is outside the scope of this book. If your company is like any other, they will try to recruit already qualified crews – they're cheaper, but once in a while they may have to take on somebody who needs a top-up as far as licences are concerned. If so, they will have to submit proper training syllabuses and include them in the ops manual if they do it regularly. If they don't intend to do type conversions, they should say so.

Actually, the trend now is to have a separate training manual, one for each fleet, in fact, but the whole thing could end up in the ops manual if it's small enough. It's for people concerned with training, including subcontractors, or even those from manufacturers converting you on to a new type, but it doesn't need to be carried on board. If you have to write one, it will need the same official stuff as the ops manual, that is, amendments, training organisation, duties, responsibilities, etc.

Licensing

As you know, an aircraft cannot fly unless it carries a properly licensed and type-rated flight crew of the numbers and descriptions required by law. Licensing and training requirements (in the UK, anyway) are covered by the ANO. CAP 54 gives a detailed look at what's required for the grant of a Professional Pilot's Licence, but a brief summary is given shortly. In Canada, look at the Pilot's Licensing Handbook.

Most people who start flying as a career do so for other reasons than money; they see themselves as being permanently engaged on their favourite hobby and being paid for the privilege. Professional flying is a bit different, though.

You must realise from the start that you need a professional attitude towards your financial rewards as well as your flying. In many cases (except when there's a shortage), you could probably get just as much satisfaction and much more money in your pocket at the end of the day from working in another field and flying for sport.

Think about it this way: to gain a CPL/IR at current rates on a full-time approved residential course costs over £100,000 ($150,000) – of *your* money (or at least somebody else's that you have to pay back in some way), assuming you do it in the minimum time. That gives you a licence that makes you employable only by an air taxi company without having extensive continuation training that may consist of anything up to thirty-five hours, depending on how good you are. An airline will require you to do a jet orientation course (JetOC) on top of your CPL, which just about takes you on-line as a co-pilot once you've done *Line-Oriented Flight Training* (LOFT) as well. Even in a simulator, where you don't actually have to fly the aeroplane to get your type rating, that will cost at least £20,000 more.

It's not that much different for helicopters – in Europe, where it's over three times more expensive and you need more hours to get your licence (700 under JARs), for the moment, anyway, anyone who can afford his own training would, in terms of pure financial reward, have to think twice before working as a pilot, because that sort of money can be considerably more productive elsewhere. Mind you, it's ultimately not that different in North America. Even though you only need 100 or 150 hours to get your ticket, you are still unemployable, unless your family owns the company (and even then the insurance companies would have something to say), so you either have to do a couple of years as a hangar rat, that is, washing windscreens until your company sees what you're like and trains you up, or buy the hours yourself. To be even remotely interesting to an employer, you need at least 1,000 hours on top of your CPL, or some sort of specialised training, such as a mountain course (preferably both) and maybe an instrument rating, depending on the job.

When you budget for your training, don't just count in the cost of your course, but the time afterwards going around companies to get hired; just sending résumés is no good at all (this could take up to four years). Note that you may well need more than the minimum hours required – certainly, as far as the PPL is concerned, the average time taken to pass is 67.7 hours, against a minimum of about 40.

To all that must be added the year's salary you don't earn while you're training, which means that you have to ensure a high enough salary that will give enough return to pay back this 'loan' of, say, £65,000 (assuming you would earn £10,000 as an 18-year old). That's as big as a mortgage, so you would need the cash flow to be able to pay yourself back around £750 per month for 25 years – and that's before you start eating! (Mind you, it could be tax-deductible).

But why be negative? Flying is the sort of profession where economics tend to take a back seat, and it's not always money that motivates people, so you will need to know that there are generally two grades of licence that entitle you to earn money as a pilot, the *Commercial Pilot's Licence* (CPL) and the *Airline Transport Pilot's Licence* (ATPL). For what people would normally think of as commercial air transport purposes (that is, where passengers or cargo are carried for money), the CPL covers you for command of aircraft up to 5,700 kg in weight and the rank of first officer for anything else (though I don't think you'll find too many CPL holders in the front end of a 747). You can't have a CPL until a certain age, but you can take the exams beforehand – some of them up to twelve months in advance.

Neither can you have an ATPL until you are much older and get a lot more hours under your belt and pass some more exams; though not necessarily in that order. The ATPL covers you for command on anything, subject to type rating.

Although the ATPL includes an instrument rating as part of its structure, the CPL may be issued without one, which makes it a useful first step, but you're generally unemployable without an IR. If you have an ATPL, but allow any of the requirements that makes it valid lapse (such as a six-monthly medical or an IR), then it reverts to a CPL. The chief pilot will have discretion to use pilots with all sorts of variations, provided a suitable training programme is established.

If you join, say, an air taxi company already type rated and with about 250 hours' charter experience, your training will be as little as possible and take the format of the Base or Proficiency Check. It will (or should) include a technical exam relating to the aircraft type. As a result, you could find yourself just completing the following in order to get on-line:

- ❑ Emergency and Lifesaving Equipment Check
- ❑ Base or Proficiency Check
- ❑ Area Competency Check
- ❑ Recent experience
- ❑ Line check

You need the emergency one first, or at least the paperwork needs to be dated that way. If you require type rating as well, you will also need a Type Technical Examination and 1179 Check (a proper training syllabus will have to be laid down for this, and will consist of a number of hours of ground and air training, typically twenty-five and five respectively), together with a minimum of two observed sectors (or 2–3 hours, whichever is the greater) before a final line check (in Canada, line checks only seem to be relevant at the airline level). If your company expects to train and convert pilots regularly, they will need to include the training syllabus as part of the ops manual. If it's a one-off occasion, a Flying Staff Instruction should cover it.

Unless the aircraft you are converting to is very similar to one you already have on your licence, you will probably also have to renew your instrument rating on type (definitely on a helicopter). If you're unlucky and not only require type rating but also have less than 250 hours' charter experience, you may find yourself doing an initial line check with at least six observed sectors (which must consist of a minimum total of about ten hours) before your final line check.

The observed sectors are not part of basic training, but are to allow you to settle down and to help check on the training procedures. All of the above is variable, however, and will change between companies.

Training in General

Unfortunately, companies don't share information readily, either for commercial reasons or lack of time, and so-called self-starters, who pay for their own training, may cause problems (no disrespect). The thing is, their training can be of varied quality, and until JAA is fully running it is possible to pass the relevant exams with the absolute minimum of training, particularly with relevance to company procedures for commercial operations.

As I said before, a typical pilot's qualifications necessarily revolve around piston-engined aircraft, whereas airlines fly jets, and the disparity can be a continual headache for training departments. When you join a company, you must be taught about high altitude, swept wing, electronic aircraft and control management, amongst a multitude of other subjects, including multi-crew co-operation and CRM. *This has to be paid for by somebody.*

If the expertise isn't already in the company to deal with this, it will have to be imported, and no accountant likes company money going outside. When the opportunity allows, the chief pilot or training captain may carry out check flights to ensure the highest possible standards are maintained, the intention being to maintain a 100 per cent safety factor within the company and keep the company's quality control procedures going. This ultimately can only be achieved by strict adherence to all rules and mandatory regulations, common sense and the co-operation of all concerned.

Every company must have a training policy, codified in a manual. It's meant to be a separate volume, but can be included in the ops manual if there's room, and one copy may need to be lodged with the authorities for reference purposes.

Training flights should take place at licensed aerodromes, and weather minima should not be less than those required for commercial air transport, although you are allowed to make one or two more instrument approaches in one session than you would normally be allowed to.

No training, checking or emergencies should be undertaken on revenue flights except final or routine line checks – in other words, training is done on non-revenue trips.

As soon as all items of any check have been completed, the person conducting the test signs all applicable licences, amends the training records and informs Operations of the results so that they can amend their own records and boards. In addition, someone of higher authority (the managing director or chief pilot) must sign check forms on behalf of the company before they become valid; for obvious reasons, the chief pilot shouldn't sign his own.

If you fail a test, the circumstances are reported and arrangements are made for repeating it. A certain amount of training may be done after consultation with a suitably appointed training captain, who will make the necessary recommendations. It will be usual for any examiner to be a fully qualified commander so that passengers can be taken home legally should a test be failed anywhere en route.

Basic flying training is carried out by a qualified instructor, as is initial training for instrument ratings or first twins. Other training may be carried out by any appointed training captain, who ought to be a TRE as well. Specialised training for specific tasks (e.g. sling work) should be given by a training captain experienced in the particular type of work.

When you get selected for commercial air transport duties, a training folder will be opened on your behalf, in which will be a personal sheet with details of your licence, qualifications, previous experience, the usual stuff, plus all the training forms that get filled in as you go along. The training captain will look at it before he gets his hands on you, and add to its contents in the shape of reports, etc.

Initial Training

As a minimum, this should include:

❏ Fire and smoke training
❏ Emergency and survival (water or otherwise)

- ❏ Ground training (handling, elementary servicing, contamination, etc.)
- ❏ Medical/first aid
- ❏ Passenger handling
- ❏ Communication
- ❏ Discipline and responsibilities (i.e. company indoctrination)
- ❏ Crew resource management (including pilot decision-making)
- ❏ Specialised tasks (slinging, water bucketing, low visibility, etc.)
- ❏ Dangerous goods

Conversion Training

Try this lot for size:

- ❏ Normal procedures
- ❏ Fire and smoke training
- ❏ Operation of doors and exits
- ❏ Evacuation slide training
- ❏ Evacuation and emergency procedures
- ❏ Crowd control
- ❏ Pilot incapacitation
- ❏ Safety equipment
- ❏ Passenger briefing/safety demonstrations

Recurrent Training

Each year, you should have sessions on:

- ❏ Emergency procedures, including pilot incapacitation
- ❏ Evacuation procedures, including crowd control
- ❏ Touch drills for opening normal and emergency exits

Checks Required

There are two things to note about checks: firstly, there is an increasing bias towards a written element, and secondly, if you take a renewal and fail it before your previous check expires, the first one expires as well!

As far as keeping your licences current is concerned, you will find yourself subject to the following checks in addition to those needed for normal licence upkeep, which you should already know about:

Emergency and Lifesaving Equipment Check

This is the one you do before everything else, and there are two versions: one done every year and another every three. The annual one is valid for twelve months, plus the remainder of the month of issue, but if you take it in the final three months, you can extend to twelve months from the previous expiry date. Similar conditions apply to the triennial.

It requires knowledge of the use and location of all emergency equipment, and must contain a written element. Usually, for small aircraft, a simple plan with boxes to put the location of any emergency equipment in will do, but increasingly two pages of multi-choice questions are in order.

Emergency training is usually organised by the flight safety officer, and should cover a range of subjects from first aid (appropriate to the aircraft) to fire and smoke drills and water survival training.

Practical experience is necessary, so expect to cover the actual donning of a lifejacket and protective breathing equipment, actual handling of fire extinguishers, instruction on the location and use of all emergency and safety equipment and exits and security procedures.

Every three years you can expect the actual operation of all types of exits, actual fire-fighting with aircraft equipment, experience the effects of smoke in an enclosed area, with actual use of all relevant equipment in a simulated smoke-filled environment, handling of pyrotechnics, real or simulated, and demonstration in the use of the life-rafts, where fitted.

If you can provide documentary evidence of all the above having been done at a previous company, you might get away with it.

Type Rating Test/Renewal Check

The type rating test must be passed after your conversion and before it goes on your licence. The renewal check is needed every six months by the ANO, where it's referred to as a Certificate of Test (but only for licensing) in order to maintain currency. As a Schedule 11 check, it must be carried out by an authorised type rating examiner (of Schedule 11 variety, who must be sponsored by a company – see later in this chapter). Some countries combine this with the base, or operator proficiency check (below) and call it a PPC, or Pilot Proficiency Certificate.

Operator Proficiency Check

Otherwise known as the Base Check, or a PPC in Canada, this is a look at your ability to carry out emergency manoeuvres at your normal flight station. It's valid for six months, plus the remainder of the month of issue. There is some talk, in Canada, at least, of replacing it with recurrent training.

It's needed on each aircraft flown and, although the statutory requirement is to assure your continued competence, it's usually also used for training, as it's a good time for practising drills and procedures that rarely arise in normal operations. It also includes an element of CRM, as do many others.

Some items in a base check will be covered by touch drills (which are normally best attended to on the ground), as well as a general discussion of operating procedures, emergencies, recognition and diagnosis of aircraft system faults, pre-flight briefing, etc. Additional precautions may be considered if you operate in extreme weather conditions. The complete list should be covered over two checks.

Occasionally, if two aircraft are very similar, OPCs may be carried out alternately on each type. On multi-engined aircraft they will also be expected to be carried out alternately at night. Some companies may have separate VFR and IFR versions.

The check must contain the 'boxed items' contained in the 1179 check form, or most of the type rating renewal check.

It is possible that a pilot who has been checked by another company may be acceptable by yours, but this will be by arrangement with your inspector (the PPC is transferable in Canada). In any case, the two companies must have similar content and procedures in their checks and the arrangements must have been agreed *before the test date* (see also Freelance Pilots, later in this chapter). However, this will not be valid in the case of a company just setting up, because it has no AOC and therefore no legal status with which to set up agreements. In Canada, this check is transferable between companies.

Instrument Approach Proficiency Check

A test of your skill in using typical instrument approach systems at aerodromes of intended landing, but most companies will just certify you on all of them for convenience. As it has the same frequency as the base check, it is normally conducted as part of one, and will form part of the IFR base check if they are split. Only really relevant if you hold . . .

Instrument Rating

This is completed at thirteen-month intervals by an instrument rating examiner and may be completed as part of a base check, or at least tagged on the end, as you're in the air anyway. If such is the case, the IRE should also be a TRE (both appointments, by the way, should be held through a company, otherwise your check will be invalid). The IR's purpose is to establish whether you're maintaining the standards necessary for safe operations in controlled airspace under IMC.

A helicopter IR is only valid on type, whereas an aeroplane one is transferable within certain limits – if you later convert to a dissimilar type, you'll probably have to renew it as well. You won't need it if you're only doing VFR work, such as pleasure flying.

Area Competence Check

The company must ensure that en route and destination facilities are such that a safe operation is run. Part of this is achieved by the area competence check, which is carried out every twelve months, plus the remainder of the month of last operation on the route. It's done with the line check for convenience, and tests your knowledge of specific route(s) or particular areas of operations.

Line Check

This is valid for twelve months plus the remainder of the month of issue, but if you take it in the final three months, you can extend to twelve months from the previous expiry date. It's a test of your performance of normal duties at your crew station, so will be done on a standard commercial flight, or at least the final line check will (initial ones only give you the status of first pilot under supervision. Lapsed line checks don't qualify, either).

It covers an entire line operation from pre-flight preparations to completion of post-flight duties, and normally must be carried out on each type of aircraft flown, although it may be done alternately where types are similar. It's not supposed to represent a particular route, but must be an adequate representation of the company's work. Line checks may be carried out by fully qualified line captains.

Although the stipulated frequency is once every twelve months, you might find a training captain hopping in on an empty seat once in a while before that. It's nothing personal, just part of Quality Control (that phrase again), and better than leaving things to the last minute and risking you being off-line because a check hasn't been done in time.

Line training, leading up to the check, is supposed to familiarise you with the routes over which you will operate, for which you will be supervised by experienced training staff. Before you can do this with passengers, you must have passed an initial line check, followed by some supervised flights, then a final line check before they let you loose on the unsuspecting public.

The supervised flights will have passengers on, so you will now become aware of commercial pressures, and these are as much a hurdle to some pilots as other training is, because you will probably also have flight director systems to use as well – you don't use those in training.

Alternative Seat Position Check

Only needed if you fly in any other seat than your normal one; you might become a line training captain, where you need to be able to fly the thing home or get it on the ground if your examinee fails en route. Also, in a helicopter you may have to do a compass swing from the other seat so that the engineer can conveniently make his adjustments, or you may be a commander who occasionally needs to be a co-pilot.

If the latter is the case, provided you still have a valid proficiency check, this one may be abbreviated at the discretion of the training captain, but not below a minimum of an engine failure after take-off, an asymmetric go-around from DH and an asymmetric landing. For whatever reason, if done, it will coincide with a proficiency check.

Crew Resource Management

CRM training will normally be addressed during line-oriented flight training (LOFT). Otherwise, you must complete elements of CRM every year, with the major elements of a full course over a three- or four-year recurrent training cycle. It will be included as part of all the above checks, and is covered more fully in a later chapter.

Recent Experience

Not a test as such, but to be considered current as a commander, you must have completed whatever it says in Chapter 5.

In addition, some companies may require some approaches or real instrument flying within a certain period. Others may even require recency on type, and will have special procedures should you be absent from the company for more than twenty-eight days.

Multi-Type Currency

Unless your company only operates simple types of aircraft (refer to your inspector), it's rare for anyone to be current on more than three types at once. Not only is this sensible, but multi-type currency causes all sorts of other problems – training costs could get out of hand, and it will be quite difficult to keep up normal twenty-eight-day currency as well (and I speak as one who was once current for over a year on six types of reasonably different helicopter or aeroplane – not easy, I can tell you).

Mixing things always causes complications. For a combination of aeroplane and helicopter, you can fly one aeroplane within the same type or class rating, and one helicopter, irrespective of maximum take-off weight or number of passengers. If types are not within the same type or class rating, you need some recency on top.

For multi-pilot aeroplanes, or those that can carry more than nineteen passengers, you cannot operate more than two types that need a separate type rating. You also need at least three months and 150 hours on the first type before the conversion for the second, on which you must do some days and hours afterwards before getting your hands on the first again. You can only fly one type in any duty period.

Otherwise, you cannot operate more than three piston types, three turbo-prop types or one turbo-prop or turbojet and one piston type.

Freelance Pilots

Freelancing need not be as precarious a living as it sounds. Like a lot of other things, it depends very much on whom you know as well as what you know. If you're known to be reliable, that is, get out of bed in the morning, turn up on time, don't crash and generally deliver passengers safely, you will always get work. Even airlines use freelancers.

If you do decide to make a living out of it (at least it gives an illusion of control over your life – you are in a position to say no, after all, especially to companies which are known to be less than enthusiastic about maintenance). The taxman will be watching to ensure that you are in fact working for more than one customer, but it doesn't pay to be too dependent on one anyway.

While their usefulness is recognised in relieving short-term problems, especially in smaller companies, the use of freelancers used to be (and still is) frowned upon as they're more difficult to keep control of, at least as far as duty hours and paperwork are concerned.

Now that aircraft are more complex, and it's increasingly difficult to hop from one machine to another with ease, all freelance pilots must be checked to the company's standards. The operative phrase is 'by or on behalf of the operator', which means that the company must maintain strict control. Provided that the ops manual says so, or a Flying Staff

Instruction is issued to cover the occasion, there's no reason why other companies' pilots and paperwork shouldn't be used, but their standards must be similar and a mutual exchange of paperwork must take place. However, the catch is that there must be a *pre-existing arrangement* for this to happen, which must be formally established in writing.

Despite the fact that everybody pinches everybody else's ops manual anyway, and the forms are therefore mostly the same, it's a legal problem – as the checks must be performed 'by or on behalf of, etc.', it could be argued that if the forms were just backdated, this will not have been done. For instance, it would be difficult to claim that tests conducted by one operator were done on behalf of another unless there was an arrangement to that effect at the time and the other operator's requirements were taken care of.

As a result, all required checks should take place and be signed up at the same time as the testing company's (for example, a TRE common to two companies should conduct a test and double up on the paperwork). The other companies' training captains will also need to be listed in your manual, which they must also have a copy of, otherwise they won't know to what standards you operate.

Company Training Captains

Qualifications for this position are naturally more stringent because of the responsibility involved. The training captain will have the normal requirements for company pilot, plus more experience on the relevant types and more total flying hours, with suitable training as a TRE or TRI. Duties and responsibilities will be down to common sense.

If the company is not large enough to have a separate training captain, the appointment may also be covered by another office holder. A list of the tests that may be carried out will be shown (possibly in a table like that below), but external pilots should not normally do company line checks:

Type	Base Check	Line Check	Area Comp	E/S Check
Capt Fred Nurk	X	X	X	X

TRI (MPA) – minimum requirements

Pass an approved TRI course, have at least 1,500 hours as PIC of multi-pilot aeroplanes, complete within the previous 12 months at least 30 route sectors, to include take-offs and landings as PIC or P2 on type, or similar, by arrangement, with up to 15 sectors done in an approved flight simulator. In addition, have conducted on a complete type rating course at least one part related to the duties of a TRI on type under the supervision of a qualified TRI.

To keep the rating, in the previous 12 months, you must have completed one part of a complete type rating course and refresher training under an authorised examiner. If it has lapsed, you must do all of the above, plus an approved course.

TRE – minimum requirements
Equal or greater licence than the applicant, with instructor privileges, qualified to act as PIC on relevant aeroplanes, meet experience requirements for the role and a certain minimum number of hours.

To keep the authorisation, you must have completed a supervised examiner skill test within the last year of authorisation.

SFI – minimum requirements
Must hold, or have held, a professional pilot licence, have completed the approved flight simulator content of the relevant type course, have at least 1,500 hours as pilot on multi-pilot aeroplanes, have completed an approved TRI course and have conducted on a complete type rating course at least one part related to the duties of a TRI on the applicable type under the supervision of a qualified TRI. In addition, in the previous year, have done a proficiency check on type in an approved flight simulator and three route sectors on type as supernumerary crew.

To keep the authorisation, you must have conducted, within the last 12 months of the authorisation, one part of a complete type rating course, or refresher training under an approved TRI. If it lapses, you must complete the flight simulator content of the applicable type rating course, successfully complete an approved TRI course, and conduct, on a complete type rating course, at least one part related to the duties of a TRI on the applicable type under the supervision of an approved TRI.

SFE – minimum requirements
Have a licence and rating the same or greater than the applicant, with suitable instructor privileges, be qualified as PIC on type, meet experience requirements for the role, plus 1,500 hours.

To keep the authorisation, you must have completed a supervised examiner skill test within the last year of authorisation.

Line training captain
Must be acceptable to the authorities.

Guidance to Training Captains

Especially in bigger aircraft, there's quite a flurry of arms and legs as flaps are taken in, hands are changed on control columns to take charge of nosewheel steering, the airspeed indicator is rebugged, etc., so definite procedures are needed to prevent accidents (however, a lot of guidance can simply be gleaned from reading the ops manual itself).

Immediately before any action takes place, the training captain should position himself to stop you applying the flying controls the wrong way and should monitor the airspeed and other indications for abnormal conditions.

Engine failures (real or otherwise) should only be practised on briefed training flights or air tests; in fact, a thorough briefing for everybody is always essential, covering such things as heights and speeds to be flown, methods of simulating whatever emergencies you're practising, etc. For those after take-off, and on single-engined approaches, the reported weather conditions at the aerodrome concerned should not be less than those required for visual manoeuvring.

The requirements of JAR Ops 1 are really geared to Performance A aircraft, so if you're in anything lower, power failure should not be simulated after take-off below V_{xse} (the best angle of climb) or V_{yse} (the best rate), unless you have a clever (or brave) training captain.

Otherwise, during take-off, the speed should always be below V_1 or V_{Toss} with the crosswind component not exceeding fifteen knots or the aircraft maximum, whichever is the smaller. After the simulated engine failure, the take-off should be abandoned, unless your machine's performance is up to scratch.

Engine shutdowns should not occur below 3,000 feet agl (or higher), or in any weather other than VMC, otherwise you may cause the very accident the training is designed to prevent. Talking of which, if you do shut down an engine on any otherwise normal flight for whatever reason in a twin-engined aircraft, only in exceptional circumstances should you not land at the nearest suitable aerodrome. You are allowed a little more flexibility if you have more than one engine left, of course.

Below the recommended minimum heights, simulated engine failure should be initiated by closing the throttle enough for a significant loss of power (in a helicopter, just lower the collective lever). However, problems may arise with propeller-driven aircraft where below a certain r.p.m. (1,000 or so), feathering cannot take place, and you would actually get better single-engined aircraft response from a failed engine with feathered blades.

The area underneath should be suitable for the exercise (over an airfield preferably, in case of a forced landing being necessary) and the call

'Practice engine failure' should be made at the time. When practising forced landings, normal low-flying rules apply.

There should be something in the ops manual to cover double engine failure under IF conditions, and the time taken to restart engine(s) having shut them down.

Entries into autorotation or the glide should be entered into above 1,000 feet agl, and (unless sure of landing correctly on a properly authorised engine-off landing area) full recovery should take place before 250 feet agl.

Before conducting accelerate/stop exercises, the training captain should ensure that the runway is not contaminated, the crosswind component is not more than 50 per cent of the limiting value for the type, the failure will be simulated before two-thirds of unstick speed, and that enough runway is available.

When practising touch and go procedures (in aeroplanes), as well as above, twice the normal TODR should be available. Before initiating the go-around, the training captain should ensure that landing flap (if used) has been converted to take-off, that the handling pilot has been advised of its position, and that in all other respects the aircraft is fit to get airborne again. The aircraft should be positively climbing before being fully cleaned up.

The aircraft should also be stopped before reconfiguration takes place, and the training captain should ensure reconfiguration before giving further instructions.

If a rejected take-off is intended, the training captain should simply state the problem, such as falling oil pressure and await events, similarly with a fire in-flight before a practice forced landing. With an engine fire after take-off, the training captain should, at a safe height, slowly close the throttle to the idle position and advise the handling pilot to restore power as soon as the emergency touch drills have been completed.

For depressurisation training a slow method of cabin pressure reduction should be used and aircraft should not be depressurised at an altitude greater than 15,000 ft (neither should an aircraft be depressurised when undergoing emergency descent).

Simulated flight conditions

If your company is lucky enough to own one, a flight simulator may be used for instrument rating renewals and instrument approach proficiency checks, provided that it has been approved for that purpose by the CAA. Simulators and procedure trainers may be used at other times for training purposes. Simulation of IF conditions in VMC for training and testing purposes will need screens or other approved apparatus. Visors are acceptable, provided the lower windows are whited out. A competent observer with a full field of vision must also be carried. Don't forget to tell ATC what's going on.

On becoming a TRE

A TRE (in the UK, anyway) is appointed for a three-year period and can only hold the appointment through a company, so if your company goes out of business, so do you, as a TRE anyway, unless you move sharply sideways to another. The application is made to the CAA, together with the usual CLM (Cheque for Lots of Money), and you are expected to undergo a training course before the appointed examiner comes to check you out. The problem is that there's no syllabus; that's the responsibility of the company concerned, so here follows an idea of the process in case they leave you on your own, as happened to me.

You are expected to conduct a complete examination, from briefing the candidate and examining documents, to sitting in the aircraft and ensuring competency to fly and signing up the forms afterwards. When you do your test, you should have a letter from the CAA, including instructions for TREs, and evidence of training. The requirements vary according to the type of aircraft you will be testing on and the type of company you will be working for, but should not realistically be less than a week, containing at least 4–5 hours' flying.

You will be examined on:

- ❏ Licence privileges, the C of T/C of E, what to look for in a licence and what they cover
- ❏ Base and line check requirements; frequency and validity
- ❏ Medical frequency and validity, ages to fly commercially
- ❏ Recency (Schedule 8)
- ❏ The need for licensed airfields
- ❏ Who can instruct and where
- ❏ The ANO with regard to flying instruction
- ❏ Status of various documents
- ❏ Performance and ANGRs
- ❏ Rules of the Air, especially 5, 6, 25 and 26
- ❏ Where to find information about the above

Preliminaries

Tests must be conducted in accordance with the operations manual if the test is for an AOC, or the Flying Order Book if for a PPL holder. The candidate must be told to ask questions if unsure about what's going on, which implies that one of the unwritten qualities of a TRE is the ability to put people at their ease – questions won't be asked if you give the impression that they're unwelcome. Remember that you are examining somebody so that they can pass a test, not to stop them passing it. In fact, your service should also include being on time, polite and respectful, well organised and businesslike. The weather must obviously be good enough, which is for the candidate to check, but if it isn't, for a commercial or otherwise normal flight to take place, you may elect to do the test anyway, provided the candidate clearly understands the position.

You need to check the licence for the following:

- ❏ Candidate's signature
- ❏ Expiry date
- ❏ Medical currency (and signature!)
- ❏ Date of last C of T

The Briefing

Should cover the following points:

- ❏ The aim of the flight – whether for Proficiency Check, 1179 or C of T
- ❏ The sequence of exercises to be covered – as you will give instructions as you go along, there is no need for the candidate to memorise them
- ❏ Responsibilities – who is the captain and when. Although the candidate is the captain, legally, you are, and the circumstances (and the methods) under which you will take control must be clearly spelt out
- ❏ Equipment usage – altimeters, icing, etc.
- ❏ ATC instructions and the following thereof
- ❏ Radio, RT and navaids – setting and tuning
- ❏ Use of checklists
- ❏ Aircraft control
  - ❏ Speeds to be used in climb, descent, approach and autorotation (if applicable)
  - ❏ Circuit heights and directions, etc.
  - ❏ Aircraft parameters – oral questions about Ts and Ps, maximum settings, r.p.m. limits, crosswind limitations, etc.
- ❏ Methods of simulating emergencies

You could also mention that any writing you do is not necessarily criticism, but an *aide-mémoire* for the debriefing. Also, the candidate shouldn't fret about mistakes so much that the rest of the test is at risk. The exercises concerned can always be done again at the end.

Based on the above, here is a sample briefing (for a helicopter flight):

'You will be required to demonstrate an accurate training circuit from and to a given area, and during the flight carry out the exercises listed on the F1179 flight test/base check form, which may be given in any order. There will be a practice engine-off in the hover, given without warning by closing the throttle.

'A limited-power take-off and landing must be demonstrated at a power setting given by me, based on what is available in the hover. There will also be a quick stop into wind from at least sixty knots, sloping-ground landings, a restricted-site landing using the full procedure for an unknown and confined area, including the relevant power checks, recces and clearing turns, followed by departure from the circuit into the local training area and subsequent rejoin. Steep turns in both directions as briefed by me, a minimum of 30° bank, normally 45°.

You will need to recognise and recover from incipient Vortex Ring. Recover to a safe configuration with minimum height loss.

At some stage you can expect a simulated engine emergency, which will result in a practice forced landing. This may be the result of a practice fire in the air. You are to continue to 500 feet agl, ensuring you manoeuvre the aircraft to safely achieve autorotation towards a suitable landing site. The appropriate checks and radio calls should be completed, but not to the detriment of the flying.

There will be an engine-off landing to a pre-agreed position on the airfield. You must be wings level, with no slip or skid and at the given autorotation speed by 300 feet. I will assist you to close the throttle if needed.

IF I CALL "I HAVE CONTROL", BE SURE TO RELEASE THE THROTTLE.'

Before starting training or examining with any candidate, you should find out exactly what they have done in the past, so that you know where the difficulties are, and can have your hands nearer the controls at the right times. Also, especially if you haven't met the candidate before, try a demonstration to show the response and procedures that are expected.

The Flight

This must take place at 90 per cent of the landing weight or RTOW, and should flow smoothly from one section to the next, because it should be as short as possible consistent with a proper examination: remember that someone is paying for it. For example, if you have sideways flight in a helicopter to do, there's no reason why it couldn't be done inside a confined area, together with a sloping-ground landing, thus combining several exercises at once. You can do this in many ways to provide smoothness and economy.

18

Crew Resource Management

Note: This is extracted from my approved single-pilot CRM course.

Aircraft are getting more reliable, so, in theory at least, accidents should happen less often. Unfortunately, this is not the case, so we need to look somewhere else for the causes. Believe it or not, accidents are very carefully planned – it's just that the results are very different from those expected! An accident is actually the end product of a chain of events, so if you can recognise the sequence it should be possible to nip any problems in the bud.

A common saying is that 'the well-oiled nut behind the wheel is the most dangerous part of any car'. Not necessarily true for aviation, perhaps, but, in looking for causes other than the hardware when it comes to accidents, it's hard not to focus on the pilot (or human factor) as the weak link in the chain – 70–90 per cent of accidents can be attributed to this, although it's also true to say that the situations some aircraft are put into make them liable to misfortunes as a matter of course, particularly helicopters – I mean, if you continually land on slippery logs in clearings with slash everywhere, something untoward is bound to happen sometime!

In Canada this training is needed to fly in visibility down to half a mile. This might not actually be due to weather, but smoke, as you might find in a forest fire – in fact, you can be nearly IMC on a hazy day in some industrial areas. However, this 'licence' for bad-weather flying does not mean you have to do it – it's not the equivalent of the amber traffic light meaning 'go faster'! You still have to be aware of the implications of what you are doing.

In other words, if you have a pilot behaving under par in an aircraft where it shouldn't be, you're just asking for trouble, and this applies to large aircraft just as much as it does to small ones. An accident-prone person, officially, is somebody to whom things happen at a higher rate than could be statistically expected by chance alone. Taking calculated risks is completely different from taking chances. Know your capabilities, and your limits.

Bad-weather visibility is associated with low ceilings, and familiarity with the area is a real help, so local flying is better than a low-level navex, at least without a GPS. This, at least, will save you changing your focus from the outside to the map inside your cockpit, which is not where it should be in such circumstances. However, GPSs produce their own problems – because they help you so much when the weather is bad, they tempt you to stretch the envelope that little bit more, which is dangerous in itself.

Most weather-based accidents involve inadvertent entry into IMC by people who have only had the basic instrument instruction required for the commercial licence. Next in line is icing.

These days, there are new concepts to consider, such as delegation, communication, monitoring and prioritisation, although they will have varying degrees of importance in a single-pilot environment. In fact, the term 'pilot error' is probably only accurate about a third of the time; all it really does is indicate where a breakdown occurred. There may have been just too much input for one person to cope with, which is not necessarily error, because no identifiable mistakes were made. Perhaps there needs to be a new phrase, occupying the same position that 'not proven' does in the Scottish legal system, which lies somewhere between guilty and not guilty.

The aim of this sort of training is to increase flight safety by showing you how to make the best use of resources available to you, which include your own body (physical and psychological factors), information, equipment and other people, whether in flight or on the ground – P2s are trained for emergencies, for example, so that they can be used instead of automatically taking over yourself when something happens – like a human autopilot, in fact. Also remember that the behaviour of people in a company is very much a reflection of the management, in our case the commander, so there is an obligation for whoever's in charge to foster a positive working environment, which, essentially, means not being a miserable sod. Like it or not, you are part of a team, even if you are the only one in the cockpit, and you have to fit into an already established system. This is geared to help you with making decisions, of which more later.

The courses are supposed to be discussion-based, which means that you are expected to participate, with the intention that your experiences will be spread around to other crews. This is because it's quite possible never to see people from one year to the next in a large organisation, and helicopter pilots in particular have no flying clubs, or at least opportunities to 'hangar fly' as the Americans say, so experience is not being passed on.

One accident which illustrates the need for CRM training was a Lockheed 1011 that flew into the Florida Everglades. A problem involving the nosewheel occupied the attention of all three members of the crew so much that they lost the big picture, and the aircraft ended up in the swamp. It was concluded that the commander should have ensured that someone was monitoring the situation, and should have delegated tasks accordingly. But was a 'mistake' actually made? Nobody pushed the wrong switches or carried out the 'wrong' actions – it was perhaps just a wrong decision.

A contribution to the Kegworth accident in the UK, where the plane ended up on the motorway, was the inability of the cabin crews to feel they were able to talk to the flight deck if they saw a problem, which puts the problem fairly and squarely at the door of the company, or at least the management. Also, a reading of the accident report on the Air Florida flight that hit a bridge and ended up in the Potomac would be instructive – the FO was clearly sure that something was wrong (icing) but didn't like to say so.

In short, Crew Resource Management (CRM) is the effective utilisa-tion of all available resources (e.g. crew members, aeroplane systems and supporting facilities) to achieve safe and efficient operation – the idea is to enhance your communication and management skills in order to achieve this. In other words, the emphasis is placed on the non-technical aspects of flight crew performance which are also needed to do your job properly. You could loosely call it airmanship, but I prefer to use the term captaincy, as flying is a lot more complex now than when the original term was more appropriate.

The elusive quality of captaincy is probably best illustrated with an example, such as the subject of the critical point. If you can think back to your pilot's exams, you will recall that it is a position where it takes as much time to go forward to your destination as it does to return whence you came, so that you can deal with emergencies in the quickest time.

In a typical pilot's exam, you will be given the departure and destina-tion points, the wind velocity and other relevant information and be asked to calculate the CP along with the PNR (Point of No Return), which is all right as far as it goes, but tells you nothing about your quali-ties as a captain, however much it may demonstrate your technical abilities as a pilot.

Now take the same question, but introduce the scenario of a flight across the Atlantic, during which you are tapped on the shoulder by a hostess who tells you that a passenger has got appendicitis. First of all, you have to know that you need the CP, which is given to you already in the previous question. Then you find out that you are only five minutes away – technically, you should turn back, but is that really such a good decision? Commercially, it would be disastrous, and here you find the difference between being a pilot and a captain, or the men and the boys, and why CRM training is becoming so important.

With regard to outside agencies, as single crew, there is only you in your cockpit, but you still have to talk to passengers and other people in your organisation, and we all work in the air transport industry. It just happens that your company is paying your wages at the moment – in this context, the word 'crew' includes anybody else who can help you deliver the end product, which is

. . . Safe Arrival!

Very few people travel just for the sake of it, unless you own a Pitts. Everything else is subordinate to this, including pride and the prospect of increasing your qualifications and experience. Remember that the general public are paying your wages.

ATC are there to help if you've got a problem. They will check that your landing gear is down, file a flight plan on your behalf and check out the weather, although a lot of this could be done by the company if it has a radio frequency.

The best way out of trouble is not to get into it, which is easier said than done with an intimidating passenger or management. You, the pilot, are the decision-maker – in fact, under the Chicago Convention (Annex 2, Chapter 2), your word is law until overturned within three months by a person with a lawful interest, regardless of what the government might say. However, the other side of the coin is that you are liable for what goes on – in fact, in aviation, the buck very definitely stops at the bottom.

Decisions, Decisions

Aviation is noticeable for its almost constant decision making. As you fly along, particularly in a helicopter, you're probably updating your next engine-off landing point every five seconds or so. Or maybe you're keeping an eye on your fuel and constantly calculating your endurance in view of unexpected weather. It all adds to the many tasks you're meant to keep up to date with, because the situation is always changing. In fact, a decision not to make a decision (i.e. wait a while for developments) is also a decision, always being aware that we don't want indecision.

The process involves not only our eyes and ears which gather data, but our attention, which should not be preoccupied all the time. The human body is not multi-tasking, and to keep track of what's going on it's necessary to split your attention for a short period between everything; typically a split second at a time. It's important not to get fixated on one thing at the expense of another, which is typically what happens when flying in bad weather (remember the L-1011). Gather all the information you can in the time available or, better still, get in the habit of updating information you're likely to need in an emergency as the flight progresses.

Each decision you make eliminates the choice of another, so, once you make a poor one, a chain of them usually follows. In fact, a decision-making chain can often be traced back up to and over fifty years, depending on whether the original cause was a design flaw. Another factor is the data itself: if it's incomplete, you can't base a proper decision on it. So:

- ❏ Don't make a decision unless you have to
- ❏ Keep it under review once you've made it
- ❏ No decision can be a decision (but watch out for indecision)

Your ability to make decisions is affected by:

- ❏ The state of your body and its performance
- ❏ Habits
- ❏ Attitudes
- ❏ Stress
- ❏ Fatigue

Each of which we will look at now.

The Body

The human body is wonderful, but only up to a point. It has limitations that affect your ability to fly efficiently, as your senses don't always tell you the truth, which is why you need extensive training to fly on instruments, as you have to unlearn so much. The classic example of this is the 'leans', where you think you're performing a particular manoeuvre, but your instruments tell you otherwise. However, you can't leave it all to machines.

If you were to ask a computer to choose between a clock that was gaining five minutes a day, and one that had stopped completely, it would probably choose the one that had stopped, because it was accurate twice a day, as opposed to once every sixty days or so. The point is that machines cannot discriminate, which is good if you just want them to report factual information, as with instruments, but not if you want them to make decisions.

Why do you need to learn about the body? Well, parts of it are used to get the information you need to make decisions with. And, of course, if it isn't working properly, you can't process the information or implement any action based on it.

Eyes

Vision is your primary source of information. It gets harder with age to distinguish moving objects; between the ages of forty and sixty-five, this ability diminishes by up to 50 per cent. This is only one of the limitations of sight, and we need to examine the eye to see how you overcome them.

The eye is nearly round, and its rotation in its socket is controlled by three pairs of external muscles. It has three coatings: the *sclerotic*, which is transparent at the front; the *choroid*, which lines the sclerotic and contains tiny blood vessels; and the *retina*, which is the light-sensitive bit that detects electromagnetic waves of the frequency of light, and converts them to electrical signals that are interpreted by the brain, and which is sensitive to hypoxia. This means that you see with the brain as well, giving you a difference between *seeing* and *perceiving*, discussed below.

Rods and Cones

The retina consists of light sensors (actually, neurons) which are called *rods* and *cones*, because of the way they are shaped. Each is more efficient than the other in different kinds of light. The point where the optic nerve joins the retina is mostly populated with cones, which work best in daylight and become less effective at night, or where oxygen levels are reduced (which is significant for smokers, whose blood has less oxygen-carrying capacity), so you get a blind spot in the direct field of vision, which is why you see things more clearly at night if you look slightly to the side of what you want to look at. Rods cannot distinguish colours, either, which is why things at night seem to be in varying shades of grey. You see colours simply because the vibrations they give out are strong enough to wake the cones up.

The more your iris is open, the less *depth of field* you have, so in darkness you find it difficult to see beyond or before a certain distance, and you may require glasses to help (the depth of field in photography is a short distance in between the camera and the subject where everything is in focus. The wider the aperture, or iris, the shorter this distance is, and vice versa).

The retina contains enormous amounts of Vitamin A, which is necessary for adapting between light and darkness. Too little Vitamin A could therefore result in *night blindness*. The changeover from light to dark takes about twenty minutes and should always be allowed for when night flying.

Refraction

The transparent part of the sclerotic is known as the *cornea*, behind which is the *lens*, whose purpose is to bend light rays inwards so that they focus on the retina. If the image is focused in front of it, *short sightedness* results. Similarly, you get *long sightedness* when the point of focus occurs behind the retina. Both conditions cause blurred vision, correctable by glasses, that vary the refraction of the light waves until they focus in the proper place.

Blurred vision can also be caused by stress, causing nervous tension, in turn causing excessive eye muscle activity leading to eyestrain. Just relaxing often helps this condition.

Optical illusions

Searching for an object in a swimming pool is difficult, because the light rays bend as they pass the surface and the object appears to be displaced. Similarly, rain on a windscreen at night gives the impression that objects are further away. A good fixed-wing example of an optical illusion is a wider runway tending to make you think the ground is nearer than it actually is; a narrow runway delays your reactions. When mountain flying, as we have seen, it's often difficult to fly straight and level because the sloping ground around you affects your judgment. Similarly, you can't judge your height when landing on a peak. Even going to the cinema is an optical illusion; still frames are shown so quickly after each other it looks as if movement is taking place – the switching is done in the brain.

Ears

These are important because an auditory stimulus is the one most often attended to. How many times do you answer the phone when you're busy, even though you've ignored everything else for hours?

Sound waves make the *eardrum* vibrate, and the vibrations are transmitted by a chain of linked bones known as the *hammer, anvil* and *stirrup* to the inner ear, which is full of fluid. There are thousands of fibres of different lengths within the inner ear which vibrate in sympathy according to different frequencies. As some of the fibres get damaged (through too severe vibration), the ability to hear that frequency goes (they do not regenerate). The fibres are linked to the brain and, as with sight, it is at this point, when the signal reaches the brain, that we 'hear'.

The *semicircular canals* are what we use to keep balanced. They use the fluid in the inner ear, which acts against sensors to send electrical signals to the brain so that you can tell which way up you are. The 'leans' happen because your semicircular canals get used to a particular sustained motion in a very short time. If you start a turn and keep it going, your canals will think this is normal, because they lag, or are slow to respond. When you straighten up, they will try to tell you you're turning, where you're actually flying straight and level. Your natural inclination is to obey your senses, but your instruments are there as a cross-reference. In fact, the whole point of instrument training is to overcome your dependence on your senses.

The *Eustachian tubes* are canals that connect the throat with the middle ear; their purpose is to equalise air pressure. When you swallow, the tubes open, allowing air to enter, which is why swallowing helps to clear the ears when changing altitude. Blocked Eustachian tubes can be responsible for split eardrums, due to the inability to equalise pressure. Since the eardrum takes around six weeks to heal, the best solution is not to go flying with a cold, but commercial pressures don't always allow this. If you have to, make sure you use a decongestant with no side effects.

Blocked sinuses
Although associated with the nose, the sinuses are actually hollow spaces or cavities inside the head surrounding the base of the nose and the eye sockets. Amongst other things, they act as sound boxes for the voice. Being hollow, they provide structural strength whilst keeping the head light; there are normally between fifteen and twenty of them. Blockages arise from fluid that can't escape through the narrow passages – any pain results from fluid pressure. Blocked sinuses can also be responsible for severe headaches.

Deafness
This can arise from many causes; in aviation, high-tone deafness from sustained exposure to jet engines is very common. Hearing actually depends on the proper working of the *eighth cranial nerve*, which carries signals from the inner ear to the brain. Obviously, if this gets damaged, deafness results. The nerve doesn't have to be severed, though; deterioration will occur if you don't get enough Vitamin B-complex (deafness is a symptom of beriberi or pellagra, for example, both diseases of Vitamin B deficiency).

You can recover from some deafness, such as that caused by illness, but not that caused by damage to the fibres in the fluid.

Disorientation
The 'leans' is the classic case, already mentioned. To combat them, close your eyes and shake your head vigorously from side to side for a couple

of seconds, which will topple the semi-circular canals. Motion sickness usually happens because of a mismatch between sight, feel and the semi-circular canals, giving unfamiliar real or apparent motion (e.g. the 'leans'). Medication can have unwelcome side effects, particularly on performance, which are normally not acceptable for flight crews.

Respiratory System

Consists of the lungs, and also the heart.

Air is drawn into the lungs from where oxygen is diffused into the blood under pressure, which carries it to every part of the body, especially the brain, the most sensitive to lack of it. Blood is pumped around by the heart. Waste products in the form of carbon dioxide go the other way. The diffusion of oxygen into the blood depends on air pressure, so as this falls, oxygen assimilation is impaired. Net result: It gets harder to breathe as you climb! Lack of oxygen leads to . . .

Hypoxia

A condition where you don't have enough oxygen in the blood, typically occurring when you climb too high to get enough, but anaemia can produce the same effect, as can alcohol (there are actually several types of hypoxia, but we won't bother with that here). From 0 to 10,000 ft you can survive on normal air; above this, an increasing amount of oxygen relative to the other ingredients is required, up to 33,700 feet, at which point you require pure oxygen to survive. Above 40,000 you need pressure breathing as well. The effects are similar to those of alcohol, but the classic signs are:

❑   Personality changes. You get jolly, aggressive and less inhibited
❑   Judgement changes. Your abilities are impaired; you think you are capable of anything and have much less self-criticism
❑   Muscle movement. Becomes sluggish, not in tune with your mind
❑   Short-term memory loss. This leads to reliance on training, or procedures established in long-term memory (see below)
❑   Sensory loss. Blindness occurs (colour first), then touch, orientation and hearing are affected
❑   Loss of consciousness. You get confused first, then semi-conscious, then unconscious

The above are *subjective* signs, in that they need to be recognised by the person actually suffering from hypoxia. External observers may notice some of them, but especially lips and fingertips turning blue and possible hyperventilation (see below) as the victim tries to get more oxygen. All are aggravated by:

- ❏ Altitude. Less oxygen available, and less pressure to keep it there
- ❏ Time. The more time you are exposed, the greater the effect
- ❏ Exercise. Increases energy usage and hence oxygen requirement
- ❏ Cold. Increases energy usage and hence oxygen requirement
- ❏ Illness. Increases energy usage and hence oxygen requirement
- ❏ Fatigue. Symptoms arise earlier
- ❏ Drugs or alcohol. Reduced tolerance
- ❏ Smoking. Carbon monoxide binds to blood cells better than oxygen

The time of useful consciousness (i.e. the time you have available to sort things out) is actually quite short: probably thirty minutes at 18,000 ft, and *two minutes* at 25,000!

Hyperventilation
This is simply overbreathing, where too much oxygen causes carbon dioxide to be washed out of the bloodstream, which then gets too alkaline, and the end result is hypoxia. Unconsciousness slows the breathing down so that the CO_2 balance is restored, but falling asleep is not often practical! The usual cause is worry, fright or sudden shock, but hypoxia can be a factor.
  Symptoms include:

- ❏ Dizziness
- ❏ Pins and needles, tingling
- ❏ Blurred sight
- ❏ Hot/cold feelings
- ❏ Anxiety
- ❏ Impaired performance
- ❏ Loss of consciousness

Pressure changes
Aside from oxygen, the body contains gases of varying descriptions in many places; some occur naturally, and some are created by the body's normal working processes. The problem is that these gases expand and contract as the aircraft climbs and descends. Some need a way out, and some need a way back as well.

- ❏ Gas in the ears is normally vented via the Eustachian tubes. If these are blocked for any reason (such as a cold), the pressure on either side of the eardrum is not balanced, which could lead (at the very least) to considerable pain, and (at worst) a ruptured eardrum

❑   Sinus cavities are also vulnerable to imbalances of pressure, and are affected in the same way as eardrums

❑   Gas in the gut can be vented from both ends

❑   Teeth may have small pockets of air in them, if filled, together with the gums. Although dentists nowadays are aware of people flying, and pack fillings properly, the general public don't fly every day, as you do, so it's best to be sure. High-altitude balloonists actually take their fillings out

Decompression sickness

Where pressures are low, nitrogen in the blood comes out of solution (typically above 18,000–25,000 feet). Bubbles can form, and are especially painful in the joints (e.g. the 'bends'). Unfortunately, these bubbles do not redissolve on descent, so if you are affected you may need to go into a decompression chamber. For this reason, diving before flight should be avoided, as extra nitrogen is absorbed while breathing pressurised gas and will dissolve out as you surface again. Don't fly for twelve hours if you have been underwater with compressed air, and twenty-four hours if you've been below thirty feet.

Heart disease

Heart disease can be grouped into three categories:

❑   *Hypertensive* – due to high blood pressure, which makes the heart work harder and become enlarged (anxiety, etc.)

❑   *Coronary*, or *arteriosclerotic* – hardening of the arteries through excessive calcium, or cholesterol, which again makes the heart work harder (bad diet)

❑   *Valvular* or *rheumatic* – where the valves are unable to open or close properly, allowing back pressure to build up (old age)

Information Processing

Physical stimuli, such as sound and sight, are received and interpreted by the brain. *Perception* at this point means converting that information into something meaningful, or realising that it's relevant to what you're doing. What comes out depends on past experience of those events, your expectations and whether you're able to cope with the information at that time. Good examples are radio transmissions from ATC, which you can understand, even if you can't hear them properly, because you expect certain items to be included, and you know from experience that they're bad anyway. The danger, of course, is that you may hear what you want to hear and not what is actually sent!

Memory

There are three types of memory:

- ❏ *Instinct*, which is what Jung called 'race memory', gives an immediate (i.e. gut reaction) response to a stimulus
- ❏ *Long-term memory*, where all our basic knowledge (e.g. memories of childhood, training, etc.) is kept. Where training is concerned, many processes can be carried out automatically, with little thinking. Repetition is used to get information into it
- ❏ *Short-term*, or *working*, *memory*, which is for data that is used and forgotten almost instantly (actually, nothing is ever forgotten, as any psychologist will tell you, but the point is that short-term memory is for 'on the spot' work, such as fuel calculations or ATC clearances). It can only cope with about seven items at a time, unless some tricks are used, such as grouping, or association. Data in short-term memory typically lasts about 10–20 seconds. It is affected by distraction

There are also two types of thinking:

- ❏ *Left brain*, or *logical*. Involves verbal and mathematical methods. It typically uses simple deduction: for example, define what the problem is *not* until you can decide what the problem must be
- ❏ *Right brain* – conceptual. The artist type

Habits

These are part of our lives; many are comforting and part of a reassuring routine that keeps us mentally the right way up. Others, however, are ones we could well do without, but the trouble is that they can be very difficult to break, because the person trying to break them is the very person trapped by them. We learn habits as children, simply in order to survive. Despite our true nature, we quickly find out that if we want food, attention or 'strokes', as the Americans say, we have to behave in certain ways, depending on the nature of our parents; in some families getting noticed demands entirely different behaviour than in others, mostly opposite to what we really are. In certain circumstances, habits can be dangerous – if we can't do anything about them, we need at least to be aware of them.

Training, which is very habit forming, is all very well, but don't let it limit your thinking. Also, don't confuse *stereotyping* with *probability*. You can always accept a probability that a certain set of actions will solve a similar problem to one you've had in the past, but stereotyping implies that the same actions work every time.

Attitudes

Flying requires considerable use of the brain, and observation/reaction to events, both inside and outside the aircraft. Psychology and aviation have been used to each other for some time; you may be familiar with selection tests and interviews. Part of why accidents happen is that some people are accidents waiting to happen! This depends on personality, amongst other things, and we will look at this now.

What Type of Person is a Pilot?

We certainly have more intelligence than the average car driver. Or do we? Passing exams doesn't mean you're capable of doing a decent job or handling a crisis. There are stupid solicitors, professors, you name it. Personally, I have flown with 17,000-hour pilots whom I wouldn't trust with a pram, and 1,000-hour types with whom I would trust anything.

Regulations and programmes such as this only go so far – if you are immature, you will not make the sort of decision that will keep you out of trouble, but this has nothing to do with age, and requires some ex-perience. The popular image of the handlebar moustache in the bar may have been correct during the Second World War, where there really was a reason to relieve stress for people who were tired, cold, frightened and inexperienced, but it is not appropriate now. Mature people do not depend on other people's opinions but rely on their own self-image.

You will agree, probably, that 95 per cent of anything is sub-standard and not worth bothering about. Take any class of objects for sale in any shop – only 5 per cent would be regarded as 'quality'. The same goes for people's opinions – they can only base them on their own experiences, so be selective when you take advice.

What is the Common Thread that Unites All Competent People?

The 'responsible position' that you, as a commander, will hold is one in which you are permitted to act with a minimum of direction but are personally responsible for the outcome of your activities. Important factors in selection are:

- ❏ Intelligence
- ❏ Personality. This can be defined as: 'The sum total of the physical, mental, emotional and social characteristics of an individual'. Generally, to be accident prone, you are either under- or over-confident. With the former, situations will tend not to be handled properly, and with the latter, situations not appreciated properly. You might also be aggressive, independent, a risk taker, anxious, impersonal, competitive, invulnerable and have a low stress tolerance, which, when you think about it, are all based on attention-seeking and fear. However, the real area where personality comes to the fore is during interactions with other people; behaviour tends to breed behaviour. Crews are frightened to deal with the captain, and captains won't deal with crews
- ❏ Leadership vs. teamwork
- ❏ Personal qualities to passengers and colleagues

On top of *personality traits*, which you are born with, the accident-prone person also has undesirable *attitudes*, which are acquired. These can include:

- ❏ Impulsivity. Doing things without proper forethought – such people don't stop to think about what they're doing. Not so fast! Apply your training! The opposite is indecisive
- ❏ Anti-authority. These people don't like being told what to do. They may either not respect the source of the authority, or are just plain ornery (with a deep source of bottled-up anger). Very often there's nothing wrong with this – if more people had questioned authority, we wouldn't have had half the wars. However, regulations have a purpose. They allow us to act with very little information, since every-thing is supposed to be predictable, although that doesn't mean that rules should blindly be obeyed – sometimes breaking the rules saves lives – apparently, the DC10 that had an engine fall off during take-off could have kept flying if the nose had been lowered a little for speed, instead of being set at the 'standard' angle of six degrees, as taught on the simulator, which, in this case, stalled the aeroplane. The opposite is brainwashed
- ❏ Invulnerability. People like this think that nothing untoward can happen to them, so they tend to take more risks, or push the envelope – humility is the antidote. Repetitive tasks must be done as if they

362

were new every time, no matter how tedious – you can practically guarantee that the one time you don't check for water in a fuel drum, it will be there! The opposite is paranoid

❏ Macho people are afraid of looking small and are always subject to peer pressure, which means they care a lot about what other people think of them, leading to the idea that they have a very low opinion of themselves. Thus, they take unnecessary chances for different reasons from so-called invulnerable people. These are typically the high-powered intimidating company executives who have houses in the middle of nowhere with no navaids within miles of the place. The opposite is wimp. You have to learn to stick up for yourself, with management and passengers. I had occasion once to ask a passenger to use the shoulder straps in the front seat of my helicopter – he had obviously become used to just using the lap strap over the years. He complained, of course, and I got hauled over the coals in front of everyone in the ops room. That was bad man-management in itself, but I had to point out that they couldn't go against the rules.

❏ Resignation. The opposite of impulsive. The thought that Allah will provide is all very well, but the Lord only helps those who helps themselves – you've got to do your bit too! The opposite is compulsive

As you can see when you compare the opposites, each side of each coin described above is as bad as the other – we should strive to be somewhere in the middle.

One way of controlling hazardous personality traits is to keep a tight hold on the factors in this mnemonic:

Stress
Weather
Exposure to risk
Aircraft
Time constraints

Flight Deck Management

This includes personal management. What sort of personality are you? Do you leave everything to the last minute? Are you a placid type, or nervous and anxious? Do you have a low self-image or are you on the arrogant side? Do you succumb to pressure? Are you strong enough to stand up to the chairman of the board who insists he must get there NOW? It's better to ask for help and look stupid, than not to ask and risk looking worse. Unfortunately, the ability to laugh at yourself and not feel uncomfortable when you've cocked things up only comes with a certain degree of maturity. As you get older, you accept that mistakes are made; there's no shame in that, even the most experienced pilot couldn't fly at one time – the trick lies in not making the same mistake twice, or at least ensuring that the ones you make aren't the fatal ones.

Communication
Defined as the ability to put your ideas into someone's head and be sure of success. Unfortunately, even under ideal conditions, only about 30 per cent is retained, due to such factors as inattention, misinterpretation, expectations and emotions.

Standard operating procedures
Drills, as per the ops manual, and checklists for your aircraft do the same thing on a different scale. Their purpose is to provide a framework on which to base good decision-making, as well as making sure you don't forget anything.

Although a checklist doesn't contain policy (as does an ops manual), it does at least stimulate activity, since the first response of most people in an emergency is to suffer acute brainfade. Either that, or you shoot from the hip, which is equally wrong. Checklists and drills are in the company's ops manual and are intended to be followed to the letter. They are not always based on the flight manual drills, which are required to be followed to comply with the requirements of the C of A. Whilst they have their uses, though, they can't cater for every situation, and you may have to think once in a while.

Stress

Flying is stressful, there's no doubt about that, but should stress be a problem? It's arguable that a little stress is good for you; it stops you slowing down and keeps you on your toes; this is the sort associated with success. Excessive stress, on the other hand, in the form of pressure (that is, stress without respite) can lead to fatigue, anxiety and inability to cope, and is associated with frustration or failure.

Stress and preoccupation have their effects; a PA31 pilot was doing a cargo flight with three scheduled stops, but he did not refuel or even shut down at any of them, so both engines stopped after the last delivery. He was anxious to get home because his wife was in hospital.

What is Excessive Stress?

Anything that has a sufficiently strong influence to take your mind off the job in hand, or to make you concentrate less well on it. Not only are you not doing your job properly, but you subconsciously feel guilty about it, too, which is enough to set up a little stress all of its own. We all like to feel we are doing the best we can possibly do, and it disturbs our self-image to feel that we're not. Consequently we get angry at ourselves for being in such a position, which increases the stress, which further takes us away from the job, and so it circulates.

Common situations that may cause this are:

- ❏ Grief
- ❏ Divorce
- ❏ Financial worries
- ❏ Working conditions (charter work)
- ❏ Management pressure
- ❏ Pride
- ❏ Anger
- ❏ Get-home-itis
- ❏ Motivation
- ❏ Doubts (about your abilities, responsibilities, weather)
- ❏ Timetable
- ❏ Passengers' expectations and timetables

All of these lead to anxiety, which is really based on fear, if you think about it. As anxiety can cause stress, you get a circulating problem. You could probably think of more. People have their own ways of dealing with stress, so what works for one does not necessarily work for someone else. This is possibly because of the evaluation of the stress that that particular person has, i.e. whether they feel they can cope and their perception of the problem.

It is *perception* of demands and abilities, rather than the actual problems, that affects the individual. If you *feel* you are capable, then your stress level will be relatively low.

Symptoms of stress include:

- ❏ Detachment from the situation
- ❏ Failure to perceive time
- ❏ Fixation of attention
- ❏ Personality changes
- ❏ Voice pitch changes

- ❏ Desire for isolation
- ❏ Reduced cognitive ability
- ❏ Poor emotional self-control
- ❏ Unsafe cavalier attitude

Coping with Stress

You can either adjust to the situation, or change the situation itself. The willingness to recognise stress and to do something about it must be there; for example, if you don't admit there's a problem at home, there's not much you can do! It is not weakness to admit you have a problem – rather, it shows lack of judgement if you do otherwise.

Stress Management

- ❏ Reduce the load
- ❏ Exercise
- ❏ Proper diet. *Hypoglycaemia* is fair enough in the short term, but long-term can be a *disease*. It happens when glucose leaves the body faster than it can be replaced – *rebound* hypoglycaemia occurs where the blood sugar level drops abnormally low after being boosted artificially with sugar products that are quickly absorbed, such as cakes, alcohol or sweets. The problem is, adrenalin is released to cope with it, which accounts for mood swings, depression, etc. Although not life-threatening, hypoglycaemia is a forerunner of many worse diseases and should be looked at. The important thing to watch appears to be the suddenness of any fall in blood sugar, and a big one can often trigger a heart attack. A high-protein diet will tend to even things out, as protein helps the absorption of fat, which is inhibited if too much insulin is about. Also check out *food combining*, where proteins and starches are not mixed due to chemical incompatibility
- ❏ Maintain a positive outlook on life

Responses

Following a decision, based on a stimulus, there is a response. However, a response due to excessive pressure is more likely to be based on insufficient data and be wrong than a more considered one, assuming time permits. Don't change a plan unnecessarily; a previously made plan based on sound thinking is more likely to work than one cooked up on the spur of the moment, provided, of course that the situation is the same or similar. A correct, rather than a rapid, reaction is appropriate.

What usually happens when an accident occurs is that the brain goes smartly into neutral whilst everything around you goes pear-shaped. Checklists can help to bridge the gap of inactivity by giving you something more or less correct to do whilst psyching yourself up and evaluating information ready for a decision. The US Navy, for example, trains pilots to stop in emergencies and reset the clock on the instrument panel, which forces them to relax, or at least, not to panic.

Response times will vary according to the complexity of the problem, or the element of expectation and hence preparedness (we are trained to expect engine failures, for example, but not locked controls, so the reaction time to the former will be less). Pushing a button as a response to a light illuminating will take about one-fifth of a second, but add another light and button and this will increase to a second or so. An unexpected stimulus will increase reaction time to nearly five seconds.

The workload in the cockpit should be moderate; we get tired when bored, and performance is poor. Similarly, performance will be poor when you're too busy, due to swamping. There is some concern over too much automation across the Atlantic, as pilots do not have enough to do. Perhaps they should have in-flight video as well!

'Judgement is the process of recognising and analysing all available information about yourself, your aircraft and the environment you are in, followed by the rational evaluation of alternatives to implement timely decisions which maximise safety. This involves the ability to evaluate risks based on knowledge, skill and experience.'

Response Checklist

❏   Gather as much data as possible
❏   Take as much time as is available
❏   Consider all possibilities; remember Sherlock Holmes – try all theories, and the one remaining, however unlikely, has to be the answer
❏   React, but continually reassess
❏   Look at the world as it really is, not as you hope it to be

Problem Solving

Get the big picture; don't concentrate on one small part. Don't be too keen to restrict the problem; start with the whole situation first, then work downwards. Try and cut the problem in half every time.

Here's a list of some keywords:

- ❏ Delegation
- ❏ Priorities
- ❏ Monitoring and cross-checking
- ❏ Communication
- ❏ Leadership

Personal Checklist

- ❏ Illness – degrades your abilities
- ❏ Attitude – be professional
- ❏ Medication – no self-prescription
- ❏ Stress – know yourself honestly
- ❏ Alcohol – bottle to throttle times
- ❏ Fatigue – be rested and unhurried
- ❏ Eating – ensure regular meals

Further Reading

Fit For Life John and Marilyn Diamond
Hypoglycaemia – A Better Approach Dr Paavo Airola

19

Glossary

ACARS

Aircraft Communications Addressing and Reporting System. Uses quick bursts of data on VHF between aircraft and ground stations, viewable on a printer in the cockpit. The ground network is operated on behalf of the airlines by a separate organisation. With ACARS, final load figures can be sent to the aircraft when taxiing out, so they don't need to be calculated at the gate, which could cause a problem when you need your rotate speed from the graphs and you still don't know what the weight is.

Adequate External Attitude Reference

Met conditions with visual cues that permit aircraft attitude and flight path to be determined without sole reference to instruments and with visual ground contact.

Aerial Work Zone

An area, delineated in an *aerial work zone plan*, in which aerial work is being conducted and is over a built-up area of a city or town or over or adjacent to an area where persons may assemble.

Aerial Work Zone Plan

A risk management plan for proposed aerial work.

Aerodrome

Adequate One where performance requirements for the expected landing weight will be met, with necessary ancillary services, such as ATC, sufficient lighting, communications, weather reporting, navaids and emergency services, and at least one let-down aid (ground radar will qualify) for an instrument approach.
Suitable An adequate aerodrome with weather reports, or forecasts, or any combination thereof, indicating that the weather conditions are likely to be at or above operating minima and the field condition reports indicate that a safe landing can be accomplished at the time of intended operation.

Aerodrome Operating Minima

The *cloud ceiling* and *runway visual range* (RVR) for take-off and the *decision height* (DH) or *minimum descent height* (MDH), RVR and visual reference for landing which are the minima for operation.

Air Ambulance flight

One where the prime reason is to transport a person who is ill or has been physically injured to a recognised medical facility, or a human organ required for a transplant is taken from one place to another. Other persons (except aircrew) are medical attendants, the patient's immediate family or next-of-kin (or a close friend).

Approach Ban
A situation where an aircraft shall not:

❏ commence or continue a descent below 1,000 feet above the height of an aerodrome where the RVR is reported to be less than the specified minima for landing, except that if this condition is reported to the aircraft commander after he has properly descended below the DH, the approach may be continued if the specified visual reference was established at DH and is maintained, provided that the approach has been made by use of an ILS *Cat I, II* or *III* until at least the time that the specified visual reference has been established, or: (in English: start or carry on with an approach where the RVR is reported to be below company minima unless you, having already made an ILS approach, are already below DH and you can see what you're doing.)

❏ commence or continue an *approach to landing* at an aerodrome outside the UK when any of the elements included in the *state minima* are reported to be below the prescribed limits and *national regulations* prohibit any attempt to land, or commence an approach to landing

❏ (start or carry on an approach to a foreign airfield where state minima are below limits and regulations forbid you to try)

❏ commence an approach to landing at any aerodrome either inside or outside the UK at which RVR is not reported, or is not available for the time being, when the met visibility or factored met visibility is less than the equivalent specified RVR, or:
(start an approach anywhere where no RVR is reported and the met vis suitably converted is less than company minima)

❏ continue an approach to landing by flying below the specified DH or MDH unless from that height the specified visual reference is established and maintained

❏ (go below DH/MDH unless you can see where you're going)

Note: An approach ban does not apply in the UK when, on a training flight, the captain elects to make a let-down followed by a missed approach procedure, having first declared such intention. Neither does it apply where the reported cloud base is below decision height – you may approach and descend to DH to assess the cloud base for yourself, but only twice. Except in emergency, you may not make a further attempt unless the controlling authority has reported a significant improvement.

Approach to landing
That portion of the flight where the aircraft is descending below 1,000 feet above the *decision height* for that particular landing.

APU
A turbine engine used as a power source for driving generators,

hydraulic pumps and other accessories and/or providing compressed air for pneumatic systems.

Avoid Curve
A graph relating to helicopter performance showing combinations of speed and height where it is dangerous to fly, being a function of blade pitch angle – if you're in flat pitch, it doesn't exist. It is actually a diagram in the *flight manual* of a helicopter showing safe combinations of speed and height from which an autorotation can safely be made or, conversely, from which they can't, covering level flight, take-off and high speed. Flight in the 'avoid' areas should be minimised. It is established by manufacturers' test pilots making a series of autorotations and confirmed by certifying authorities.

Balanced Field Length
The distance within which an aircraft can either accelerate to V_1 and then either stop or continue to a height of thirty-five (or whatever) feet with one engine out at $V_{1.3}$.

Category I (Cat I) Operation
A precision instrument approach and landing using ILS, MLS or PAR with a decision height of above 200 ft and with an RVR above 550 m.

Category II operation
A precision instrument approach and landing using ILS or MLS with a *decision height* (DH) below 200 ft but not lower than 100 ft, and a minimum RVR of 300 m.

Category III operations
Sub-divided as follows:

❏ a Category IIIA operation is a precision instrument approach and landing using ILS or MLS with a *decision height* lower than 100 ft and a *runway visual range* not less than 200 m

❏ a Category IIIB operation is a precision approach and landing using ILS or MLS with a decision height lower than 50ft, or no decision height, and RVR between 75 and 200 m

Circling
Circling describes the visual phase of an instrument approach to bring an aeroplane into position for landing on a runway which is not suitably located for a straight-in approach.

Circling Minima
The lowest conditions of circling heights and in-flight visibility in which a circuit (using visual reference only) may be carried out within a fixed radius or sector of an aerodrome at which landing is intended (RVR is that for the landing runway). Circling minima apply to any instrument approach for landing on another runway than that directly served by the approach aid being used ('directly served' means the final heading of the approach is within 30° of the runway QDM), purely visual approaches where you decide to dispense with an available let-down aid and visual circuits following overshoots from either instrument or visual approaches.

Climb Compliance
With reference to take-off, covers the situation after an engine failure at V_1 or later during take-off with requirements for reasonable climbout on one engine. The take-off weight of an aircraft may be limited by climb

compliance in one of the take-off segments.

Cloud Base
The lowest reported cloud level (reported as FEW).

Cloud Ceiling
The vertical distance from the elevation of the aerodrome to the lowest part of any cloud visible from the aerodrome which is sufficient to obscure more than one half of the sky above the elevation of the aerodrome (reported as BKN).

Dead Man's Curve
See *Avoid Curve*

Decision Altitude/Height (DA/H)
A specified altitude in a precision approach at which a missed approach must be initiated if the required visual reference to continue the approach has not been established.

Defined Area
The whole of a circle of 4 nm radius centred on the aerodrome, or a prescribed segment of this circle if visual manoeuvring can be confined to a smaller area to avoid a predominant obstruction.

Dispatch
The point at which an aircraft first moves under its own power for the purpose of commencing a flight, at which the provisions of the MEL will cease to apply and from which the commander must be solely responsible for ensuring that the flight can be made safely.

Dry Operating Mass (DOM)
The total mass of the aeroplane ready for a specific type of operation, excluding all usable fuel and traffic load. This mass includes:

❏ crew and crew baggage
❏ catering and removable passenger service equipment, and
❏ potable water and lavatory chemicals

EADI
Electronic Attitude Director Indicator. Equipment replacing the artificial horizon.

ELT
Emergency Locator Transmitter. These emit a distinctive siren-like sound on 121.5 or 243.0 MHz, which should be detectable by satellite. They should work for about forty-eight hours on a set of batteries and can be operated manually or switched on in the event of a crash by a G-switch.

EPR
Engine Pressure Ratio. A measurement of thrust, or the difference between air pressure coming into the engine and the pressure of that coming out of the back.

ETOPS
Extended Range Twin OPerationS. Those conducted over a route with a point further than one hour's flying time (still air), at the normal one-engine-inoperative cruise speed, from an adequate aerodrome. When, alternatively, a *threshold distance* has been agreed with the authority, all non-ETOPS flights shall remain within the threshold distance of an *adequate aerodrome*. Authorisation for ETOPS times of 120 and 180 minutes from an adequate aerodrome are available, subject to the operator showing compliance with the laid-down

operational criteria, and the aeroplane airframe/engine combination having the appropriate type design approval.

ETOPS Segment

The portion of an *ETOPS* flight that begins when the aeroplane is first more than the threshold distance from an *adequate aerodrome* and ends when the aeroplane is last more than threshold distance from an adequate aerodrome.

Extended Range Entry Point

The point on the aeroplane's outbound route which is one hour's flying time at the approved single-engine-inoperative cruise speed (under standard conditions in still air) from an adequate aerodrome.

Final Approach

That part of an instrument approach procedure which commences at the specified final approach fix or point, or where such a fix or point is not specified, at the end of the last procedure turn, base turn or inbound turn of a racetrack procedure, if specified, or at the point of interception of the last track specified in the approach procedure, and ends at a point in the vicinity of an aerodrome from which a landing can be made or a missed approach procedure is initiated.

Flight Manual

The document required for type certification and approved by the authorities.

Height/Velocity Envelope

See *Avoid Curve*.

High Seas

Any body of water, frozen or otherwise, not within the territorial waters of any state.

Indirect Approach

A circling procedure established for some airfields (notably French), where prescribed tracks are flown to establish an approach on the runway in use after an approach to another runway. Similar to *circling minima*, but more precise.

In-flight Visibility

As seen from the cockpit. As a guide for a circling approach, an IFV equal to the diameter of a Rate 1 turn is required. A reasonably accurate assessment is given by the formula:

$$\text{IFV (metres)} = 20 \times \text{circuit speed (knots)}$$

Inoperative

Equipment is inoperative if it malfunctions in such a way that it cannot accomplish its intended purpose and/or is not consistently functioning within its designated operating limits or tolerances.

Long-Range Flight

Over water in helicopters, where the overwater sector exceeds 30 nm.

Low Visibility Take-Off

Where the reported RVR is less than 400 m. These requirements must be satisfied:

❏ if RVR is between 150 and 400 m (200–400 m Cat D aeroplanes) the PIC must be satisfied that the runway lighting and markings are satisfactory and appropriate low visibility procedures (LVPs) are in force

❏ when reported RVR is below 150 m (200 m Cat D aeroplanes) additional runway features, crew training, lateral guidance in the aeroplane for the lower RVRs and approval are required

Low Visibility Procedures (LVPs)

Ground procedures at the aerodrome designed to prevent the entry of ground vehicles and taxiing aircraft into take-off and landing areas. In addition, they protect the sensitive areas of the aerodrome's ILS or MLS transmissions and regulate the flow of air traffic on the approach. ATC at the aerodrome will ensure these procedures have been implemented by the time the cloud ceiling is below 200 ft or the RVR has dropped to below 600 m.

Maximum Zero Fuel Mass

The maximum permissible mass of an aeroplane with no usable fuel. The fuel contained in particular tanks must be included in the zero fuel mass when it is explicitly mentioned in *Flight Manual* limitations.

Maximum Structural Landing Mass

The maximum permissible total aeroplane mass upon landing under normal circumstances.

Maximum Structural Take-Off Mass

The maximum permissible total aeroplane mass at the start of the take-off run.

Minimum Descent Altitude/Height (MDA/H)

A specified altitude/height in a *non-precision* or *circling approach* below which descent may not be made without visual reference.

Minimum Weather Conditions

In relation to an aerodrome, the *cloud ceiling* and RVR for take-off, and *decision height* and RVR for landing, below which you cannot safely take off and land.

Missed Approach Point (MAP)

That point in an instrument approach procedure at or before which the prescribed missed approach procedure must be initiated in order to ensure that the minimum obstacle clearance is not infringed.

Non-precision Approach and Landing Operations

An instrument approach and landing which does not utilise electronic glide-path guidance. That is, there is no vertical guidance, and all altitudes associated with the procedure are minimum IFR ones, or not to be descended below. 1,000 feet clearance is provided above the highest obstacle in the initial segment, 500 in the intermediate segment and down to 250 feet in the final segment (from final approach fix to *missed approach point*).

Notified

'As set forth in a document entitled "Aeronautical Information Publication" or "NOTAM" published by the Civil Aviation Authority (for the UK) or by a country other than the UK (when abroad) for the time being in force.'

Obstacle Clearance Altitude/Height (OCA/H)

The lowest altitude (OCA), or the lowest height above the elevation of the relevant runway threshold or above the aerodrome elevation as applicable (OCH), used in establishing compliance with appropriate obstacle clearance criteria.

Obstacle Clearance Limit (OCL)

The height above aerodrome elevation below which the minimum vertical clearance cannot be maintained either on approach or in the event of a missed approach.

Precision Approach and Landing Operations

An instrument approach and landing using precision azimuth and glide path guidance with minima as determined by the *category* of operation.

Positioning

The practice of transferring crews from place to place as passengers in surface or air transport at the behest of the operator.

Rule Distance

The distance in still air in the *rule time*, at one-engine-inoperative cruise speed.

Rule Time

The maximum diversion time any point on the route may be, from a suitable aerodrome, as per the maximum authorised diversion time. e.g. 120, 180 minutes.

Runway Visual Range (RVR)

The range over which the pilot of an aeroplane on the centreline of a runway can see its surface markings or the lights delineating it.

Reported RVR

The RVR communicated to the commander of an aeroplane, by or on behalf of the person in charge of the aerodrome.

Sector

The time between an aircraft first moving under its own power until it next comes to rest after landing.

Short-range flights

For helicopters, where the overwater sector is 10–30 nm.

Specified

In relation to aircraft means specified by the operator in, or ascertainable by reference to, the operations manual.

State Minima

In some countries (e.g. France), the controlling authority lays down mandatory minimum weather conditions for take-off and landing, which may relate to the type of aircraft and nature of the operation as well as the aids in use. The more stringent restrictions between state and company minima apply.

System

A group of directly related components which perform a specified function.

Threshold Distance

The distance travelled in still air in sixty minutes by an aeroplane, at the one-engine-inoperative cruise speed.

Traffic load

The total mass of passengers, baggage and cargo.

Visible Moisture

An atmospheric environment containing water in any form that can be seen in natural or artificial light, such as clouds, fog, rain, etc.

Visual Approach

An approach by an IFR flight when either part or all of an instrument approach procedure is not completed, but executed by visual reference (not below 800 m RVR).

Visual Contact Flight

A flight conducted under VFR (or IFR) such that the aircraft remains below and clear of cloud and during which the crew are in continuous visual contact with the surface, so they must be able to assess the aircraft attitude and separation from the surface by external reference by day, and a clearly distinguishable external horizon by night.

Visual Reference

For descent below DH, a continuous or successive reference to a segment of at least seven consecutive approach or runway lights, or a combination of both, or a segment of the runway established to be not less than 1,000 feet (300 m) long, including the touchdown point.

When the approach has been made with a full ILS or PAR, the consecutive lights can be reduced to six; for a visual or part circuit based on circling minima, a pilot should have continuous sight of ground features which will enable him to establish the position of the aircraft in relation to the aerodrome and subsequently to remain within the notified visual manoeuvring area.

V-speeds

Significant aircraft speeds, calculated for every take-off, and varying with aircraft weight or mass. Here are some:

Speed	Meaning
V_s	Stall speed.
V_a	Manoeuvring speed. The maximum speed at which you can make abrupt, full-scale deflections of the controls without causing damage, or the speed at which the aircraft will either stall or break.
V_{mca}	Minimum control speed, or minimum speed at which it is possible to control the aircraft in the air, with one engine inoperative and the other at take-off thrust.
V_1	Take-off decision speed, before which you can stop safely inside the remaining runway length, or the speed above which the take-off is continued, and below which it is abandoned, in the case of engine failure, unless you think the aircraft is unsafe to fly. Of course, this guarantees you will go off the end of the runway
V_r	Rotation speed, at which the aircraft is rotated to the take-off attitude. V_r must not be less than V_1 or $1.05 \times V_{mc}$. It must also be high enough to allow V_2 to be attained before reaching screen height.
V_2	Take-off safety speed, or minimum safe flying speed if you lose an engine after take-off, to be achieved before screen height.
V_{so}	Stall speed in landing configuration.
V_{ref}	Chosen speed to be maintained on the approach.

Abbreviations

A/H	Altitude/height	ATS	Air Traffic System
ACAS	Airborne Collision and Avoidance Systems	ATT	Ambulance Taxi Transport
ADF	Automatic Direction Finder	BPA	British Parachute Association
AFCS	Automatic Flight Control System	CofA	Certificate of Airworthiness
AFTN	Aeronautical Fixed Telecommunications Network	C of E	Certificate of Experience
		C of G	Centre of Gravity
		C of T	Certificate of Test
AI	Altitude Indicator	CAA	Civil Aviation Authority
AIC	Aeronautical Information Circular	CANP	Civil Aviation Notification Procedure
AIP	Aeronautical Information Publication	CAP	Capacity
ANGR	Air Navigation (General) Rules	CAR	Canadian Aviation Regulations
ANO	Air Navigation Order	CASS	Commercial Air Service Standards
AOC	Air Operator's Certificate	CAT	Commercial Air Transport
AP	Authorised Person	CB	Cumulonimbus Cloud
APS	Air Pictorial Service	CDL	Configuration Deviation List
ARA	Airborne Radar Approach	CDP	Critical Decision Point
ARB	Air Registration Board	CP	Critical Point
ASI	Airspeed Indicator	CPL	Commercial Pilot's Licence
ATC	Air Transport Control		
ATCC	Air Traffic Control Centre	CPL(H)	Commercial Pilot's Licence (Helicopter)
ATL	Air Transport Licence	CRM	Crew Resource Management
ATPL	Airline Transport Pilot's Licence		
		CSU	Constant Speed Unit
ATPL(H)	Airline Transport Pilot's Licence (Helicopter)	CVDR	Cockpit Voice Data Recorder

CVR	Cockpit Voice Recorder	HEMS	Helicopter Emergency Medical Service
DA	Decision Altitude	HI	Heading Indicator
DD	Deferred Defects (Sheet)	HIGE	Hover Ceiling In Ground Effect
DH	Descent Height		
DI	Directional Indicator	HISL	High-Intensity Strobe Lights
DME	Distance Measuring Equipment		
DOM	Dry Operating Mass	HOGE	Hover Performance Out of Ground Effect
DR	Dead Reckoning		
DRA	Defence Research Agency	IAA	Inner Approach Area
		IAS	Indicated Airspeed
EDA	Emergency Distance Available	IATA	International Air Transport Association
EDB	Ethylene dibromide	ICAO	International Civil Aviation Organisation
EGT	Exhaust Gas Temperature	ICO	Idle Cut-off
ELT	Emergency Landing Technique	ICT	Intensive Care Transport
		IFR	Instrument Flight Rules
EPR	Exhaust Pressure Ratio	IFV	In-Flight Visibility
ETA	Estimated Time of Arrival	ILS	Instrument Landing System
ETOPS	Extended Range Twin Operations	IMC	Instrument Meteorological Conditions
FAA	Federal Aviation Administration	INS	Inertial Navigation System
FAR	Federal Aviation Regulations	IR	Instrument Rating
FATO	Final Approach and Take-off Area	IRE	Instrument Rating Examiner
FDP	Flying Duty Period	ISA	International Standard Atmosphere
FO	First Officer		
FOD	Foreign Object Damage	ISO	International Standards Organisation
FSI	Flying Staff Instruction		
FSO	Flight Safety Officer	JAA	Joint Aviation Authorities
FTL	Flight Time Limitations		
GA	General Aviation	JAR	Joint Airworthiness Requirements
GASIL	General Aviation Safety Information Leaflet		
		LAMS	Light Aircraft Maintenance Schedule
GPS	Global Positioning System	LATCC	London Air Traffic Control Centre
GPU	Ground Power Unit		
GPWS	Ground Proximity Warning System	LDA	Landing Distance Available
HAA	Helicopter Acceleration Area	LDAH	Landing Distance Available (Helicopters)

LDP	Latest Decision Point	OGE	Out of Ground Effect
LDR	Landing Distance Required	OMEGA	Very low frequency navigation system based on 8 transmitters covering the world
LOFT	Line-oriented Flight Training		
LVP	Low Visibility Procedure	OPC	Operator Proficiency Check
MAP	Missed Approach Point		
MAUW	Maximum All-up Weight	OTS	Organised Track System
MDA	Minimum Descent Altitude	P1	Pilot in Command
		P2	Second Pilot
MDH	Minimum Descent Height	PA	Pressure Altitude
		PAOM	Police AOC and Ops Manual
MEA	Minimum En route Altitude	PAR	Precision Approach Radar
MEL	Minimum Equipment List	PEC	Pressure Error Correction
METAR	Meteorological Actual (Weather) Report	PH	Pilot Handling
		PIC	Pilot in Command
MLS	Microwave Landing System	PNH	Pilot Non-handling
MNPS	Minimum Navigation Performance Specification	PNR	Point of No Return
		PPC	Pilot Proficiency Certificate
MOC	Minimum Obstacle Clearance Altitude	PPL	Private Pilot's Licence
		QDM	Magnetic Heading To
MORA	Mimimum Off-Route Altitude	QFE	Height Above Touchdown
MORS	Mandatory Occurrence Reporting Scheme	QGH	Telephony Code for sea-level pressure
MPA	Multi Pilot Aeroplane	QNH	Barometric Pressure reported by a particular station
MSA	Minimum Safe Altitude		
MTBF	Mean Times Between Failures		
		RA	Resolution Advisory
MTOW	Maximum Take-off Weight	RAS	Radar Advisory Service
		RNAV	Area Navigation
N_1	Gauge – Engine RPM	ROC	Rate of Climb
NDB	Non-Directional Beacon	ROD	Rate of Descent
NFP	Net Flight Path	RTOW	Restricted (or Regulated) Take-off Weight
NOTAM	Notice to Airmen		
NR	Number	RVR	Runway Visual Range
OAT	Outside Air Temperature	SA	Safety Area
OBS	Omni-bearing Selector	SAR	Search and Rescue
OCH	Obstacle Clearance Height	SARBE	Search and Rescue Beacon
OCL	Obstacle Clearance Limit	SDR	Special Drawing Rights

SFE	Simulator Flight Examiner	TLOF	Touchdown and Lift-off Area
SFI	Simulator Flight Instructor	TMA	Terminal Manoeuvring Area
SI	Statutory Instrument	TOC	Top of Climb
SID	Standard Instrument Departure	TOD	Top of Descent
		TODA	Take-off Distance Available
SRA	Special Rules Area		
SRE	Surveillance Radar Element of Precision	TODAH	Take-off Distance Available (Helicopters)
SSA	Sector Safety Altitude	TODR	Take-off Distance Required
STAR	Standard Terminal Arrival Route	TORA	Take-off Run Available
STC	Supplemental Type Certificate	TOT	Turbine Outlet Temperature
SWL	Safe Working Load	TRE	Type Rating Examiner
TA	Traffic Advisory	TRI	Type Rating Instructor
TA	Take-off Area	V_1	Take-off Decision Speed
TAF	Aerodrome Weather Forecast	V_2	Take-off Safety Speed Best angle of climb Best rate of climb
TAS	True Airspeed	VASI	Visual Approach Slope Indicator
TBO	Times Between Overhaul		
TCAS	Traffic Alert and Collision Avoidance Systems	VFR	Visual Flight Rules
		VMC	Minimum Control Speed
		VOR	Very High Frequency Omndirectional Range
TCDS	Type Certificate Data Sheet	VSI	Vertical Speed Indicator
TDP	Take-off Decision Point	WAT	Weight, Altitude and Temperature
TEL	Tetra-ethyl lead		

Index

Index

Index

Index

rapelling 213
Recollections of an Airman 12–13
records, maintenance of 99
rectification away from base 191
refuelling 47, 99–103, 220
reimbursement 292–297, 331 *see also*
   payment for charter
relief, in-flight 38
rescue equipment 218–219, 226–227
rescue helicopter 168, 170
respiratory system 357–359
responses 366–368
responsible position 361–362
rest periods 32, 36–37, 38
restricted take-off weight (RTOW) 85,
   159
résumé (CV) xvii, 325–327, 329
returned flight documentation, inspecting
   6–7
rostering limits 32, 41
rotor blades 263–264, 265
rotor disc 134, 136, 242–243, 246, 260
Route Competency Certificate 56
runway lights 63, 68
Runway Visual Range (RVR) 62, 63–64,
   67–68, 69, 70–71, 75, 76, 123,
   373–374, 375
runways 48, 55, 56, 77, 124–125, 128–129,
   156–157,158–159

SAR *see* Search and Rescue
SARBE *see* Search And Rescue Beacon
SFE 342
SFI 342
SKC 77
safety, cabin 133–134 *see also* flight safety
safety, handling procedures related to
   104–106
Safety Area 222
safety belts/harnesses 130, 131, 133, 136,
   137, 138
sandstorms 126
scheduled flying xviii-xix, xx
Schermuly flares 246–247
sea state 166, 167
Search and Rescue (SAR) 168, 170
Search And Rescue Beacon (SARBE)
   164, 166, 168, 169, 170

second pilot (P2) 13–14, 23–24, 26, 131,
   138, 139, 350
sectors 38, 375
security 49, 179–182
seeding 211–212
self-briefing file 56, 58
self-control 236
shutdown checks 142
Silverstone 225, 226
simulated flight conditions 344–345
single-pilot operation 71, 73
sinuses, blocked 356
site support 256–258
skids 249, 250
skin contamination 210
slush 124, 125
smoking 136, 137, 138, 151, 152, 358
snow 61, 119–120, 123–125, 244, 247,
   248, 251, 253
special events 225–227
Special VFR 109
split duty 37, 43
spray booms 209, 211
spray drift 210–211
Squirrel 205
standard mass values 86–88
standby duty 39
statements 290
static electricity 198, 250
Statutory Instruments 282–283, 284
Stopway 156, 157
stress 364–366
sub-charters 49–50
sun tables 251–252
supervision of company operations 16
supervisors 20–21
Supplemental Type Certificate 278
surface temperature (ISA) 51
survival kit 145, 169, 171
swells 166, 167

TAFs (aerodrome weather forecasts)
   78–79
TAS 235
TCAS *see* Traffic Alert and Collision
   Avoidance Systems
TCDS *see* Type Certificate Data Sheet
TDP *see* Take-off Decision Point
TLOF *see* Touch-down and Lift-off Area